WHAT INTELLIGENCE TESTS MISS

What Intelligence Tests Miss

The Psychology of Rational Thought

KEITH E. STANOVICH

YALE UNIVERSITY PRESS NEW HAVEN AND LONDON

Published with assistance from the Mary Cady Tew Memorial Fund.

Set in Electra type by Tseng Information Systems, Inc..
Printed in the United States of America.

The Library of Congress has cataloged the hardcover edition as follows:
Stanovich, Keith E., 1950–
What intelligence tests miss : the psychology of rational thought / Keith E. Stanovich.
p. cm.
Includes bibliographical references and index.
ISBN 978-0-300-12385-2 (hardcover : alk. paper) 1. Intelligence tests.
2. Thought and thinking. I. Title.
BF431.S687 2009
153.9—dc22 2008037325

ISBN 978-0-300-16462-6 (pbk.)

A catalogue record for this book is available from the British Library.

10 9 8 7 6 5 4 3 2 1

For Paula,
who has never measured a person's worth in IQ points

CONTENTS

Preface ix

Acknowledgments xiii

ONE
Inside George W. Bush's Mind: Hints at What IQ Tests Miss 1

TWO
Dysrationalia: Separating Rationality and Intelligence 8

THREE
The Reflective Mind, the Algorithmic Mind,
and the Autonomous Mind 20

FOUR
Cutting Intelligence Down to Size 45

FIVE
Why Intelligent People Doing Foolish Things Is No Surprise 59

SIX
The Cognitive Miser: Ways to Avoid Thinking 70

CONTENTS

SEVEN

Framing and the Cognitive Miser 86

EIGHT

Myside Processing: Heads I Win—Tails I Win Too! 101

NINE

A Different Pitfall of the Cognitive Miser:
Thinking a Lot, but Losing 115

TEN

Mindware Gaps 129

ELEVEN

Contaminated Mindware 152

TWELVE

How Many Ways Can Thinking Go Wrong? A Taxonomy of Irrational
Thinking Tendencies and Their Relation to Intelligence 172

THIRTEEN

The Social Benefits of Increasing Human Rationality—and
Meliorating Irrationality 195

Notes 213

Bibliography 243

Index 303

In 2002, cognitive scientist Daniel Kahneman of Princeton University won the Nobel Prize in Economics for work done with his longtime collaborator Amos Tversky (who died in 1996). The press release for the award from the Royal Swedish Academy of Sciences drew attention to the roots of the award-winning work in "the analysis of human judgment and decision-making by cognitive psychologists." Kahneman was cited for discovering "how human judgment may take heuristic shortcuts that systematically depart from basic principles of probability. His work has inspired a new generation of researchers in economics and finance to enrich economic theory using insights from cognitive psychology into intrinsic human motivation."

In short, Kahneman and Tversky's work was about how humans make choices and assess probabilities, and they uncovered some very basic errors that are typical in decision making. Their work includes some of the most influential and highly cited studies in all of psychology, and it deserved to be honored with the Nobel Prize. One reason that this work was so influential was that it addressed deep issues concerning human rationality. As the Nobel announcement noted, "Kahneman and Tversky discovered how judgment under uncertainty systematically departs from the kind of rationality postulated in traditional economic theory." The thinking errors uncovered by Kahneman and Tversky are thus not trivial errors in a parlor game. Being rational means acting to achieve one's own life goals using the best means possible. To violate the thinking rules examined by Kahneman and Tversky thus has the practical consequence that we are less satisfied with our lives than we might be.

The work of Kahneman and Tversky, along with that of many other investigators, has shown how the basic architecture of human cognition makes all of us prone to these errors of judgment and decision making. But being prone to these errors does not mean that we always make them. Every person, on some occasions, overrides the tendency to make these reasoning errors and instead makes the rational response. It is not that we always make errors all the time. Even more important, it has been shown that there are systematic differences among individuals in the tendency to make errors of judgment and decision making. My own research group has tried to find out what predicts these individual differences.

The fact that there are systematic individual differences in the judgment and decision-making situations studied by Kahneman and Tversky means that there are variations in important attributes of human cognition related to rationality—how efficient we are in achieving our goals. It is a curious fact that none of these critical attributes of human thinking are assessed on IQ tests (or their proxies such as the SAT test). This fact is curious for two related reasons. First, most laypeople are prone to think that IQ tests are tests of, to put it colloquially, good thinking. Scientists and laypeople alike would tend to agree that "good thinking" encompasses good judgment and decision making—the type of thinking that helps us achieve our goals. In fact, the type of "good thinking" that Kahneman and Tversky studied was deemed so important that research on it was awarded the Nobel Prize. Yet assessments of such good thinking are nowhere to be found on IQ tests.

A second, and related, point is that when people use the term *intelligence* (again, laypersons and psychologists alike), they often talk as if the concept of intelligence encompassed rationality. For example, many conceptions of intelligence define it as involving adaptive decision making. Adaptive decision making is the quintessence of rationality, but the items used to assess intelligence on widely accepted tests bear no resemblance to measures of rational decision making. This creates some curious phenomena that we do in fact tend to notice. We do tend to notice, and to find mildly perplexing, "smart people doing dumb things." But the way that we have historically measured intelligence makes this phenomenon not perplexing at all. If by smart we mean IQ-test smart and by dumb we mean poor decision making, then the source of the phenomenon is clear. IQ tests do not measure adaptive decision making. So if we are surprised at a high-IQ person acting foolishly, it can only mean that we think that all good mental attributes must co-occur with high intelligence—in this case, that rational thinking must go with high intelligence. However, research is increasingly bringing this assumption into question. Rational thinking skills of the type studied by Kahneman and Tversky show only small-to-medium correlations with intelligence test performance—not surprisingly, because tests of the latter make no direct assessment of the former.

In the present book, I explore the issue of whether they should. Judgment and decision-making skills—the skills of rational thought—are at least as important as the attributes that are assessed on IQ tests. Like intelligence, rational thinking skills relate to goal achievement in the real world. Yet we fail to teach them in schools or to focus our attention on them as a society. Instead, we keep using intelligence proxies as selection devices in educational institutions from exclusive preschools to graduate schools. Corporations and the military are likewise excessively focused on IQ measures. The lavish attention devoted to intelligence (raising it, praising it, worrying when it is low, etc.) seems wasteful when we virtually ignore another set of mental skills with just as much social consequence.

The thinking skills studied by Kahneman and Tversky cash out in terms of real-world behaviors that affect people's happiness and well-being. They are just as important as the cognitive skills assessed on IQ tests. Intelligence tests are thus radically incomplete as measures of cognitive functioning. Because of their vast influence, IQ tests have both explicitly and implicitly defined, for the layperson and psychologist alike, what cognitive attributes to value. These are important abilities, to be sure, but the tests leave out huge domains of cognitive functioning. We do not need to stretch to noncognitive domains— to notions such as emotional intelligence or social intelligence—to see important lacunae in the tests. That would be implicitly conceding too much. It would seem to concede that the tests cover the cognitive domain quite well and that we need to go outside the cognitive domain, or at least straddle it (into things like emotion, creativity, aesthetic sensibility, interpersonal skills) in order to find things that IQ tests miss. I believe we need not look so far afield. The skills of judgment and decision making are cognitive skills that are the foundation of rational thought and action, and they are missing from IQ tests.

This book, then, is an extended meditation on the scientific and social consequences of a historical irony of the behavioral sciences: The Nobel Prize was awarded for studies of cognitive characteristics that are entirely missing from the most well-known mental assessment device in the behavioral sciences—the intelligence test.

M y intellectual debts in writing this book are immense and are represented in the wide literature that I cite. Nonetheless, I would single
out several foundational influences. Decades ago, the work of Daniel Kahneman and Amos Tversky inspired my interest in rational thinking tasks that
were new to psychology at the time. More recently, the work of Jonathan
Evans and David Over provoked me to make my own contributions to dual-
process theory. I have long admired Jonathan Baron's use of the heuristics
and biases literature to illuminate public policy issues. I thank David Perkins
for coining the term *mindware*, which I have used liberally in this book. From
the standpoint of my interest in individual differences in cognitive functioning, the work of Robert Sternberg has been influential. The key points in
several chapters of this book were inspired by his theoretical and empirical
contributions. I say this in full awareness that he will dislike several of my
arguments. Nevertheless, I thank him for his relentless probing of the intelligence construct and his willingness to mix it up with me over the dysrationalia concept a decade ago.

My literary agent, Susan Arellano, is thanked for her patience in helping me work out what would be the central themes of this book. She aided
me greatly in seeing what should be central and what should be peripheral.
My editor at Yale University Press, Keith Condon, is thanked for his enthusi-
asm for the project and for making important structural suggestions for the

book. Susan Laity was very helpful with manuscript editing, and Katherine Scheuer did wonderful work with the copyediting.

This book was crafted in many places with great views: in my ninth-floor office overlooking downtown Toronto and Lake Ontario; in St. Ives, Cornwall, overlooking the Atlantic; and on the Oregon coast overlooking the Pacific. Two people have been with me in all of these settings. Richard West, my colleague of thirty years, has been a continuous sounding board for these ideas. Many nights on my balcony in Toronto and down in the clearing have done wonders for my morale. Paula Stanovich has been the shining light behind all of the work that I do. She has helped me build the life that made this work possible.

David Over of the University of Durham, Maggie Toplak of York University, and an anonymous reviewer read the entire manuscript and provided many discerning comments. Three conferences were seminal in allowing me to discuss these ideas at length: the Fourth International Thinking Conference in Durham, England; the Conference on Dual-Process Theories of Reasoning and Rationality in Cambridge, England, organized by Jonathan Evans and Keith Frankish; and a workshop on dual-process theory at the University of Virginia organized by Tim Wilson and Jonathan Evans.

The Chairs of my Department while this book was being written, Janet Astington and Esther Geva, and my Deans, Michael Fullan and Jane Gaskell, provided great administrative support for this work. Mary Macri, our Department's business officer, took care of my technical and logistical needs with extraordinary dedication, as did my secretaries Diana Robinson and Marisa Freire. My empirical research on some of the issues discussed in this volume was made possible by support received from the Social Sciences and Humanities Research Council of Canada and by the Canada Research Chairs program. Marilyn Kertoy and Anne Cunningham are always part of my personal and intellectual support team.

Most members of the Stanovich/West lab (a joint lab linking the University of Toronto and James Madison University) in the past decade have contributed in some way to the research of our own that is cited in this volume. Leaders in the lab now well into their post-Ph.D. careers are represented by Caroline Ho, Robyn Macpherson, Walter Sá, and Maggie Toplak. Other lab members thanked for their participation are Maria Grunewald, Carol Kelley, Judi Kokis, Eleanor Liu, Russ Meserve, Laura Page, George Potworowski, Jason Riis, Rachel Ryerson, Robin Sidhu, Ron Stringer, Rebecca Wells-Jopling, and Joan Wolforth.

ONE

Inside George W. Bush's Mind:
Hints at What IQ Tests Miss

I'm also not very analytical. You know I don't spend a lot of time thinking about myself, about why I do things.
— *President George W. Bush, aboard Air Force One, June 4, 2003*

For years, there have been debates about George W. Bush's intelligence. His many opponents never seem to tire of pointing out his mental shortcomings. The president's strangled syntax, goofy phrasing ("Too many good docs are getting out of the business. Too many OB-GYNs aren't able to practice their love with women all across this country." — Sept. 6, 2004), and lack of familiarity with many issues have been used as evidence by his opponents to argue that this is a man of truly inferior intelligence. Even Bush's supporters often implicitly concede the point by arguing that although he lacks "school smarts" he makes up for it with "street smarts." Therefore, it came as something of a surprise when scores on various college placement exams and Armed Forces tests that the president had taken over the years were converted into an estimated IQ score. The president's score was approximately 120 — roughly the same as that of Bush's opponent in the 2004 presidential election, John Kerry, when Kerry's exam results from young adulthood were converted into IQ scores using the same formulas.[1]

These results surprised many critics of the president (as well as many of his supporters), but I, as a scientist who studies individual differences in cognitive skills, was not surprised. Virtually all commentators on the president's cognition, including sympathetic commentators such as his onetime speechwriter David Frum, admit that there is something suboptimal about the president's thinking. The mistake they make is assuming that all intellectual deficiencies are reflected in a lower IQ score.

In a generally positive portrait of the president, Frum nonetheless notes that "he is impatient and quick to anger; sometimes glib, even dogmatic; often uncurious and as a result ill-informed" (2003, p. 272). Conservative commentator George Will agrees, when he states that in making Supreme Court appointments, the president "has neither the inclination nor the ability to make sophisticated judgments about competing approaches to construing the Constitution" (2005, p. 23).

In short, there is considerable agreement that President Bush's thinking has several problematic aspects: lack of intellectual engagement, cognitive inflexibility, need for closure, belief perseverance, confirmation bias, over-confidence, and insensitivity to inconsistency. These are all cognitive characteristics that have been studied by psychologists and that can be measured with at least some precision. However, they are all examples of thinking styles that are not tapped by IQ tests. Thus, it is not surprising that someone could suffer from many of these cognitive deficiencies and still have a moderately high IQ.

Bush's cognitive deficiencies do not impair performance on intelligence tests, but they do impair rational decision making. His cognitive deficiencies instead are the causes of "dysrationalia" (an analogue of the word "dyslexia"), which is a term that I coined in the mid-1990s in order to draw attention to what is missing in IQ tests. I define dysrationalia as the inability to think and behave rationally despite having adequate intelligence. The president is, in fact, not unintelligent, but he may well be dysrationalic.

And he is not alone. Many people display the systematic inability to think or behave rationally despite the fact that they have more than adequate IQs. One of the reasons that many of us are dysrationalic to some extent is that, for a variety of reasons, we have come to overvalue the kinds of thinking skills that IQ tests measure and undervalue other critically important cognitive skills, such as the ability to think rationally.

Although most people would say that the ability to think rationally is a clear sign of a superior intellect, standard IQ tests devote no section to rational thinking as cognitive scientists would define the term. To think rationally means adopting appropriate goals, taking the appropriate action given one's goals and beliefs, and holding beliefs that are commensurate with available evidence. Although IQ tests do assess the ability to focus on an immediate goal in the face of distraction, they do not assess at all whether a person has the tendency to develop goals that are *rational* in the first place. Likewise, IQ tests are good measures of how well a person can hold beliefs in short-term memory and manipulate those beliefs, but they do not assess at all whether a person has the tendency to *form* beliefs rationally when presented with evidence. And again, similarly, IQ tests are good measures of how efficiently a person processes information that has been provided, but they do not at all assess whether the person is a *critical assessor* of information as it is gathered in the natural environment.

Given that IQ tests measure only a small set of the thinking abilities that people need, it is amazing that they have acquired the power that they have. IQ tests determine, to an important degree, the academic and professional careers of millions of people in the United States. University admissions offices depend on indicators that are nothing but proxies for IQ scores, even if the admissions office dare not label them as such. The vaunted SAT test has undergone many name changes (from Scholastic Achievement Test, to Scholastic Aptitude Test, to Scholastic Assessment Test, to simply the letters SAT) in order to disguise one basic fact that has remained constant throughout these changes — it is a stand-in for an IQ test.[2] It is the same in law school, business school, and medical school — admission assessment devices are often simply disguised proxies for IQ. Young children in affluent neighborhoods are given IQ tests to determine which of them will be admitted to exclusive preschools. Older children are given IQ tests to determine whether they will be allowed to enter a gifted program. Corporations and the military as well are dependent on assessment and sorting devices that are little more than disguised intelligence tests. Even the National Football League in the United States gives prospective quarterbacks an IQ test.[3]

Perhaps some of this attention to intelligence is necessary, but what is not warranted is the ignoring of capacities that are of at least equal importance — the capacities that sustain rational thought and action. It is ludicrous for society to be so fixated on assessing intelligence and to virtually ignore rationality when it is easy to show that the societal consequences of irrational thinking are profound. And yet, oddly enough, I have discovered that there is enormous resistance to the idea of giving full value to mental abilities other than intelligence. For instance, when I lecture on how I think society has overvalued mental traits like intelligence and undervalued other traits such as rationality, someone in the audience will invariably respond with a variant of the rhetorical question "Well, would you want someone with an IQ of 92 doing surgery?" My answer is that perhaps not—but that I also would not want someone with a rationality quotient (RQ) of 93 serving on the judicial bench, someone with an RQ of 91 heading a legislature, someone with an RQ of 76 investing my retirement funds, someone with an RQ of 94 marketing the home I am selling, or a guidance counselor with an RQ of 83 advising the children in my school district.

Of course, currently, we do not have a rationality quotient, as we have an IQ, an intelligence quotient, which might explain, at least to some extent, why IQ has acquired such value in relation to other equally important cognitive skills. In our society, what gets measured gets valued. But what if we could turn things around? What if we could actually devise tests of rationality? In fact, as I will discuss in the book, there is now enough knowledge available so that we could, in *theory*, begin to assess rationality as systematically as we do IQ. There is no such thing as the Wechsler or Stanford Rationality Test published by The Psychological Corporation. There is no RQ test. But the point is that there *could* be, using the same criteria used to justify current IQ tests (psychometric criteria such as reliability of measurement and the ability to predict relevant behavior). If not for professional inertia and psychologists' investment in the IQ concept, we could choose tomorrow to more formally assess rational thinking skills, focus more on teaching them, and redesign our environment so that irrational thinking is not so costly.

Whereas just thirty years ago we knew vastly more about intelligence than we knew about rational thinking, this imbalance has been redressed in the last few decades because of some remarkable work in behavioral decision theory, cognitive science, and related areas of psychology. In the past two decades cognitive scientists have developed laboratory tasks and real-life performance indicators to measure rational thinking tendencies such as sensible goal prioritization, reflectivity, and the proper calibration of evidence.

People have been found to differ from each other on these indicators. These processes have also been found to be separable from the kinds of cognitive operations tapped by intelligence tests. Interestingly, some people can have very high IQs but be remarkably weak when it comes to the ability to think rationally.

What This Book Is *Not* About

At this point the reader probably expects me to reveal that this book is about the importance of the emotions (so-called emotional intelligence), or about the importance of social skills (of so-called social intelligence), or about the importance of creativity or some other supracognitive characteristic. Further, many readers might well expect me to say that IQ tests do not measure anything important, or that there are many different kinds of intelligence, or that all people are intelligent in their own way.

In fact, I will be saying *none* of these things—and in many instances I will be saying just the opposite. First, this is not a book about social or emotional skills. Because I questioned the comprehensiveness of standard IQ tests at the outset of this chapter, some may have thought that this was a signal that I was going to emphasize noncognitive domains. This is the strategy most commonly employed by critics of intelligence as it is conventionally measured with standard IQ tests. Critics of intelligence as it is conventionally defined often point out that IQ tests fail to assess many domains of psychological functioning that are essential. For example, many largely noncognitive domains such as socioemotional abilities, motivation, empathy, and interpersonal skills are almost entirely unassessed by tests of cognitive ability. However, these standard critiques of intelligence tests often contain the unstated assumption that although intelligence tests miss certain key noncognitive areas, they encompass most of what is important cognitively. It is this unstated assumption that I am challenging. In fact, intelligence, as conventionally measured, leaves out many critical *cognitive* domains—domains of thinking itself. Some of the thinking domains that are missing are related to the ability to make optimal decisions at important choice points in life.

In short, there is no need to look outside of the cognitive domain for things that IQ tests miss. However, when I say that intelligence, as measured with standard IQ tests, leaves something out, I do not mean to "blow off" conventional views of intelligence as is common in many popular books. It is fashionable to say that intelligence has nothing to do with real life, or that the items on IQ tests are just parlor games related only "school smarts." Decades of research in psychology contradicts this view. IQ tests measure something that is cognitively real and that does relate to real life.

In fact, the way we use the term *intelligence* in day-to-day discourse reveals that we do not think that it is so trivial after all. People are termed "bright" and "quick" and "smart" in ways that clearly indicate that it is not social or emotional qualities that we are talking about. And these terms are used often and nearly universally with positive connotations. In fact, "bright" and "quick" and "sharp" are used in general discourse to pick out precisely a quality assessed on standard IQ tests (something termed "fluid g" in the psychological literature). It may not be politically correct to laud IQ at certain cocktail parties, but all the parents at those same cocktail parties do want that quality for their children. When their children have behavioral/cognitive difficulties, parents are much more accepting of diagnostic categories that do not have "low IQ" attached.[4] In short, we seem very confused about intelligence. We value it in private, but would never say so in public.

The Source of the Confusion about Bush's Intelligence

It is telling to note that President Bush's supporters were as surprised by his pro-rated IQ results as were his detractors. Like his detractors, they did not expect him to do well on the tests. So *both* groups were confused about what the tests show and do not show. Bush's detractors described him as taking disastrously irrational actions, and they seemed to believe that the type of poor thinking that led to those disastrous actions would be picked up by the standard tests of intelligence. Otherwise, they would not have been surprised when his scores were high rather than low. Thus, the Bush detractors must have assumed that a mental quality (rational thinking tendencies) could be detected by the tests that in fact the tests do not detect at all.

In contrast, Bush's supporters like his actions but admit that he has "street smarts," or common sense, rather than "school smarts." Assuming his "school smarts" to be low, and further assuming that IQ tests pick up only "school smarts," his supporters were likewise surprised by the high pro-rated IQ scores that were indicated. Thus, his supporters missed the fact that Bush would excel on something that *was* assessed by the tests. The supporters assumed the tests measured only "school smarts" in the trivial pursuit sense ("who wrote *Hamlet?*") that is easily mocked and dismissed as having nothing to do with "real life." That the tests would actually measure a quality that cast Bush in a favorable light was something his supporters never anticipated. For different reasons from those of the detractors, Bush's supporters were quite confused about what such tests do and do not measure.

There is more, however. It is not just that people are confused about what IQ tests assess and what they do not assess. People are also very confused about the concept of intelligence itself. The so-called folk language (everyday usage) of the term *intelligence* is an utterly inconsistent mess. It is a unique confluence of inconsistent terminology, politically infused usage, and failure to assimilate what science has found out about the nature of human cognitive abilities. A desire to help to clarify this situation was what led me to invent the term *dysrationalia*.

It is important to point out, however, that Bush is not a typical case of dysrationalia, in the sense that he would not be the first example to come to mind. Dysrationalia is the inability to think and behave rationally despite having adequate intelligence. People were surprised when informed of Bush's measured intelligence. In more clear-cut cases of dysrationalia, people are in *no doubt* about the intelligence of the individual in question. It is the blatantly irrational acts committed by people of obvious intelligence that shock and surprise us and that call out for explanation. These are the most obvious cases of dysrationalia.

In the next chapter I will discuss some of these more clear-cut cases and explain why we should not expect them to be rare. That we are surprised when we hear about such cases indicates that we have confused views about what intelligence is and what IQ tests measure—and that we undervalue human rationality because we tend to deify intelligence.

Dysrationalia:
Separating Rationality and Intelligence

Rationality gives us greater knowledge and greater control over our own actions and emotions and over the world. . . . It enables us to transform ourselves and hence transcend our status as mere animals, actually and also symbolically.

—*Robert Nozick*, The Nature of Rationality, *1993*

John Allen Paulos is a smart man. He is a professor of mathematics at Temple University and the author of several popular books, including the best-selling *Innumeracy*. On any existing intelligence test, Professor Paulos would score extremely high. Nevertheless, Paulos did a very stupid thing—in fact, a whole sequence of stupid things. The sequence began with a single action that, itself, may or may not have been stupid: Professor Paulos bought the stock of WorldCom at $47 per share in early 2000.

Whether or not that act was wise, the act of buying even more of the stock when it had fallen to $30 later in the year seems much less prudent. As Paulos tells us in his book *A Mathematician Plays the Stock Market*, by that time, the problem of overcapacity in the long-distance phone industry was becoming clear. However, Paulos admits that he "searched for the good news, angles, and analyses about the stock while avoiding the less sanguine indications" and flatly confesses that "my purchases were not completely rational" (p. 13).

His purchases became even *less* rational later in October 2000, when the stock was at $20 and he continued to buy ("I bought more shares even though I knew better," he says, p. 24) when mounting evidence indicated that he should have been selling rather than buying ("there was apparently a loose connection between my brain and the buy button on my Schwab online account," p. 24). As things got steadily worse, Paulos concealed from his wife that he had been buying stock on margin (buying with borrowed money). After the stock price was halved yet again, Paulos began e-mailing the CEO of WorldCom in a desperate attempt to gain control of the situation (he offered to write copy for the company so that it could more effectively "state its case" to the investment world).

By late 2001, Professor Paulos could not stand to be out of contact with the stock's price for even an hour. As late as April 2002 he was still in thrall to the idea that he would keep buying as the stock went down and then re-coup some of his losses when it bounced back up. He was still buying when the price was $5. However, on April 19 the stock rose to over $7, and Paulos did finally resolve to sell. However, it was Friday, and he did not get back from a lecture in northern New Jersey until after the market closed. By the next Monday, the stock had lost a third of its value, and he finally ended the ordeal, selling at a huge loss. WorldCom eventually collapsed to a worth of 9¢ after accounting fraud was revealed. In his fascinating book, Paulos medi-tates on the mental states that led him to violate every principle of sound investing (diversification, etc.). He has no trouble telling you that he was a smart man who acted foolishly (he says that "the thought of the stock even now sometimes momentarily unhinges me," p. 150).

David Denby's story is, if anything, even stranger than that of Paulos. Denby is also a very intelligent man. He is a staff writer and film critic for *The New Yorker* who has written a very well received book on — and titled — *Great Books*. He lived in a valuable New York apartment and wanted to continue to own it after his divorce. That meant buying out his ex-wife. Except that the numbers didn't add up. The apartment was worth $1.4 million, and there were a lot of other complications and, well, Denby decided that he would try to make $1 million in the stock market in the year 2000. That makes sense, doesn't it? Exactly the sort of thing for any reasonable fellow to do, right?

In his hilarious book *American Sucker*, Denby tells us how, in late 1999 and early 2000 he liquidated all of his conservative investment vehicles (index stock funds, bonds, insurance policies) and invested in technology funds and dot-com stocks. His entire 401(k) accumulation was rolled over into a fund that invested in nothing but volatile NASDAQ companies. All this took place in late 1999 and early 2000, remember (the NASDAQ peaked at over 5000 in March 2000 — in May 2004 it was trading under 2000, and in May 2007 it was still under 3000). All this was done even though Denby admitted, "I was ignorant. I understood only the most rudimentary things about the stock market; I knew nothing of the new communications technologies. . . . I knew damn well that a large part of the current boom, at least in the Internet sector, was sheer desire. . . . But doubt was overwhelmed by hope," pp. 18, 28). Throughout 2000 and 2001, he continued to buy companies with business "models" but without revenues, sales, or profits.

At first Denby was successful, and he admitted that he heard, but ignored, very clear warnings even from market enthusiasts to "take some off the table" because the types of stocks he held were outrageously overvalued. He describes how he clearly processed, but willfully ignored, the warning of one investment specialist from the Wharton School of Business, who noted that the NASDAQ had doubled in five months without any change at all in earnings projections. But these early days of success were brief. Denby tells us that by October 2002, sitting on $900,000 worth of losses, he was asking himself the question "Was I insane in 2000?" (p. 320).

Both David Denby and John Allen Paulos took actions over an extended period of time that were disastrous. Neither verbal cognitive ability (Denby) nor quantitative cognitive ability (Paulos) in large amounts seemed to have helped much here. Denby and Paulos provide vivid examples of smart people acting foolishly, and we are surprised at such cases. We are amazed when a physician loses all his pension funds in a speculative financial venture. We are astounded that there are highly trained scientists who are creationists. We cannot figure out why an educated professional would ignore proven medical treatment and instead go to Mexico for a quack therapy. We are puzzled when we hear that some Holocaust deniers are university professors with degrees in history. When our neighbors, who are high school teachers, ask us to become involved in a pyramid sales scheme, we are flabbergasted. In short, we find it paradoxical when smart people believe preposterous things and take disastrous actions.

In fact, we are wrong to be surprised by such cases. There is really nothing remarkable about smart people acting stupidly—once we understand what this colloquialism means in the language of modern cognitive science. Our tendency to see something remarkable in this phenomenon reflects flaws in our folk language of mental life—flaws that are fostered by the confusing ways that psychologists themselves speak about concepts such as intelligence.

What to Call These Cases?

There are a variety of folk phrases to describe cases like those with which I opened this chapter. For example, Robert Sternberg once edited a book titled *Why Smart People Can Be So Stupid*, considered the logic of the volume's title, and found it wanting! A typical dictionary definition of the adjectival form of the word *smart* is "characterized by sharp quick thought; bright" or "having or showing quick intelligence or ready mental capacity." Thus, being smart seems a lot like being intelligent, according to the dictionary. Sternberg points out that the same dictionaries tell us that a stupid person is "slow to learn or understand; lacking or marked by lack of intelligence." Thus, if a smart person is intelligent, and stupid means a lack of intelligence and, by the law of contradiction, someone cannot be intelligent and not intelligent, the "smart people being stupid" phrase seems to make no sense.

But if we look at the secondary definitions of the term, we see what is motivating the phrase "smart but acting stupid." The second definition of the word *stupid* in Dictionary.com is "tending to make poor decisions or careless mistakes"—a phrase which attenuates the sense of contradiction. A similar thing happens if we analyze the word *dumb* to see if the phrase, "smart but acting dumb," makes sense. The primary definition describes "dumb" as the antonym of "intelligent," again leading to a contradiction. But in phrases referring to decisions or actions such as "what a dumb thing to do!" we see a secondary definition like that of stupid: tending to make poor decisions or careless mistakes. These phrases pick out a particular meaning of "stupid" or "dumb"—albeit not the primary one.

For this reason, Sternberg suggested that a better phrasing for these examples is that they represent smart people acting foolishly.[1] Harvard cognitive scientist David Perkins likewise prefers the term *folly* to characterize what is being described in these examples. A foolish person is a person "lacking good sense or judgment; showing a lack of sense; unwise; without judgment or discretion." This picks out the aspect of "stupid" and "dumb" that we wish to focus on here—the aspect that refers not to intelligence (general mental "brightness"), but instead to the tendency to make judicious decisions (or, rather, injudicious ones).

I am not at all concerned with arguing about the terminology here. However we phrase it—"smart but acting dumb," "smart but acting foolish," or whatever—it is only essential that the phrase pick out the phenomenon that we are discussing: intelligent people taking injudicious actions or holding unjustified beliefs.

The Broad versus Narrow Intelligence Debate

There is just one problem here. Some conceptualizations of intelligence define it, at least in part, as the ability to adapt to one's environment.[2] But surely the tendency to make judicious decisions that serve one's goals is part of what we mean by adaptation to the environment. Thus, we are right back at the problem of contradiction again. If we are concerned with cases where intelligent people make foolish decisions (decisions that do not serve their goals), and intelligence is in part the tendency to make decisions that serve one's goals, then we have a contradiction—smart people can't *possibly* have the (general) tendency to act foolishly.[3]

What is happening here is that we are bumping up against an old controversy in the study of cognitive ability—the distinction between broad and narrow theories of intelligence. Broad theories include aspects of functioning that are captured by the *vernacular* term *intelligence* (adaptation to the environment, showing wisdom and creativity, etc.), whether or not these aspects are actually measured by existing tests of intelligence. Narrow theories, in contrast, confine the concept of intelligence to the set of mental abilities actually tested on extant IQ tests. Narrow theories adopt the operationalization of the term that is used in psychometric studies of intelligence, neurophysiological studies using brain imaging, and studies of brain disorder. This definition involves a statistical abstraction from performance on established tests and cognitive ability indicators. It yields a scientific concept of general intelligence usually symbolized by g or, in cases where the fluid/crystallized theory is adopted, fluid intelligence (Gf) and crystallized intelligence (Gc). I am referring here to the Cattell/Horn/Carroll theory of intelligence—as close as there is to a consensus view in the field of intelligence research.[4] Sometimes called the theory of fluid and crystallized intelligence (symbolized Gf/Gc theory), this theory posits that tests of mental ability tap a small number of broad factors, of which two are dominant. Fluid intelligence (Gf) reflects reasoning abilities operating across of a variety of domains—in particular, novel ones. It is measured by tasks of abstract reasoning such as figural analogies, Raven Matrices, and series completion (for example, what is the next number in the series 1, 4, 5, 8, 9, 12, __?). Crystallized intelligence (Gc) reflects declarative knowledge acquired from acculturated learning experiences. It is measured by vocabulary tasks, verbal comprehension, and general knowledge measures. The two dominant factors in the fluid/crystallized theory reflect a long history of considering two aspects of intelligence: intelligence-as-process (Gf) and intelligence-as-knowledge (Gc).

The narrow view of intelligence then takes these operationally defined constructs—g, Gf, Gc—and validates them in studies of brain injury, educational attainment, cognitive neuroscience, developmental trends, and information processing. These constructs of the narrow theory are grounded in the types of mental abilities measured on traditional tests of intelligence.

It might help the discussion of broad versus narrow views if we mark these abilities with an easily remembered acronym—MAMBIT (to stand for: the mental abilities measured by intelligence tests). The narrow view of the intelligence concept, in viewing intelligence as MAMBIT, differs from the broad view in expressly *not* including in its primary definition a host of things that appear in broad theories: adaptation to the environment, real-life decision making, showing wisdom and creativity, etc. Notice that the contradictions that I discussed above in the phrases "smart but acting dumb" or "smart but acting foolish" do not occur if a narrow definition of intelligence is adopted— but they present a paradox if a broad view is adopted. On the former view, the "smart but acting foolish" phenomenon might occur quite frequently. Why? Simple really. On the narrow view, smart and foolish are two different things. Smart refers to the mental faculties that are specifically tapped by IQ tests (MAMBIT; most likely Gf). MAMBIT does not encompass variation in the qualities that lead to behavioral acts that we call dumb, stupid, or foolish—failure to show: judicious decision making, adequate behavioral regulation, wise goal prioritization, sufficient thoughtfulness, or the proper calibration of evidence. If smart is just MAMBIT and dumb refers to a set of characteristics not encompassed by MAMBIT, then the phrase "smart but acting dumb" simply marks a case where two different mental faculties are out of kilter (one is high and one is low).

In contrast, the broad view of intelligence creates problems of interpretation. The broad view has trouble articulating just what it is that the phrase "smart but acting dumb" is drawing our attention to. A broad view that defines "smart" (intelligence) as encompassing adaptation to the environment or judicious decision making has no place for a smart person repeatedly acting foolishly (maladaptively, injudiciously, or unwisely). Under the broad view, smart people who continually act foolishly are simply not as smart as we thought they were.

Why do people resist this conclusion? Why does folk psychology not dispense with the notion of "smart but acting stupid" and simply treat "smart but acting stupid" people as "not smart"? I conjecture it is because we have noticed that such people possess a lot of that quality that is assessed, narrowly, on existing IQ tests, and that folk psychology has evolved to mark and value this mental capacity.

What I am suggesting is that there is an inconsistency in the folk view of intelligence. Studies of people's folk theories of intelligence have found that people tend to take a broad view of intelligence.[5] But, nonetheless, people seem to find something odd in the "smart but acting dumb" phenomenon. I suggest that the folk theory finds something worth noting in the phenomenon because the folk theory *does* recognize MAMBIT. That people are surprised when this quality (MAMBIT) is out of kilter with adaptive behavior shows that people have a so-called g-model lodged in their broad folk theory of intelligence—a model that dictates that all aspects of mental functioning should vary together (if high on one, high on the other).

In short, the folk theory overvalues MAMBIT by viewing as odd any case where other good mental qualities do not go together with high MAMBIT. In this way, the folk theory undervalues other mental faculties by giving pride of place to MAMBIT in defining what is "odd." In fact, some psychologists have encouraged this folk psychological tendency by adopting broad definitions of intelligence that, ironically, impede us from giving proper recognition to other mental faculties. I say ironically because many of these same psychologists have adopted broad definitions in an explicit attempt to reduce the importance of "the part of intelligence that IQ tests measure." However, in adopting a broad definition they have fostered just the opposite—they have encouraged the concept of intelligence to become an imperialist power in the language of the mental. This is not the best strategy for scientific purposes—and it has untoward social implications as well.

Rationality—the Missing Element

Broad definitions of intelligence conflate the two individual difference factors in the phrase "smart but acting foolishly" into one concept. The "smart" part is MAMBIT. The foolish part refers to tendencies to take or not take judicious actions, make sensible decisions, or behave appropriately to the situation. Broad theories conjoin the two (MAMBIT and sensible decision making) under the umbrella term *intelligence*. Such broad views of intelligence lead to the privileging of MAMBIT and the devaluing of the non-MAMBIT parts of the broad definition. This is because MAMBIT has a name (IQ), is measured explicitly (by IQ tests), and has a one-hundred-year history that many people know at least a little about. If we would name (and measure) the other things (and not just call them part of intelligence), we would be better able to give them proper emphasis. And we do have an omnibus name for these other things. Adaptive behavioral acts, judicious decision making, efficient behavioral regulation, sensible goal prioritization, reflectivity, the proper calibration of evidence—all of the characteristics that are lacking when we call an action foolish, dumb, or stupid—are precisely the characteristics that cognitive scientists study when they study rational thought.

Dictionary definitions of rationality tend to be rather lame and unspecific ("the state or quality of being in accord with reason"), and some critics who wish to downplay the importance of rationality have promulgated a caricature of rationality that involves restricting its definition to artificial skills such as solving logic problems of the type found in textbooks. The meaning of rationality in modern cognitive science is, in contrast, much more robust and important.[6]

Cognitive scientists recognize two types of rationality: instrumental and epistemic. The simplest definition of instrumental rationality—the one that emphasizes most that it is grounded in the practical world—is: Behaving in the world so that you get exactly what you most want, given the resources (physical and mental) available to you. Somewhat more technically, we could characterize instrumental rationality as the optimization of the individual's goal fulfillment. Economists and cognitive scientists have refined the notion of optimization of goal fulfillment into the technical notion of expected utility. The model of rational judgment used by decision scientists is one in which a person chooses options based on which option has the largest expected utility.[7] One discovery of modern decision science is that if people's preferences follow certain patterns (the so-called axioms of choice) then they are behaving as if they are maximizing utility—they are acting to get what they most want. This is what makes people's degrees of rationality measurable by the experimental methods of cognitive science. The deviation from the optimal choice pattern is an (inverse) measure of the degree of rationality.

The other aspect of rationality studied by cognitive scientists is termed epistemic rationality. This aspect of rationality concerns how well beliefs map onto the actual structure of the world.[8] The two types of rationality are related. Importantly, a critical aspect of beliefs that enter into instrumental calculations (that is, tacit calculations) is the probabilities of states of affairs in the world. Although many people feel (mistakenly or not) that they could do without the ability to solve textbook logic problems (which is why the caricatured view of rationality works to undercut its status), virtually no person wishes to eschew epistemic rationality and instrumental rationality, properly defined. Virtually all people want their beliefs to be in some correspondence with reality, and they also want to act to maximize the achievement of their goals.

Rationality and MAMBIT are two different things. So under a narrow view of intelligence, the notion of smart people acting foolishly presents no conceptual problem. Under a broad view—one that folds rationality into the concept of intelligence—smart people who continually act foolishly simply are not as smart as we thought they were. That there is a certain reluctance to actually *call* such people unintelligent has led me to believe that by taking the broad view we will not be successful in attenuating the tendency to over-value MAMBIT. My strategy is the opposite—to press the implications of a narrow view of intelligence, and to thus oppose the tendency of intelligence to rule an imperialist empire in the conceptual landscape of human mental faculties.

Dysrationalia as an Intuition Pump

Rationality is different from intelligence defined in the narrow sense as MAMBIT. Thus, it is not surprising for rationality and intelligence to be dissociated—for an individual to be low on one and high on the other. I gave one such dissociation a name in two articles I published in the early 1990s. In those articles, I coined the name for the disability based on the fundamental idea that underlies the concept of a learning disability in educational psychology: the idea of selective cognitive deficit as defined by a discrepancy from measured intelligence. We can see the discrepancy notion at work in, for example, the diagnostic criterion for developmental reading disorder in the *Diagnostic and Statistical Manual of Mental Disorders* IV (*DSM* IV) of the American Psychiatric Association. The criterion for reading disorder is: "Reading achievement that falls substantially below that expected given the individual's chronological age, measured intelligence, and age-appropriate education" (p. 48). The idea of defining a disability as an aptitude/achievement discrepancy (performance on some domain that is unexpectedly below intelligence) spread widely during the early years of the development of the learning disability concept. Note that the discrepancy idea contains the assumption that all good things should go with high intelligence. When a high IQ-test score is accompanied by subpar performance in some other domain, this is thought "surprising," and a new disability category is coined to name the surprise. So, similarly, the diagnostic criterion for mathematics disorder (sometimes termed dyscalculia) in *DSM* IV is that "Mathematical ability that falls substantially below that expected for the individual's chronological age, measured intelligence, and age-appropriate education" (p. 50).

The logic of discrepancy-based classification based on IQ-test performance has created a clear precedent whereby we are almost obligated to create a new disability category when an important skill domain is found to be somewhat dissociated from intelligence. It is just this logic that I exploited in creating a new category of disability—dysrationalia. The proposed definition of the disability was as follows:

> Dysrationalia is the inability to think and behave rationally despite adequate intelligence. It is a general term that refers to a heterogeneous group of disorders manifested by significant difficulties in belief formation, in the assessment of belief consistency, and/or in the determination of action to achieve one's goals. Although dysrationalia may occur concomitantly with other handicapping conditions (e.g., sensory impairment), dysrationalia is not the result of those conditions. The key diagnostic criterion for dysrationalia is a level of rationality, as demonstrated in thinking and behavior, that is significantly below the level of the individual's intellectual capacity (as determined by an individually administered IQ test).

Of course, it is easy to recognize that this definition was formulated to contain linguistic and conceptual parallels with the disability definitions devised by the National Joint Committee on Learning Disabilities and American Psychiatric Association.[9] My purpose was to use the concept of dysrationalia as an "intuition pump." The term *intuition pump* was coined by philosopher Daniel Dennett to refer to "a device for provoking a family of intuitions by producing variations on a thought experiment. An intuition pump is not, typically, an engine of discovery, but a persuader or pedagogical tool—a way of getting people to see things your way" (1980, p. 429). Dysrationalia is my intuition pump to help people see that rationality and intelligence are two different things, and that it should not be surprising that the two often dissociate.

But why do we need such an intuition pump? Most psychologists realize that IQ tests do not encompass all of the important mental faculties. Most educators also would know this if asked explicitly. Yet despite this, I still contend that *most of the time most people forget this fact*. In short, I think that

IQ tests do fool most of the people most of the time—including psychologists who should know better. By acknowledging the frequent occurrence of dysrationalia, we create the conceptual space to value abilities at least as important as MAMBIT—abilities to form rational beliefs and to take rational action.

THREE

The Reflective Mind, the Algorithmic Mind, and the Autonomous Mind

We engage in our share of rather mindless routine behavior, but our important acts are often directed on the world with incredible cunning, composing projects exquisitely designed under the influence of vast libraries of information about the world.
    —*Daniel Dennett*, Darwin's Dangerous Idea, 1995

As a concept in our cultural discourse, intelligence will not be disappearing anytime soon. Nor should it. At the same time, many of the long-standing debates surrounding intelligence will, in fact, gradually disappear. This is already happening. Over a decade ago Richard J. Herrnstein and Charles Murray published their book titled *The Bell Curve*, and it caused a sensation. That will not happen again. No book on intelligence will cause such a sensation again because, although the public is as yet unaware of it, the seemingly interminable IQ debate is over. All of the major questions about intelligence have been answered to a first order of approximation.[1] For example, we know that intelligence is roughly 50 percent heritable (due to genetics) and roughly 50 percent determined by a host of environmental factors. We know that an important portion of the variance in life outcomes (why some people do better than others) is associated with intelligence, but not the majority of the variance. The new debates are about mental abilities beyond those measured on IQ tests. Among those abilities are some that, when missing, cause dysrationalia.

Some critics of the intelligence concept like to imply that intelligence tests are just parlor games that measure nothing important. Alternatively, other critics allow that there may be something to the intelligence concept but that "we're all intelligent in our own way"—which amounts to the same thing. All of these critics are wrong. In addition, critics often imply that IQ does not predict behavior in the real world. That claim is also wrong.[2] Correspondingly, however, the positions of some of the more vociferous champions of the traditional intelligence concept are not without their flaws. For example, some of these IQ advocates like to imply that IQ tests capture most of what is important in cognition. I will cite in this book dozens of studies that are a refutation of this idea. In short, research is rendering obsolete the arguments of the harshest critics of IQ tests, along with those of their counterparts—the vociferous cheerleaders for a traditional concept of IQ.

Discussions of intelligence often go off the rails at the very beginning by failing to set the concept within a general context of cognitive functioning, thus inviting the default assumption that intelligence is the central feature of the mind. I will try to preclude this natural default by outlining a model of the mind and then placing intelligence within it. Cognitive scientists have made remarkable progress in sketching out the basics of how the mind works in the last twenty years. Indeed, ten years ago, cognitive scientist Steven Pinker titled a very influential book *How the Mind Works*. Twenty years before his book, the use of this title would have been viewed as laughably overreaching. Now that is no longer true. Nevertheless, the generic models of the mind developed by cognitive scientists often give short shrift to a question that the public is intensely interested in—how and why do people *differ* from each other in their thinking? In an attempt to answer that question, I am going to present a gross model of the mind that is true to modern cognitive science but that emphasizes individual differences in ways that are somewhat new. My model builds on a current consensus view of cognition termed dual-process theory.

Type 1 and Type 2 Processing

Evidence from cognitive neuroscience and cognitive psychology is converging on the conclusion that the functioning of the brain can be characterized by two different types of cognition having somewhat different functions and different strengths and weaknesses. That there is a wide variety of evidence converging on this conclusion is indicated by the fact that theorists in a diverse set of specialty areas (including cognitive psychology, social psychology, cognitive neuroscience, and decision theory) have proposed that there are both Type 1 and Type 2 processes in the brain.[3]

The defining feature of Type 1 processing is its autonomy. Type 1 processes are termed autonomous because: 1) their execution is rapid, 2) their execution is mandatory when the triggering stimuli are encountered, 3) they do not put a heavy load on central processing capacity (that is, they do not require conscious attention), 4) they are not dependent on input from high-level control systems, and 5) they can operate in parallel without interfering with each other or with Type 2 processing. Type 1 processing would include behavioral regulation by the emotions; the encapsulated modules for solving specific adaptive problems that have been posited by evolutionary psychologists; processes of implicit learning; and the automatic firing of overlearned associations.[4] Type 1 processing, because of its computational ease, is a common processing default. Type 1 processes are sometimes termed the adaptive unconscious in order to emphasize that Type 1 processes accomplish a host of useful things—face recognition, proprioception, language ambiguity resolution, depth perception, etc.—all of which are beyond our awareness. Heuristic processing is a term often used for Type 1 processing—processing that is fast, automatic, and computationally inexpensive, and that does not engage in extensive analysis of all the possibilities.

Type 2 processing contrasts with Type 1 processing on each of the critical properties that define the latter. Type 2 processing is relatively slow and computationally expensive—it is the focus of our awareness. Many Type 1 processes can operate at once in parallel, but only one Type 2 thought or a very few can be executing at once—Type 2 processing is thus serial processing. Type 2 processing is often language based and rule based. It is what psychologists call controlled processing, and it is the type of processing going on when we talk of things like "conscious problem solving."

One of the most critical functions of Type 2 processing is to override Type 1 processing. This is sometimes necessary because Type 1 processing is "quick and dirty." This so-called heuristic processing is designed to get you into the right ballpark when solving a problem or making a decision, but it is not designed for the type of fine-grained analysis called for in situations of unusual importance (financial decisions, fairness judgments, employment decisions, legal judgments, etc.). Heuristic processing depends on benign environments. In hostile environments, it can be costly.

All of the different kinds of Type 1 processing (processes of emotional regulation, Darwinian modules, associative and implicit learning processes) can produce responses that are irrational in a particular context if not overridden. In subsequent chapters, we shall discuss how humans act as cognitive misers by engaging in attribute substitution—the substitution of an easy-to-evaluate characteristic for a harder one even if the easier one is less accurate. For example, the cognitive miser will substitute the less effortful attributes of vividness or salience for the more effortful retrieval of relevant facts. But when we are evaluating important risks—such as the risk of certain activities and environments for our children—we do not want to substitute vividness for careful thought about the situation. In such situations, we want to employ Type 2 override processing to block the attribute substitution of the cognitive miser.

In order to override Type 1 processing, Type 2 processing must display at least two related capabilities. One is the capability of interrupting Type 1 processing and suppressing its response tendencies. Type 2 processing thus involves inhibitory mechanisms of the type that have been the focus of recent work on executive functioning.[5]

But the ability to suppress Type 1 processing gets the job only half done. Suppressing one response is not helpful unless there is a better response available to substitute for it. Where do these better responses come from? One answer is that they come from processes of hypothetical reasoning and cognitive simulation that are a unique aspect of Type 2 processing.[6] When we reason hypothetically, we create temporary models of the world and test out actions (or alternative causes) in that simulated world.

In order to reason hypothetically we must, however, have one critical cognitive capability—we must be able to prevent our representations of the real world from becoming confused with representations of imaginary situations.

For example, when considering an alternative goal state different from the one we currently have, we must be able to represent our current goal and the alternative goal and to keep straight which is which. Likewise, we need to be able to differentiate the representation of an action about to be taken from representations of potential *alternative* actions we are trying out in cognitive simulations. But the latter must not infect the former while the mental simulation is being carried out. Otherwise, we would confuse the action about to be taken with alternatives that we were just simulating.

Cognitive scientists call the confusion of representational states representational abuse, and it is a major issue for developmental psychologists who are trying to understand the emergence of pretense and pretend play in children (for example, a child saying "this banana is a phone"). Playing with the banana as a phone must take place without actual representations of banana and phone in the mind becoming confused. In a famous article, developmental psychologist Alan Leslie modeled the logic of pretense by proposing a so-called decoupling operation, which is illustrated in Figure 3.1.[7] In the figure, a primary representation is one that is used to directly map the world and/or is also directly connected to a response. Leslie modeled pretense by positing a so-called secondary representation that was a copy of the primary representation but that was decoupled from the world so that it could be manipulated—that is, be a mechanism for simulation.

As Leslie notes, the ongoing simulation leaves intact the tracking of the world by the primary representation: "Meanwhile the original primary representation, a copy of which was raised to a second order, continues with its definite and literal reference, truth, and existence relations. It is free to continue exerting whatever influence it would have on ongoing processes" (1987, p. 417). Nonetheless, dealing with secondary representations—keeping them decoupled—is costly in terms of cognitive capacity. Evolution has guaranteed the high cost of decoupling for a very good reason. As we were becoming the first creatures to rely strongly on cognitive simulation, it was especially important that we not become "unhooked" from the world too much of the time. Thus, dealing with primary representations of the world always has a special salience for us. An indication of the difficulty of decoupling is a behavior such as closing one's eyes while engaged in deep thought (or looking

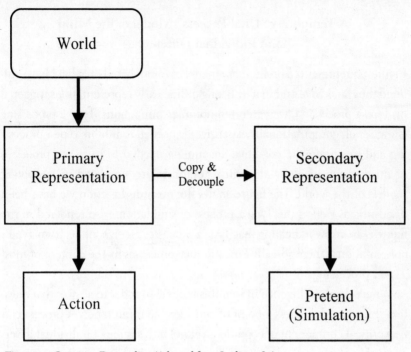

Figure 3.1. Cognitive Decoupling (Adapted from Leslie, 1987)

up at the sky or averting one's gaze). Such behaviors are attempts to prevent changes in our primary representations of the world from disrupting a secondary representation that is undergoing simulation.

We have, in Leslie's conception, a mechanistic account of how pretence, and mental simulation in general, are carried out without destabilizing primary representations. Other investigators have called the mental space where simulations can be carried out without contaminating the relationship between the world and primary representations a "possible world box." The important issue for our purposes here is that decoupling secondary representations from the world and then maintaining the decoupling while simulation is carried out is a Type 2 processing operation. It is computationally taxing and greatly restricts the ability to do any other Type 2 operation. In fact, decoupling operations might well be a major contributor to a distinctive Type 2 property—its seriality.

A Temporary "Dual-Process" Model of the Mind
and Individual Differences

Figure 3.2 represents a preliminary model of mind, based on what I have outlined thus far. I have said that by taking offline early representations triggered by Type 1 processing, we can often optimize our actions. Type 2 processing (slow, serial, computationally expensive) is needed to inhibit Type 1 processing and to sustain the cognitive decoupling needed to carry out processes of imagination whereby alternative responses are simulated in temporary models of the world. The figure shows the override function we have been discussing as well as the Type 2 process of simulation. Also rendered in the figure is an arrow indicating that Type 2 processes receive inputs from Type 1 computations. These so-called preattentive processes fix the content of most Type 2 processing.

Where does intelligence fit into this model? In order to answer that question, I first need to stress a point of considerable importance. A process can be a critical component of cognition, yet not be a source of individual differences (because people do not tend to vary much in the process). Such is the case with many Type 1 processes. They help us carry out a host of useful information processing operations and adaptive behaviors (depth perception, face recognition, frequency estimation, language comprehension, reading the intentions of others, threat detection, emotive responses, color perception, etc.)—yet there are not large individual differences among people on many of these processes. This accounts for some of the confusion surrounding the use of the term *intelligence* in cognitive science.

In a magazine article or textbook on cognitive science, the author might describe the marvelous mechanisms we have for recognizing faces and refer to this as "a remarkable aspect of human intelligence." Likewise, a book on popular science might describe how we have mechanisms for parsing syntax when we process language and also refer to this as "a fascinating product of the evolution of the human intellect." Finally, a textbook on evolutionary psychology might describe the remarkably intelligent mechanisms of kin recognition that operate in many animals, including humans. Such processes—face recognition, syntactic processing, detection of gaze direction, kin recognition—are all parts of the machinery of the brain. They are also sometimes

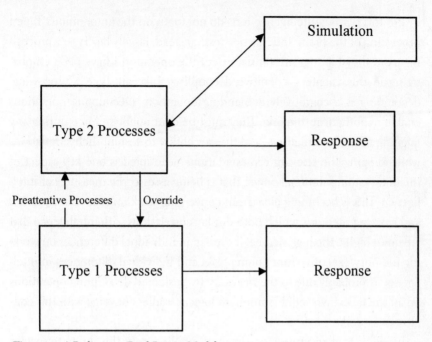

Figure 3.2. A Preliminary Dual-Process Model

described as being part of human intelligence. Yet none of these processes are ever tapped on intelligence tests. What is going on here? Is there not a contradiction?

In fact, there is not a contradiction at all if we understand that intelligence tests assess *only those aspects of cognitive functioning on which people tend to show large differences*. What this means is that intelligence tests will not routinely assess *all* aspects of cognitive functioning. There are many kinds of Type 1 processing that are important for us as a species, but on which there tend not to be large differences *between* people in the efficiency of functioning. Face recognition, syntactic processing, gaze direction detection, and kin recognition provide four examples of such domains.[8] This is why such processes are not assessed on intelligence tests. Intelligence tests are a bit like the personal ads in the newspaper — they are about the things that distinguish people, not what makes them similar. That is why the personals contain entries like "enjoy listening to Miles Davis" but not "enjoy drinking when I'm thirsty."

For this reason, intelligence tests do not focus on the autonomous Type 1 processing of the brain. Intelligence tests, instead, largely tap Type 2 processing. And they tap to a substantial extent the operation I have been emphasizing in this chapter—cognitive decoupling. Like all Type 2 processing, decoupling is a cognitively demanding operation. Decoupling operations enable hypothetical thinking. They must be continually in force during any ongoing mental simulations, and the raw ability to sustain such simulations while keeping the relevant representations decoupled is one key aspect of the brain's computational power that is being assessed by measures of intelligence. This is becoming clear from converging work on executive function and working memory, which both display correlations with intelligence that are quite high.[9] The high degree of overlap in individual differences on working memory/executive functioning tasks and individual differences in intelligence is probably due to the necessity for sustained decoupling operations on all the tasks involved. Neurophysiological studies converge with this conclusion as well.

In saying that an important aspect of intelligence is the ability to sustain cognitive decoupling, I really should be saying instead: an important aspect of *fluid* intelligence.[10] I am referring here to the Cattell/Horn/Carroll theory of intelligence mentioned in the previous chapter. Fluid intelligence (Gf) reflects reasoning abilities operating across a variety of domains—in particular, novel ones. Crystallized intelligence (Gc) reflects declarative knowledge acquired from acculturated learning experiences. Thus, Type 2 processes are associated with Gf. I shall work Gc into the model shortly, but will first turn to an even more critical complication.

Thinking Dispositions versus Cognitive Ability

At this point, we need to back up and think about how we explain behavior in the world. We will begin with an example of a lady walking on a cliff and imagine three incidents, three stories. The three stories are all sad—the lady dies in each. The purpose of this exercise is to get us to think about how we explain the death in each story. In incident A, a woman is walking on a cliffside by the ocean, and a powerful and totally unexpected wind gust blows her off the cliff; she is crushed on the rocks below. In incident B, a woman is walking on a cliffside by the ocean and goes to step on a large rock, but the rock is not a rock at all. Instead, it is actually the side of a crevice, and she falls down the crevice and dies. In incident C, a woman attempts suicide by jumping off an ocean cliff and dies when she is crushed on the rocks below.

In all three cases, at the most basic level, when we ask ourselves for an explanation of why the woman died, the answer is the same. The same laws of physics in operation in incident A (the gravitational laws that describe why the woman will be crushed upon impact) are also operative in incidents B and C. However, we feel that the laws of gravity and force somehow do not provide a complete explanation of what has happened in incidents B and C. This feeling is correct. The examples each call for a different level of explanation if we wish to zero in on the *essential* cause of death.

In incident A it is clear that *nothing more* than the laws of physics are needed (the laws of wind force, gravity, and crushing). Scientific explanations at this level—the physical level—are important, but for our purposes here they are relatively uninteresting. In contrast, the difference between incidents B and C is critical to the subsequent arguments in this book.

In analyzing incident B, a psychologist would be prone to say that when processing a stimulus (the crevice that looked somewhat like a rock) the woman's information processing system malfunctioned—sending the wrong information to response decision mechanisms which then resulted in a disastrous motor response. Cognitive scientists refer to this level of analysis as the algorithmic level.[11] In the realm of machine intelligence, this would be the level of the instructions in the abstract computer language used to program the computer (FORTRAN, COBOL, etc.). The cognitive psychologist works largely at this level by showing that human performance can be explained by positing certain information processing mechanisms in the brain (input coding mechanisms, perceptual registration mechanisms, short- and long-term-memory storage systems, etc.). For example, a simple letter pronunciation task might entail encoding the letter, storing it in short-term memory, comparing it with information stored in long-term memory, if a match occurs making a response decision, and then executing a motor response. In the case of the woman in incident B, the algorithmic level is the right level to explain her unfortunate demise. Her perceptual registration and classi-fication mechanisms malfunctioned by providing incorrect information to response decision mechanisms, causing her to step into the crevice.

Incident C, on the other hand, does not involve such an algorithmic-level information processing error. The woman's perceptual apparatus accurately recognized the edge of the cliff, and her motor command centers quite accu-rately programmed her body to jump off the cliff. The computational pro-cesses posited at the algorithmic level of analysis executed quite perfectly. No error at this level of analysis explains why the woman is dead in inci-dent C. Instead, this woman died because of her overall goals and how these goals interacted with her beliefs about the world in which she lived.

In 1996, philosopher Daniel Dennett wrote a book about how aspects of the human mind were like the minds of other animals and how other as-pects were not. He titled the book *Kinds of Minds* to suggest that within the brains of humans are control systems of very different types—different kinds of minds. In the spirit of his book, I am going to say that the woman in inci-dent B had a problem with the algorithmic mind and the woman in inci-dent C had a problem with the reflective mind. This terminology captures the fact that we turn to an analysis of goals, desires, and beliefs to understand a case such as C. The algorithmic level provides an incomplete explanation of behavior in cases like incident C because it provides an information pro-cessing explanation of how the brain is carrying out a particular task (in this case, jumping off a cliff) but no explanation of *why* the brain is carrying out this particular task. We turn to the level of the reflective mind when we ask questions about the *goals* of the system's computations (*what* the system is attempting to compute and *why*). In short, the reflective mind is concerned with the goals of the system, beliefs relevant to those goals, and the choice of action that is optimal given the system's goals and beliefs. It is only at the level of the reflective mind that issues of rationality come into play. Impor-tantly, the algorithmic mind can be evaluated in terms of efficiency but not rationality.

This concern for the efficiency of information processing as opposed to its rationality is mirrored in the status of intelligence tests. They are measures of efficiency but not rationality—a point made clear by considering a distinction that is very old in the field of psychometrics. Psychometricians have long distinguished typical performance situations from optimal (sometimes termed maximal) performance situations.[12] Typical performance situations are unconstrained in that no overt instructions to maximize performance are given, and the task interpretation is determined to some extent by the participant. The goals to be pursued in the task are left somewhat open. The issue is what a person would typically do in such a situation, given few constraints. Typical performance measures are measures of the reflective mind—they assess in part goal prioritization and epistemic regulation. In contrast, optimal performance situations are those where the task interpretation is determined externally. The person performing the task is instructed to maximize performance and is told how to do so. Thus, optimal performance measures examine questions of efficiency of goal pursuit—they capture the processing efficiency of the algorithmic mind. All tests of intelligence or cognitive aptitude are optimal performance assessments, whereas measures of critical or rational thinking are often assessed under typical performance conditions.

The difference between the algorithmic mind and the reflective mind is captured in another well-established distinction in the measurement of individual differences—the distinction between cognitive abilities and thinking dispositions. The former are, as just mentioned, measures of the efficiency of the algorithmic mind. The latter travel under a variety of names in psychology—thinking dispositions or cognitive styles being the two most popular. Many thinking dispositions concern beliefs, belief structure, and, importantly, attitudes toward forming and changing beliefs. Other thinking dispositions that have been identified concern a person's goals and goal hierarchy. Examples of some thinking dispositions that have been investigated by psychologists are: actively open-minded thinking, need for cognition (the tendency to think a lot), consideration of future consequences, need for closure, superstitious thinking, and dogmatism.[13]

The literature on these types of thinking dispositions is vast, and my purpose is not to review that literature here. It is only necessary to note that the types of cognitive propensities that these thinking disposition measures reflect are: the tendency to collect information before making up one's mind, the tendency to seek various points of view before coming to a conclusion, the disposition to think extensively about a problem before responding, the tendency to calibrate the degree of strength of one's opinion to the degree of evidence available, the tendency to think about future consequences before taking action, the tendency to explicitly weigh pluses and minuses of situations before making a decision, and the tendency to seek nuance and avoid absolutism. In short, individual differences in thinking dispositions are assessing variation in people's goal management, epistemic values, and epistemic self-regulation—differences in the operation of reflective mind. They are all psychological characteristics that underpin rational thought and action.

The cognitive abilities assessed on intelligence tests are not of this type. They are not about high-level personal goals and their regulation, or about the tendency to change beliefs in the face of contrary evidence, or about how knowledge acquisition is internally regulated when not externally directed. As we shall see in the next chapter, people have indeed come up with *definitions* of intelligence that encompass such things. Theorists often define intelligence in ways that encompass rational action and belief but, despite what these theorists argue, *the actual measures of intelligence in use assess only algorithmic-level cognitive capacity.* No current intelligence test that is even moderately used in practice assesses rational thought or behavior.

The algorithmic mind, assessed on actual IQ tests, is relevant in determining what happened in the case of lady B above, but it does not provide sufficient explanation of the case of lady C. To understand what happened in the case of lady C, we need to know about more than her processes of memory and speed of pattern recognition. We need to know what her goals were and what she believed about the world. And one of the most pressing things we want to know about lady C was whether there was some sense in her jumping off the cliff. We do not want to know whether she threw herself off with the greatest efficiency possible (an algorithmic-level question). We want to know whether it was *rational* for her to jump.

Moving toward a Tripartite Model of Mind

We have now bifurcated the notion of Type 2 processing into two different things—the reflective mind and the algorithmic mind. If we give Type 1 processing its obvious name—the autonomous mind—we now have a tripartite view of thinking that departs somewhat from previous dual-process views because the latter tended to ignore individual differences and hence to miss critical differences in Type 2 processing. The broken horizontal line in Figure 3.3 represents the location of the key distinction in older, dual-process views. The figure represents the classification of individual differences in the tripartite view, and it identifies variation in fluid intelligence (Gf) with individual differences in the efficiency of processing of the algorithmic mind. In contrast, thinking dispositions index individual differences in the reflective mind. The reflective and algorithmic minds are characterized by continuous individual differences. Continuous individual differences in the autonomous mind are few. Disruptions to the autonomous mind often reflect damage to cognitive modules that result in very discontinuous cognitive dysfunction such as autism or the agnosias and alexias.[14]

Figure 3.3 highlights an important sense in which rationality is a more encompassing construct than intelligence. To be rational, a person must have well-calibrated beliefs and must act appropriately on those beliefs to achieve goals—both properties of the reflective mind. The person must, of course, have the algorithmic-level machinery that enables him or her to carry out the actions and to process the environment in a way that enables the correct beliefs to be fixed and the correct actions to be taken. Thus, individual differences in rational thought and action can arise because of individual differences in intelligence (the algorithmic mind) or because of individual differences in thinking dispositions (the reflective mind). To put it simply, the concept of rationality encompasses two things (thinking dispositions of the reflective mind and algorithmic-level efficiency) whereas the concept of intelligence—at least as it is commonly operationalized—is largely confined to algorithmic-level efficiency.

The conceptualization in Figure 3.3 has two great advantages. First, it conceptualizes intelligence in terms of what intelligence tests actually measure. That is, all current tests assess various aspects of algorithmic efficiency (including the important operation that I have emphasized here—the ability to sustain cognitive decoupling). But that is all that they assess. None attempt to measure directly an aspect of epistemic or instrumental rationality, nor do

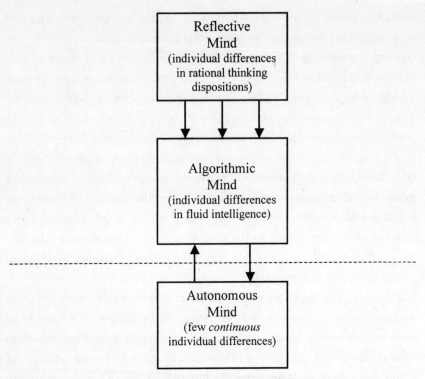

Figure 3.3. Individual Differences in the Tripartite Framework

they examine any thinking dispositions that relate to rationality. It seems perverse to define intelligence as including rationality when no existing IQ test measures any such thing! The second advantage is that the model presented in Figure 3.3 explains the existence of something that folk psychology recognizes—smart people doing dumb things (dysrationalia).

It is clear from Figure 3.3 why rationality and intelligence can come apart, creating dysrationalia. As long as variation in thinking dispositions is not perfectly correlated with intelligence, then there is the statistical possibility of dissociations between rationality and intelligence. Substantial empirical evidence indicates that individual differences in thinking dispositions and intelligence are far from perfectly correlated. Many different studies involving thousands of subjects have indicated that measures of intelligence display only moderate to weak correlations (usually less than .30) with some thinking dispositions (for example, actively open-minded thinking, need for cognition) and near zero correlations with others (such as conscientiousness, curiosity, diligence).[15]

Psychologist Milton Rokeach, in his classic studies of dogmatism, puzzled over why his construct displayed near-zero correlations with intelligence test scores. He mused that "it seems to us that we *are* dealing here with intelligence, although not the kind of intelligence measured by current intelligence tests. Apparently, intelligence tests do not tap the kinds of cognitive functioning we have been describing in this work. This seems paradoxical. For the current work is concerned with the very same cognitive processes with which intelligence tests are allegedly concerned" (1960, p. 407). The paradox that Rokeach was noticing was the drastic mismatch between the *claims* for the concept of intelligence and the cognitive processes that tests of the construct actually measure. In the current view, Rokeach's measure of dogmatism is indeed an important thinking disposition of the reflective mind, but there is no reason to consider it an aspect of intelligence. Dogmatism/openness is instead an aspect of the reflective mind that relates to rationality.

It is important to note that the thinking dispositions of the reflective mind are the psychological mechanisms that underlie rational thought. Maximizing these dispositions is not the criterion of rational thought itself. Rationality involves instead the maximization of goal achievement via judicious decision making and optimizing the fit of belief to evidence. The thinking dispositions of the reflective mind are a means to these ends. Certainly high levels of such commonly studied dispositions as reflectivity and belief flexibility are needed for rational thought and action. But "high levels" does not necessarily mean the maximal level. One does not maximize the reflectivity dimension for example, because such a person might get lost in interminable pondering and never make a decision. Likewise, one does not maximize the thinking disposition of belief flexibility either, because such a person might end up with a pathologically unstable personality. Reflectivity and belief flexibility are "good" cognitive styles (in that most people are not high enough on these dimensions, so that "more would be better"), but they are not meant to be maximized.

Thinking Dispositions as Predictors of
Rational Thought and Action

There is a further reason to endorse the tripartite structure I am proposing here—an empirical reason. In order to statistically predict rational thought and action to a maximum extent, one needs to take into account aspects of the reflective mind in addition to intelligence. For example, an important aspect of epistemic rationality is the ability to calibrate evidence appropriately to belief. One rule of such calibration is that ambiguous evidence should lead to tentative belief. People often violate this stricture, particularly when myside bias is operating. Research has found that the tendency to follow this stricture is more strongly related to two thinking dispositions—the tendency to believe in certain knowledge and the need for cognition—than it is to intelligence.

In my own laboratory, we have developed an argument evaluation task in which we derive an index of the degree to which argument evaluation is associated with argument quality independent of prior belief.[16] Intelligence did in fact correlate with the ability to avoid belief bias in our task. Nonetheless, we have consistently found that, *even after statistically controlling for intelligence*, individual differences on our index of argument-driven processing can be predicted by a variety of thinking dispositions, including: measures of dogmatism and absolutism; categorical thinking; flexible thinking; belief identification; counterfactual thinking; superstitious thinking; and actively open-minded thinking.

It is likewise with other aspects of rational thinking. For example, researchers have studied situations where people display a particular type of irrational judgment—they are overly influenced by vivid but unrepresentative personal and testimonial evidence and are under-influenced by more representative and diagnostic statistical evidence.[17] We have studied a variety of such situations in my own laboratory and have consistently found that dispositions toward actively open-minded thinking are consistently associated with reliance on the statistical evidence rather than the testimonial evidence. Furthermore, this association remains even after intelligence has been statistically controlled for. Similar results have obtained for a variety of other rational thinking tendencies that we have studied.[18]

Not only is rational thought itself predicted by thinking dispositions after intelligence is controlled, but the *outcomes* of rational thought are likewise predicted by variation in characteristics of the reflective mind.[19] In an important study, Angela Duckworth and Martin Seligman found that the grade point averages of a group of eighth graders were predicted by measures of self-discipline (that is, indicators of response regulation and inhibition at the reflective level) after the variance due to intelligence was partialled out. A longitudinal analysis showed that self-discipline was a better predictor of the changes in grade point average across the school year than was intelligence. The personality variable of conscientiousness—which taps the higher-level regulatory properties of the reflective mind—has been shown to predict, independent of intelligence, academic performance and measures of performance in the workplace. Political psychologist Philip Tetlock studied expert political forecasters, all of whom had doctoral degrees (and hence were presumably of high intelligence), and found that irrational overconfidence was related to thinking dispositions that tapped epistemic regulation. Wandi Bruine de Bruin and colleagues recruited a sample of 360 citizens who resembled the demographics of the 2000 U.S Census for their area and administered to them a battery of rational thinking tasks similar to those to be discussed in this book. They formed a composite score reflecting overall rational thinking skill and found that it was correlated (negatively) with a composite measure of poor decision making outcomes (for instance, bouncing checks, having been arrested, losing driving privileges, credit card debt, eviction). Importantly, Bruine de Bruin and colleagues found that variance in their decision outcome measure was predicted by rational thinking skill after the variance due to cognitive ability had been controlled.

Across the range of tasks I have been reviewing here (and more that will be discussed in later chapters), it is the case that performance on the rational thinking tasks was moderately correlated with intelligence. Nevertheless, the magnitude of the associations with cognitive ability left much room for systematic variation to be explained by thinking dispositions. Furthermore, if anything, the studies I have reviewed *over*estimate the linkage between intelligence and rational thinking. This is because many of these studies have given the subjects helpful instructions—for example, that they are to put aside their prior opinion and reason in an unbiased manner. There is a pattern in the literature indicating that when subjects are not given such in-structions—when they are left free to reason in a biased or unbiased manner according to their wish (as we all do in real life)—then the correlations be-tween unbiased reasoning and intelligence are nearly zero (as opposed to the modest .30–.40 correlations that obtain when such instructions are given).[20]

For example, in a series of studies, developmental psychologist Paul Klac-zynski has shown that when evaluating evidence, if subjects are not given explicit instructions to decontextualize—that is, to set aside their prior opinion—there is little correlation between intelligence and the tendency to reason in an unbiased manner.[21] My research group has produced evi-dence consistent with this finding. In one study, Maggie Toplak and I had subjects generate arguments relevant to a controversial issue (should people be allowed to sell their internal organs?). We also assessed where individu-als stood on the issues in question. We found a substantial myside bias on the task (people tended to give more arguments in favor of their position than against), but the degree of myside bias was not correlated with cognitive ability.

In short, our research converges with that of other researchers in indicating that in informal reasoning situations where people are not told to put aside their prior beliefs, intelligence is unrelated to the tendency to reason in an unbiased manner. That such ambiguous situations (without explicit instruc-tions to be unbiased) are common in real life means that the literature might actually be overestimating the contribution of intelligence to rationality be-cause many tasks in the experimental literature contain explicit instructions on the task requirements and how to reason in order to fulfill them. More in-telligent people appear to reason better only when you tell them in advance what good thinking is! This makes little sense given the structure in Figure 3.2. It becomes more explicable from within the expanded model presented in Figure 3.4.

The override capacity is a property of the algorithmic mind, and it is indi-cated by the arrow labeled A in Figure 3.4. However, previous dual-process theories have tended to ignore the higher-level cognitive function that *initi-ates* the override function in the first place. This is a dispositional property of the reflective mind that is related to rationality. In the model in Figure 3.4, it is represented by arrow B, which represents, in machine intelligence terms,

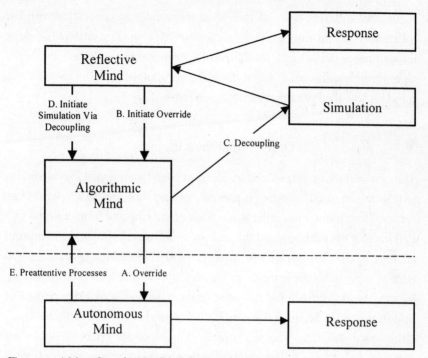

Figure 3.4. A More Complete Model of the Tripartite Framework

the call to the algorithmic mind to override the Type 1 response by taking it offline. This is a different mental function from the override function itself (arrow A), and I have presented evidence indicating that the two functions are indexed by different types of individual differences—the ability to sustain the inhibition of the Type 1 response is indexed by measures of fluid intelligence, and the tendency to initiate override operations is indexed by thinking dispositions such as reflectiveness and need for cognition.

Figure 3.4 represents another aspect of cognition somewhat neglected by previous dual-process theories. Specifically, the override function has loomed large in dual-process theory, but less so the simulation process that computes the alternative response that makes the override worthwhile. Figure 3.4 explicitly represents the simulation function as well as the fact that the call to initiate simulation originates in the reflective mind. The decoupling operation (indicated by arrow C) itself is carried out by the algorithmic mind and the call to initiate simulation (indicated by arrow D) by the reflective mind.

Again, two different types of individual differences are associated with the initiation call and the decoupling operator—specifically, rational thinking dispositions with the former and fluid intelligence with the latter. Finally, the algorithmic mind receives inputs from the computations of the autonomous mind via so-called preattentive processes (arrow E).

Don't Forget the Mindware!

The term *mindware* was coined by Harvard cognitive scientist David Perkins to refer to the rules, knowledge, procedures, and strategies that a person can retrieve from memory in order to aid decision making and problem solving.[22] Perkins uses the term to stress the analogy to software in the brain/computer analogy. Each of the levels in the tripartite model of mind has to access knowledge to carry out its operations, as illustrated in Figure 3.5. As the figure indicates, the reflective mind not only accesses general knowledge structures but, importantly, accesses the person's opinions, beliefs, and reflectively acquired goal structure. The algorithmic mind accesses micro-strategies for cognitive operations and production system rules for sequencing behaviors and thoughts. Finally, the autonomous mind not only accesses evolutionarily compiled encapsulated knowledge bases, but also retrieves information that has become tightly compiled and available to the autonomous mind due to overlearning and practice.

It is important to note that what is displayed in Figure 3.5 are the knowledge bases that are *unique* to each mind. Algorithmic- and reflective-level processes also receive inputs from the computations of the autonomous mind (see arrow E in Figure 3.4). The mindware available for retrieval, particularly that available to the reflective mind, is in part the product of past learning experiences. And here we have a direct link to the Cattell/Horn/Carroll theory of intelligence mentioned earlier. The knowledge structures available for retrieval by the reflective mind represent Gc, crystallized intelligence (intelligence-as-knowledge). Recall that Gf, fluid intelligence (intelligence-as-process), is already represented in the figure. It is the general computational power of the algorithmic mind—importantly exemplified by the ability to sustain cognitive decoupling.

The Gf/Gc theory is the most comprehensive theory of intelligence

Knowledge Structures

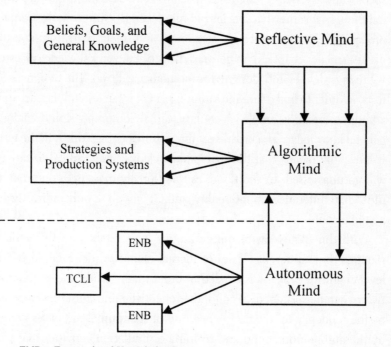

ENB = Encapsulated Knowledge Base
TCLI = Tightly Compiled Learned Information

Figure 3.5. Knowledge Structures in the Tripartite Framework

available that has extensive scientific validation. It is thus important to see how both of its major components miss critical aspects of rational thought. Fluid intelligence will, of course, have some relation to rationality because it indexes the computational power of the algorithmic mind to sustain decoupling. Because override and simulation are important operations for rational thought, Gf will definitely facilitate rational action in some situations. Nevertheless, the tendency to initiate override (arrow B in Figure 3.4) and to initiate simulation activities (arrow D in Figure 3.4) are both aspects of the reflective mind unassessed by intelligence tests, so the tests will miss these components of rationality.

The situation with respect to Gc is a little different. It is true that much of the mindware of rational thought would be classified as crystallized intelligence in the abstract. But is it the kind of crystallized knowledge that is specifically assessed on the tests? The answer is no. The mindware of rational thought is somewhat specialized mindware (it clusters in the domains of probabilistic reasoning, causal reasoning, and scientific reasoning, as I will discuss in later chapters). In contrast, the crystallized knowledge assessed on IQ tests is deliberately designed to be nonspecialized. The designers of the tests, in order to make sure the sampling of Gc is fair and unbiased, explicitly attempt to *broadly* sample vocabulary, verbal comprehension domains, and general knowledge. The broad sampling insures unbiasedness in the test, but it inevitably means that the specific knowledge bases critical to rationality will go unassessed. In short, Gc, as traditionally measured, does not assess individual differences in rationality, and Gf will do so only indirectly and to a mild extent.

With this discussion of mindware, we have established that rationality requires three different classes of mental characteristic. First, algorithmic-level cognitive capacity is needed in order that override and simulation activities can be sustained. Second, the reflective mind must be characterized by the tendency to initiate the override of suboptimal responses generated by the autonomous mind and to initiate simulation activities that will result in a better response. Finally, the mindware that allows the computation of rational responses needs to be available and accessible during simulation activities. Intelligence tests assess only the first of these three characteristics that determine rational thought and action. As measures of rational thinking, they are radically incomplete.

Scoping Out the President's Brain

Now that we have the sketch of a tripartite model of mind on the table, we can revisit the example that started this book—the thought processes of President George W. Bush. American politics is so polarized, however, that a quick caveat is needed. In such domains, people tend not to agree on the facts of the matter. However, I would argue that at this late date—after eight years of the Bush presidency—we have such a wealth of consistent testimony and commentary that, in science, it would be called a convergence of evidence.

In fact, no one doubts—*not even the president's supporters*—that the aspects of his cognition that I will describe here are characteristic of him. His supporters, in numerous books, have described exactly these characteristics. In Chapter 1, I mentioned the characterizations of the president by David Frum and George Will, two conservative commentators not unsympathetic to many of Bush's policies. Frum, the president's onetime speechwriter, has a view of Bush's intellect ("sometimes glib, even dogmatic; often uncurious and as a result ill-informed," p. 272) that is exactly mirrored by that of John McCain, the Republican senator whom Bush defeated for the Republican nomination in 2000 but who was one of the president's most important allies on the issue of the war in Iraq. McCain was asked if Bush ever asks his opinion. McCain replied, "No, no, he hasn't. As a matter of fact he's not intellectually curious" (Woodward, 2006, p. 419). Reporters Evan Thomas and Richard Wolffe in *Newsweek* magazine fill in other parts of the pattern in their coverage of how Bush handled the war in Iraq. One of our senior officials in Baghdad had observed Bush in various videoconferences and noticed how the president's "obvious lack of interest in long, detailed discussions, had a chilling effect" (p. 37). The reporters note, "by all accounts, he is not intellectually curious. Occasionally outsiders brought into the Bush Bubble have observed that faith, not evidence, is the basis for decision making" (p. 37). Numerous other commentators echo these descriptions.[23]

Nonetheless, many of the same commentators who criticize President Bush's thinking insist that he does not lack intelligence. Ronald McCallum, a friend of Bush's from Yale, says that Bush was "extraordinarily intelligent, but was not interested in learning unless it had practical value" (Kessler, 2004, p. 27). The prime minister of Great Britain, Tony Blair, found that Bush had a quality that President Clinton had lacked, reliability, and Blair repeatedly told his associates that Bush was "very bright" (Barnes, 2006, p. 56).

What Blair is referring to with the phrase "very bright" is the same thing—fluid intelligence (Gf)—that allowed Bush to do well in his youth on tests that were intelligence proxies.[24] However, the presence of that fluid intelligence did not prevent him from displaying irrational thought tendencies well known to psychologists. The president has only one of the three characteristics that determine rational thought—algorithmic-level cognitive capacity. He lacks two essential factors—the mindware that supports rational action and the thinking dispositions of the reflective mind that support rational thought. In fact, his case shows how important are the intellectual qualities that IQ tests leave out.

There are published and well-investigated scales or tasks for most of the thinking dispositions suggested in the characterizations of George Bush's thinking. The technology of rationality assessment is so far advanced that we could imagine, for example, testing President Bush (long before his presidency) and in fact predicting exactly the thinking attributes that are now known to be so tellingly characteristic of the him. Using the terms for the actual scales and tasks in the literature, formal tests of rational thinking might have revealed that the president is: overconfident; low in typical intellectual engagement; low in openness to experience; high in belief perseverance; high in confirmation bias; high in faith in intuition; high in impulsiveness; high in one-sided thinking; low in need for cognition; low in openness to experience; does not engage in counterfactual thinking; treats beliefs as possessions (has high belief identification); is high in need for closure, and low in thought flexibility.

The directions of Bush's score on all of these thinking dispositions is in the direction associated with lower rationality.[25] Fluid intelligence provided no inoculation against a confluence of problematic intellectual traits. President Bush is an intelligent person—consistent with his test scores and consistent with what many people close to him insist. But he is not a very rational person.

FOUR

Cutting Intelligence Down to Size

In U.S. society, cognitive skills have become practically equated with intellectual skills—the mental bases of intelligence. This equation is a mistake.
—*Robert J. Sternberg*, Wisdom, Intelligence, and
Creativity Synthesized, *2003b*

I totally agree with the epigraph from Robert Sternberg that leads this chapter. We are missing something important by treating intelligence as if it encompassed all cognitive abilities. I coined the term *dysrationalia* over a decade ago in order to draw attention to a large domain of cognitive life (rational thinking) that intelligence tests fail to assess. The idea that IQ tests do not measure all of the important human faculties is not new. This is precisely what broad theorists of intelligence[1] have been emphasizing all these years, so in one sense I align myself with the critics who wish to stop the overvaluing of MAMBIT (the mental abilities measured by intelligence tests). However, my strategy for taming MAMBIT is different from that of critics such as Howard Gardner and Robert Sternberg.[2] These critics want to broaden the term *intelligence* (practical intelligence, bodily-kinesthetic intelligence, etc.) in order to signal that MAMBIT is not all of intelligence in their view. Even though I am in sympathy with some of the goals of these critics, I think their strategy is mistaken. Here is why.

Broad theorists inflate the concept of intelligence. By inflation I mean putting into the term more than what the IQ tests measure. One very strong tendency among broad theorists is to use adjectives to differentiate the more encompassing parts of their intelligence concept from the "IQ-test part." Major theorists such as Sternberg and Gardner talk about practical intelligence, creative intelligence, interpersonal intelligence, bodily-kinesthetic intelligence, etc. In such usages, the word *intelligence* becomes a marker for "optimal or expert behavior in the domain of." So, for instance, when Sternberg discusses high practical intelligence it can be translated to mean "optimal behavior in the domain of practical affairs" or when Gardner talks about high bodily-kinesthetic intelligence he means little more than high functioning in the bodily-kinesthetic domain. The word *intelligence* is actually superfluous. It is there merely to add status to the domain in question (to put it on equal footing with MAMBIT). The strategy seems to be something like the following: Because intelligence is a valued trait and we want bodily-kinesthetic talent to be valued too, we'll fuse the term *intelligence* onto it in order to transfer some of the value from intelligence to bodily-kinesthetic talent. Indeed, this is why educators have been so enthusiastic about the "multiple intelligences" idea. Its scientific status is irrelevant to them. They use it as a motivational tool—to show that "everyone is intelligent in some way." The same is true for the coinages of social intelligence or emotional intelligence.[3]

However, there are unintended consequences—some of them quite ironic—of this strategy, consequences that have been insufficiently appreciated. Labeling different mental entities with the same name will encourage just the assumption that many broad theorists want to attack—it will inflate the esteem given to MAMBIT. In a sense, broad theorists seek to break a rule of construct validity—and of common sense: things that are named the same should go together. If these things really are separate mental faculties, and we wish to emphasize their separateness, then we should not suggest just the opposite by calling them all "intelligences." However, by their profligate use of the term *intelligence*, the broad theorists subvert their very purpose of isolating "the IQ-test part of intelligence" (MAMBIT) as only one aspect of many cognitive virtues that we may wish to value (spatial ability, creative ability, fluency in practical affairs). People will continue to make the assumption that MAMBIT will correlate with all of these other things (in psychometric terms, an assumption of positive manifold).[4]

By inflating the word *intelligence,* by associating it with more and more valued mental activities and behaviors, broad theorists will succeed in doing just the opposite of what many of them intend—cutting "the IQ-test part of intelligence" down to size. If you inflate the conceptual term *intelligence* you will inflate all its close associates as well—and 100 years of mental testing makes it a simple historical fact that the closest associate of the term *intelligence* is "the IQ-test part of intelligence."

Intelligence Imperialism

In commenting on the history of his multiple intelligences theory, Howard Gardner relates that he considered other terms such as *skills* or *capacities* but then realized "that each of these words harbored pitfalls, I finally elected to take the bold step of appropriating a word from psychology and stretching it in new ways. . . . I was proposing an expansion of the term intelligence so that it would encompass many capacities that had been considered outside its scope" (1999, pp. 33, 34). Likewise, Robert Sternberg argues that "the time perhaps has come to expand our notion and everyone's notion of what it means to be intelligent" (2003b, p. 69). Clearly one of the goals here is to emphasize that there are aspects of cognitive life that are important outside of MAMBIT. This is a goal that I share with many broad theorists.[5] However, I do not see why everything in human nature, cognitively speaking, has to have the label *intelligence*—particularly when there are readily existing labels (both scientific labels and folk labels) for some of those things (rationality, creativity, wisdom, critical thinking, open-minded thinking, reflectivity, sensitivity to evidence).

In fact, I feel that if we continue this tendency to label every positive cognitive trait with the term *intelligence,* that will just add to the inappropriate societal deification of MAMBIT that Sternberg, Gardner, and I are united in deploring. Consider a thought experiment. Imagine that someone objected to the emphasis given to horsepower (engine power) when evaluating automobiles. They feel that horsepower looms too large in people's thinking. In an attempt to deemphasize horsepower, they then begin to term the other features of the car things like "braking horsepower" and "cornering horsepower" and "comfort horsepower." Would such a strategy serve to make people less likely to look to engine power as an indicator of the "goodness" of a car? I think not. I think it would instead serve to make more salient just the feature that the person wished to deemphasize. Just as calling "all good car things" horsepower would serve to emphasize engine power, I would argue that calling "all good cognitive things" intelligence will contribute to the deification of MAMBIT.[6]

Such a strategy will impede educational efforts to foster other cognitive characteristics. For example, critical thinking skills vanish under broad definitions of intelligence. All critical thinking or rationality assessments become part of intelligence if the latter is conceptualized broadly. And again, intelligence-test producers gain from these broad definitions because people will continue to associate the broad concept of intelligence with these tests. How could they not? The tests carry the label *intelligence*, and the producers of the tests are not eager to discourage the association with broad theories. For example, it took real chutzpah for David Wechsler to define intelligence in his book as "the aggregate or global capacity of the individual to act purposefully, to think rationally and to deal effectively with his environment" (1958, p. 7) despite authoring an IQ test with his name on it that measured no such thing!

A Different Strategy: Using Dysrationalia to Tame the Intelligence Concept

My strategy is different from that of the broad theorists. It is to let MAMBIT carve what it can out of nature in scientific terms, label that *intelligence*, and restrict intelligence to that. We can tame intelligence in folk psychology by pointing out that there are legitimate scientific terms as well as folk terms for the other valued parts of cognitive life and that some of these are measurable. This strategy uses to advantage a fact of life that many IQ-test critics have lamented—that intelligence tests are not going to change any time soon.[7] The tests have the label *intelligence* and thus MAMBIT will always be dominant in the folk psychology of intelligence. I would argue that it is a mistake to ignore this fact.

Instead, my strategy is to open up some space for rationality in the lexicon of the mental and, in doing so, tame the intelligence concept. My strategy in proposing dysrationalia was to prevent intelligence from absorbing the concept of rationality—something that IQ tests do not measure. I confine the term *intelligence* to MAMBIT, a practice having the not inconsiderable advantage of getting usage in line with the real world of measurement and testing. We have coherent and well-operationalized concepts of rational action and belief formation. We have a coherent and well-operationalized concept of MAMBIT. No scientific purpose is served by fusing these concepts, because they are very different. To the contrary, scientific progress is made by *differentiating* concepts. Dysrationalia, and the fact that it is not rare, highlights the fact that "all good things" (rationality in this case) do not always go with MAMBIT.

Broad views of intelligence that spread the term over a variety of other constructs are in part motivated by a desire to tame the valuation and prestige of IQ tests. The strategy seems to be to downplay the importance of IQ tests by broadening the definition of intelligence to make them (IQ tests) only a small part of this larger concept—a strategy of dilution. But stretching the intelligence concept by dumping into it other positively valued things will not succeed in breaking the link with IQ tests for two reasons. The first reason is that the effects of the one-hundred-year history of associating MAMBIT with the concept intelligence are not going to be easily attenuated. Second, even in the expanded concept of the broad view, MAMBIT remains the easiest component to measure—and the most measurable component will always end up dominating all other components no matter how broad or encompassing the concept.

If I am right, then the strategy of the broad theorists ends up giving us the worst of all worlds—an intelligence concept more prestigious than ever (because all kinds of other good things have now been associated with it) and the value of MAMBIT further inflated through its association with the new broadened view of intelligence! More important, short shrift is given to the concept of rationality because it is not separately named (but instead conflated with and lost within the intelligence concept). There is no imperative to actually assess rationality, because its semantic space has been gobbled up by the broadened view of intelligence. It will be even harder than it already is to stress that MAMBIT does not measure rational thinking. Although most people recognize that IQ tests do not encompass all of the important mental faculties, we often act (and talk) as if we have forgotten this fact. Where else does our surprise at smart people doing foolish things come from if not from the implicit assumption that rationality and intelligence should go together? The concept of dysrationalia (and the empirical evidence indicating that the condition is not rare) should help to attenuate our surprise at this phenomenon and to create conceptual space in which we can value abilities at least as important as MAMBIT—abilities to form rational beliefs and to take rational action.

MAMBIT: The Engine of the Brain without a Driver

Professional psychologists will immediately recognize my proposal to identify intelligence only as MAMBIT as a version of E. G. Boring's infamous dictum—and this recognition may cause some of them to balk at my proposal. Boring's dictum was that we should define intelligence as what the intelligence tests measure. However, what made Boring's suggestion objectionable was that neither he nor anyone else at the time (1923) knew what the tests measured. Because of this, Boring's definition of intelligence was truly circular. The situation now is totally different. We now know—from the standpoint of information processing and cognitive neuroscience—what the tests measure.

Unlike some critics of the traditional intelligence concept, I think there has been some justification in the inertia of the psychometric establishment regarding changes in IQ tests and in the (narrow) intelligence concept itself. Traditional intelligence research is a progressive research program in the sense that philosophers of science use that term. There is every indication that work in the traditional paradigm is carving nature at its joints.[8] First, the field has a consensus model in the form of the theory of fluid and crystallized intelligence. Much work has gone into uncovering the cognitive subcomponents of fluid intelligence. We now know that there is substantial overlap in the variance in Gf and the variance in measures of working memory capacity.[9] Importantly, the computational features of working memory have also been identified during the same period. The most critical insight has been that the central cognitive function tapped by working memory tasks is cognitive decoupling—the ability to manipulate secondary representations that do not track the world in one-to-one fashion as do primary representations.

Cognitive decoupling appears to be the central cognitive operation accounting for individual differences in Gf and, because of its role in simulation and hypothetical thinking, cognitive decoupling is a crucial mental capacity. Thus, traditional intelligence tests—and MAMBIT—converge on something important in mental life. They represent the fruits of a scientific research program that is progressively carving nature at an appropriate and important joint.[10]

I do not wish to minimize the importance of cognitive decoupling—the central individual difference component of MAMBIT. Decoupling operations help us carry out cognitive reform: the evaluation of our own beliefs and the critique of our own desires. Nevertheless, cognitive decoupling as measured on these tests is still a property of the algorithmic mind that is assessed under maximal rather than typical conditions. Such measures do not assess how *typical* it is for a person to engage in decoupling operations. They do not assess the propensity of the reflective mind to use such decoupling abilities for cognitive self-critique. They do not assess the *tendency* to engage in hypothetical thinking to aid problem solving. The *ability* to sustain cognitive decoupling does not guarantee rationality of behavior or thought. When we measure Gf we measure a critical aspect of the engine of the brain but not the skill of the driver.

Intelligence Misdefined as Adaptation

One type of broad definition of intelligence that has strong imperialist tendencies is represented by those definitions that emphasize intelligence as "adaptation to the environment" like that of Wechsler quoted above. Such definitions appropriate large areas of instrumental rationality into the definition of intelligence. To define intelligence as adaptation to the environment when the best known tests of the construct do not assess any such thing creates tremendous potential for confusion.

Such confusion is apparent in discussions of the so-called Flynn effect in the study of intelligence. Two decades ago, James Flynn systematically documented what some restandardizations of IQ tests had merely suggested—that IQs were rising over time. Overall IQs seem to have risen about 3 points per decade since about 1930. The gains are larger for Gf than for Gc. Cognitive psychologist Ulric Neisser edited a book commissioned by the American Psychological Association concerned with various explanations for the Flynn effect. The explanations considered were nutrition, urbanization, schooling, television, and preschool home environment, among others.[11] Interestingly, in his own chapter in the book, Flynn himself favored none of these explanations. Instead, he believed that the intelligence gains are in some sense not "real." In short, he believed that there have been IQ gains but not intelligence gains, according to his definition. As evidence for his position, he pointed to the lack of cultural flowering that he felt would result from a true intelligence increase. For him, contrary trends were indicated by the fact that "the number of inventions patented in fact showed a sharp decline over the last generation" (1998, p. 35) and that Who's Who books of eminent scientists were not bursting at the seams.

But why one would expect such things from an increase in MAMBIT is unclear. The tests do not measure rationality or creativity—things that might really lead to a cultural explosion of the type that Flynn is looking for. In fact, Flynn had tacitly adopted some sort of environmental adaptation definition of intelligence which MAMBIT does not meet. Thus, what some see as a paradox created by the Flynn effect (that IQ gains over the past generation have not been paralleled by concomitant societal achievements) I see as no paradox at all. It is puzzling only because we find it hard to keep in mind that, although our folk concept of intelligence might include adaptation to the environment, the tests on which the gains have been shown do not measure that at all. The tests measure MAMBIT—cognitive decoupling ability that is a critical mental skill, but one that is only one of three components needed for fully rational thought and behavior. The other two are the mindware and thinking dispositions that foster rational thought. That the Flynn effect is thought to present a puzzle shows how difficult it is not to deify intelligence by broadening the definition of it beyond what the tests measure.

The Dark Side of the Deification of Intelligence

Such deification of intelligence can have a truly perverse moral consequence that we often fail to recognize—the denigration of those low in MAMBIT. Such denigration goes back to the very beginnings of psychometrics as an enterprise. Sir Francis Galton would hardly concede that those low in IQ could feel pain: "The discriminative facility of idiots is curiously low; they hardly distinguish between heat and cold, and their sense of pain is so obtuse that some of the more idiotic seem hardly to know what it is. In their dull lives, such pain as can be excited in them may literally be accepted with a welcome surprise" (1883, p. 28).

Milder and subtler versions of this denigration continue down to the modern day. In 2004 author Michael D'Antonio published a book titled *The State Boys Rebellion* about the ill treatment of boys in the Walter E. Fernald School for the Feebleminded and how a group of boys residing at the school rebelled against this treatment. Disturbingly, however, reviews of the book tended to focus on the stories of those boys who later were found to have normal IQs. The *New York Times Book Review* (June 27, 2004) titled its review "A Ledger of Broken Arms: Misdiagnosis and Abuse at a School for the 'Feebleminded' in the 1950s." We might ask what in the world does "misdiagnosis" have to do with the issue of highlighting the ill treatment in these institutions? The implication here is that somehow it was less tragic for those "properly diagnosed"—whatever that may mean in this context. Shades of Galton, and of the dark side of the deification of intelligence, are revealed in the reactions to this book.

The historical tendency that Robert Sternberg has noted—the "tendency to conflate scores on tests of intelligence with some kind of personal value" (2003b, p. 13)—appears in modern life in many guises. As Sternberg suggests, intelligence has come to signify something like one's personal essence—some indication of personal worth. The deification of IQ and the denigration of low intelligence is now so complete that people would rather have a high IQ than almost any other physical or mental quality. Note, for example, how the diagnosis of intellectual disability has been reduced by almost half in the last 3–4 decades and the explosion of the incidence of disabilities whose definitions—particularly those definitions aimed at parents—stress the presence of normal IQ during the same period (e.g., learning disabilities, ADHD, Asperger's syndrome).[12] This shift is in part a function of social changes, consumerism infecting diagnostic categories, and ascertainment biases introduced by schools, clinicians, and parents. Many parents, for example, are much more accepting of diagnostic categories that do not have "low IQ" attached. Never mind that the life problems associated with some emotional and behavioral disorders are often much greater than those associated with many forms of moderate/mild intellectual disability. As physician G. Robert DeLong notes, "in my work I encounter youngsters whose mental retardation is insignificant as compared with their severe disorders of behavior. Finally, it is the behavioral disorder and not intellectual retardation that is decisive and destructive to family life. This suggests a fundamental flaw in the concept of mental retardation: 'mental' life constitutes not only intellectual ability (as measured by IQ tests)" (2004, p. 515).

This comment leads us to an ironic implication of accepting a broad definition of intelligence. If a broad definition is accepted, particularly one that emphasizes the "adaptation to the environment" criterion, then all of the categories of disability that have exploded in recent years will have to be regarded in a new light. Many cases of emotional disorders, behavioral disorders, and ADHD would *also* now represent cases of low intelligence, because it is almost the defining feature of these disabilities that they represent poor adaptations to the environment. It is fascinating to speculate about whether some of these categories of disability would have become so popular had the broad theorists won the day several decades ago. Imagine that the behavior of an ADHD child was routinely termed "low intelligence" in folk psychology. A response to the thought experiment might be that we would still notice "some difference" between an ADHD child (or even an emotionally disturbed child) and a child with intellectual disability. If we are tempted to give this response, think about what it means. It means that we can notice and label MAMBIT in folk psychology. As indicated earlier in this chapter, scientific evidence does converge on the conclusion that MAMBIT picks out a class of mental operations of considerable importance. The problem is just that folk psychology values those mental operations—and the tests used to measure them—too much. Gf is a mechanism, not a soul.

Folk Psychology Can Distinguish Intelligence and Rationality

Finally, my argument is, essentially, that we would value MAMBIT less if we would take care to label the things it is not (rationality) and not let the term *intelligence* incorporate those other things. I think that folk psychology does now differentiate between rationality and intelligence somewhat, but that folk psychology could be reformed to do this even more.

My feeling that folk psychology could be reformed to further mark the intelligence/rationality distinction is based on a study I conducted with my longtime colleague Richard West some years ago. We had subjects write, in a quite open-ended manner, about what they thought that intelligence was. That is, we asked them to discourse on the following: "What does it mean to say that a person is thinking or behaving intelligently? That is, explain what you mean when you use the term 'intelligence.' What are the characteristics of intelligent thinking and behavior?" Replicating earlier studies of the folk psychology of intelligence, we found that students had broad theories of intelligence that often incorporated aspects of rationality. However, the theories of intelligence were somewhat less broad when the subjects had previously been asked to give their folk theories of rationality with the following probes: "What does it mean to say that a person is thinking or behaving rationally? That is, explain what you mean when you use the term 'rationality.' What are the characteristics of rational thinking and behavior?"

Even more convincing was a third part of our questionnaire where, after responding with their personal definitions of intelligence and rationality (half the subjects were asked for the former first and half for the latter), the subjects were asked whether or not they differentiated between intelligence and rationality. Specifically, they were presented with the following probe: "Are rationality and intelligence related? Please explain." Overwhelmingly, subjects *did* see a difference between the two—often mentioning the "smart but acting dumb" phenomenon (dysrationalia) that I have discussed. Examples of typical responses are the following:

Subject 9:
Rationality and intelligence are definitely related in that their definitions largely overlap. Both include an ability to reason or think logically. They

go together in a sense that one who is rational is usually intelligent. They differ dramatically when looking at the inverse. For example, one can be intelligent (clever, bright) but in no way rational (behaving in an acceptable, reasonable manner). In the minds of many, Saddam Hussein is intelligent but is not rational. They differ in their expressions. Being rational or irrational is definitely more observable through one's actions and behaviors rather than through their thoughts.

Subject 10:

Rationality and intelligence are both related and unrelated. I feel that in order to behave rationally one must have intelligence in order to think about their behavior. Since rational behavior is behavior ruled by the head intelligence does play a part. The reason I think they are unrelated is that very intelligent people can and do exhibit irrational behavior. This is most often done when people's emotions take a hold and people act on them without intelligently thinking them through.

Subject 13:

Rationality and intelligence are related in certain ways; However, a person can be very rational and not very intelligent at the same time and vice versa. Many people have good or common sense abilities which would be rational ones; however, a lot of these people are not considered to be vastly intelligent. Although they have good rationale, thinking and behavior ability, they may have difficulty understanding, perceiving, and processing information (i.e., they may not be book smart, but are very street smart or good at everyday situations.) On the other hand there are many intelligent people who have the ability to easily comprehend information or stimulus but could not think or reason themselves out of a shoe box. I feel rationality and intelligence are definitely different; they are related at times, but a person could easily have the ability to be one or the other.

Subject 17:

Rationality and intelligence are related in that they both use reasoning and understanding. However, I believe intelligence, or one's capacity to obtain knowledge is somewhat innate whereas rationality is learned. An individual can learn to make rational decisions from being exposed to one's environment and its expectations. I do feel that rationality and intelligence are related in that if a person is intelligence [sic] then they can grasp rationality faster. They will understand concepts, experiences, and other things in a different manner than if they were unintelligent.

Subject 30:

Rationality and intelligence are very closely related. Both require the ability to look at subjects from each perspective and to be able to take these subjects apart and analyze each part. . . . Rationality, however, is expressly the ability at a specific time to keep all emotions out of the decision making process. In this respect someone who is intelligent may do irrational things at times. Also, someone who is rational and even tempered will have the ability to think things through but may not have the ability to see how his/her decisions will affect the future situation. In some senses, rationality and intelligence seem related, but in other areas they are quite different.

These responses indicate that folk psychology does seem to recognize dysrationalia, and in doing so it signals that it does distinguish between intelligence and rationality. Of course, this might have been more true in our experiment because previous questions drew attention to the concept of rationality and perhaps suggested the possibility of separating it from intelligence. But this is just my point. When they were given the term *rationality* (which they do not tend to think of spontaneously) our subjects had no trouble differentiating rationality from intelligence and then saw little difficulty in explaining the observation of smart people acting foolishly.

I hope now that the title of the chapter—Cutting Intelligence Down to Size—has been contextualized. What needs to be cut down to size is our conceptualization of intelligence—the tendency to incorporate all important mental qualities into it or to append it to every valued mental quality that we wish to praise or highlight. Instead, we should conceptualize intelligence as MAMBIT. By constricting the term *intelligence* we will create conceptual space for other qualities (rational thinking) that are currently given short shrift because they are not measured on IQ tests. Our culture's fixation on the intelligence concept has obscured other mental qualities that society needs at least as much. The failure to develop these mental qualities leads to dysrationalia. In the next several chapters we will see why dysrationalia occurs and why it is not rare — in short, we will see why intelligence is no inoculation against irrational thought and behavior.

Why Intelligent People Doing Foolish Things Is No Surprise

My counterfactual, introspective, and hard-thinking ancestor would have been eaten by a lion while his nonthinking but faster-reacting cousin would have run for cover. . . . Evidence shows that we do much less thinking than we believe we do.

—*Nassim Nicholas Taleb*, The Black Swan, 2007

In effect, all animals are under stringent selection pressure to be as stupid as they can get away with.

—*Peter Richerson and Robert Boyd*, Not by Genes Alone, 2005

You do not need to look far for examples of dysrationalia. In the domain of personal finance, the cases of John Paulos and David Denby discussed in Chapter 2 are not atypical. We now know why intelligent people like Paulos and Denby tend to lose a lot in the market during bad times, and why even during good markets many intelligent people do not make much money. Consider for a moment a very volatile period of the stock market, from the beginning of 1998 to the end of 2001. During that period, the Firsthand Technology Value mutual fund did very well. Its annualized total return for this period was 16 percent—that is, its average gain for this period was 16 percent *per year*. Yet the average investor who invested in this fund *lost* 31.6 percent of his or her money over this same four-year period.[1] From 1998 through 2001, a period in which the annualized return of the fund was +16 percent, investors lost a total of $1.9 billion (yes, that's billion with a b) by investing in this fund. How could this be true? How could investors have lost money in a fund whose investments showed an annualized gain of 16 percent over the same period?

The answer dawns after a moment of reflection. The +16 percent annualized return of the fund would have been the gain for any investor who was in the fund at the beginning of 1998 and stayed in it continuously through the end of 2001. But most investors did not stay in the fund throughout that period. They invested in the fund at different points and they cashed out of the fund at different points—and often the same investor came in and out of the fund multiple times. The Firsthand Technology Value fund was a very volatile fund during this period. When it gained, it gained a lot, and when it lost, it lost a lot. And now the seeming paradox is easily explained (in a way that says something about the prevalence of dysrationalia). Investors lost a tremendous amount of money in the fund because *they invested and cashed out at exactly the wrong times.* In other words, they bought the fund when it was high and sold when it was low. And because when it was high it was very high, and when it was low it was very low, such behavior resulted in extremely large losses to the individuals engaging in it.

Such self-defeating behavior was not limited to the Firsthand Technology Value fund. For example, during the same time period, Janus Mercury fund had an annualized return of +13.9 percent, but its investors lost money (annualized return of −7.4 percent); Fidelity Aggressive Growth earned an annualized return of +2.8 percent, but its investors realized an annualized loss of 24.1 percent; and the Invesco Dynamics fund had an annualized return of +7.0 percent, but its investors nevertheless lost money (−14.4 percent annualized return). Reporting on a study of 700 mutual funds during 1998–2001, financial reporter Jason Zweig notes that "to a remarkable degree, investors underperformed their funds' reported returns—sometimes by as much as 75 percentage points a year" (2002, p. 112). Zweig tells us that across the 700 funds the average total return was +5.7 percent annualized, but that the average investor earned only +1.0 percent. Zweig quotes Lawrence Siegel of the Ford Foundation as saying that "if investors earned the rates of return that the funds report, we'd all be rich. And why aren't we all rich? Because people keep shooting themselves in the foot" (p. 113). People who "keep shooting themselves in the foot" are irrational. Because most stock investors are high-income individuals and high incomes are associated with higher educational attainment, we can be assured that this gargantuan example of suboptimal behavior (investors lost over $200 billion of potential gains) represents dys-rationalia on a truly massive scale.

Cognitive scientists now know quite a bit about the psychological processes that sustain such widespread dysfunctional behavior. For example, many people suffer from overconfidence in their knowledge calibration. They think that they know more than they do, and they think they can process new information better and faster than others. This is an astoundingly bad mental trait to have as a stock market investor, because major markets are simply crawling with talented individuals analyzing financial data with sophisticated technological aids. Most of what these analysts have figured out about the market in general and about specific stocks in particular is already represented in the market price for a specific security. For "weekend investors" to think that they can figure out something about the market for a particular stock that these analysts have missed and use it to advantage is pure folly, yet thousands of investors (many with quite substantial IQs) are afflicted with this dysfunctional thinking trait. As a result, they display an investment behavior that lowers their overall return: they trade too much. Their too-frequent trading incurs additional transaction costs and, because their behavior is *not* based on any superior knowledge, their attempts at "market timing" (going in and out of the market repeatedly) also lower their return. Ironically, less confident investors tend to default more to a "buy and hold" strategy that has been judged superior by personal finance professionals. Psychologists have developed ways to measure this mental trait—the tendency toward overconfidence—that has such a significant effect on investing behavior.

The second psychological characteristic that leads people to make investment mistakes can quite often be useful. Our brains have evolved in such a way that they engage in a relentless search for patterns in the world. We seek relationships, explanations, and meaning in the things that happen around us. This characteristic is obviously very adaptive, but it backfires on us by encouraging us to expend effort trying to explain chance events. This is exactly what happens to some investors in the stock market. Markets generally, and individual companies more specifically, are buffeted constantly by small un-predictable events that move stock prices somewhat but really have no effect on a company's ability to pay future dividends over the long term (the factor that critically determines the value of its stock). It is a mistake to try to ex-plain these chance events and react to them, yet some investors have a very low threshold for doing so (they tend to over-react to chance events). The psychological disposition to seek explanations for chance events leads people to trade too much, thus reducing their overall long-term return (by incurring excessive transaction costs).

The third factor that leads to overtrading is called myopic loss aversion. It represents part of the work for which cognitive scientist Daniel Kahneman won the 2002 Nobel Prize in Economics. As part of their prospect theory of judgment and decision making, Kahneman and his colleague Amos Tversky posited that the expected subjective valuation of losses is roughly twice as strong as that of expected gains. That is, the pain that people feel they will experience when losing $100 is roughly twice as strong as the pleasure that they feel they will derive from gaining $100. That is where the term *loss aver-sion* comes from.[2] The "myopic" part of the phrase refers to our tendency to monitor investments on a time scale that is out of sync with the life span of the investment. For example, a 40-year-old individual invested for retirement would display myopic monitoring if she checked her investments hourly or daily (or even weekly). Professionals would recommend that such an indi-vidual check her investments monthly at most (more optimally, only 4–5 times a year).

Wait—isn't more information always better? What could be wrong with monitoring frequently? Plenty, actually. The stock market is volatile. There are many ups and downs. People are quite scared of losses (recall loss aver-sion) and thus tend to react strongly to downward price spikes. Each dip that is observed becomes a temptation to cash out and avoid or limit the loss. Individuals monitoring more frequently are presented with many more such opportunities and, not surprisingly, they are more likely to succumb to this temptation than are those monitoring infrequently. Then, once cashed out, individuals who frequently monitor are also more likely to have noticed when things have calmed down and prices are up—in short, when things seem safe. And, once they buy back into the market under these conditions, they have completed a cycle that perfectly illustrates what not to do in the stock market: sell low and buy high.

The factors discussed here—overconfidence, over-reacting to chance, and myopic loss aversion—are now accepted explanations of maladaptive behavior in the domain of personal finance. Work in cognitive psychology has shown that people vary in each of these processing styles and that this variation can be measured with laboratory tasks. Furthermore, that variation is known to be largely independent of intelligence—leading to a truly colossal example of dysrationalia: millions of quite intelligent investors losing billions of dollars of potential gains. Dysrationalia is clearly widespread. Why is this the case?

Humans as Cognitive Misers

The human brain has two broad characteristics that make it less than rational. One is a processing problem and one is a content problem. Intelligence provides insufficient inoculation against both.

The processing problem is that we tend to be cognitive misers in our thinking. The finding that humans are cognitive misers has been a major theme throughout the past 30 years of research in psychology and cognitive science.[3] When approaching any problem, our brains have available various computational mechanisms for dealing with the situation. These mechanisms embody a tradeoff, however. The tradeoff is between power and expense. Some mechanisms have great computational power—they can solve a large number of problems and solve them with great accuracy. However, this power comes with a cost. These mechanisms take up a great deal of attention, tend to be slow, tend to interfere with other thoughts and actions we are carrying out, and require great concentration that is often experienced as aversive. In contrast, other brain mechanisms are low in computational power but have the advantage that they are low in cost. These mechanisms cannot solve a wide range of problems and do not permit fine-grained accuracy, but they are fast-acting, do not interfere with other ongoing cognition, require little concentration, and are not experienced as aversive. They are the Type 1 processes discussed in Chapter 3, which are sometimes also termed heuristic processes.

Humans are cognitive misers because their basic tendency is to default to Type 1 processing mechanisms of low computational expense. Using less computational capacity for one task means that there is more left over for another task if they both must be completed simultaneously. This would seem to be adaptive. Nevertheless, this strong bias to default to the simplest cognitive mechanism—to be a cognitive miser—means that humans are often less than rational. Increasingly, in the modern world we are presented with decisions and problems that require more accurate responses than those generated by heuristic processing. Type 1 processes often provide a quick solution that is a first approximation to an optimal response. But modern life often requires more precise thought than this. Modern technological societies are in fact hostile environments for people reliant on only the most easily computed automatic response. Think of the multi-million-dollar advertising industry that has been designed to exploit just this tendency. Modern society keeps proliferating situations where shallow processing is not sufficient for maximizing personal happiness—precisely because many structures of market-based societies have been designed explicitly to *exploit* such tendencies. Being cognitive misers will seriously impede people from achieving their goals.

Why We Are Cognitive Misers

We humans will find any way we can to ease our cognitive load and process less information, but this is why we are often less rational than we might be. But why are we cognitive misers and as a result less than fully rational? In a word—evolution. Our cognitive mechanisms were designed by evolution, and evolution does not operate to produce humans who are perfectly rational.

There are a number of reasons why evolution would not be expected to guarantee perfect human rationality.[4] One reason is that rationality is defined in terms of maximization (for example, in the case of instrumental rationality, maximizing the expected utility of actions). In contrast to maximization, natural selection works on a "better than" principle. As Richard Dawkins puts it, "Natural selection chooses the better of present available alternatives.... The animal that results is not the most perfect design conceivable, nor is it merely good enough to scrape by. It is the product of a historical sequence of changes, each one of which represented, at best, the better of the alternatives that happened to be around at the time" (1982, p. 46). In short, the variation and selective retention logic of evolution "designs" for the reproductive advantage of one organism over the next, not for the optimality of any one characteristic (including rationality). It has been said that evolution should be described as the survival of the *fitter* rather than as the survival of the fittest.

Organisms have evolved to increase the reproductive fitness of genes, not to increase the rationality of humans. Increases in fitness do not always entail increases in rationality. Take, for example, the domain of beliefs. Beliefs need not always track the world with maximum accuracy in order for fitness to increase (see the epigraph from Nassim Nicholas Taleb that introduces this chapter). Thus, evolution does not guarantee perfect epistemic rationality. For example, evolution might fail to select out epistemic mechanisms of high accuracy when they are costly in terms of organismic resources (for example, in terms of memory, energy, or attention). An additional reason that belief-forming mechanisms might not be maximally truth preserving is that "a very cautious, risk-aversive inferential strategy—one that leaps to the conclusion that danger is present on very slight evidence—will typically lead to false beliefs more often, and true ones less often, than a less hair-trigger one that waits for more evidence before rendering a judgment. Nonetheless, the unreliable, error-prone, risk-aversive strategy may well be favored by natural selection. For natural selection does not care about truth; it cares only about reproductive success" (Stich, 1990, p. 62).

It is likewise in the domain of goals and desires. The purpose of evolution was not to maximize the happiness of human beings. As has become clear from recent research on the topic of affective forecasting, people are remarkably bad at making choices that make themselves happy.[5] This should be no surprise. The reason we have pleasure circuits in our brains is to encourage us to do things (survive and reproduce, help kin) that propagate our genes. The pleasure centers were not designed to maximize the amount of time we are happy.

The instrumental rationality of humans is not guaranteed by evolution for two further reasons. First, many genetic goals that have been lodged in our brain no longer serve our ends because the environment has changed. For example, thousands of years ago, humans needed as much fat as they could get in order to survive. More fat meant longer survival and because few humans survived beyond their reproductive years, longevity translated directly into more opportunities for gene replication. In short, our mechanisms for storing and utilizing energy evolved in times when fat preservation was efficacious. These mechanisms no longer serve the goals of people in our modern technological society where there is a McDonald's on practically every corner—the goals underlying these mechanisms have become detached from their evolutionary context. Finally, the cultural evolution of rational standards is apt to occur at a pace markedly faster than that of human evolution—thus providing ample opportunity for mechanisms of utility maximization to dissociate from local genetic fitness maximization.[6] Our evolutionary history does not guarantee that all of our brain defaults are rational.

As I discussed in Chapter 3, research on multiple-process theories of mind has been increasingly suggesting that some processes in our brains are at war with other processes. Parts of our minds are more oriented toward instrumental rationality—toward fulfilling our goals as people. In contrast, some brain processes are more directly oriented (in a short-leashed manner) to fulfilling ancient genetic goals that might not be current personal goals (many Type 1 processes, for instance). Some of the tendencies of the cognitive miser are evolutionary defaults. They were "good enough" in their day (our environment of evolutionary adaptation of thousands of years ago), but might not be serving us well now when our environments have radically changed.

Why Dysrationalia Is Widespread

In short, our brains are naturally lazy. Thus, in ordinary situations—when not specifically cued to avoid minimal information processing (as we are when taking tests, for example)—all people are subject to the irrationalities entailed when one is a cognitive miser. However, there is variation in the use of many of the information processing strategies of the cognitive miser. This means that there will be variation among people in their degree of rationality, as there is for almost any other cognitive/behavioral characteristic. Furthermore, we will see that this variation displays only a weak correlation with intelligence.

Earlier in this chapter, I said that the human brain is characterized by two broad traits that make it less than rational—one a processing problem and one a content problem. The processing problem is that we are cognitive misers. The content problem comes about because we need to acquire some very specific knowledge structures in order to think and act rationally. When knowledge structures that are needed to sustain rational behavior are not present, I will term this a mindware problem, again following Perkins's use of this term to refer to the rules, knowledge, procedures, and strategies that a person can retrieve from memory in order to aid decision making and problem solving. In Chapters 10 and 11, I will discuss mindware problems that cause much human irrationality.

Rational standards for assessing human behavior are social and cultural products that are preserved and stored independently of the genes. The development of probability theory, concepts of empiricism, logic, and scientific thinking throughout the centuries have provided humans with conceptual tools to aid in the formation and revision of belief and in their reasoning about action. They represent the cultural achievements that foster greater human rationality when they are installed as mindware. As societies evolve, they produce more of the cultural tools of rationality and these tools become more widespread in the population. A college sophomore with introductory statistics under his or her belt, if time-transported to the Europe of a few centuries ago, could become rich "beyond the dreams of avarice" by frequenting the gaming tables (or by becoming involved in insurance or lotteries).

The tools of rationality—probabilistic thinking, logic, scientific reasoning—represent mindware that is often incompletely learned or not acquired at all. This incomplete learning represents a class of causes of irrationality that I label a "mindware gap." A different type of mindware problem arises because not all mindware is helpful—either to attaining our goals (instrumental rationality) or to having accurate beliefs (epistemic rationality). In fact, some acquired mindware can be the direct cause of irrational actions that thwart our goals. This type of problem I term "contaminated mindware."

Being a cognitive miser is a universal human psychological characteristic—it is typical of everyone's thinking.[7] Likewise, mindware problems of some degree are characteristic of most individuals. In short, all people are cognitive misers and all experience mindware problems. Thus, irrational behavior and thinking will be characteristic of all humans to some extent. Nevertheless, there exists variability in the extent to which people process information as cognitive misers, the extent to which people have mindware gaps, and the extent to which they have been infected by contaminated mindware. None of this variation is explicitly assessed on intelligence tests. Those with higher IQs are only slightly less likely to be cognitive misers or to have mindware problems.[8] Statistically, this fact guarantees that dysrationalia will be a widespread phenomenon. To put it another way, if irrationality is common and only mildly correlated with intelligence, then irrational behavior among those of high intelligence should not be rare.

Thinking Errors and Rational Thought

Even though this is a book about rationality—the psychology of optimal thinking—several of the following chapters will be focused on the causes of thinking *errors*. The reason is that rationality is a multifarious concept. It requires the presence of many different types of mindware. It requires the acquisition of various dispositions of the reflective mind, all of which help in avoiding the shortcuts of the autonomous mind when they are nonoptimal. It is hard to measure the optimal functioning of all these components—that is, to specify whether "perfect" rationality has been attained. Researchers have found it much easier to measure whether a particular rational stricture is being *violated*—that is, whether a person is committing a thinking error— rather than whether his or her thinking is as good as it can be. This is much like our judgments at a sporting event where, for example, it might be difficult to discern whether a quarterback has put the ball perfectly on the money, but it is not difficult at all to detect a bad throw.

In fact, in many domains of life this is often the case as well. It is often difficult to specify what the best type of performance might be, but performance errors are much easier to spot. Essayist Neil Postman has argued, for instance, that educators and other advocates of good thinking might adopt a stance more similar to that of physicians or attorneys.[9] He points out that doctors would find it hard to define "perfect health" but, despite this, they are quite good at spotting disease. Likewise, lawyers are much better at spotting injustice and lack of citizenship than defining "perfect justice" or ideal citizenship. Postman argues that, like physicians and attorneys, educators might best focus on instances of poor thinking, which are much easier to identify, as opposed to trying to define ideal thinking. The literature on the psychology of rationality has followed this logic in that the empirical literature has focused on identifying thinking errors, just as physicians focus on disease.

The next several chapters take up in turn the multifarious requirements of rationality. To jointly achieve epistemic and instrumental rationality, a person must display judicious decision making, adequate behavioral regulation, wise goal prioritization, sufficient thoughtfulness, and proper evidence calibration. For example, epistemic rationality—beliefs that are properly matched to the world—requires probabilistic reasoning and the ability to calibrate theories to evidence. Instrumental rationality—maximizing goal fulfillment—requires adherence to all of the axioms of rational choice. People fail to fulfill the many different strictures of rational thought because they are cognitive misers, because they lack critical mindware, and because they have acquired contaminated mindware. These errors can be prevented by acquiring the mindware of rational thought and the thinking dispositions that prevent the overuse of the strategies of the cognitive miser.

SIX

The Cognitive Miser: Ways to Avoid Thinking

The rule that human beings seem to follow is to engage the brain only when all else fails—and usually not even then.
    —*David Hull*, Science and Selection: Essays on Biological Evolution
                    and the Philosophy of Science, 2001

C onsider the following problem, taken from the work of Hector Levesque and studied by my research group. Try to answer before reading on:

Jack is looking at Anne but Anne is looking at George. Jack is married but George is not. Is a married person looking at an unmarried person?

A) Yes   B) No   C) Cannot be determined

Answer A, B, or C before you look ahead.

Over 80 percent of the people who respond to this problem answer incorrectly. The vast majority of people answer C (cannot be determined) when in fact the correct answer is A (yes). The answer is easily revealed once we engage in what in the psychological literature is called fully disjunctive reasoning.[1] Fully disjunctive reasoning involves considering all possible states of the world when deciding among options or when choosing a problem solution in a reasoning task. Disjunctive reasoning is slow and systematic and represents the Type 2 processing I have discussed previously.

To solve the problem, it is necessary to consider both possibilities for

Anne's marital status (married and unmarried) to determine whether a conclusion can be drawn. If Anne is married, then the answer is "Yes" because she would be looking at George, who is unmarried. If Anne is not married, then the answer is still "Yes" because Jack, who is married, would be looking at Anne. Considering all the possibilities (the fully disjunctive reasoning strategy) reveals that a married person is looking at an unmarried person whether Anne is married or not. The fact that the problem does not *reveal* whether Anne is married or not suggests to people that nothing can be determined. That is the easiest conclusion to draw. Unfortunately, it happens to be an incorrect one. The shallow, Type 1 processing that is characteristic of the cognitive miser—namely, the tendency not to look for information that can be inferred but is not explicitly stated—results in the preponderance of "cannot be determined" responses to this problem. People make the easiest (incorrect) inference from the information given and do not proceed with the more difficult (but correct) inference that follows from fully disjunctive reasoning.

Fully disjunctive reasoning requires subjects to override their tendencies to be cognitive misers; that is, to avoid giving the response that is suggested to them on the basis of the most shallow type of information processing. The truth is that most people can carry out fully disjunctive reasoning when they are explicitly *told* that it is necessary. But it is also true that most do not automatically do so. We might expect high-IQ individuals would excel at disjunctive reasoning when they know it is required for successful task performance. But high-IQ people are only slightly more likely to *spontaneously* adopt this type of processing in situations that do not explicitly require it. Note that the instructions in Levesque's Anne problem do not cue the subject to engage in fully disjunctive reasoning. My research group found that people of high intelligence were no more likely to solve the Anne problem and similar problems than were people of lower intelligence. If told to reason through all of the alternatives, the subjects of higher intelligence would have done so more efficiently. However, without that instruction, they defaulted to computationally simple cognition when solving problems—they were cognitive misers like everyone else. Intelligence and the tendency toward *spontaneous* disjunctive reasoning can be quite unrelated.

We often do not realize that we are failing to think fully disjunctively (failing to think through all the possibilities) because the Type 1 processing takes place so rapidly. Daniel Kahneman and colleague Shane Frederick described a simple experiment in which people were asked to consider the following puzzle:[2]

A bat and a ball cost $1.10 in total. The bat costs $1 more than the ball. How much does the ball cost?

Many people emit the response that first comes to mind—10¢—without thinking further and realizing that this cannot be right. The bat would then have to cost $1.10 and the total cost would then be $1.20 rather than the required $1.10. People often do not think deeply enough to make this simple correction, though, and many students at very selective universities will answer incorrectly and move on to the next problem before realizing that their shallow processing has led them to make an error. They will not realize that they have failed to trump Type 1 thinking with Type 2 thinking. Frederick found that large numbers of brilliant students at MIT, Princeton, and Harvard were cognitive misers like the rest of us when given this and other similar problems.

Attribute Substitution:
The Generic Trick of the Cognitive Miser

Kahneman and Frederick describe a trick that we cognitive misers use all the time in order to lighten our cognitive load. The trick is called attribute substitution, and it occurs when a person needs to assess attribute A but finds that assessing attribute B (which is correlated with A) is easier cognitively and so uses B instead. In simpler terms, attribute substitution amounts to substituting an easier question for a harder one.

Many times there is no problem with attribute substitution as a cognitive strategy. If two different strategies can get you in the same ballpark of an answer, why not use the simpler one and avoid having to think so hard? Even if the attribute substituted is not quite as good a cue, it might get you so close to the right answer that it is not worth switching to the computationally more expensive attribute A. However, in certain situations in real life, overgeneralizing the attribute-substitution strategy can lead us seriously astray.

One rather drastic mistake that people can make is to violate a dominance relationship. The latter is a technical term in decision theory, but what it is and why it is bad are easy to understand. Suppose you turn down my offer to give you $100 for successfully picking a spade or a heart out of a deck of cards on the first try and instead accept someone else's offer to give you $100 if you draw a heart. By spurning my offer and accepting the other, you have—beyond dispute—made a very, very bad decision. You have made a bad decision because you have violated a dominance relationship. My offer dominates the other offer because if you win the other one you win mine too, but there are *additional* ways you can win mine.

Dominance relationships occur when one set of outcomes contains the other. Violations of the dominance principle occur when people judge the probability or value of the smaller set of outcomes to be higher than the larger set. Kahneman and Frederick provide a number of examples of how attribute substitution can lead people to violate dominance relationships. Here is one of the simplest examples. One group of subjects was asked to estimate the number of murders that occurred in Michigan during a particular year. This is a tough task, and people cannot retrieve this information from memory. However, to complete the task, they must retrieve relevant facts (the population of the state, what they have heard about the crime there, and other cues) that they can then put together to come up with an estimate. That people were not working too hard in coming up with information with which to derive an estimate (that they were cognitive misers) is suggested by the fact that another group of subjects who were asked to estimate the number of murders in Detroit in a year came up with an estimate that was twice as large as the Michigan group's!

This is a dominance violation, of course (all Detroit murders are also in Michigan), and the reason for it is clear. People are not working very hard to retrieve relevant information at all—they are using crude affect-laden images of the localities in question to generate a high or low number. Because the image of Detroit is associated with more affect-laden murder imagery than is the image of Michigan, the former as a stimulus generates a higher murder number even though on a logical or empirical basis this could not be the case. For similar reasons, forecasters assigned a higher probability to "an earthquake in California causing a flood in which more than 1,000 people will drown" than to "a flood somewhere in the United States in which more than 1,000 people will drown." Of course, an image of a California earthquake is very accessible, and its ease of accessibility affects the probability judgment.[3]

A large body of research in decision science has indicated that one attribute that is regularly substituted for an explicit assessment of decision costs and benefits is an affective valuation of the prospect at hand.[4] This is often a very rational attribute to substitute—affect does convey useful signals as to the costs and benefits of outcomes. A problem sometimes arises, however, when affective valuation is not supplemented by any analytic processing and adjustment at all. For example, sole reliance on affective valuation can make people insensitive to probabilities and to quantitative features of the outcome that should effect decisions. One study demonstrated that people's evaluation of a situation where they might receive a shock is insensitive to the probability of receiving the shock because their thinking is swamped by affective evaluation of the situation. People were willing to pay almost as much to avoid a 1 percent probability of receiving a shock as they were to pay to avoid a 99 percent probability of receiving a shock. Clearly the affective reaction to the thought of receiving a shock was overwhelming the subjects' ability to evaluate the probabilities associated.

Likewise, research by resource economists studying the public's valuation of environment damage indicates again that affective reaction interferes with people's processing of numerically important information. It was found that people would pay little more to save 200,000 birds from drowning in oil ponds (mean estimate $88) than they would pay to save 2000 birds ($80). The authors speculated that the affective reaction to a bunch of birds drowning in oil is determining the response here—that the actual number of birds involved has become overwhelmed by the affect-laden imagery. Christopher Hsee and colleagues confirmed this interpretation in a study where they had subjects respond to a hypothetical situation in which a group of university researchers had found pandas in a remote Asian region and the subjects were asked how much they would donate to save four pandas. Another group was asked what they would donate to save one panda. Both groups simply received a paragraph without supplemental visual information. Because the numbers are lower here than in the bird study, they were easier to evaluate and think about and, in these conditions, subjects would donate more to save four pandas (a mean of $22.00) than to save one (a mean of $11.67). In two comparable conditions, groups evaluated their prospective donations to save pandas in the presence of pictures of cute pandas. When the questions were accompanied by affect-laden photos, subjects donated no more to save four pandas than to save one. The quantitative aspect of thinking in the situation was lost because it was overwhelmed by a judgment determined solely by affect valuation.

Affect substitution is implicated in the difficulty that people have following the standard advice to buy low and sell high in stock market investing. When the stock market is high, euphoria reigns and a positive affect hangs over stock investing—encouraging nonprofessionals (and many professionals as well!) whose judgment is primed by affective cues to buy. The opposite happens when the market has fallen. People have lost money, and fear of more loss dominates the evaluative atmosphere. Thinking of the stock market triggers negative affective reactions and people do not buy, and often they are prompted to sell. Thus, affect valuation primes people to buy high and sell low—just the opposite of what they should do. And, in this domain, being a cognitive miser can be costly. As illustrated in the example of the mutual funds discussed in the last chapter, people lost billions of dollars in forgone gains during the period 1998–2001 because they bought high and sold low. Affect substitution is one cognitive characteristic (others are loss aversion, overconfidence, and over-explaining chance) that contributes to this costly irrational behavior.

Tools of the Cognitive Miser:
Vividness, Salience, and Accessibility

The cognitive miser is very sensitive to vivid presentations of information. The inability to override the influence of vivid but unrepresentative data is a recurring cause of dysrationalic behavior and beliefs in the real world. Here is an example. A friend drives you 20 miles to the airport where you are getting on a plane for a trip of about 750 miles. Your friend is likely to say, "Have a safe trip," as you part. This parting comment turns out to be sadly ironic, because your friend is *three times more likely to die in a car accident on the 20-mile trip back home than you are on your flight of 750 miles.* Driving automobiles is an extremely dangerous activity, compared to almost any other activity in our lives, yet the deaths due to automobile crashes are not presented as vividly and saliently as the crash of a large airliner.[5] It is the way we are biased toward vivid information that accounts for the apparent irrationality of person A's wishing person B safety, when it is person A who is in more danger.

Subsequent to the terrorist attacks of September 11, 2001, travel by airlines decreased because people were afraid of flying. Of course, people continued to travel. They did not just stay home. They simply took their trips by other means—in most cases by automobile. Since automobile travel is so much more dangerous than flying, it is a statistical certainty that more people died because they switched to driving. In fact, researchers have estimated that over 300 more people died in the final months of 2001 because they took trips by car rather than flew. One group of researchers were able to come up with a vivid statistic to convey just how dangerous driving is. They calculated that for driving to be as dangerous as flying, an incident on the scale of September 11 would have to occur once a month!

Misleading personal judgments based on the vividness of media-presented images are widespread in other areas as well. For example, risks that we face such as the possibility of developing diabetes cause less worry than risks such as developing staph infections in hospitals, even though the former will affect 45 million Americans and the latter only 1500 in a year. This is despite the fact that, personally, we can do something about the former (by changing our diet and exercising) but not the latter.

The cognitive miser relies on the easily processed cue of salience, but this can lead the cognitive miser astray. Certain formats for information appear to be more salient than others. A study by Kimihiko Yamagishi demonstrated a similar phenomenon by showing that people rated a disease that killed 1286 out of 10,000 people as more dangerous than one that killed 24.14 percent of the population. Again, the vividness of representing 1286 actual people rather than an abstract percentage is what triggers an affective response that leads to a clearly suboptimal judgment. Pointing to the potentially important practical implications of such a finding, Yamagishi titled his article "When a 12.86% Mortality Is More Dangerous than 24.14%: Implications for Risk Communication."[6]

Of course, even more vivid than a frequency statistic is a picture or a photograph—that is, something that turns a statistic into a person. Cognitive scientist Paul Slovic reported a study in which people were asked to donate money to the charity Save the Children. In one condition, termed the Statistical Victims condition, subjects were given statistical information such as the following: "Food shortages in Malawi are affecting more than 3 million children; In Zambia, severe rainfall deficits have resulted in a 42% drop in maize production from 2000; As a result, an estimated 3 million Zambians face hunger; More than 11 million people in Ethiopia need immediate food assistance." Subjects were asked to donate money to help ease these problems. In another condition, termed the Identifiable Victim condition, subjects were shown a photograph of an individual and told a story about the person containing information like the following: "Rokia, a 7-year-old girl from Mali, Africa, is desperately poor and faces a threat of severe hunger or even starvation. Her life will be changed for the better as a result of your financial gift." Twice as much money was donated in the Identifiable Victim condition as in the Statistical Victims condition.

One salience-related effect that has been studied by behavioral economists is called the money illusion.[7] This illusion occurs when people are overly influenced by nominal monetary value. Simply put, it is when the cognitive miser responds only to the face value of a monetary amount without contextualizing it with factors that affect actual buying power such as inflation, time, and currency exchange rates. The most stunning example of the money illusion was reported in a study where it was found that people underspend in a foreign currency when the foreign currency is a multiple of the home currency (for example, 1 US dollar = 4 Malaysian ringgits) and overspend when the foreign currency is a fraction of the home currency (for instance, 1 US dollar = .4 Bahraini dinar). This effect shows that there is an influence of the face value of the currency: items look expensive if they cost a multiple of the home currency (and thus people attenuate spending), and they look cheap when they cost a fraction of the home currency (and thus people are enticed to spend). The effect shows that people cannot suppress the miserly tendency to respond to the face value of the currency even though they know that its face value prior to conversion to the home currency is irrelevant.

The money illusion has some very real public policy consequences. Throughout 2006 and early 2007 there was consternation (and calls for po-

litical action) in the United States as gasoline prices spiked to the unprecedented price of over $3 per gallon. There was just one problem. These prices
were not unprecedented. Throughout 2006 and early 2007 the price of gas
remained below its inflation-adjusted price in 1981. In fact, in terms of afford-
ability (price adjusted for income) the price of gasoline in 2006 was substantially below what it was in 1978–1981.

Heuristic Processing:
Quantity versus Quality in Decision Making

By giving examples of the thinking shortcuts taken by the cognitive miser
and their pitfalls, I do not mean to imply that using such shortcuts is always
wrong. To the contrary, there is a rich literature in psychology showing that
in many situations such heuristic processing is quite useful.[8] Heuristic processing is a term often used for Type 1 processing—processing that is fast,
automatic, and computationally inexpensive, and that does not engage in
extensive analysis of all the possibilities. Thus, one way to describe cognitive
misers is to say that they rely to a large extent on heuristic processing.

So certainly I do not wish to deny the usefulness of heuristic processing.
Nevertheless, my emphasis will be the opposite—to highlight the dangers of
using these heuristics in too many situations, including those that modern
society has deliberately designed in order to trap cognitive misers. When we
are over-reliant on heuristic processing we lose personal autonomy. Being a
cognitive miser makes us vulnerable to exploitation. We give up our thinking
to those who manipulate our environments, and we let our actions be determined by those who can create the stimuli that best trigger our shallow automatic processing tendencies. We make the direction of our lives vulnerable
to deflection by others who control our symbolic environment. This is what
makes defaulting to such heuristics a two-edged sword. Being a cognitive
miser preserves processing capacity for other tasks. At the same time, heuristics can be over-generalized to situations that require not a quick approximation but, rather, precise calculating.

The number of situations where the use of heuristics will lead us astray
may not be large, but such situations may be of unusual importance. The
importance of a thinking strategy is not assessed by simply counting the num-

ber of instances in which it is engaged. We cannot dismiss conscious analytic thinking by saying that heuristics will get a "close enough" answer 98 percent of the time, because the 2 percent of the instances where heuristics lead us seriously astray may be critical to our lives. This point is captured in an interview in *Money Magazine* with Ralph Wanger, a leading mutual fund manager. Wanger says, "The point is, 99 percent of what you do in life I classify as laundry. It's stuff that has to be done, but you don't do it better than anybody else, and it's not worth much. Once in a while, though, you do something that changes your life dramatically. You decide to get married, you have a baby—or, if you're an investor, you buy a stock that goes up twentyfold. So these rare events tend to dominate things" (Zweig, 2007, p. 102).

In short, a small subset of all the decisions we will make in our lives might end up being the dominating factors in determining our life satisfaction. Deciding what occupation to pursue, what specific job to take, whom to marry, how to invest, where to locate, how to house ourselves, and whether to have children may, when we look back on our lives decades later, turn out to have determined everything. In terms of raw numbers, these might represent only 20–30 decisions out of thousands that we have made over many years. But the thousands are just the "laundry of life," to use Wanger's phrase. These 20 are what count. The 20 "nonlaundry" decisions may also be quite unique, and this may render heuristics unhelpful for two reasons. Events that are small in number and not recurring give unconscious implicit learning mechanisms no chance to abstract information that could be used heuristically. Second, if they are unique, they are probably unprecedented from an evolutionary point of view, and thus there is no chance that unconscious modules that are evolutionary adaptations could help us. For both of these reasons, it is doubtful that heuristics will be adequate. The "quick and dirty" answers that heuristics are likely to provide in the "nonlaundry" part of life could lead us seriously astray.

Cognitive Shortcuts and Personal Autonomy

Consider how some very useful processing heuristics can be easily turned around to work against us because they are too easy to trigger. Several decades ago Amos Tversky and Daniel Kahneman discovered the so-called anchoring and adjustment heuristic.[9] The anchoring and adjustment process comes into play when we have to make a numerical estimation of an unknown quantity. In this strategy, we begin by anchoring on the most easily retrievable relevant number that we know. Then we adjust that anchor up or down based on the implications of specific facts that we may know.

This does not seem to be such a bad procedure. A problem arises, however, when the number most available to anchor on is not relevant to the calculation at hand. In a classic experiment, Tversky and Kahneman demonstrated that the anchoring tendency is much too miserly—that it does not bother to assess for relevance. They had subjects watch a spinning wheel and, when the pointer landed on a number (rigged to be the number 65), asked them whether the percentage of African countries in the United Nations was higher or lower than this percentage. After answering higher or lower to this question, the subjects then had to give their best estimate of the percentage of African countries in the United Nations. For another group of subjects it was arranged that the pointer land on the number 10. They were also asked to make the higher or lower judgment and then to estimate the percentage of African countries in the United Nations. Now it is clear that because a spinning wheel was used, the number involved in the first question is totally irrelevant to the task of answering the second question. Yet the number that came up on the spinning wheel affected the answer to the second question. The mean estimate of the first group (the group where the spinning wheel stopped at 65) turned out to be significantly larger (45) than the mean estimate (25) for the second group.

It is clear what is happening here. Both groups are using the anchoring and adjustment heuristic—the high anchor group adjusting down and the low group adjusting up—but their adjustments are "sticky." They are not adjusting enough because they have failed to fully take into account that the anchor is determined in a totally *random* manner. The anchoring and adjustment heuristic is revealing a miserly tendency to rely on an anchor regardless of its relevance.

Even when the anchor is not randomly determined, the cognitive miser tends to rely on it too much because using it is easier than trying to retrieve from memory facts about the situation that are actually relevant. It has been found that even experienced real estate agents are overly affected by the listing price of a home when trying to assess its actual value. Anchoring and adjustment is also a critical feature in sales of new automobiles. The salesperson wants the customer to anchor on the MSRP (the manufacturer's suggested retail price) and bargain down from there—knowing that the adjustment will be "sticky," that is, that it will be overly influenced by the MSRP and not move far enough from it. Consumer magazines and websites recommend, in contrast, that the customer obtain the invoice price (what the dealer paid the manufacturer for the car) and bargain up from there. For used cars, a similar thing happens. The salesperson wants to bargain from the advertised price. Consumer publications recommend bargaining from a "bluebook" price. Both the salesperson and the consumer magazines are correct. Both know that where the negotiation starts will have a primary influence on where it ends up. Both know that whoever controls the anchor will largely control the negotiation.

Heuristically relying on anchors has been shown to affect such important contexts as judicial decisions and awards. Likewise, in personal injury cases, the amount of compensation requested affects the judgment itself as well as the amount awarded to the plaintiff. Also, it has been shown that, statistically, prosecution requests for sentences affect the sentencing by judges as well as bail decisions. Judges appear to be cognitive misers too—they succumb to simple heuristics that promise to lighten the cognitive load.

Anchoring effects are related to the mindless use of reference points. Such mindless processing can result in absurd behavior. For example, it can lead people to prefer getting less to getting more (that is, to prefer $5 to $6). How is this possible? A study by Slovic and colleagues provides an example. They found that people rated a gamble with 7/36 chance to win $9 and 29/36 to lose 5¢ more favorably than a gamble with 7/36 chance to win $9 and 29/36 chance to win nothing. Indeed, they report that the latter gamble was even rated less desirable than a gamble having a 7/36 chance to win $9 and 29/36 to lose 25¢. In the two loss conditions, the 5¢ and 25¢ provide reference points against which the $9 looks very large. The no-loss condition does not provide a readily usable small reference point and hence is not rated as favorably. Note that the subjects in this study violated the dominance stricture discussed above, a very fundamental rule of rational choice.[10]

Status Quo Bias: The Default Heuristic

Another tendency of the cognitive miser that robs us of personal autonomy is the overuse of the so-called default heuristic.[11] This heuristic operates via a simple rule: If you have been given a default choice, stick with it. That humans have such a heuristic is suggested by two decades of work on status quo biases in decision making. That humans overuse the default heuristic to the point of failing to maximally achieve their goals is also demonstrated in these same two decades of research. People who overuse the default heuristic give up their autonomy by ceding control of their lives to those with the power to set the defaults.

The default heuristic operates in many real-life contexts of economic and public policy choice. One group of investigators described a survey conducted by Pacific Gas and Electric in the 1980s. Because of various geographic factors (urban-rural, etc.), service reliability varied in the company's service area. Some of their customers suffered more outages than others. Customers with unreliable service were asked whether they would be willing to pay for more reliable service and, if so, whether they would accept increases of various percentages. Customers with reliable service were asked if they would be willing to accept somewhat less reliable service and receive a discount on their bills of a certain percentage (in fact, the same percentages as the other group, only a decrease instead of an increase). Although there were not income differences between these groups of customers, neither group wanted to change. People overwhelmingly wanted to stay with whatever their status quo was. The service difference between the two groups was large. The unreliable service group suffered 15 outages per year of 4 hours' average duration and the reliable service group suffered 3 outages per year of 2 hours' average duration, yet very few customers wanted to switch!

Hostile and Benign Environments for Heuristics

Of course, I do not mean to imply that the use of heuristics *always* leads us astray. As I argued above, they often give us a useful first approximation to the optimal response in a particular situation, and they do so without stressing cognitive capacity. In fact, they are so useful that one group of influential psychologists has been led to extol their advantages even to the extent of minimizing the usefulness of the formal rules of rationality.[12] Most psychologists, though, while still acknowledging the usefulness of heuristics, think that this view carries things too far. Here is why.

The usefulness of the heuristics that the cognitive miser relies upon to lighten the cognitive load is dependent on a benign environment. By a benign environment, I mean an environment that contains useful cues that can be exploited by various heuristics (for example, affect-triggering cues, vivid and salient stimulus components, convenient anchors). Additionally, for an environment to be classified as benign, it also must contain no other individuals who will adjust their behavior to exploit those relying only on heuristics. In contrast, a hostile environment for heuristics is one in which there are no cues that are usable by heuristic processes. Another way that an environment can turn hostile for the cognitive miser is if other agents discern the simple cues that are triggering the miser's heuristics and the other agents start to arrange the cues for their own advantage (for example, advertisements, or the deliberate design of supermarket floor space to maximize revenue).

Take as an example one chapter in an edited book extolling the usefulness of the so-called recognition heuristic.[13] The chapter is subtitled "How Ignorance Makes Us Smart." The idea behind such "ignorance-based decision making," as it is called, is the fact that some items of a subset are unknown can be exploited to aid decisions. In short, the yes/no recognition response can be used as an estimation cue. For example, novice tennis fans correctly predicted the winners of 72 percent of all the men's matches at the 2003 Wimbledon by using the simple recognition heuristic of: If you recognize one player's name and not the other's, predict that the one you recognize will win. This heuristic does just as well as Wimbledon experts' rankings.

With ingenious simulations, Gerd Gigerenzer and colleagues have demonstrated how certain information environments can lead to such things as less-is-more effects: where those who know less about an environment can display more inferential accuracy in it. One is certainly convinced after reading material like this that the recognition heuristic is efficacious in some situations. But one immediately begins to worry when one ponders how it relates to a market environment specifically designed to exploit it. If I were to rely solely on the recognition heuristic as I went about my day tomorrow, I could easily be led to:

1. buy a $3 coffee when in fact a $1.25 one would satisfy me perfectly well
2. eat in a single snack the number of fat grams I should have in an entire day
3. pay the highest bank fees
4. incur credit card debt rather than pay cash
5. buy a mutual fund with a 6 percent sales charge rather than a no-load fund

None of these behaviors serves my long-term goals at all. Yet the recognition heuristic triggers these and dozens more that will trip me up as I try to make my way through the maze of modern society. The commercial environment of my city is not a benign environment for a cognitive miser.

The danger of such miserly tendencies and the necessity of relying on Type 2 processing in the domain of personal finance is suggested by the well-known finding that consumers of financial services overwhelmingly purchase high-cost products that underperform in terms of investment return when compared to the low-cost strategies recommended by true experts (for example, dollar-cost averaging into no-load index mutual funds). The reason is, of course, that the high-cost fee-based products and services are the ones with high immediate recognizability in the marketplace, whereas the low-cost strategies must be sought out in financial and consumer publications. An article in a British publication illustrates the situation by asking "Can 70 per cent of people be wrong?" and answers "yes, it seems." In the article we learn that, at that time, seven out of ten people in Britain had money in checking accounts earning 0.10 percent with one of the big four banks (Barclays, HSBC, Lloyds TSB, and Royal Bank of Scotland) when interest rates more than 30 times that amount were available from checking accounts recommended in the Best Buy columns of leading consumer publications. The reason millions of people were losing billions of dollars in interest is clear—the "big four" were the most recognizable banks and the cognitive miser defaulted to them. The marketplace of personal finance is not benign. It requires that the investor avoid behaving like a cognitive miser and instead consciously—sometimes disjunctively—think through the alternatives.[14]

Just how easy it is to exploit the miser tendency to rely on easily processed stimuli is illustrated in a study by Marwan Sinaceur and colleagues.[15] They presented subjects with the following hypothetical situation: "Imagine that you have just finished eating your dinner. You have eaten a packaged food product made with beef that was bought at the supermarket. While listening to the evening news on the television, you find out that eating this packaged food may have exposed you to the human variant of bovine spongiform encephalopathy (BSE)." After reading this, the subjects were asked to respond on a seven-point scale to the following questions: "After hearing this, to what extent would you decrease your consumption of this type of packaged beef?" and "To what extent would you alter your dietary habits to de-emphasize red meats and increase the consumption of other foods?" Not surprisingly, after hearing this hypothetical situation, subjects felt that they would decrease their consumption of beef. However, another group of subjects was even *more* likely to say they would decrease their consumption of beef when they heard the same story identically except for the very last words. Instead of "human variant of bovine spongiform encephalopathy (BSE)" the second group read "human variant of Mad Cow Disease." It is clear what is going on here. Our old friend vividness is rearing its head again. Mad Cow Disease conjures creepy imagines of an animal-borne disease in a way that bovine spongiform encephalopathy does not. In short, when we are being cognitive misers, our actions and thoughts are readily influenced by small changes in wording that alter the vividness and affective valence of our reactions. It is a pretty sure bet that Social Security taxes would be less if Social Security was called instead Welfare for the Elderly.

In short, extreme cognitive misers literally do not have "a mind of their own." What their mind will process is determined by the most vivid stimulus at hand, the most readily assimilated fact, or the most salient cue available. The cognitive miser is easily exploited by those who control the labeling, who control what is vivid, who control the anchor. We shall see even more dramatic examples of how over-reliance on shallow Type 1 processing threatens our autonomy as independent thinkers in the next chapter when we consider framing effects.

SEVEN

Framing and the Cognitive Miser

Decision makers are generally quite passive and therefore inclined to accept any frame to which they are exposed.
—*Daniel Kahneman*, Choices, Values, and Frames, 2000

Edward McCaffery, a professor of law and economics, and Jonathan Baron, a cognitive psychologist, have collaborated on extensive studies of people's attitudes toward aspects of the tax system.[1] They have found, to put it bluntly, that people's thinking about taxes is incoherent. I am going to focus on one particular type of incoherence that they have studied, because it illustrates a critical pitfall of the cognitive miser.

Focus for a moment on how you would set up an idealized tax system in a hypothetical country. Imagine that in this country a family with no children and an income of $35,000 pays $4,000 in tax and that a family with no children and an income of $100,000 pays $26,000 in tax. Imagine that it is proposed in this hypothetical country that there be a $500 tax reduction for having a child for a family with an income of $35,000. Thus, that family's tax would go from $4,000 to $3,500 when they had one child. The question is, should the reduction for the family with an income of $100,000 be the same? Should their tax go from $26,000 to $25,500 or should they be given more of a reduction because of their higher income?

Nobel Prize–winning economist Thomas Schelling notes that there are some arguments for the latter (giving the higher-income family a larger tax reduction): "One way to make the case is that the high-income families spend much more on children and the 'cost' of raising their children is much more" (1984, p. 19). In short, the high-income family is going to output more money in raising their children, so they deserve more of a reduction. Perhaps you do not find this argument to be convincing. Most people don't. Most people reject this argument outright and respond instead that the reduction for having a child should be at least the same for low-income households as for those with high income and, if anything, it should probably be higher for the lower-income households.

This is where economist Schelling steps in and teaches us that we have not thought hard enough about the logic of this situation—that we have not, in particular, thought about alternative ways that it might be framed. He points out that it is arbitrary that we originally framed the issue starting at the rate for a childless household. In thinking about setting up this hypothetical system, we could just as well have started from a different baseline—for example, the baseline of a "typical" family of four (two adults and two children). Of course, as before, children affect the rates, so we would have to figure out the fair tax for families with one child or no children (and for 3, 4, etc.).

Imagine that in this hypothetical country, a family with two children and an income of $35,000 pays $3,000 in tax and that a family with two children and an income of $100,000 pays $25,000 in tax. What would the rates be here for one child and zero children? We would adjust the rates upward because families without children can afford to pay more. Instead of speaking of a reduction for children, we might call this type of adjustment in the tax schedule the "penalty for the childless." And here I am giving away a hint at what Schelling is teaching us about framing and tax policy (and what McCaffery and Baron have studied empirically)—every "reduction" (tax credit, or deduction) for a family with a certain characteristic (children, home ownership, farm status, self-employment status, and all the many other characteristics in the tax code) is in effect a penalty for those who do not share the characteristic (because there is a fixed number representing what the sum total of government services has cost, and this must be paid even if the government must borrow).

So let us imagine in this case that the family with an income of $100,000 and one child has their taxes set at $26,000 and the same family with no children has their taxes set at $27,000. That is, there is a childless penalty of $1000 per child who does not reside in the family. The question is, should the poorer family which makes $35,000 and has no children also pay the same $2000 childless penalty as the richer family—should the poorer family's taxes go from $3000 to $5000 as the richer family's taxes went from $25,000 to $27,000?

Most people have the instinctive feeling that this is not right. Most people feel that the $2000 penalty represents a much more severe hardship for the poorer family and that it should be less than the penalty paid by the richer family with no children. But this judgment does not square with people's feelings about whether the reduction for children should be the same for rich and poor families. People want the "bonus" for children to be equal for low- and high-income families, but they do not want the "penalty" for lacking children to be the same for high and low income. This is incoherent thinking, because the bonus and the penalty are *exactly the same thing*—just with different names that direct the focus of attention in different directions. And this is the point of the example, and of this chapter—that cognitive misers allow their attention to be focused by others. Cognitive misers let the structure of the environment determine how they think. The miser accepts whichever way the problem is presented and thinks from there, often never realizing that a different presentation format would have led to a different conclusion.

In cognitive science, the tendency to give different responses to problems that have surface dissimilarities but that are really formally identical is termed a framing effect. Framing effects are very basic violations of the strictures of rational choice. In the technical literature of decision theory, the stricture that is being violated is called descriptive invariance—the stricture that choices should not change as the result of trivial rewordings of a problem.[2] Subjects in framing experiments, when shown differing versions of the same choice situation, overwhelmingly agree that the differences in the problem representations should not affect their choice. If choices flip-flop based on problem characteristics that the *subjects themselves* view as irrelevant—then the subjects can be said to have no stable, well-ordered preferences at all. If a person's preference reverses based on inconsequential aspects of how the problem is phrased, the person cannot be described as maximizing expected utility. Thus, such failures of descriptive invariance have quite serious implications for our view of whether or not people are rational.

Tax policy is a good domain in which to see framing effects operating because reframing can be done so easily, yet the possibility of reframing often goes completely unnoticed. The idea of a "tax deduction" seems to most people such an unequivocally good thing that any policy attached to the term is usually endorsed. It is rarely noticed by anyone other than economists that a tax deduction for citizens having a certain characteristic is the equivalent of a penalty for those not sharing the characteristic. As two economists describe the situation, "by requiring higher tax rates, subsidies cause everything else to be penalized. . . . The point is that these features are enormously popular because they have been enshrined as 'tax reductions,' but these exact same features probably wouldn't stand a chance as stand-alone policies" (Slemrod and Bakija, 1996, pp. 113, 141). This quote draws attention to the fact that no matter what amount of government services (be it national defense, health care, roads, or payments to the elderly) we deem appropriate, there is some fixed sum of money that must be raised to pay for it—either now or in the future (the latter if the government takes on debt to pay for the services). Thus, deductions for certain classes of taxpayer necessarily mean that those not qualifying for the deduction will pay more.

Consider the tax deduction for home mortgage interest. On its surface it seems like a good thing, but it would seem less benign if we were to describe it as "the rent payer's penalty." When we recognize that this is an equivalent reframing, we realize the sense in which phrasing the issue as "should there be a deduction allowed for home mortgage interest paid?" biases the question. Rephrasing the question as "Should renters pay more tax in order that home owners can pay less?" is an equivalent framing biased in the other direction. Likewise, a lower tax rate for capital gains sounds less benign when counter-phrased as "the wage earner's penalty."

Framing and Personal Autonomy

The fact that our opinion of a tax policy can be changed by a mere reframing of the policy clearly illustrates that we lose personal autonomy when we act as cognitive misers. We literally allow whoever chose the framing to "make up our minds" for us.

Decision scientists have studied the so-called equality heuristic in decision making.[3] In a typical experiment, the critical comparison involves that between two different groups of subjects. One group of subjects is asked to allocate the profits in a firm of partners where the partners themselves had generated unequal revenue—some have earned more for the firm than others. The most common allocation strategy among this group of subjects was to allocate each partner an equal share of the profits. A common rationale for this allocation choice was that "they're all in it together."

That this rationale was not very thoughtfully derived was indicated by the results from the second group of subjects. This group of subjects was also asked to make a judgment about the allocation in a firm of partners where the partners themselves had generated unequal revenue. However, this time, the subjects were told to allocate the firm's *expenses* for the year (rent, secretarial salaries, etc.) rather than the profits. The most common allocation strategy used by this group of subjects was to allocate each partner an equal share of the expenses. Of course, allocating the expenses equally results in unequal profits. Likewise the subjects in the first group, in opting for equal profits, were implicitly opting for unequal expenses. Both quantities cannot be equalized. Interestingly, in the second condition, where subjects made profits unequal by equalizing expenses, they tended to give the very same rationale ("they're all in it together") as did the subjects in the first condition!

These results suggest that people were not thoughtfully deciding upon equal profit outcomes (in the first condition) or thoughtfully deciding that equality of fixed costs is really fair (in the second condition) but were instead just settling on a cognitively undemanding heuristic of "equal is fair." The "equalizing" subjects in these experiments had not thought through the problem enough to realize that there is more than one dimension in play and all cannot be equalized at once. Instead, they ended up equalizing the one dimension that was brought to their attention by the way the problem was framed.

There is no doubt that people who use the heuristic of "divide things equally" think they are making a social decision and they think it is a fair one. But the design logic of these experiments reveals that people are not making a social or ethical judgment at all. Think of what the logic of these experiments has done. It has turned people into Marxists (the first condition) or into advocates of the *Wall Street Journal* editorial page (the second condition) at a whim—by simply rephrasing the question. These experiments reinforce my earlier warning that framing effects are a threat to personal autonomy (as are other cognitive miser tendencies). One of the implications of these experiments and those of McCaffery and Baron is that those who pose the questions—those who frame them—may have more control over your political and economic behavior than you do.

There is the unsettling idea latent here that people's preferences come from the outside (from whoever has the power to shape the environment and determine how questions are phrased) rather than from internal preferences based in their unique psychologies. Since most situations can be framed in more than one way, this means that rather than a person's having stable preferences that are just elicited in different ways, the elicitation process itself can totally *determine* what the preference will be!

Professor of medicine Peter Ubel has studied how the overuse of the equality heuristic can lead to irrational framing effects in decisions about the allocation of scarce medical resources. Subjects were asked to allocate 100 usable livers to 200 children awaiting a transplant.[4] When there were two groups of children, Group A with 100 children and Group B with 100 children, there was an overwhelming tendency to allocate 50 livers to each group. The equality heuristic seems reasonable here. Even though the nature of the groups was unspecified, it is reasonable to assume that Group A and Group B refer to different geographic areas, different hospitals, different sexes, different races, or some other demographic characteristic. However, in another condition of Ubel's experiments with colleague George Loewenstein, the equality heuristic seems much more problematic. It was found that some subjects applied it when the groups referred to children having differing prognoses. Group A was a group of 100 children with an 80 percent average chance of surviving if transplanted, and Group B was a group of 100 children with only a 20 percent average chance of surviving if transplanted.

More than one quarter of Ubel's subjects nevertheless allocated the livers equally—50 livers to Group A and 50 to Group B. This decision results in the unnecessary deaths of 30 children (the 80 that would be saved if all 100 were allocated to Group A minus the 50 that will be saved if the equality heuristic is used).

Before condemning the equality heuristic, though, perhaps we should ask whether subjects had a rationale for it. Perhaps they viewed other principles as being at work here beyond sheer numbers saved. It turns out that many subjects did indeed have rationales for their 50/50 split. Common justifications for using the equality heuristic were that "even those with little chance deserve hope" and that "needy people deserve transplants, whatever their chance of survival." We must wonder, though, whether such justifications represent reasoned thought or mere rationalizations for using the first heuristic that came to mind—the equality heuristic. Another condition in Ubel's experimentation suggests the latter. Ubel notes that when the candidates for transplant were ranked from 1 to 200 in terms of prognoses (that is, listed as individuals rather than broken into groups), "people are relatively comfortable distributing organs to the top 100 patients . . . yet if the top 100 patients are called group 1 and the bottom 100 group 2, few people want to abandon group 2 entirely" (2000, p. 93). This finding makes it seem that the mere word "group" is triggering the equality heuristic in some subjects. The finding also suggests that the rationale "even those with little chance deserve hope" is actually a rationalization, because subjects do not tend to think of this rationale when the patients "with little chance" are not labeled as a "group." Again, the trouble with heuristics is that they make our behavior, opinions, and attitudes subject to radical change based on how a problem is framed for us by others.

Now You Choose It—Now You Don't:
Research on Framing Effects

In discussing the mechanisms causing framing effects, Daniel Kahneman has stated that "the basic principle of framing is the passive acceptance of the formulation given" (2003a, p. 703). The frame presented to the subject is taken as focal, and all subsequent thought derives from it rather than from alternative framings because the latter would require more thought. Kahneman's statement reveals framing effects as a consequence of cognitive miser tendencies, but it also suggests how to avoid such effects.

In laboratory experiments conducted on framing effects, when subjects are debriefed and the experiment is explained to them, they are often shown the alternative versions of the task. For example, in the tax example above they would be shown both the "reduction for children" and the "penalty for the childless" version. It is almost uniformly the case that, after being debriefed, subjects recognize the equivalence of the two versions, and also they realize that it is a mistake (an incoherence in people's political attitudes) to respond differently to the two versions simply because they have been framed differently. This finding suggests that what people need to learn to do is to think from more than one perspective—to learn to habitually reframe things for themselves. The debriefing results show that once they do so, people will detect discrepancies in their responses to a problem posed from different perspectives and will take steps to resolve the discrepancies. People seem to recognize that consistency is an intellectual value. What they do not do, however, is habitually generate the perspective shifts that would highlight the inconsistencies in their thinking. Their inability to do so makes them subject to framing effects—a violation of descriptive invariance signaling a basic irrationality in people's choice patterns.

In some of the earliest and most influential work on framing effects it was not surprising that subjects would acknowledge that the different versions of the problem were equivalent because the equivalence was very transparent once pointed out. One of the most compelling framing demonstrations is from the early work of Tversky and Kahneman.[5] Give your own reaction to Decision 1:

Decision 1. Imagine that the United States is preparing for the outbreak of an unusual disease, which is expected to kill 600 people. Two alternative programs to combat the disease have been proposed. Assume that the exact scientific estimates of the consequences of the programs are as follows: If Program A is adopted, 200 people will be saved. If Program B is adopted, there is a one-third probability that 600 people will be saved and a two-thirds probability that no people will be saved. Which of the two programs would you favor, Program A or Program B?

Most people when given this problem prefer Program A—the one that saves 200 lives for sure. There is nothing wrong with this choice taken alone. It is only in connection with the responses to another problem that things really become strange. The experimental subjects (sometimes the same group, sometimes a different group—the effect obtains either way) are given an additional problem. Again, give your own immediate reaction to Decision 2:

Decision 2. Imagine that the United States is preparing for the outbreak of an unusual disease, which is expected to kill 600 people. Two alternative programs to combat the disease have been proposed. Assume that the exact scientific estimates of the consequences of the programs are as follows: If Program C is adopted, 400 people will die. If Program D is adopted, there is a one-third probability that nobody will die and a two-thirds probability that 600 people will die. Which of the two programs would you favor, Program C or Program D?

Most subjects when presented with Decision 2 prefer Program D. Thus, across the two problems, the most popular choices are Program A and Program D. The only problem here is that Decision 1 and Decision 2 are really the same decision—they are merely redescriptions of the same situation. Program A and C are the same. That 400 will die in Program C implies that 200 will be saved—precisely the same number saved (200) in Program A. Likewise, the two-thirds chance that 600 will die in Program D is the same two-thirds chance that 600 will die ("no people will be saved") in Program B. If you preferred Program A in Decision 1 you should have preferred Program C in Decision 2. But many subjects show inconsistent preferences—their choice switches depending on the phrasing of the question.

What this example shows is that subjects were risk averse in the context of gains and risk seeking in the context of losses. They found the sure gain of 200 lives attractive in Decision 1 over a gamble of equal expected value. In contrast, in Decision 2, the sure loss of 400 lives was unattractive compared with the gamble of equal expected value. Of course, the "sure loss" of 400 here that subjects found so unattractive is exactly the same outcome as the "sure gain" of 200 that subjects found so attractive in Decision 1! This is an example of a problem with very transparent equivalence. When presented with both versions of the problem together, most people agree that the problems are identical and that the alternative phrasing should not have made a difference. As I discussed above, such failures of descriptive invariance guarantee that a person cannot be a utility maximizer—that is, cannot be rational in the sense that cognitive scientists define that term.

A theory of why these framing effects occur was presented in the prospect theory of Kahneman and Tversky—the theory that in part led to the Nobel Prize in Economics for Kahneman in 2002. In the disease problem, subjects coded the outcomes in terms of contrasts from their current position—as gains and losses from a zero point (*however* that zero point was defined for them). This is one of the key assumptions of prospect theory. Another of the other key assumptions is that the utility function is steeper (in the negative direction) for losses than for gains.[6] This is why people are often risk averse even for gambles with positive expected values. Would you flip a coin with me—heads you give me $500, tails I give you $525? Most people refuse such favorable bets because the potential loss, although smaller than the potential gain, looms larger psychologically.

Consider a series of studies by Nicholas Epley and colleagues in which subjects were greeted at the laboratory and given a $50 check.[7] During the explanation of why they were receiving the check, one group of subjects heard the check described as a "bonus" and another group heard it described as a "tuition rebate." Epley and colleagues conjectured that the bonus would be mentally coded as a positive change from the status quo, whereas the rebate would be coded as a return to a previous wealth state. They thought that the bonus framing would lead to more immediate spending than the rebate framing, because spending from the status quo is more easily coded as a relative loss. This is exactly what happened. In one experiment, when the subjects were contacted one week later, the bonus group had spent more of the money. In another experiment, subjects were allowed to buy items from the university bookstore (including snack foods) at a good discount. Again, the subjects from the bonus group spent more in the laboratory discount store.

Epley, a professor in the University of Chicago's Graduate School of Business, demonstrated the relevance of these findings in an op-ed piece in the *New York Times* of January 31, 2008. Subsequent to the subprime mortgage crisis of 2007–2008, Congress and the president were considering mechanisms to stimulate a faltering economy. Tax rebates were being considered in order to get people spending more (such tax rebates had been used in 2001, also as a stimulative mechanism). Epley pointed out in his op-ed piece that if the goal was to get people to spend their checks, then the money would be best labeled tax bonuses rather than tax rebates. The term *rebates* implies that money that is yours is being returned—that you are being restored to some status quo. Prospect theory predicts that you will be less likely to spend from the status quo position. However, describing the check as a tax bonus suggests that this money is "extra"—an increase from the status quo. People will be much more likely to spend such a "bonus." Studies of the 2001 program indicated that only 28 percent of the money was spent, a low rate in part caused by its unfortunate description as a "rebate."

Epley's point illustrates that framing issues need to be more familiar among policy analysts. In contrast, advertisers are extremely knowledgeable about the importance of framing. You can bet that a product will be advertised as "95% fat free" rather than "contains 5% fat." The *providers* of frames well know their value. The issue is whether you, the *consumer* of frames, will come to understand their importance and thus transform yourself into a more autonomous decision maker.

Economist Richard Thaler has described how years ago the credit card industry lobbied intensely for any differential charges between credit cards and cash to be labeled as a *discount* for using cash rather than a surcharge for using the credit card.[8] They were implicitly aware that any surcharge would be psychologically coded as a loss and weighted highly in negative utility. The discount, in contrast, would be coded as a gain. Because the utility function is shallower for gains than for losses, forgoing the discount would be psychologically easier than accepting the surcharge. Of course, the two represent exactly the same economic consequence. The industry, merely by getting people to accept the higher price as normal, framed the issue so that credit card charges were more acceptable to people.

The fact that human choices are so easily altered by framing has potent social implications as well. James Friedrich and colleagues describe a study of attitudes toward affirmative action in university admissions.[9] Two groups of subjects were given statistical information about the effect of eliminating affirmative action and adopting a race-neutral admissions policy at several universities. The statistics were real ones and they were accurate. One group of subjects, the percentage group, received the information that under race-neutral admissions the probability of a black student being admitted would decline from 42 percent to 13 percent and that the probability of a white student being admitted would rise from 25 percent to 27 percent. The other group, the frequency group, received the information that under race-neutral admissions, the number of black students being admitted would drop by 725 and the number of white students being admitted would increase by 725. The statistics given to the two groups were mathematical equivalents—the results of the very same policy simply expressed in different ways (they are different framings). The difference in the pairs of percentages in the percentage condition (a 29 percent decrease for black students versus a 2 percent increase for white students) follows from the fact that many more applicants to the institutions were white.

Support for affirmative action was much higher in the percentage condition than in the frequency condition. In the percentage condition, the damage to black students from a race-neutral policy (42 percent admitted decreasing to only 13 percent admitted) seems extremely large compared to the benefit that white students would receive (an increase from 25 percent to only 27 percent admitted). The frequency condition, in contrast, highlights the fact that, on a one-to-one basis, each extra black student admitted under affirmative action means that a white student is denied admission. Both conditions simply represent different perspectives on exactly the same set of facts, but which perspective is adopted strongly affects opinions on this policy choice.

Many political disagreements are largely about alternative framings of an issue because all parties often know that whoever is able to frame the issue has virtually won the point without a debate even taking place. What many reformers are trying to do is to illustrate that the conventional wisdom is often just a default framing that everyone has come to accept. Cognitive psychologist George Lakoff has done several well-known analyses of the framing inherent in political terminology. He has drawn attention to the disciplined consistency with which, early in his first term, George W. Bush's White House operatives used the term *tax relief.* Lakoff pointed out how once this term becomes accepted, the debate about the level of taxation is virtually over. Start first with the term *relief.* Lakoff notes that "for there to be relief there must be an affliction, an afflicted party, and a reliever who removes the affliction and is therefore a hero. And if people try to stop the hero, those people are villains for trying to prevent relief. When the word tax is added to relief, the result is a metaphor: Taxation is an affliction. And the person who takes it away is a hero, and anyone who tries to stop him is a bad guy" (Lakoff, 2004, pp. 3–4). Of course, a well-known example is the inheritance tax, with Democrats preferring the term *estate tax* (most people do not view themselves as possessing "estates") and Republicans preferring the term *death tax* (which implies—incorrectly—that everyone is taxed at death).

Equal Opportunity Framing

Of course, framing would be less of an issue if we were not such cognitive misers. Perhaps frame-free politics, where issues could be decided on their real merits, is too much to ask for in the near term. But personally autonomous decision making that is free of arbitrary framing effects is *not* too much to ask for. The mental operations that are necessary if we are to avoid framing instability are not difficult to acquire.

Framing effects are the source of much dysrationalia, because, interestingly, the tendency to respond passively to the frame as given is largely independent of intelligence. Here a brief word about research methodology is needed. Framing experiments—and most other experiments on rational thinking—can be run either between subjects or within subjects. For the disease framing problem discussed previously, for example, in a between-subjects design one group of subjects would be presented with the gain version ("200 will be saved") and a different group of subjects would be presented with the loss version ("400 will die"). Random assignment of subjects to conditions ensures that the two groups are roughly equivalent and that the response patterns obtained from them are comparable. In a within-subjects design, each subject responds to both versions of the problem. Usually the two versions are separated in time so that the relation between the problems is not completely transparent. Of course, in within-subjects experiments the two versions are counterbalanced—one half of the subjects receive the gain version first and the other half of the subjects receive the loss version first.

Not surprisingly, between-subjects experiments show large framing effects because this design contains no cue that there is an issue of consistency at stake. Interestingly, however, the magnitude of the framing effect is not at all related to intelligence in this design.[10] So when given no cue that they should be consistent, the higher-IQ people in the research sample are just as likely to be framed by irrelevant context as the lower-IQ people.[11] The results with within-subjects designs are slightly different. Framing effects still occur in these designs, although they are not as large as those obtained in between-subjects designs. Also, in within-subjects designs, there is a statistically significant association between the magnitude of the framing effect and intelligence—higher-IQ individuals are slightly less likely to show a framing effect.

In short, subjects of higher intelligence are somewhat less likely to show irrational framing effects when cued (by the appearance of both problem versions) that an issue of consistency is at stake; but they are *no* more likely to avoid framing without such cues. We need to stop here and ponder one implication of the between/within findings regarding intelligence. I need to draw out the implications of the findings by speaking of them in a more colloquial way. The point is that, increasingly, cognitive science is coming to a shocking conclusion—a conclusion so important in its ramifications that it deserves to be set apart:

Intelligent people perform better only when you tell them what to do!

I am referring here specifically to the domain of rational thought and action. If you tell intelligent people what a rational requirement is—if you inform them about a particular stricture of rational thought (avoid intransitivity, avoid framing, do not be overconfident in your own knowledge, etc.)—and then give them a task that requires following the stricture, higher-IQ individuals will adhere to the stricture better than individuals of lower intelligence. However, if you give people tasks without warning them that a particular rational principle is involved—if they have to notice *themselves* that an issue of rationality is involved—individuals of higher intelligence do little better than their counterparts of lower intelligence.

It is true that there is a statistically significant relationship between intelligence and framing avoidance in within-subjects designs, but it is quite modest, leaving plenty of room for dysrationalia in this domain. It is likewise with some of the characteristics of the cognitive miser discussed in the last chapter—attribute substitution, vividness effects, failures of disjunctive reasoning. None of these characteristics are strongly correlated with intelligence.[12] All of the characteristics discussed in this and the previous chapter are critical for achieving rationality of thought and action, yet none of these characteristics are assessed on intelligence tests. If they were, some people would be deemed more intelligent and some people less intelligent than they are now. Why? Because of the empirical evidence that I just mentioned—these processing characteristics show little relation to intelligence. That certainly holds true as well for one of the most defining features of the cognitive miser, to be discussed in the next chapter—myside processing.

EIGHT

Myside Processing:
Heads I Win — Tails I Win Too!

If it's at all feasible then your brain will interpret the question in a way that suits you best.
    — *Cordelia Fine*, A Mind of Its Own, 2006

I n a recent study my colleague Richard West and I presented one group of subjects with the following thought problem:

> According to a comprehensive study by the U.S. Department of Transportation, a particular German car is 8 times more likely than a typical family car to kill occupants of another car in a crash. The U.S. Department of Transportation is considering recommending a ban on the sale of this German car.

Subjects then answered the following two questions on a scale indicating their level of agreement or disagreement: (1) Do you think that the United States should ban the sale of this car? (2) Do you think that this car should be allowed on U.S. streets, just like other cars? We found that there was considerable support for banning the car — 78.4 percent of the sample thought that the German car should be banned and 73.7 percent thought that it should not be allowed on the streets like other cars.

The statistics on dangerousness of the car in the example happen to be real statistics, but they are not the statistics for a German car. They are actu-

ally the statistics for the Ford Explorer, which happens to be a very dangerous vehicle indeed, for the passengers of *other* cars.[1] In the scenario just presented, subjects were evaluating the social policy of allowing a dangerous
German vehicle on American streets. A second group of subjects in our study
evaluated the reverse—the policy of allowing a dangerous American vehicle
on German streets. This group of subjects received the following scenario:

> According to a comprehensive study by the U.S. Department of Trans-
> portation, Ford Explorers are 8 times more likely than a typical family
> car to kill occupants of another car in a crash. The Department of Trans-
> portation in Germany is considering recommending a ban on the sale
> of the Ford Explorer in Germany. Do you think that Germany should
> ban the sale of the Ford Explorer? Do you think that the Ford Explorer
> should be allowed on German streets, just like other cars?

Subjects responded on the same scale, and when they did we found that
51.4 percent thought that the Ford Explorer should be banned and 39.2 percent thought that it should not be allowed on the German streets like other
cars. Statistical tests confirmed that these percentages were significantly
lower than the proportion of subjects who thought a similar German vehicle
should be banned in the United States.

Our study illustrates what has been termed in the literature a myside bias.
That is, people tend to evaluate a situation in terms of their own perspective. They judge evidence, they make moral judgments, and they evaluate
others from a standpoint that is biased toward their own situation. In this
case, they saw the dangerous vehicle as much more deserving of banning if
it were a German vehicle in America than if it were an American vehicle in
Germany.

Myside bias is a ubiquitous phenomenon, and it has been revealed in a
variety of ingenious psychological studies. Drew Westen and colleagues have
used an interesting task to study myside processing in contradiction detection.[2] Subjects were asked to read materials which revealed a contradiction
between a person's words and actions. Some of the materials concerned political figures. For example, subjects read a statement by George W. Bush

about Ken Lay, the CEO of Enron. The statement was made when Bush was a candidate in 2000: "First of all, Ken Lay is a supporter of mine. I love the man. I got to know Ken Lay years ago, and he has given generously to my campaign. When I'm President, I plan to run the government like a CEO runs a country. Ken Lay and Enron are a model of how I'll do that." Subjects where then presented with a fact about Bush's (then current) actions with respect to Lay. The fact was: "Mr. Bush now avoids any mention of Ken Lay and is critical of Enron when asked." Subjects were then asked to consider whether the statement and action were inconsistent with each other on a 1 to 4 scale running from 1 (strongly disagree that the action and statement are inconsistent) to 4 (strongly agree that the action and statement are inconsistent).

There were other similar items about different political figures. For example, subjects were told: "During the 1996 campaign, John Kerry told a *Boston Globe* reporter that the Social Security system should be overhauled. He said Congress should consider raising the retirement age and means-testing benefits. 'I know it's going to be unpopular,' he said. 'But we have a generational responsibility to fix this problem.'" Subjects were then presented with a fact about Kerry's actions that contradicted his statement: "This year, on *Meet the Press*, Kerry pledged that he will never tax or cut benefits to seniors or raise the age for eligibility for Social Security." Subjects then answered on the same scale reporting whether or not they believed the action and earlier statement were inconsistent.

Myside bias in this contradiction detection paradigm was massive. Subjects' political beliefs influenced whether they were able to detect the contradictions. For example, for Bush contradictions like the example given, self-identified Democrats gave a mean rating of roughly 3.79 (strongly agree that the statement and action are inconsistent). In contrast, self-identified Republicans gave Bush contradictions a mean rating of roughly 2.16 (disagree that the statement and action are inconsistent). Conversely, for Kerry contradictions like the example given, self-identified Republicans gave a mean rating of roughly 3.55 (strongly agree that the statement and action are inconsistent). In contrast, self-identified Democrats gave Kerry contradictions a mean rating of roughly 2.60 (neutral on whether the statement and action are inconsistent). In short, people could see the contradictions of the *other* party's candidate but not the contradictions of their own.

People not only *evaluate* arguments in a biased manner, they *generate* arguments in a biased manner as well. My colleagues Maggie Toplak, Robyn Macpherson, and I had subjects explore arguments both for and against various public policy propositions. When the subjects were instructed to be balanced and unbiased, or when they did not have an extremely strong prior opinion on the issue (for example, "People should be allowed to sell their internal organs"), they generated arguments for both sides of the issue that were roughly equal in quality and quantity. But when subjects (university students) had a strong opinion on the issue (for instance, "Tuition should be raised to cover the full cost of a university education"), even when they were given explicit instructions to be unbiased in their reasoning, they generated many more arguments on their side of the issue than for the opposite position.

Myside processing undermines our ability to evaluate evidence as well as generate it. In several studies, Paul Klaczynski and colleagues presented subjects with flawed hypothetical experiments that led to conclusions that were either consistent or inconsistent with prior positions and opinions.[3] The subjects ranged from young adults to elderly individuals. Subjects were then asked to critique the flaws in the experiments (which were most often badly flawed). Robust myside bias effects were observed—subjects found many more flaws when the experiment's conclusions were inconsistent with their prior opinions than when the experiment's conclusions were consistent with their prior opinions and beliefs.

We have known for some time that it is cognitively demanding to process information from the perspective of another person.[4] It is thus not surprising that people are reluctant to engage in it, and that myside processing is a fundamental property of the cognitive miser. Nonetheless, we sometimes underestimate the costs of myside processing and/or fail to recognize it as the source of much irrational thought and action. Finally, as we shall see, intelligence is no inoculation against the perils of myside processing.

Overconfidence: On Thinking We Know What We Don't

We will begin this section with a little test. For each of the following items, provide a low and high guess such that you are 90 percent sure the correct answer falls between the two. Write down your answers:

1. I am 90 percent confident that Martin Luther King's age at the time of his death was somewhere between ___ years and ___ years.
2. I am 90 percent confident that the number of books in the Old Testament is between ___ books and ___ books.
3. I am 90 percent confident that the year in which Wolfgang Amadeus Mozart was born was between the year ____ and the year ____.
4. I am 90 percent confident that the gestation period (in days) of an Asian elephant is between ____ days and ____ days.
5. I am 90 percent confident that the deepest known point in the oceans is between _____ feet and _____ feet.

These questions relate to another important aspect of cognition in which people are myside processors. That domain of cognition concerns how people monitor confidence in their own beliefs. Psychologists have done numerous studies using the so-called knowledge calibration paradigm.[5] In this paradigm, a large set of probability judgments of knowledge confidence are made. Of course, a single probability judgment by itself is impossible to evaluate. How would I know if you were correct in saying there is a 95 percent chance that your nephew will be married in a year? However, a large *set* of such judgments *can* be evaluated because, collectively, the set must adhere to certain statistical criteria.

For example, if the weather forecaster says there is a 90 percent chance of rain tomorrow and it is sunny and hot, there may be nothing wrong with that particular judgment. The weather forecaster might have processed all the information that was available and processed it correctly. It just happened to be unexpectedly sunny on that particular day. However, if you found out that on half of the days the weatherperson said there was a 90 percent chance of rain it did not rain, then you would be justified in seriously questioning the accuracy of weather reports from this outlet. You expect it to rain on 90 percent of the days that the weatherperson says have a 90 percent chance of rain. You accept that the weatherperson does not know on *which* 10 percent of the days it will not rain (otherwise she would have said she was 100 percent certain), but overall you expect that if, across the years, the weatherperson has predicted "90 percent chance of rain" on 50 different days, that on about 45 of them it will have rained.

The assessment of how well people calibrate their knowledge proceeds in exactly the same way as we evaluate the weatherperson. People answer multiple choice or true/false questions and, for each item, provide a confidence judgment indicating their subjective probability that their answer is correct. Epistemic rationality is apparent only when one-to-one calibration is achieved—that the set of items assigned a subjective probability of .70 should be answered correctly 70 percent of the time, that the set of items assigned a subjective probability of .80 should be answered correctly 80 percent of the time, etc. This is what is meant by good knowledge calibration. If such close calibration is not achieved, then a person is not epistemically rational because his or her beliefs do not map on to the world in an important way. Such epistemic miscalibration will make it impossible to choose the best actions to take.

The standard finding across a wide variety of knowledge calibration experiments has been one of overconfidence. Subjective probability estimates are consistently higher than the obtained percentage correct. So, for example, people tend to get 88 percent of the items correct on the set of items on which they say they are 100 percent sure that they were correct. When people say they are 90 percent sure they are correct, they actually get about 75 percent of the items correct, and so on. Often, people will say they are 70 to 80 percent certain when in fact their performance is at chance—50 percent in a true/false paradigm.

The overconfidence effect in knowledge calibration is thought to derive at least in part from our tendency to fix on the first answer that comes to mind, to then assume "ownership" of that answer, and to cut mental costs by then privileging that answer as "our own" in subsequent thinking. Subjects make the first-occurring answer a focal hypothesis (akin to a myside bias) and then concentrate attention on the focal hypothesis, thereby leading to inattention to alternative, or nonfocal, answers. In short: "one reason for inappropriately high confidence is failure to think of reasons why one might be wrong" (Baron, 2000, p. 132). The evidence retrieved for each of the alternatives forms the basis for the confidence judgments, but the subject remains unaware that the recruitment of evidence was biased—that evidence was recruited only for the favored alternative. As a result, subjects end up with too much confidence in their answers.

You can see if you were subject to the phenomenon of overconfidence by looking at the answers to the questions that were presented at the beginning of this section:[6]

1. 39 years;
2. 39 books;
3. the year 1756;
4. 645 days;
5. 36,198 feet.

Recall that you were forewarned about the phenomenon of overconfidence by the title of this section. Because you were forming 90 percent confidence intervals, 90 percent of the time your confidence interval should contain the true value. Only one time in 10 should your interval fail to contain the actual answer. So because you answered only five such questions, your intervals should have contained the correct answer each time—or, at the very most, you should have answered incorrectly just once. Chances are, based on past research with these items, that your confidence intervals missed the answer more than once, indicating that your probability judgments were characterized by overconfidence (despite the warning in the title) like those of most people.

Overconfidence effects have been found in perceptual and motor domains as well as in knowledge calibration paradigms. They are not just laboratory phenomena, but have been found in a variety of real-life domains such as the prediction of sports outcomes, prediction of one's own behavior or life outcomes, and economic forecasts. Overconfidence is manifest in the so-called planning fallacy—the fact that it is a ubiquitous fact of human behavior that we routinely underestimate the time it will take to complete projects in the future (for example, to complete an honors thesis, to complete this year's tax forms, to finish a construction project). Nobel Prize winner Daniel

Kahneman tells a humorous story of how intractable the planning fallacy is, even among experts who should know better. Years ago, with such a group of decision experts, Kahneman was working on a committee to develop a curriculum to teach judgment and decision making in high schools. The group was meeting weekly to develop the curriculum and to write a textbook. At one point in the series of meetings, Kahneman asked the group, which included the Dean of Education, to estimate how long they thought it would take them to deliver the curriculum and textbook that they were writing. The range of estimates, including those made by the Dean and Kahneman himself, was between eighteen months and two and half years. At that point it occurred to Kahneman that, because it was the early 1970s and many curriculum and textbook initiatives had been taking place, he should ask the Dean about the many other curriculum groups that the Dean had chaired. He asked the Dean to think back to previous groups concerned with similar projects. How long did it take them to finish? The Dean pondered a bit, then looked a little embarrassed, and told the group that roughly 40 percent of the groups in the past had never finished! Noting the discomfort in the room, Kahneman asked the Dean of those that finished, how long did it take them? The Dean, again looking somewhat embarrassed, told the committee that he could not think of any group that finished in less than seven years![7]

The cognitive bias of overconfidence in knowledge calibration has many real-world consequences. People who think they know more than they really do have less incentive to learn more or to correct errors in their knowledge base. People who think their motor or perceptual skills are excellent are critical of the performance of other people but do not subject their own behavior to criticism. For example, surveys consistently show that most people think that their driving skill is above average. Consider a survey by the Canada Safety Council in which 75 percent of drivers admitted to either talking on the phone, eating, shaving, or applying makeup while driving. Oddly, 75 percent of the same people said they were frustrated and appalled by *other* drivers they saw eating or talking on the phone! Similarly, thousands of people overconfidently think that their driving is unimpaired by talking on their cell phones. This failure of epistemic rationality (beliefs tracking reality) is proving increasingly costly as inattention-based accidents increase due to the addition of more technological distractions to the driver's environment.

The failure to achieve good probabilistic calibration represents an epistemic irrationality in humans that appears to be widespread and that may have pervasive consequences. For example, overconfidence among physicians is a pervasive and dangerous problem.[8]

The poor calibration of driving abilities relates to a larger area of social psychological research that has been focused on biased self-assessments. People systematically distort self perceptions, often but not always in self-enhancing ways.[9] In a self-evaluation exercise conducted with 800,000 students taking the SAT Test, less than 2 percent rated themselves less than average in leadership abilities relative their peers. Over 60 percent rated themselves in the top 10 percent in the ability to get along with others. In a study by Justin Kruger and David Dunning it was found that the bottom 25 percent of the scorers on a logic test thought, on average, that they were at the 62nd percentile of those taking the test. In short, even the very lowest scorers among those taking the test thought that they were above average!

There is a final recursive twist to this myside processing theme. Princeton psychologist Emily Pronin has surveyed research indicating that there is one additional domain in which people show biased self-assessments. That domain is in the assessment of their own biases.[10] Pronin summarizes research in which subjects had to rate themselves and others on their susceptibility to a variety of cognitive and social psychology biases that have been identified in the literature, such as halo effects and self-serving attributional biases (taking credit for successes and avoiding responsibility for failures). Pronin and colleagues found that across eight such biases, people uniformly felt that they were less biased than their peers. In short, people acknowledge the truth of psychological findings about biased processing—with the exception that they believe it does not apply to them.

In explaining why this so-called bias blind spot exists, Pronin speculated that when estimating the extent of bias in others, people relied on lay psychological theory. However, when evaluating their own bias, she posited, they fell back on an aspect of myside processing—monitoring their own conscious introspections. Modern lay psychological theory allows for biased processing, so biased processing is predicted for others. However, most social and cognitive biases that have been uncovered by research operate unconsciously. Thus, when we go on the introspective hunt for the processes operating to bias our own minds we find nothing. We attribute to ourselves via the intro-spective mechanism much less bias than we do when we extrapolate psycho-logical theory to others.

Another important aspect of myside processing is our tendency to have misplaced confidence in our ability to control events. Psychologist Ellen Langer has studied what has been termed the illusion of control—that is, the tendency to believe that personal skill can affect outcomes determined by chance. In one study, two employees of two different companies sold lot-tery tickets to their co-workers. Some people were simply handed a ticket, whereas others were allowed to choose their ticket. Of course, in a random drawing, it makes no difference whether a person chooses a ticket or is as-signed one. The next day, the two employees who had sold the tickets ap-proached each individual and attempted to buy the tickets back. The subjects who had chosen their own tickets demanded four times as much money as the subjects who had been handed their tickets! In several other experiments, Langer confirmed the hypothesis that this outcome resulted from people's mistaken belief that skill can determine the outcome of random events.

People subject to a strong illusion of control are prone to act on the basis of incorrect causal theories and thus to produce suboptimal outcomes. That this is a practical outcome of acting on illusory feelings of control is well illus-trated in a study by Mark Fenton-O'Creevy and colleagues. They studied 107 traders in four different investment banks in the City of London. The degree of illusory control that characterized each trader was assessed with an experi-mental task. The subjects pressed keys that they were told either might or might not affect the movement of an index that changed with time. In reality, the keys did not affect the movement of the index. The degree to which sub-jects believed that their key presses affected the movement of the index was the measure of the degree to which subjects' thought processes were charac-terized by an illusion of control. Fenton-O'Creevy and colleagues found that differences in feelings of illusory control were (negatively) related to several measures of the traders' performance. Traders who were high in the illusion of control earned less annual remuneration than those who were low in the illusion of control. A one standard deviation increase in illusion of control was associated with a decrease in annual remuneration of £58,000.[11]

Myside Processing: Egocentrism in Communication and Knowledge Assumptions

Myside processing biases can disrupt our communication attempts, especially in certain settings. Kruger and colleagues have studied egocentrism in e-mail communication.[12] Of course, any written communication requires some perspective-taking on our part because we know that the normal cues of tone, expression, and emphasis are not present. E-mail may be particularly dangerous in this respect, because its ease, informality, and interactiveness might encourage us to think that it is more like face-to-face communication than it really is. In their first study, Kruger and colleagues had one group of subjects send e-mail messages to another group of subjects who then interpreted the messages. Half of the messages sent were sarcastic ("I really like going on dates because I like being self-conscious") and half were not. Receivers were asked to judge which were sarcastic and which were not, and senders were asked to estimate whether they thought the receiver would properly classify each particular message. Senders were quite optimistic that the receivers could decode virtually every message—the senders thought that the receivers would achieve 97 percent accuracy in their classification. In fact, the receivers correctly interpreted only 84 percent of the messages. Senders had a difficult time adjusting their myside perspective in order to understand that without expressive cues and intonation, it was hard to see that some of these messages were sarcastic.

That the difficulty people have in understanding the possibility of miscommunication in e-mail really is due to egocentrism was suggested by another experiment. This experiment was one in which the senders read their e-mail messages aloud. However, the oral recordings were not sent to the receiver. Just as in the previous experiment, the receiver interpreted e-mails alone. The purpose of the oral recording was to induce a less egocentric mindset in one group of senders. One group of senders recorded the messages in a manner consistent with their meaning—the senders read sarcastic messages sarcastically and serious messages seriously. The other group, however, read the messages inconsistently—sarcastic messages were read seriously and serious messages sarcastically. As Kruger and colleagues put it, "Our reasoning was simple. If people are overconfident in their ability to communicate over e-mail partly because of the difficulty of moving beyond their own perspective, then forcing people to adopt a perspective different from their own ought to reduce this overconfidence. As a result, participants who vocalized the messages in a manner inconsistent with the intended meaning should be less overconfident than those who vocalized the messages in a manner consistent with the intended meaning" (p. 930).

Replicating the earlier studies, the consistent group showed a very large overconfidence effect. Their receivers correctly identified only 62.2 percent of the messages, whereas the senders had thought that 81.9 percent of their messages would be accurately interpreted. In contrast, in the inconsistent group, while the receivers correctly identified 63.3 percent of the messages, the senders had been much less optimistic about how many would be interpreted correctly. These senders had predicted (correctly) that only 62.6 percent of their messages would be accurately interpreted.

What the Kruger findings illustrate is how automatically we egocentrically project what we know into the minds of others. Indeed, their studies were inspired by an even more startling demonstration of this tendency. They describe a doctoral dissertation study by Elizabeth Newton in which subjects were asked to tap out the rhythm of a popular song to a listener. The tapper then estimated how many people would correctly identify the song from the taps if the taps were presented to a large group of listeners. The tappers estimated that roughly 50 percent of the listeners would be able to identify the song they were tapping. Actually, only 3 percent of the listeners were able to identify the song from the tapping. We all know this phenomenon. The song is just so clear in our own mind, we can't believe our cryptic hums or taps do not immediately trigger it in our listener. Even knowing about such myside biases does not inoculate us from this illusion—that what is in our heads does not loom as large to other people as it does to us.

Myside thinking of this type is implicated in the phenomena of "feature creep" and "feature fatigue" discussed in the consumer literature on electronic devices.[13] As more and more complicated features are added to electronic products, the devices become less useful because consumers cannot afford the time that it takes to master the appliance. One study done by the Philips Electronics company found that one half of their returned products had nothing wrong with them. Instead, in half the cases, the problem was that the consumer could not figure out how to use the device.

Many companies are designing products with additional features that actually make the product less useful in the end. Writer James Surowiecki mentions the obvious example of Microsoft Word 2003, which has 31 toolbars and over 1500 commands. Why does this feature creep occur? The problem arises because the designers of the products cannot avoid falling into myside thinking. The myside bias of the designers is well described by cognitive scientist Chip Heath, who notes that he has "a DVD remote control with 52 buttons on it, and every one of them is there because some engineer along the line knew how to use that button and believed I would want to use it, too. People who design products are experts. . . . and they can't imagine what it's like to be as ignorant as the rest of us" (Rae-Dupree, 2007, p. 3).[14]

Intelligence and Myside Processing

In this chapter, I have discussed only a small sampling of the many different ways that psychologists have studied myside processing tendencies.[15] Myside processing is ubiquitous. Is high intelligence an inoculation against myside processing bias?

In several studies of myside bias like that displayed in the Ford Explorer problem that opened this chapter, my colleague Richard West and I have found absolutely no correlation between the magnitude of the bias obtained and intelligence. The subjects above the median intelligence in our sample were just as likely to show such biases as the subjects below the median. It is likewise with the argument generation paradigm that I described ("Tuition should be raised to cover the full cost of a university education"). The tendency to generate more myside arguments than otherside arguments was unrelated to intelligence.[16] In several studies, Klaczynski and colleagues found that the higher-IQ subjects in experiments were just as likely to evaluate experimental evidence in a biased manner as were the lower-IQ subjects. Overconfidence effects have been modestly associated with intelligence in a few studies. Subjects with higher intelligence have been shown to display slightly lower overconfidence. Again, though, these are statistically significant but modest associations—ones that leave plenty of room for the dissociation that defines dysrationalia in this domain (highly unwarranted overconfidence in an individual of high intelligence).

Most of the myside situations for which we have the strongest evidence for the lack of a link to intelligence involve what West and I call natural myside bias paradigms. These are situations where people show a tendency to evaluate propositions from within their own perspective when given no explicit instructions or cues to avoid doing so. It is probably important to note that these studies did not strongly instruct the subject that myside thinking was to be avoided or that multiple perspective-taking was a good thing. It is likely that the higher-intelligence subjects in the experimental sample would have been better able to comply with these instructions.

The findings surveyed here on myside bias suggest exactly the same ironic conclusion that was mentioned in the previous chapter on framing effects: Intelligent people perform better only when you tell them what to do. If you tell an intelligent person what a rational requirement is—in the case of this chapter, if you tell them to avoid myside bias or in the case of the last chapter you tell them to avoid framing effects—and then give them a task that requires following that stricture, individuals with higher intelligence will adhere to the stricture better than individuals of lower intelligence.

It is important to note that the literature in education that stresses the importance of critical thinking actually tends to focus on avoiding *natural* myside bias. It is thus not surprising that we observe massive failures of critical thinking among, for example, university students. They have been selected, in many cases, by admissions instruments that are proxies for intelligence, but such instruments contain no measures of critical thinking defined in this way. Note that, in theory, the tests *could* contain such assessments. I have just discussed a very small and select sample of tasks that are used to assess myside processing. There are many more. They represent ways to examine an important aspect of rational thought that is not tapped by intelligence tests. Such an aspect of thought (myside bias) represents an important part of cognition that intelligence tests miss.

NINE

A Different Pitfall of the Cognitive Miser:
Thinking a Lot, but Losing

The prosperity of modern civilization contrasts more and more sharply with people's choice of seemingly irrational, perverse behaviors, behaviors that make many individuals unhappier than the poorest hunter/gatherer. As our technical skills overcome hunger, cold, disease, and even tedium, the willingness of individuals to defeat their own purposes stands in even sharper contrast. In most cases these behaviors aren't naive mistakes, but the product of robust motives that persist despite an awareness of the behaviors' cost
—*George Ainslie*, Breakdown of Will, 2001

One evening, in July 1999, John F. Kennedy Jr. set off for Martha's Vineyard in a small aircraft with his wife and sister-in-law and, just miles from his destination, piloted the aircraft into the ocean after he became disoriented in the dark and haze. Journalist Malcolm Gladwell describes Kennedy's errors as an instance of override failure.[1] Kennedy could not trump Type 1 tendencies with Type 2 thinking. He could not trump normal thinking defaults with the rules he had learned about instrument flying. Specifically, he could not keep his wings level when he could not find lights marking the horizon, did not realize that the plane was in a bank, and ended up with his plane in a spiral dive.

Without a visible horizon, a bank is undetectable through felt gravitational forces and the pilot *feels* level, although in fact he is not. This is just the situation that creates the necessity for an override by our conscious minds—

brain subsystems are signaling a response that is nonoptimal, and they must be overridden by acquired knowledge. In this case, the nonoptimal response was to navigate the plane up and down in an effort to escape the clouds and haze and thus reveal the horizon. The acquired knowledge and correct response was to use the instruments to keep the plane level, but this is what Kennedy could not bring himself to do consistently. According to Gladwell, "Kennedy needed to think, to concentrate on his instruments, to break away from the instinctive flying that served him when he had a visible horizon" (p. 90). Instead, the learned tendencies of instrument flying lost a war with basic perceptual instincts not applicable to the situation. By the end, "he had fallen back on his instincts—on the way the plane *felt*—and in the dark, of course, instinct can tell you nothing" (p. 90). The National Transportation Safety Board report on the crash, which details the plane's movements in the last few minutes, reveals a desperate attempt to find the horizon visually—the natural tendency built into us. But night flying requires that this tendency be overridden and other learned behaviors be executed instead.

In previous chapters, I have discussed many situations where the cognitive miser fails to consciously process information and unthinkingly uses default processing modes that lead to irrational responses in some situations. The Kennedy case seems not quite like this. It seems not quite like passively accepting a frame that is provided (Chapter 7) or thoughtlessly responding to a novel problem like the Levesque problem of Chapter 6 ("Jack is looking at Anne but Anne is looking at George. Jack is married but George is not"). Kennedy was not a cognitive miser in the sense that he failed to think at all. Plus—he *knew* the right things to do. Kennedy had been taught what to do in this situation and, given that his life and the lives of others were at stake, he clearly was thinking a *lot*. What happened was that the right behavioral patterns lost out to the wrong ones. The right response was probably in Kennedy's mind at some point (unlike the case of the Levesque problem), but it lost out to the wrong response. Kennedy was thinking, but the right thinking lost out—which of course raises the question: lost out to whom? Given that *all* thinking is going on in the same brain, this suggests the possibility that there are different minds in the same brain—precisely what the tripartite model discussed in Chapter 3 suggested. There are many different nonconscious subsystems in the brain that often defeat the reflective, conscious parts of our brains.[2] In Kennedy's case, he lost out to ancient evolutionarily adapted modules for balance, perception, and orientation. This is a common occurrence, but an even *more* common one is the tendency of rational response tendencies to lose out to a suite of evolutionarily adapted modules related to emotional regulation.

The Trolley Problem: Overriding the Emotions

To get ourselves warmed up for thinking about the emotions, let's contemplate killing someone. Do not get too upset, though—it will be for a good cause. I would like to discuss a hypothetical situation that is well traveled in moral philosophy—the trolley problem. There are many variants in the literature,[3] but basically it goes like this. Imagine you are watching a runaway trolley that has lost its brakes and is rolling down a hill toward five people standing on the tracks below, who will certainly be killed by it. The only way to avoid this tragedy is for you to hit a nearby switch. This switching device will send the trolley down an alternative track on which there is only one person standing who will be killed by the trolley. Is it correct for you to hit the switch?

Most people say that it is—that it is better to sacrifice one person in order to save five.

Consider now an alternative version of this hypothetical studied by Harvard psychologist Joshua Greene, who has done work on the cognitive neuroscience of moral judgment. This alternative version is called the footbridge problem. As before, a runaway trolley that has lost its brakes is rolling down a hill and is certain to kill five people on the tracks below. This time you are standing on a footbridge spanning the tracks in between the trolley and the five people. A large stranger is leaning over the footbridge and if you push him over the railing he will land on the tracks, thus stopping the trolley and saving the five people (and no one will see the push). Should you push him over? Most people say no.

We all certainly can understand why there is a *tendency* to say no in the second case. The second case is just . . . yucky . . . in a way the first case is not.

So, the fact that we all have these intuitions is understandable. The problem comes about when some people want to *justify* these intuitions, that is, to say that *both* intuitions are right—that it is right to sacrifice one to save five in the first case and not right to sacrifice one to save five in the second. As Greene notes, "while many attempts to provide a consistent, principled justification for these two intuitions have been made, the justifications offered are not at all obvious and are generally problematic. . . . These intuitions are not easily justified. . . . If these conclusions aren't reached on the basis of some readily accessible moral principle, they must be made on the basis of some kind of intuition. But where do these intuitions come from?" (2005, p. 345).

To address this question, Greene and colleagues ran studies in which subjects responded to a variety of dilemmas like the trolley problem (termed less personal dilemmas) and a variety of dilemmas like the footbridge dilemmas (termed more personal dilemmas) while having their brains scanned. The brain scanning results confirmed that the more personal dilemmas were more emotionally salient and activated to a greater extent brain areas associated with emotion and social cognition: the posterior cingulate cortex, amygdala, medial prefrontal cortex, and superior temporal sulcus. The less personal dilemmas, in contrast, "produced relatively greater neural activity in two classically 'cognitive' brain areas associated with working memory function in the inferior parietal lobe and the dorsolateral prefrontal cortex" (Greene, 2005, p. 346). These are brain areas associated with overriding the decisions of the unconscious mind.

One interesting finding concerned the subjects who defied the usual pattern and answered yes to the footbridge-type problems—who sacrificed one to save five even in the highly personal dilemmas. They took an inordinately long time to make their responses. Greene and colleagues looked deeper into this finding and compared the brain scans on slow trials on which subjects said yes to footbridge-like problems (save the five) to the brain scans on fast trials on which subjects gave the majority response on such personal problems (the no response—don't save the five). The brain looked different on yes trials. The areas of the brain associated with overriding the emotional brain—the dorsolateral prefrontal cortex and parietal lobes—displayed more activity on those trials. What was happening for these individuals was that they were using Type 2 processing to override Type 1 processing coming from brain centers that regulate emotion. These subjects were realizing that if it was correct to divert the train toward one person to save five, it was also the right thing to do to push the large man over the footbridge in order to save five.

Most subjects are not like these subjects, however—they do not override the emotions in the footbridge dilemma. They engage in a cognitive struggle but their "higher" mind loses out to the emotions. It is thus not surprising that at a later time these subjects can find no principled reason for not sacrificing for greater gain in the footbridge case—because no principle was involved. The part of their minds that deals with principles lost out to the emotional mind. These people were left in a desperate attempt to make their two totally contradictory responses cohere into some type of framework—a framework that their conscious minds had not actually used during their responses to the problems.

It is a general fact of cognition that subjects are often unaware that their responses have been determined by their unconscious minds, and in fact they often vociferously defend the proposition that their decision was a conscious, principled choice. We tend to try to build a coherent narrative for our behavior despite the fact that we are actually unaware of the brain processes that produce most of it. The result is that we tend to confabulate explanations involving conscious choice for behaviors that were largely responses triggered unconsciously, a phenomenon on which there is a large literature.[4] The tendency to give confabulated explanations of behavior may impede cognitive reform that can proceed only if we are aware of the autonomous nature of certain of our brain subsystems.

Fighting "Cold" Heuristic Tendencies and Still Losing

Psychologists differentiate thought that is affect-laden from thought that is relatively free of affect. Trying to think in ways that override the contaminating effects of the emotions is an example of what psychologists term *hot cognition*. But our conscious thinking can lose out to unconscious thinking even when the emotions are not involved—that is, when we are engaged in purely cold cognition.[5] We can, in fact, let nonconscious processing determine our behavior even when, consciously, we know better. For example, would you rather have a 10 percent chance of winning a dollar or an 8 percent chance of winning a dollar? A no-brainer? But consider that if you are like many people in experiments by psychologist Seymour Epstein and colleagues you would have actually chosen the latter.[6]

Yes—Epstein found that it is actually possible to get subjects to prefer an 8 percent chance of winning a dollar over a 10 percent chance of winning a dollar. Here's how. Subjects in several of his experiments were presented with two bowls of jelly beans. In the first were nine white jelly beans and one red jelly bean. In the second were 92 white jelly beans and 8 red. A random draw was to be made from one of the two bowls and if a red jelly bean was picked, the subject would receive a dollar. The subject could choose which bowl to draw from. Although the two bowls clearly represent a 10 percent and an 8 percent chance of winning a dollar, a number of subjects chose the 100-bean bowl, thus reducing their chance of winning. The majority did pick the 10 percent bowl, but a healthy minority (from 30 to 40 percent of the subjects) picked the 8 percent bowl. Although most of these subjects were aware that the large bowl was statistically a worse bet, that bowl also contained more enticing winning beans—the 8 red ones. Many could not resist trying the bowl with more winners despite some knowledge of its poorer probability. That many subjects were aware of the poorer probability but failed to resist picking the large bowl is indicated by comments from some of them such as the following: "I picked the one with more red jelly beans because it looked like there were more ways to get a winner, even though I knew there were also more whites, and that the percents were against me" (Denes-Raj and Epstein, 1994, p. 823). In short, the tendency to respond to the absolute number of winners, for these subjects, trumped the formal rule (pick the one with the best percentage of reds) that they knew was the better choice.

Perhaps you think that you would have picked the small bowl, the correct one (you are probably right—the majority do in fact pick that bowl). Perhaps you do not feel that this was a problem of cold cognition that involved much of a struggle for you. Then maybe you will experience more of a struggle—of a cognitive battle that "you" may well lose—in the next example.

Consider the following syllogism. Ask yourself if it is valid—whether the conclusion follows logically from the two premises:

Premise 1: All living things need water
Premise 2: Roses need water
Therefore, Roses are living things

What do you think? Judge the conclusion either logically valid or invalid before reading on.

If you are like about 70 percent of the university students who have been given this problem, you will think that the conclusion is valid. And if you did think that it was valid, you would be wrong.[7] Premise 1 says that all living things need water, not that all things that need water are living things. So, just because roses need water, it does not follow from Premise 1 that they are living things. If that is still not clear, it will probably become clear after you consider the following syllogism with exactly the same structure:

Premise 1: All insects need oxygen
Premise 2: Mice need oxygen
Therefore, Mice are insects

Now it seems pretty clear that the conclusion does not follow from the premises.

If the logically equivalent "mice" syllogism is solved so easily, why is the "rose" problem so hard? Well, for one thing, the conclusion (roses are living things) seems so reasonable and you know it to be true in the real world. And that is the rub. Logical validity is not about the believability of the conclusion—it is about whether the conclusion necessarily follows from the premises. The same thing that made the rose problem so hard made the mice problem easy. The fact that "mice are insects" is false in the world we live in made it easier to see that the conclusion did not follow logically from the two premises.

In both of these problems, prior knowledge about the nature of the world (that roses are living things and that mice are not insects) is becoming implicated in a type of judgment that is supposed to be independent of content: judgments of logical validity. In the rose problem, prior knowledge was interfering, and in the mice problem prior knowledge was facilitative. The rose syllogism is an example of cold cognition involving a conflict between a natural response and a more considered rule-based response. Even if you answered it correctly, you no doubt felt the conflict. If you did not answer it correctly, then you have just experienced a situation in which you thought a lot but lost out to a more natural processing tendency to respond to believability rather than validity.

Syllogisms where validity and prior knowledge are in conflict assess an important thinking skill—the ability to maintain focus on reasoning through a problem without being distracted by our natural tendency to use the easiest cue to process (our natural tendency to be cognitive misers). These problems probe our tendencies to rely on attribute substitution when the instructions tell us to avoid it. In these problems, the easiest cue to use is simply to evaluate whether the conclusion is true in the world. Validity is the harder thing to process, but it must be focused on while the easier cue of conclusion believability is ignored and/or suppressed.

It is important to realize that the rose-type syllogism is not the type of syllogism that would appear on an intelligence test. It is the type of item more likely to appear on a *critical thinking* test, where the focus is on assessing thinking tendencies and cognitive styles. The openness of the item in terms of where to focus (on the truth of the conclusion or the validity of the argument) would be welcome in a critical thinking test, where the relative reliance on reasoning versus context may well be the purpose of the assessment. This openness would be unwanted on an intelligence test, where the focus is on (ostensibly) the raw power to reason when there is no ambiguity about what constitutes optimal performance. On an intelligence test (or any aptitude measure or cognitive capacity measure) the syllogism would be stripped of content into "all As are Bs" form. Alternatively, unfamiliar content would be used, such as this example with the same form as the "rose" syllogism:

Premise 1: All animals of the hudon class are ferocious
Premise 2: Wampets are ferocious
Therefore, Wampets are animals of the hudon class

Items like this strip away the "multiple minds in conflict" aspect of the problem that was the distinguishing feature of the rose syllogism. Problems that do not involve such conflict tap only the power of the algorithmic mind and fail to tap important aspects of the reflective mind. For example, research has shown that performance on rose-type syllogisms is correlated somewhat with intelligence. However, thinking dispositions that are part of the reflective mind—dispositions such as cognitive flexibility, open-mindedness, context independence, and need for cognition—can predict variance in conflict syllogisms that intelligence cannot.[8]

Finally, although the rose syllogism may seem like a toy problem, it is indexing a cognitive skill of increasing importance in modern society—the ability to reason from the information *given* and at least temporarily to put aside what we thought before we received new information. For example, many aspects of the contemporary legal system put a premium on detaching prior belief and world knowledge from the process of evidence evaluation. There has been understandable vexation at the rendering of odd jury verdicts that had nothing to do with the evidence but instead were based on background knowledge and personal experience. Two classic cases from the 1990s provide examples. If the polls are to be believed, a large proportion of Americans were incensed at the jury's acquittal of O. J. Simpson. Similar numbers were appalled at the jury verdict in the first trial of the officers involved in the Rodney King beating. What both juries failed to do was to detach the evidence in their respective cases from their prior beliefs.

The need to detach knowledge and prior belief from current action characterizes many work settings in contemporary society. Consider the common admonition in the retail service sector that "the customer is always right." This admonition is often interpreted to include even instances where customers unleash unwarranted verbal assaults on the employee. Knowledge that the customer is wrong in this instance must be set aside, and the peculiar logic of the retail sector must be carried out by the employee or she will be fired. The service worker is supposed to remain polite and helpful and realize that this is the socially constructed domain of the market-based transaction. The worker must realize that he or she is not in an *actual* social interaction with this person, but in a special, indeed unnatural, realm where different rules apply.

I am not arguing that it is always better to ignore what you know. Obviously, most of the time we bring to bear all the prior knowledge we can in order to solve a problem. I am simply pointing to the fact that modernity is creating more and more situations where such unnatural decontextualization is required. The science on which modern technological societies is based often requires "ignoring what we know or believe." Testing a control group when you fully expect it to underperform an experimental group is a form of ignoring what you believe. The necessity for putting aside prior knowledge is not limited to science and the law. Modernity increasingly requires decontextualizing in the form of stripping away what we personally "know" by its emphasis on such characteristics as: fairness, rule-following despite context, even-handedness, sanctioning of nepotism, unbiasedness, universalism, inclusiveness, contractually mandated equal treatment, and discouragement of familial, racial, and religious discrimination.

Visceral Urges and Willpower: Thinking an *Awful* Lot and *Still* Losing

The tendencies that we have toward miserly information processing are often not apparent to us. When people are presented with a problem, they are often not even aware that there is an alternative framing. They are not aware that they are failing to think as much as they could. When people are engaged in myside thinking, they often are not aware of alternative ways of processing information. When we use anchoring and adjustment or have our thinking affected by vividness, we are rarely aware of alternative ways of thinking. This makes sense. The purpose of the cognitive shortcuts used by the cognitive miser is to provide answers without taxing awareness. If we were aware of having chosen between alternative strategies, then these would not be cognitive shortcuts! Their purpose is subverted if we are *aware* of choosing alternative ways of decision making and problem solving.

The situations discussed in the current chapter are different, however. If you felt that you would have chosen the 8 percent bowl in the Epstein jelly bean task, you were at least aware that the 10 percent was probably a better bet. If you thought that it was wrong to push the man over the footbridge in that version of the trolley problem, you were at least aware of a conflicting argument for doing so — you were aware of the argument that you were sentencing four more people to death because you failed to push the man over. On the rose syllogism if you defaulted to the easy solution of just saying "valid" when you saw the phrase "roses are living things" you were probably aware that you had been a bit lazy and not thought about the premises of the problem all that much. People are aware that there is a conflict in these situations between what we might call hard thinking and easy thinking. They have some awareness that the hard thinking is pulling them in one direction and the easy thinking in the other direction.

There are still other situations where people have no trouble at all realizing that they are made up of multiple minds. In fact, the struggle between minds is almost the defining feature of these situations. They are situations where we have to resist temptation: where we have to get up and make breakfast despite wanting to sleep; have to resist an extra $3 coffee in the afternoon because we know the budget is tight this month; are on a diet and know that our snack should be carrots and not chips; know the garage needs to be cleaned this Saturday, but the Michigan–Notre Dame game is on; have to study for a mid-term but there are two parties this weekend; are at a casino having promised to lose no more than $100 and are $107 down now and we really should stop but . . .

It is only *too* apparent to us in these instances that there are parts of our brains at war with each other. Our natural language even has a term to designate the hard thinking that is attempting to overcome the easy thinking in these instances: willpower. Willpower is a folk term, but in the last two decades cognitive researchers have begun to understand it scientifically.[9]

The Kennedy airplane crash incident that opened this chapter was an example where basic perceptual and cognitive processes needed to be overridden. However, these are not the situations in which we usually refer to willpower. Instead, our colloquial notion of willpower usually refers to the ability to delay gratification or to override visceral responses prompting us to make a choice that is not in our long-term interests. The inability to properly value immediate and delayed rewards is a source of irrationality that keeps many people from maximizing their goal fulfillment. The logic of many addictions, such as alcoholism, overeating, and credit card shopping, illustrate this point. From a long-term perspective, a person definitely prefers sobriety, dieting, and keeping credit card debt low. However, when immediately confronted with a stimulus that challenges this preference—a drink, a dessert, an item on sale—the long-term preference is trumped by the short-term desire. There are a whole variety of so-called self-control problems that fall into this class: drug abuse, smoking, over-eating, over-spending, gambling, procrastination.

Psychologists have studied this issue using delayed-reward paradigms in which people have been shown to display an irrationality called intertemporal preference reversal.[10] It is an irrational pattern of preference because it prevents us from getting what we most want over the long term. For example, imagine that you have the choice of receiving $100 immediately or $115 in one week's time (it is assumed that the money is held in escrow by the federal government, so that the thought experiment eliminates issues concerning the probability of receiving the money). Not all people choose the $115 when given this choice. For whatever reasons, some prefer to receive the $100 immediately. The same subjects who were given the first choice now receive another choice: receive $100 in 52 weeks or $115 in 53 weeks. Almost all subjects—regardless of the choice made earlier—prefer the $115 in this comparison. But for the people who chose the $100 in the earlier example, this is a rank inconsistency. In 52 weeks they will be in exactly the situation of the first example—they could be receiving $100 immediately or waiting one week for $115.

Why does waiting one week seem substantial at one time (so substantial that it is worth $15 to avoid) and insubstantial at another (making the decision one year in advance)? The answer is that humans display this inconsistency because they have so-called hyperbolic discount curves. These are simply the functions that determine how rapidly we discount a reward that is at a distance. Our functions are hyperbolic for sound evolutionary reasons. The only problem is that however well this type of function might have served genetic fitness, it is not a rational discount function for a human trying to maximize personal utility (an exponential curve is the right function for optimal human choice). Hyperbolic functions cause us to overvalue rewards that are close in time and thus to sometimes neglect longer-term goals. They cause us to reverse our preferences across time. From the standpoint of any planner of projects or actions this is suboptimal. Plans for a project made at an earlier point in time will be abandoned at a later point—and, at a still later point, this abandonment will be regretted!

Our hyperbolic discount functions account for many of the temptations that are dysfunctional when we succumb to them. We set the alarm for 7 A.M. when we go to bed at midnight because we judge that the tasks of the next day are better served by getting up at this time than by arising at 9 A.M. But when the alarm rings at 7 A.M. and we press the snooze button, we have reversed our earlier judgment—and later we will regret the reversal. We stock our fridges with expensive diet foods anticipating a period of weight loss, then find ourselves almost instinctively saying yes to the question "supersize that, sir?" at the fast-food counter. We must override the short-term response in situations like this, and the failure to do so is what folk psychology has labeled "lack of willpower."

Consider an example of willpower related in *Newsweek* magazine. In a profile of the wife of Senator John Edwards, Elizabeth Edwards, the writer reveals an anecdote from the 2004 presidential election campaign. Mrs. Edwards was struggling to stay on the South Beach Diet. The writer reports that while she was on a connecting flight, an airline attendant came by with the dessert tray and asked Mrs. Edwards if she would like a brownie. Mrs. Edwards replied: "The answer is yes. But if you go away I'll be happier in the long run" (Henneberger, 2004, p. 31). Mrs. Edwards exercised so-called willpower here, but she also may have used a cognitive tool that is an example of mindware that supports rational thought. She could have called up a so-called bundling strategy well described by psychologists George Ainslie and Howard Rachlin.[11] We want to pursue a long-term goal (weight loss through dieting) but a short-term reward (a brownie) tempts us. We know that we should not be eating a brownie every day. That would surely thwart our preeminent goal—weight loss through dieting. On the other hand, we find, in the heat of the moment, that visceral responses to the short-term goal are dominant. And they even have on their side another argument: Why not have the brownie now and start the diet tomorrow? In short, why not get the benefits of the brownie now *and* have the benefits of the long-term diet? Our ability to create alternative worlds—a key feature of the Type 2 processing carried out by the algorithmic and reflective minds—tells us why not: Tomorrow, we will be in exactly the same position as we are now, and we will opt for the brownie then as well, and so on, and so on.

At this point we could do some hard thinking and go one more step. We could create a rule that reclassifies the meaning of having a brownie today: Having a brownie today stands for having a brownie on every day of the future. This rule makes it clear that having the brownie today totally thwarts our preeminent goal of dieting. If I have a brownie—even this one—my *whole* weight-loss plan is threatened. The total loss is now magnified so that it can at least compete with the over-valued short-term gain from eating the brownie.

We now have a reframing of the problem that has the motivational force to at least compete with short-term visceral interests (this is of course not to say that the rule will win; only that it has the force now to make this a genuine struggle—an overtime game rather than a blowout, to use a sports analogy). Using our facility for language, we can instantiate rules that have the effect of "bundling" together behavioral actions to be taken in the future so that they can acquire the motivational force to override an action that *right now* threatens our long-term goals.

The example here points up an important issue that leads us to the topic of the next chapter. Overriding the responses primed by our unconscious minds is a process that utilizes content. Declarative knowledge and strategic rules (linguistically coded strategies) are brought to bear during the override process. This mindware is often a language-based proposition with motivational force that can prime a response system. We might upload such information as basic and simple as near universally understood aphorisms—"a penny saved is a penny earned," "beauty is only skin deep"—all in an effort to damp response priming from visceral or emotion modules.

A problem arises, though, in cases where the relevant mindware has not been learned by the individual—it is not available as an alternative control system that could influence behavior. There are thus situations where the individual might wish to override automatic responses but not have the appropriate mindware installed for the situation. This is a mental problem that causes irrational behavior and that I have called a mindware gap.

TEN

Mindware Gaps

Debates about rationality have focused on purely cognitive strategies, obscuring the possibility that the ultimate standard of rationality might be the decision to make use of superior tools.

—*Richard Larrick*, Blackwell Handbook of Judgment
and Decision Making, 2004

We cannot defy the laws of probability, because they capture important truths about the world.

—*Amos Tversky and Daniel Kahneman*, Judgment under Uncertainty:
Heuristics and Biases, 1982

I n the past several chapters, I have sketched some of the characteristics of the cognitive miser. But being a cognitive miser is not the only cause of poor thinking. People also fail to reach their goals because of mindware problems. Mindware is a generic label for the rules, knowledge, procedures, and strategies that a person can retrieve from memory in order to aid decision making and problem solving. Good thinking may be impossible because people have failed to acquire important mindware—they might lack the rules, strategies, and knowledge that support rational thinking. A second mindware problem arises because some knowledge can actually be the cause of irrational behavior and thought. The first problem, what I call mindware gaps, is the focus of this chapter. The second problem, termed contaminated mindware, is the subject of the next.

Mindware Problems in the Real World: Two Tragic Examples of the Effects of Mindware Gaps

Autism is a developmental disability characterized by impairment in reciprocal social interaction, delayed language development, and a restricted repertoire of activities and interests. The noncommunicative nature of many autistic children, who may be normal in physical appearance, makes the disorder a particularly difficult one for parents to accept. It is therefore not hard to imagine the excitement of parents of autistic children when, in the late 1980s and early 1990s, they heard of a technique coming out of Australia that enabled autistic children who had previously been totally nonverbal to communicate.

This technique for unlocking communicative capacity in nonverbal autistic individuals was called facilitated communication, and it was uncritically trumpeted in such highly visible media outlets as 60 *Minutes*, *Parade* magazine, and the *Washington Post*. The claim was made that autistic individuals and other children with developmental disabilities who had previously been nonverbal had typed highly literate messages on a keyboard when their hands and arms had been supported over the typewriter by a sympathetic "facilitator." Not surprisingly, these startling verbal performances on the part of autistic children who had previously shown very limited linguistic behavior spawned incredibly high hopes among their parents. It was also claimed that the technique worked for individuals with severe intellectual disability who were nonverbal. The excitement of the parents was easy to understand, and everyone sympathized with their hope.

Sadly, though, this story has no happy ending. Throughout the early 1990s, behavioral science researchers the world over watched in horrified anticipation, almost as if observing cars crash in slow motion, while a predictable tragedy unfolded before their eyes—predictable because the researchers had much experience with trying to fill (via teaching) the mindware gap that made the tragedy inevitable.

That mindware gap was a failure to appreciate some of the most critical features of scientific thinking—most notably the feature of testing alternative explanations by using a control group. The claims for the efficacy of facilitated communication were disseminated to hopeful parents before any controlled studies had been conducted. The need for controlled studies was imperative in this situation because there were many obvious alternative explanations for the phenomenon being observed. The facilitator, almost always a sympathetic individual who was genuinely concerned that the child succeed, had numerous opportunities to consciously or unconsciously direct the child's hand to the vicinity of keys on the keyboard. The fact that cuing by the facilitator might have been occurring was also suggested by the additional observation that the children sometimes typed out complicated messages while not even looking at the keyboard. Additionally, highly literate English prose was produced by children who had not previously been exposed to the alphabet.

By now, over a decade's worth of controlled studies have been reported that have tested the claims of facilitated communication by using appropriate experimental controls.[1] Each study has unequivocally demonstrated the same thing: The autistic child's performance depended on tactile cuing by the facilitator. Many of these studies set up a situation in which the child and the facilitator were each presented with a drawing of an object but neither could see the other's drawing. When both child and facilitator were looking at the same drawing, the child typed the correct name of the drawing. However, when the child and the facilitator were shown different drawings, the child typed the name of the facilitator's drawing, not the one at which the child was looking. Thus, the responses were being determined by the facilitator rather than the child. It is no overstatement to say that facilitated communication did indeed result in tragedy. For example, at some centers, during facilitated sessions on the keyboard, clients reported having been sexually abused by a parent in the past. Children were subsequently removed from their parents' homes, only to be returned later when the charges of abuse proved to be groundless.

The clinicians responsible for the facilitated communication tragedy were not unintelligent people. Nevertheless, their beliefs and behavior were irrational and caused great harm because they had a mindware gap. They lacked critical thinking strategies that would have prevented them from making mistaken causal inferences. They were smart people acting foolishly because of a mindware gap.

Another mindware gap was exposed with consequences just as tragic, in an even more recent set of cases. In 2003, Sally Clark, an English attorney, was released from prison when her conviction for killing her two young infants was overturned. Five months later, pharmacist Trupti Patel from Maidenhead, England, had her conviction for murdering her children overturned as well.[2] Mrs. Clark and Mrs. Patel had many things in common. They both had suffered recurring infant deaths in their families. They both had been charged with killing their infants. The evidence against both of the mothers was quite ambiguous. And—finally—both were convicted because the judge, the jury, and, most notably, an expert witness at their trials suffered from mindware gaps.

The expert witness who testified in both cases was a pediatrician. His theory was that both mothers suffered from Munchausen syndrome by proxy, a form of child abuse in which a parent subjects a child to unnecessary medical procedures. More convincing to the juries than this theory, however, was a probability presented to them during the pediatrician's testimony. The pediatrician testified that the odds against two babies dying of cot death (the term used in Britain for sudden infant death syndrome) in the same family was 73 million to 1. This figure greatly impressed the juries because it made the probability of these deaths happening by chance seem quite small. But the pediatrician had missed a basic rule of applied probability that operates in cases like this. To get his 73,000,000:1 figure, he had simply squared the probability of a single cot death. But this is the correct formula *only* under the assumption that the two deaths were independent events. That assumption is likely false in the case of sudden infant death syndrome where various genetic and environmental factors have been studied that would increase the probability of these deaths happening in the same family.

Shortly after the conviction of Mrs. Clark, the *British Medical Journal* published an essay titled "Conviction by Mathematical Error?" pointing out the errors in the logic of probability in the pediatrician's trial testimony. In one sense, the error in probabilistic reasoning is trivial. Once it is pointed out to most people, they understand it. That the "square the probabilities" rule requires that the events be independent is stressed by every introductory statistics instructor. But in another sense, the problem seems larger. The mindware of basic probability theory is very inadequately distributed. The pediatrician had failed to learn it, and it was also probably unknown to the judge and jury. Most people leave high school without knowing the multiplication rule of probability, and only a subset of university students takes courses in which it is taught. Intelligence tests do not assess it. Research in cognitive psychology has shown that our natural thinking tendencies (what the cognitive miser relies on) will not yield the right estimates when processing probabilistic information of this type.[3] Many important rules of probability theory are not in the stored mindware of most people because they have not been learned through formal instruction. In short, the lack of knowledge of probability theory is a mindware gap that is widespread and thus the source of much irrational thought and action.

In these two examples (facilitated communication and the convictions due to improper use of probabilities), I have illustrated how missing mindware can lead to irrational decisions and action. The two classes of missing mindware that I have illustrated here—rules of scientific thinking and probabilistic thinking, respectively—were chosen deliberately because they account for much irrational thinking. The presence or absence of this mindware determines whether people are rational or not. It is mindware that is often missing even among people of high intelligence (due to lack of exposure or instruction) and thus is a cause of dysrationalia. That is, because the tests do not assess probabilistic reasoning, many people who are deemed highly intelligent might still be plagued by irrational probabilistic judgments. Although many IQ tests do examine whether people have acquired certain types of factual information (for example, vocabulary), the mindware of scientific thinking and probability is not assessed by the tests. If it were, some people would be deemed more intelligent than they are by current tests and other people less so.

The Reverend Thomas Bayes to the Rescue!

The scientific thinking principle illustrated in the facilitated communication example—the necessity of considering alternative hypotheses—has enormous generality. The most basic form of this reasoning strategy—one that might be termed "think of the opposite"—is in fact mindware that can be used in a variety of problems in daily life. Imagine that there is an intriguing-looking restaurant in your neighborhood that you have never visited. One thing that has kept you away is that several of your discerning friends have said that they have eaten there and that it is not very good. Rightly or wrongly (your friends may be unrepresentative—and you may be overly influenced by the vividness of their testimony) you (implicitly) put the probability that the restaurant is any good at .50—that is, 50 percent. Later that month you are at the hairdresser getting a cut, and the proprietor of the restaurant happens to be there as well. The proprietor, recognizing you from the neighborhood, asks you why you have never been in the restaurant. You make up a lame excuse. Perhaps detecting some reluctance on your part, the proprietor says, "Come on, what's the matter? Ninety-five percent of my customers never complain!"

Does this put you at ease? Does this make you want to go there? Is this evidence that the restaurant is good?

The answer to all of these questions is of course a resounding no. In fact, the proprietor's statement has made you, if anything, even more hesitant to go there. It certainly hasn't made you want to raise your implicit probability that it is any good above 50/50. What is wrong with the proprietor's reasoning? Why is the proprietor wrong in viewing his or her statement as evidence that the restaurant is good and that you should go to it?

The formal answer to this question can be worked out using a theorem discovered by the Reverend Thomas Bayes of Tunbridge Wells, England, in the eighteenth century.[4] Bayes' formula is written in terms of just two fundamental concepts: the focal hypothesis under investigation (labeled H) and a set of data that are collected relevant to the hypothesis (labeled D). In the formula I will show you below, you will see an additional symbol, ~H (not H). This simply refers to the alternative hypothesis: the mutually exclusive alternative that must be correct if the focal hypothesis, H, is false. Thus, by convention, the probability of the alternative hypothesis, ~H, is one minus the probability of the focal hypothesis, H. For example, if I think the probability that the fish at the end of my line is a trout is .60, then that is the equivalent of saying that the probability that the fish at the end of my line is not a trout is .40.

Here I should stop and say that this is the most mathematical and technical part of this book. However, it is not the math but the concepts that are important, and they should be clear throughout the discussion even if you are math-phobic and wish to ignore the numbers and formulas. This is a key point. You need not learn anything more than a way of thinking—some verbal rules—in order to be a Bayesian thinker. Formal Bayesian statistics involve calculation to be sure, but to escape the thinking errors surrounding probability you only need to have learned the *conceptual* logic of how correct thinking about probabilities works.

So, in the formula to come, P(H) is the probability estimate that the focal hypothesis is true prior to collecting the data, and P(~H) is the probability estimate that the alternative hypothesis is true prior to collecting the data. Additionally, a number of conditional probabilities come into play. For example, P(H/D) represents the probability that the focal hypothesis is true subsequent to the data pattern being actually observed, and P(~H/D) represents the complement of this—the posterior probability of the alternative hypothesis, given the data observed. P(D/H) is the probability of observing that particular data pattern given that the focal hypothesis is true, and P(D/~H) (as we shall see below, a very important quantity) the probability of observing that particular data pattern given that the alternative hypothesis is true. It is important to realize that P(D/H) and P(D/~H) are *not* complements (they do not add to 1.0). The data might be likely given both the focal and alternative hypotheses or unlikely given both the focal and alternative hypotheses.

We will focus here on the most theoretically transparent form of Bayes' formula—one which is written in so-called odds form:

$$\frac{P(H/D)}{P(\sim H/D)} = \frac{P(D/H)}{P(D/\sim H)} \times \frac{P(H)}{P(\sim H)}$$

In this ratio, or odds form, from left to right, the three ratio terms represent: the posterior odds favoring the focal hypothesis (H) after receipt of the new data (D); the so-called likelihood ratio (LR) composed of the probability of the data given the focal hypothesis divided by the probability of the data given the alternative hypothesis; and the prior odds favoring the focal hypothesis. Specifically:

posterior odds = $P(H/D)/P(\sim H/D)$
likelihood ratio = $P(D/H)/P(D/\sim H)$
prior odds = $P(H)/P(\sim H)$

The formula tells us that the odds favoring the focal hypothesis (H) after receipt of the data are arrived at by multiplying together the other two terms—the likelihood ratio and the prior odds favoring the focal hypothesis:

posterior odds favoring the focal hypothesis = LR × prior odds

It is very important to understand, though, that no one is saying that people are irrational if they do not know Bayes' rule. No one is expected to know the formula. Instead, the issue is whether people's natural judgments of probabilities follow—to an order of approximation—the dictates of the theorem. It is understood that people making probabilistic judgments are making spontaneous "guesstimates"—the experimental evidence concerns whether these spontaneous judgments capture some of the restrictions that Bayes' theorem puts on probabilities. When we fall to the ground, our body can be described as behaving according to a law of Newton's. We do not consciously *calculate* Newton's law as our falling behavior is taking place—but we can in fact be described *as if* we were adhering to that law. The analogous question here is whether people's judgments can be described as adhering to the model of rational reasoning provided by Bayes' rule. The probability judgments of people might be described as consistent with Bayes' rule without their having *any* knowledge of the formula or being aware of any conscious calculation.

There are several ways in which reasoning has been found to deviate from the prescriptions of Bayes' rule, but in this section I concentrate on just one:[5]

Often, when evaluating the diagnosticity of evidence, $[P(D/H)/P(D/\sim H)]$, people fail to appreciate the relevance of the denominator term $[P(D/\sim H)]$. They fail to see the necessity of evaluating the probability of obtaining the data observed if the focal hypothesis were *false*.

This is the formal reason why failing to "think of the opposite" leads to serious reasoning errors. Let's go back to the proprietor of the restaurant described above. Anyone who thinks that the proprietor's argument is a good one is making this error. Here is why the proprietor's reasoning is wrong.

In Bayesian terms, what is happening is that the proprietor is providing you only with information about P(D/H) [the probability of less than 5 percent complaints if the restaurant is good] and ignoring P(D/~H) [the probability of less than 5 percent complaints if the restaurant is not good]. He or she wants you to raise your probability because he has presented you with a high P(D/H), but you are reluctant to do so because you (rightly) see that the critical posterior odds depend on more than this. You, in turn (if you are thinking correctly) are making some assumptions about the term he is *not* giving you—P(D/~H)—and realizing that the evidence he is presenting is not very good. In this simple example, you recognize the necessity of obtaining evidence about P(D/~H). In other words, what is the probability that only 5 percent of the customers would complain directly to the proprietor if the restaurant were not good?

What is happening in Bayesian terms is this. Recall the basic formula. Conceptually, it is:

posterior odds = likelihood ratio × prior odds

Let us suppose that you put your prior probability that the restaurant is good at .50—the same probability, .50, that it is bad. The prior odds in favor of the restaurant being good are thus .5/.5, or 1 to 1—even money, in racetrack terms.

What is the likelihood ratio (LR) here? Taking the proprietor at face value, the datum is the fact that: 95 percent of the customers never complain. So the likelihood ratio might be portrayed as this:

P(at least 95% of the customers never complain/the restaurant is good)
divided by
P(at least 95% of the customers never complain/the restaurant is bad)

Given that a restaurant is good, it is highly likely that at least 95 percent won't complain. In fact a 5 percent complaint rate is pretty high for any restaurant to stay in business with, so it's probably at least .99 probable that a good restaurant will have more than 95 percent walking away without complaint. The key to the proprietor's error is in the term in the denominator—$P(D/\sim H)$: Given that a restaurant is bad, what is the probability that more than 95 percent of its customers wouldn't complain? There are many problems here. Most bad restaurants are not bad all the time. Additionally, most are bad not because customers are gagging on the food (such restaurants close quickly), but because they are consistently mediocre or worse than average for their neighborhood. It is because they are "blah" restaurants—not that they are poisoning people. Add to this the fact that, for a host of social reasons, people rarely publicly complain when they are mildly dissatisfied. It seems quite likely that at a bad restaurant—a restaurant that would not poison us, but that we would not want to go to—*most people would leave without complaining*. This is why the 95 percent figure is unimpressive.

Given it is a bad restaurant, there might be a .90 probability that at least 95 percent of the customers will still leave without complaining. So what happens in Bayes' theorem when we plug in these numbers for the likelihood ratio is this:

posterior odds = likelihood ratio × prior odds
posterior odds = $(.99/.90) \times (.5/.5)$
posterior odds = 1.1

The odds favoring its being a good restaurant are still only 1.1 to 1 (the probability that it is a good restaurant has gone from 50 percent to only 52.4 percent[6]). Thus, on the best possible interpretation, it is still not very probable that this is a good restaurant.

The restaurant proprietor has tried to lure us into a thinking error. The proprietor's sleight of hand involves three parts:

1. Producing a datum, D, guaranteed to yield a high $P(D/H)$,
2. Hoping that we will fail to consider $P(D/\sim H)$, and
3. Implying that the high $P(D/H)$ alone implies a high probability for the focal hypothesis.

A large research literature has grown up demonstrating that the tendency to ignore the probability of the evidence given that the nonfocal hypothesis is true—P(D/~H)—is a ubiquitous psychological tendency. For example, psychologist Michael Doherty and colleagues used a simple paradigm in which subjects were asked to imagine that they were a doctor examining a patient with a red rash.[7] They were shown four pieces of evidence, and the subjects were asked to choose which pieces of information they would need in order to determine the probability that the patient had the disease "Digirosa." The four pieces of information were:

The percentage of people with Digirosa.
The percentage of people without Digirosa.
The percentage of people with Digirosa who have a red rash.
The percentage of people without Digirosa who have a red rash.

These pieces of information corresponded to the four terms in the Bayesian formula: P(H), P(~H), P(D/H), and P(D/~H). Because P(H) and P(~H) are complements, only three pieces of information are necessary to calculate the posterior probability. However, P(D/~H)—the percentage of people who have a red rash among those without Digirosa—clearly must be selected because it is a critical component of the likelihood ratio in Bayes' formula. Nevertheless, 48.8 percent of the individuals who participated in a study by Doherty and colleagues failed to select the P(D/~H) card. Thus, to many people presented with this problem, the people with a red rash but without Digirosa do not seem relevant—they seem (mistakenly) to be a nonevent.

The importance of P(D/~H) is not something that is automatically installed in our brain as mindware, so the fact that it is absolutely necessary information often seems counterintuitive. People have to be taught that it is important, or else their default is to ignore it. Thus, for many people, failure to realize the importance of processing P(D/~H) represents a mindware gap.

A Critical Mindware Gap—Ignoring the Alternative Hypothesis

The failure to attend to the alternative hypothesis—to the denominator of the likelihood ratio when receiving evidence—is not a trivial reasoning error. Paying attention to the probability of the observation under the alternative hypothesis is a critical component of clinical judgment in medicine and many other applied sciences. It is the reason we use control groups. It is essential to know what would have happened if the variable of interest had not been changed. Both clinical and scientific inference are fatally compromised if we have information about only the treated group.

This is perhaps one of many things that went seriously awry in the facilitated communication case which was characterized by failure to think about the necessity of testing alternative hypotheses. Psychologists have done extensive research on the tendency for people to ignore essential comparative (control group) information. For example, in a much researched covariation detection paradigm, subjects are shown data from an experiment examining the relation between a treatment and patient response.[8] They might be told, for instance, that:

200 people were given the treatment and improved
75 people were given the treatment and did not improve
50 people were not given the treatment and improved
15 people were not given the treatment and did not improve

These data represent the equivalent of a 2 × 2 matrix summarizing the results of the experiment. In covariation detection experiments, subjects are asked to indicate whether the treatment was effective. Many think that the treatment in this example is effective. They focus on the large number of cases (200) in which improvement followed the treatment. Secondarily, they focus on the fact that more people who received treatment showed improvement (200) than showed no improvement (75). Because this probability ($200/275 = .727$) seems high, subjects are enticed into thinking that the treatment works. This is an error of rational thinking.

Such an approach ignores the probability of improvement given that treatment was *not* given. Since this probability is even higher ($50/65 = .769$) the particular treatment tested in this experiment can be judged to be completely *ineffective*. The tendency to ignore the outcomes in the no-treatment condition and focus on the large number of people in the treatment/improvement group seduces many people into viewing the treatment as effective. Disturbingly, this nonoptimal way of treating evidence has been found even among those who specialize in clinical diagnosis such as physicians.

More Mindware of Scientific Thinking: Falsifiability

Just as people have difficulty learning to assess data in light of an *alternative* hypothesis, people have a hard time thinking about evidence and tests that could *falsify* their *focal* hypotheses. Instead, people tend to seek to confirm theories rather than falsify them. One of the most investigated problems in four decades of reasoning research illustrates this quite dramatically. The task was invented by Peter Wason, one of the most creative scientists to study human rationality in the modern era, and has been investigated in dozens, if not hundreds, of studies.[9] Try to answer it before reading ahead: Imagine four rectangles, each representing a card lying on a table. Each one of the cards has a letter on one side and a number on the other side. Here is a rule: If a card has a vowel on its letter side, then it has an even number on its number side. Two of the cards are letter-side up, and two of the cards are number-side up. Your task is to decide which card or cards must be turned over in order to find out whether the rule is true or false. Indicate which cards must be turned over. The four cards confronting you have the stimuli K, A, 8, and 5 showing.

This task is called the four-card selection task and has been intensively investigated for two reasons—most people get the problem wrong and it has been devilishly hard to figure out why. The answer seems obvious. The hypothesized rule is: If a card has a vowel on its letter side, then it has an even number on its number side. So the answer would seem to be to pick the A and the 8—the A, the vowel, to see if there is an even number on its back, and the 8 (the even number) to see if there is a vowel on the back. The problem is that this answer—given by about 50 percent of the people completing the problem—is wrong. The second most common answer, to turn over the A card only (to see if there is an even number on the back)—given by about 20 percent of the responders—is also wrong. Another 20 percent of the responders turn over other combinations (for example, K and 8) that are also not correct.

If you were like 90 percent of the people who have completed this problem in dozens of studies during the past several decades, you answered it incorrectly too (and in your case, you even missed it despite the hint given by my previous discussion of falsifiability!). Let's see how most people go wrong. First, where they don't go wrong is on the K and A cards. Most people don't choose the K and they do choose the A. Because the rule says nothing about what should be on the backs of consonants, the K is irrelevant to the rule. The A is not. It could have an even or odd number on the back, and although the former would be consistent with the rule, the latter is the critical potential outcome—it could prove that the rule is false. In short, in order to show that the rule is not false, the A must be turned. That is the part that most people get right.

However, it is the 8 and 5 that are the hard cards. Many people get these two cards wrong. They mistakenly think that the 8 card must be chosen. This card is mistakenly turned because people think that they must check to see if there is a vowel rather than a nonvowel on the back. But, for example, if there were a K on the back of the 8, it would not show that the rule is false because, although the rule says that vowels must have even numbers on the back, it does *not* say that even numbers must have vowels on the back. So finding a nonvowel on the back says nothing about whether the rule is true or false. In contrast, the 5 card, which most people do not choose, is absolutely essential. The 5 card might have a vowel on the back and, if it did, the rule would be shown to be false because all vowels would *not* have even numbers on the back. In short, in order to show that the rule is not false, the 5 card must be turned.

In summary, the rule is in the form of an "if P then Q" conditional, and it can be shown to be false only by showing an instance of P and not-Q, so the P and not-Q cards (A and 5 in our example) are the only two that need to be turned to determine whether the rule is true or false. If the P and not-Q combination is there, the rule is false. If it is not there, then the rule is true.

Why do most people answer incorrectly when this problem, after explanation, is so easy? Many theories exist, but one of the oldest theories that certainly plays at least a partial role in the poor performance is that people focus on confirming the rule. This is what sets them about turning the 8 card (in hopes of confirming the rule by observing a vowel on the other side) and turning the A card (in search of the confirming even number). What they do *not* set about doing is looking at what would falsify the rule—a thought pattern that would immediately suggest the relevance of the 5 card (which might contain a disconfirming vowel on the back). As I have noted, there are many other theories of the poor performance on the task, but regardless of which of these descriptive theories explains the error, there is no question that a concern for falsifiability would rectify the error.

As useful as the falsifiability principle is in general reasoning, there is a large amount of evidence indicating that it is not a natural strategy. The reason is that the cognitive miser does not automatically construct models of alternative worlds, but instead models the situation as given. This is why, for most people, the mindware of seeking falsifying evidence must be taught.

Another paradigm which illustrates the problems that people have in dealing with falsification is the so-called 2-4-6 task, another famous reasoning problem invented by Peter Wason.[10] In the 2-4-6 task, subjects are told that the experimenter has a rule in mind that classifies sets of three integers (triplets). They are told that the triplet 2-4-6 conforms to the rule. The subjects are then to propose triplets and, when they do, the experimenter tells them whether their triplet conforms to the rule. Subjects are to continue proposing triplets and receiving feedback until they think they have figured out what the experimenter's rule is, at which time they should announce what they think the rule is.

The experimenter's rule in the 2-4-6 task is actually "any set of three increasing numbers." Typically, subjects have a very difficult time discovering this rule because they initially adopt an overly restrictive hypothesis about what the rule is. They develop rules like "even numbers increasing" or "numbers increasing in equal intervals" and proceed to generate triplets that are consistent with their overly restrictive hypothesis. Subjects thus receive much feedback from the experimenter that their triplets are correct, and when they announce their hypothesis they are often surprised when told it is not correct. For example, a typical sequence is for the subject to generate triplets like: 8-10-12; 14-16-18; 40-42-44. Receiving three confirmations, they announce the rule "numbers increasing by two." Told this is incorrect, they then might proceed to generate 2-6-10; 0-3-6; and 1-50-99 — again receiving confirmatory feedback. They then proceed to announce a rule like "the rule is that the difference between numbers next to each other is the same" —

which again is incorrect. What they fail to do with any frequency is to generate sequences seriously at odds with their hypothesis so that they might falsify it—sequences like 100-90-80 or 1-15-2.

That subjects are not seriously attempting to refute their focal hypothesis is suggested by one manipulation that has been found to strongly facilitate performance. Ryan Tweney and colleagues ran an experiment in which the subject was told that the experimenter was thinking of *two* rules—one rule would apply to a group of triplets called DAX and the other to a set of triplets called MED. Each time the subject announced a triplet he or she was told whether it was DAX or MED. The subject was told that 2-4-6 was a DAX, and the experiment proceeded as before. DAX was defined, as before, as "any set of three increasing numbers" and MED was defined as "anything else." Under these conditions, the subjects solved the problem much more easily, often alternating between positive tests of DAX and MED. Of course—now—a positive test of MED is an attempt to falsify DAX. The subject is drawn into falsifying tests of DAX because there is another positive, salient, and vivid hypothesis to focus upon (MED). Because the alternative exhausts the universe of hypotheses and it is mutually exclusive of the old focal hypothesis, each time the subjects try to get a confirmation of one they are simultaneously attempting a falsification of the other. In this way, the subjects were drawn to do something they did not normally do—focus on the alternative hypothesis and falsify the focal hypothesis. Of course, the fact that they had to be lured into it in this contrived way only serves to reinforce how difficult it is to focus on the focal hypothesis *not* being true.

Thus, the bad news is that people have a difficult time thinking about the evidence that would falsify their focal hypothesis. The good news is that this mindware is teachable. All scientists go through training that includes much practice at trying to falsify their focal hypothesis, and they automatize the verbal query "What alternative hypotheses should I consider?"

Base Rates: More Bayesian Mindware

Assigning the right probability values to future events is another critical aspect of rational thought. Interestingly, research has shown that people are quite good at dealing *implicitly* with probabilistic information (when it needs only to be tracked by the autonomous mind), but at the same time, when probabilities must be reasoned about *explicitly* people have considerable difficulty. Consider a problem that concerns the estimation of medical risk and has been the focus of considerable research, including some involving medical personnel:[11]

Imagine that the XYZ virus causes a serious disease that occurs in 1 in every 1000 people. Imagine also that there is a test to diagnose the disease that always indicates correctly that a person who has the XYZ virus actually has it. Finally, imagine that the test has a false-positive rate of 5 percent. This means that the test wrongly indicates that the XYZ virus is present in 5 percent of the cases where the person does not have the virus. Imagine that we choose a person randomly and administer the test, and that it yields a positive result (indicates that the person is XYZ-positive). What is the probability (expressed as a percentage ranging from 0 to 100) that the individual actually has the XYZ virus, assuming that we know nothing else about the individual's personal or medical history?

Don't read on until you have taken a stab at the problem. Do not feel that you must calculate the answer precisely (although if you think you can, go ahead). Just give your best guesstimate. The point is not to get the precise answer so much as to see whether you are in the right ballpark. The answers of many people are not. They show a tendency to overweight concrete and vivid single-case information when it must be combined with more abstract probabilistic information.

The most common answer is 95 percent. The *correct* answer is approximately 2 percent! People vastly overestimated the probability that a positive result truly indicates the XYZ virus. Although the correct answer to this problem can again be calculated by means of Bayes' rule, a little logical reasoning can help to illustrate the profound effect that base rates have on probabilities. We were given the information that, of 1000 people, just one will actually be XYZ-positive. If the other 999 (who do not have the disease) are tested, the test will indicate *incorrectly* that approximately 50 of them have the virus (.05

multiplied by 999) because of the 5 percent false-positive rate. Thus, of the 51 patients testing positive, only 1 (approximately 2 percent) will actually be XYZ-positive. In short, the base rate is such that the vast majority of people do not have the virus. This fact, combined with a substantial false-positive rate, ensures that, in absolute numbers, the majority of positive tests will be of people who do not have the virus.

In this problem there is a tendency to overweight individual-case evidence and underweight statistical information. The case evidence (the laboratory test result) seems "tangible" and "concrete" to most people—it is more vivid. In contrast, the probabilistic evidence seems, well—probabilistic! This reasoning is of course fallacious because case evidence itself is always probabilistic. A clinical test misidentifies the presence of a disease with a certain *probability*. The situation is one in which *two* probabilities, the probable diagnosticity of the case evidence and the prior probability, must be combined if one is to arrive at a correct decision. There are right and wrong ways of combining these probabilities, and more often than not—particularly when the case evidence gives the illusion of concreteness—people combine the information in the wrong way.

I cannot emphasize enough that I do not wish to imply in this discussion of Bayesian reasoning that we do, or should, actually calculate using the specific Bayesian formula in our minds.[12] It is enough that people learn to "think Bayesian" in a qualitative sense—that they have what might be called "Bayesian instincts," not that they have memorized the rule, which is unnecessary. It is enough, for example, simply to realize the importance of the base rate. That would allow a person to see the critical insight embedded in the XYZ virus problem—that when a test with a substantial false alarm rate is applied to a disease with a very small base rate, then the majority of individuals with a positive test will not have the disease. This is all the knowledge of the Bayesian mindware regarding base rate that is needed (of course, greater depth of understanding would be an additional plus). Such a qualitative understanding will allow a person to make a guesstimate that is close enough to prevent serious errors in action in daily life. It is likewise with $P(D/\sim H)$. Good thinkers need not always actually calculate the likelihood ratio. They only need enough conceptual understanding to recognize the reason why the restaurant proprietor's argument is a poor one.

Mindware for Probability Assessment

Consider another problem that is famous in the literature of cognitive psychology, the so-called Linda problem.[13]

Linda is 31 years old, single, outspoken, and very bright. She majored in philosophy. As a student, she was deeply concerned with issues of discrimination and social justice, and also participated in anti-nuclear demonstrations. Please rank the following statements by their probability, using 1 for the most probable and 8 for the least probable.

    a. Linda is a teacher in an elementary school ____

    b. Linda works in a bookstore and takes Yoga classes ____

    c. Linda is active in the feminist movement ____

    d. Linda is a psychiatric social worker ____

    e. Linda is a member of the League of Women Voters ____

    f. Linda is a bank teller ____

    g. Linda is an insurance salesperson ____

    h. Linda is a bank teller and is active in the feminist movement ____

Most people make what is called a "conjunction error" on this problem. Because alternative h (Linda is a bank teller and is active in the feminist movement) is the conjunction of alternatives c and f, the probability of h cannot be higher than that of either c (Linda is active in the feminist movement) or f (Linda is a bank teller). All feminist bank tellers are also bank tellers, so h cannot be more probable than f—yet often over 80 percent of the subjects in studies rate alternative h as more probable than f, thus displaying a conjunction error. It is often argued that attribute substitution is occurring when subjects answer incorrectly on this problem. Rather than think carefully and see the problem as a probabilistic scenario, subjects instead answer on the basis of a simpler similarity assessment (a feminist bank teller seems to overlap more with the description of Linda than does the alternative "bank teller").

Of course, logic dictates that the subset (feminist bank teller)/superset (bank teller) relationship should trump assessments of similarity when judgments of probability are at issue. If the relevant probability relationships are well learned, then using similarity reflects an error of the cognitive miser. In contrast, if the relevant rules of probability are not learned well enough for this problem to be perceived as within the domain of probabilistic logic, then the thinking error might be reclassified as a case of a mindware gap (rather than one of attribute substitution based on similarity and vividness).

An additional error in dealing with probabilities—one with implications for real-life decision making—is the inverting of conditional probabilities. The inversion error in probabilistic reasoning is thinking that the probability of A, given B, is the same as the probability of B, given A. The two are not the same, yet they are frequently treated as if they are. For example, Robyn Dawes described an article in a California newspaper that had a headline implying that a survey indicated that use of marijuana led to the use of hard drugs. The headline implied that the survey was about the probability of a student's using hard drugs, given previous smoking of marijuana. But, actually, the article was about the inverse probability: the probability of having smoked marijuana, given that the student was using hard drugs. The problem is that the two probabilities are vastly different. The probability that students use hard drugs, given that they have smoked marijuana, is much, much smaller than the probability of having smoked marijuana given that students are using hard drugs. The reason is that most people who smoke marijuana do not use hard drugs, but most people who use hard drugs have tried marijuana.

An important domain in which the inversion of conditional probabilities happens quite often is medical diagnosis. It has been found that both patients and medical practitioners can sometimes invert probabilities, thinking, mistakenly, that the probability of disease, given a particular symptom, is the same as the probability of the symptom, given the disease (as a *patient*, you are concerned with the former).

Strategic Mindware

Much of the mindware discussed so far represents declarative knowledge. However, not all mindware is declarative knowledge. Some of it would be classified as procedural knowledge by cognitive scientists—that is, as strategies and dispositions to process information in a certain way. For example, many of the principles of probabilistic reasoning I have discussed so far would be classified as declarative knowledge, whereas the tendency toward disjunctive thinking would represent strategic mindware.

Varying tendencies for regulating processing, for information pickup, and for belief calibration are dispositions of the reflective mind that are sometimes, but not always, measured by questionnaires.[14] For example, the thinking disposition need for cognition affects our tendency to engage the reflective mind in problem solving. It is measured by questionnaire items that ask a person to agree or disagree with statements such as: "The notion of thinking abstractly is appealing to me," and "I would prefer a task that is intellectual, difficult, and important to one that is somewhat important but does not require much thought." My research group has studied a thinking disposition termed *belief identification:* whether belief change in order to get closer to the truth is an important goal or whether retaining current beliefs is a more important goal. It is measured by questionnaire items that ask a person to agree or disagree with statements such as: "Beliefs should always be revised in response to new information or evidence," and "It is important to persevere in your beliefs even when evidence is brought to bear against them."

Some thinking dispositions are measured by performance-based tasks. For example, the reflectivity/impulsivity disposition is assessed by performance on the Matching Familiar Figures Test (MFFT). In the MFFT, participants are presented with a target picture of an object, and their task is to find the correct match from an array of six other pictures that are quite similar. Participants' time to respond and number of errors are measured. Reflective people have long response times and few errors, whereas impulsive people have short response times and numerous errors.

Other thinking dispositions of the reflective mind that can be assessed by either questionnaire or performance-based measures are: typical intellectual engagement, need for closure, belief perseverance, confirmation bias, overconfidence, openness to experience, faith in intuition, counterfactual thinking, categorical thinking, superstitious thinking, and dogmatism. The commonality among these types of mindware is that they are closer to strategies, tendencies, procedures, and dispositions than to declarative knowledge structures.

Dysrationalia Due to a Mindware Gap

Irrational behavior due to a mindware gap occurs when the right mindware (cognitive rules, strategies, and belief systems) is not available to use in reasoning and decision making. However, in order to constitute a case of dysrationalia, the mindware gap must occur in an individual of substantial intelligence. How likely is this? Mindware gaps most often arise because of lack of education or experience. Thus, it is not surprising that there is a positive correlation between the acquisition of some of the mindware discussed in this chapter and intelligence.[15] But the correlation is far from perfect. Many individuals of high intelligence lack critical mindware, and many individuals of low intelligence use mindware to make rational responses. For example, if we look at the subset of subjects in a university sample who are all above the median SAT for their institution, we find that less than half of them can use the base rate correctly in situations such as the XYZ virus problem discussed in this chapter.

So while there are modest correlations between rational thinking mindware and intelligence, there is still plenty of room for the dissociation that defines dysrationalia to occur. Although it is true that highly intelligent individuals learn more things than the less intelligent, there are other factors involved.[16] The explicit teaching of some of the mindware discussed in this chapter is very spotty and inconsistent. That such principles are taught very inconsistently means that some intelligent people fail to learn such important aspects of critical thinking. The studies showing that people often fail to think of alternative possibilities for events, ignore P(D/~H), commit the conjunction fallacy, fail to use base rates, and invert conditional probabilities often employ as subjects university students—most of whom are presumably of high intelligence. This must also have been the case in the example that I gave at the outset of the chapter regarding the pediatrician who wrongly testified about the probabilities involved in sudden infant death syndrome (although he probably had thinking problems that *combined* a mindware gap with tendencies toward overconfidence).

Training on such mindware remains rare even later in life. As legal scholar Jeffrey Rachlinski argues, "In most professions, people are trained in the jargon and skill necessary to understand the profession, but are not necessarily given training specifically in making the kind of decisions that members of the profession have to make. Thus, even though some psychologists have argued that certain types of reasoning can be taught quickly and easily, such training is extremely rare. Generalized training that allows people to avoid a wide range of cognitive errors also seems unavailable" (2006, p. 220). In summary, although we might expect mindware gaps to occur somewhat less frequently in individuals of high intelligence, the powerful mindware that prevents irrational thought and action is often inadequately learned by many people regardless of their cognitive ability.

The mindware of rational thinking—strategies for dealing with probabilities, for thinking about causes, for thinking about what conclusions follow from arguments—currently goes unassessed on intelligence tests. If these strategies were assessed, the tests would identify some individuals as more intelligent than do current tests and some as less so. Intelligence tests would be measuring rational functioning, and rationality would be part of MAMBIT (the mental abilities measured by intelligence tests). But as the tests are currently constructed, they do not—and because they do not, we have dysrationalia due to a mindware gap.

ELEVEN

Contaminated Mindware

Civilizations have *never* gotten along healthily, and *cannot* get along healthily, without large quantities of *reliable factual information*. They also cannot flourish if they are beset with troublesome infections of *mistaken* beliefs.
— *Harry Frankfurt*, On Truth, 2006

We as human beings are also irrational animals, unique among animals in our capacity to place faith in bizarre fictions of our own construction.
— *Robert Fogelin*, Walking the Tightrope of Reason, 2003

The country of Albania was a communist dictatorship for many decades. It was also one of the poorest countries in Europe, but by 1991–1992 it had started to turn itself around, granting more personal and economic freedoms. Economic strides were made from 1992 to 1997. The International Monetary Fund lauded the country's progress during this period as markets opened, GDP increased, inflation eased, the budget moved closer to balancing, and foreign investment went up. This economic and social improvement came to an end in early 1997 when the economy collapsed, lawlessness broke out, army depots were plundered by irregular armed bands, and the government lost control of a large part of the country. In 1997, Albania collapsed — basically, because of mass dysrationalia.

Albanian society imploded in 1997 because by that time over one-half of its population had become involved in Ponzi schemes, and in the early months of that year the schemes—as they always do—collapsed.[1] Ponzi schemes offer extremely large rates of return to initial investors. In a Ponzi scheme, no assets are actually owned by those running the scheme (thus it is insolvent from its first day of operation), but that does not mean that the early investors are not paid their promised return. Early investors in fact are paid off with the money put into the scheme by later investors. The high returns paid to the early investors spawn (usually by word of mouth) a rush of new investors who in turn cause more excitement, and the scheme runs on this self-reinforcing basis for a time. Of course, mathematics eventually catches up with the scheme, and at some point the pyramid collapses—usually after the originators have managed to skim off a considerable amount of money from gullible investors.

Usually prospective investors are given a complicated explanation for the high returns. Some of the scam artists operating in Albania explained to their investors that the high rates of return were generated by foreign currency speculation; others claimed complex mining schemes were behind the profits; and one even proclaimed that the returns were generated from investment in California hotels. In Ponzi schemes, it is often the case that the more complex and exotic the purported scheme for generating the profits, the more enticing the scheme seems to potential investors.

Ponzi schemes operate all over the world, but it was the sheer magnitude of the Albanian schemes that was noteworthy. They had become popular by offering interest rates of 30 percent *monthly* on money invested—when real banks and real companies offered investment opportunities of only a tiny fraction of that return. Once the early schemes became popular, they spawned many newer competitors. However, in order to entice investors, the newer schemes had to offer even better rates. At the end of 1996, many of the Ponzis (which of course traveled under the names of legitimate-sounding companies) were offering interest rates of 50–60 percent monthly, and one was actually offering 100 percent. Of course, the higher the rate of return, the quicker the scheme collapses because it eventually becomes impossible to recruit enough new money to pay off the obligations owed to earlier investors.

By 1997, fully one half of Albania's adult population was participating in such schemes! People took out mortgages on their homes in order to participate. Others sold their homes. Many put their entire life savings into the schemes. At their height, an amount equal to 50 percent of the country's GDP was invested in Ponzi schemes. Before the schemes collapsed, they actually began to compete with wage income and distort the economy. For example, one business owner saw his workforce quickly slip from 130 employees to 70 because people began to think they could invest in the Ponzi schemes instead of actually working for their income.

Ponzi schemes are related to pyramid schemes in that the latter often operate by giving recruits to the system (who pay a fee to join) a commission for bringing in new recruits—who then in turn try to recruit new members on the same logic. The combinatorial explosion ensures that the schemes will exhaust themselves after just a few iterations, leaving approximately 80 percent of the recruits (the latest ones) at a loss. In pyramid schemes there is often a nominal product being sold, but the focus is always on the new recruits, not the product supposedly being sold. A Ponzi scheme instead involves no recruiting at all for commissions. There is no product. It is a simple case of paying returns to early investors from the investments of the newer investors. At some point, the promised returns cannot be delivered to everyone who is owed them, and those running the scheme usually try to abscond with the remaining money.

How could people have thought that such a system could continue once everyone was participating in this manner? Likewise, how can people ignore the mathematical implications of a pyramid scheme where 15 people recruit 15 people and so on? (After 15 people recruit to seven levels, over half the population of the United States would be involved!)

People ignore the mathematics because they have become prisoners of contaminated mindware. The underlying logic behind Ponzi and pyramid schemes is essentially the same: the people hosting such contaminated mindware come to believe that the laws of economics—laws that they see all around them and that they have experienced throughout their lives—can be defied. They come to believe that there is a way to obtain returns on investments that are orders of magnitude greater than those in traditional financial instruments and that such a scheme involves no risk. The scheme is usually justified with a clever explanation, but however clever the justification, belief in Ponzi and pyramid schemes is bad mindware. It leads people to take actions that they will come to regret.

Thousands of Albanians lost their entire savings and their homes when the schemes collapsed. The country descended into chaos as riots broke out. The government could not guarantee the investments of the population because at the time of the collapse the five largest companies operating the Ponzis had $49 million in assets to cover $475 million worth of liabilities—and the latter figure was twice the value of the country's GDP. As is usual in such fraud, much of the actual money had disappeared into foreign banks, and many of those who perpetrated the fraud had fled or were being held in jail but claiming bankruptcy along with the other investors.

Because such a large segment of the population was participating in these schemes, we can be certain that many of the individuals caught up in this economic hysteria were highly intelligent people and thus were exhibiting dysrationalia.[2] They had acquired irrational economic beliefs—they were dysrationalic due to contaminated mindware. Certainly mindware gaps are involved too, but since in the last chapter I discussed problems that those lead to, here I would like to focus our attention on situations where mindware is acquired but where that mindware is maladaptive.

Contaminated mindware can often spread and sweep through a specific population like an epidemic. In the late 1980s, encouraged by therapists who themselves were in the grip of some complicated mindware, many patients in psychotherapy began to remember being sexually abused, usually by family members, as small children. The psychotherapists who encouraged these reports had theories about why these memories had been forgotten and then remembered subsequent to therapy. The favored explanation was one of dissociation in childhood, and this led to an epidemic of diagnoses of multiple personality disorder. As Elaine Showalter explains:

> Therapists maintained that children dealt with the pain, fear, and shock
> of sexual abuse through splitting or dissociation. The memory of abuse
> was always there but contained in another personality or many person-
> ality fragments—"alters" who sprang into being to contend with the
> trauma. Therapists could contact these alters through hypnosis, using the

Inner Self-Helper, an alter who mediates between the various fragments. Then they could reach a child alter, who might testify to sexual abuse as well as to other suppressed or repressed aspects of the host personality. (1997, p. 159)

Professional associations spread these ideas in the absence of any research evidence that this theory was correct. And these interrelated sets of theories linking recovered memory with multiple personality disorder replicated quite quickly throughout various therapeutic communities. Prior to 1970 there had been fewer than a dozen cases of multiple personality disorder reported in the United States in the previous fifty years. The disorder did not even become an official diagnosis of the American Psychiatric Association until 1980. Yet by the 1990s thousands of such cases had been identified.[3]

As this so-called recovered memory phenomenon gained steam, the claims made by the patients in therapy sessions became more and more bizarre. Some patients began to report that they were not only sexually abused as children but that they had been victims of satanic ritual abuse. Showalter describes the case of a woman, SRB, in her forties, who had a degree in biochemistry from Yale. Subsequent to therapy sessions, she began to believe that her parents had belonged to a ring of child pornographers who used children in rituals with satanic overtones. She recalled having been sold into prostitution and being tortured with electricity and drugs. She also thought that she had become pregnant as a seventh grader and had been compelled to have an abortion.

The literature contains dozens of such examples, many of them are more lurid than this one, and virtually all share a problematic aspect of SRB's case—there is no independent evidence that any of the events occurred. The patients involved had had no memories of this abuse prior to entering therapy. This was true in SRB's case. She had endured many years of unsuccessful therapies for various phobias, but prior to 1986 had reported no memories of any sexual abuse. In 1986 she attended a workshop for survivors of child abuse and in therapy began to present three different personalities. It was there that her stories of sexual abuse and satanic rituals began to emerge. No one questioned the accuracy of SRB's stories—even though there was no independent evidence to corroborate them. This was because the belief systems of the therapists had been shaped so as to not ask for independent evidence ("if the patient thinks she was abused then she was"). The mindware represented by this belief system requires only that the patient and therapist believe in the coherence of the narrative. But these narratives were not so innocent. People were convicted of abuse charges because of them.

Both the patients and the therapists in the recovered memory epidemic of the 1980s and 1990s were the victims of contaminated mindware—mindware that leads to maladaptive actions but that resists evaluation. This and the Ponzi scheme example illustrate that not all mindware is helpful. When discussing mindware gaps, one can easily get the impression that more mindware is always better. The examples of Ponzi schemes and the recovered memory epidemic illustrate that people can acquire mindware that not only fails to prevent irrational action, but is actually the *cause* of the irrational action.

"If That Man Had Two Brains He'd Be Twice as Stupid"

The title of this section is the punch line to an Irish joke told to me by Desmond Ryan. I cannot remember the rest of the joke, but this funny line summarizes the implication of the existence of dysrationalia—that having more brainpower in the form of intelligence is no guarantee against foolish behavior. This is especially true of irrational action caused by contaminated mindware.

Contaminated mindware is often acquired because it is wrapped in an enticing narrative, one that often has some complexity to it. This complexity is probably not the best "sell" to those of lower intelligence. Instead, complex mindware probably sounds most enticing to those of moderate to high intelligence. Search the Internet for examples of conspiracy theories, tax evasion schemes, get-rich-quick schemes, schemes for "beating" the stock market, and procedures for winning the lottery. You will quickly see that many of them are characterized by enticing complexity. For example, many get-rich-quick schemes involve real-estate transactions that interact in a complex manner with the tax system. Many win-the-lottery books contain explanations (wrong ones!) employing mathematics and probabilities. "Beat the market" stock investment advice often involves the mathematics and graphics of so-called technical analysis.

The intuition that those taken in by fraudulent investment schemes are probably not of low intelligence is confirmed by the results of a study commissioned by the National Association of Securities Dealers.[4] The study examined the beliefs and demographic characteristics of 165 people who had lost over $1000 in a fraudulent investment scheme, and compared them with those of a group of individuals who had not been victims of financial fraud. The study found that the investment fraud victims had significantly more education than the comparison group—68.6 percent of the investment fraud victims group had at least a BA degree compared to just 37.2 percent in the control group. The proportion of the investment victim group with incomes over $30,000 was 74.1 percent compared with 56.4 percent in the other group. We can infer from the education and income statistics that the victims of investment fraud are not more likely to be of low intelligence. This type of contaminated mindware may, if anything, be more enticing to those of higher intelligence.

Much truly mischief-making mindware that supports the irrational behavior we observe in society is concocted by and infects those of moderate to high intelligence. As a result, there are numerous examples of famous individuals, noted for their intelligence, who displayed persistently irrational behavior. Philosopher Martin Heidegger, a conceptual thinker of world renown, was a Nazi apologist and used the most specious of arguments to justify his beliefs. He organized paramilitary camps for his students and often signed correspondence "Heil Hitler." Famed scientist William Crookes, discoverer of the element thallium and a Fellow of the Royal Society, was repeatedly duped by spiritualist "mediums," but never gave up his belief in spiritualism. Arthur Conan Doyle, creator of Sherlock Holmes, was likewise a notorious dupe for "mediums." Poet Ezra Pound (who was surely no slouch in the verbal domain) spent most of World War II ranting Fascist propaganda on Italian radio broadcasts. These examples could be extended almost indefinitely.[5]

Many truly evil ideas have been promulgated by people of considerable intelligence. Several of the Nazi war criminals tried at Nuremberg were given IQ tests and scored above 125, and eight of the fourteen men who planned the Final Solution had doctoral degrees. Studies of leading Holocaust deniers have revealed that their ranks contain the holder of a master's degree from Indiana University in European history, the author of several well-known biographies of World War II figures, a professor of literature at the University of Lyon, an author of textbooks used in Ivy League universities, a professor of English at the University of Scranton, a professor at Northwestern University, and the list goes on.[6] Of course, the ranks of creationist advocates include many with university degrees as well.

Cognitive scientists have uncovered some of the reasons why intelligent people can come to have beliefs that are seriously out of kilter with reality. One explanation is in terms of so-called knowledge projection tendencies. The idea here is that in a natural ecology where most of our prior beliefs are true, processing new data through the filter of our current beliefs will lead to faster accumulation of knowledge.[7] This argument has been used to explain the presence of the belief bias effect in syllogistic reasoning. Cognitive scientist Jonathan Evans and colleagues argued that because belief revision has interactive effects on much of the brain's belief network, it may be computationally costly. Thus, they posit that a cognitive miser might be prone to accept conclusions that are believable without engaging in logical reasoning at all. Only when faced with unbelievable conclusions do subjects engage in logical reasoning about the premises. They argue that this could be an efficacious strategy when we are in a domain where our beliefs are largely true.

But the assumption here—that we are in a domain where our beliefs are largely true—is critical. We use current knowledge structures to help to assimilate new ones more rapidly. To the extent that current beliefs are true, then, we will assimilate further true information more rapidly. However, when the subset of beliefs that the individual is drawing on contains substantial amounts of false information, knowledge projection will *delay* the assimilation of the correct information. And herein lies the key to understanding the creationist or Holocaust denier. The knowledge projection tendency, efficacious in the aggregate, may have the effect of isolating certain individuals on "islands of false beliefs" from which they are unable to escape. In short, there may be a type of knowledge isolation effect when projection is used in particularly ill-suited circumstances. Thus, knowledge projection, which in the aggregate might lead to more rapid induction of new true beliefs, may be a trap in cases where people, in effect, keep reaching into a bag of beliefs which are largely false, using these beliefs to structure their evaluation of evidence, and hence more quickly assimilating additional incorrect beliefs for use in further projection.

Knowledge projection from an island of false beliefs might explain the phenomenon of otherwise intelligent people who get caught in a domain-specific web of falsity and because of projection tendencies cannot escape. Such individuals often use their considerable computational power to rationalize their beliefs and to ward off the arguments of skeptics.[8] When knowledge projection occurs from an island of false belief, it merely results in a belief network even more divergent from that of individuals not engaged in such projection or with less computational power. This may be the reason why some of the most pernicious contaminated mindware was invented by and acquired by some of the most intelligent individuals ("if that man had two brains he'd be twice as stupid!"). Indeed, such people "had twice the brain and ended up twice as stupid."

Skepticism about Contaminated Mindware

But isn't there something inherently wrong with the idea of contaminated mindware? Why would people believe something that is bad for them? Don't all beliefs serve *some* positive purpose?

These are all reasonable questions and reflect a commonsense reaction to the idea of contaminated mindware. This commonsense worry about the idea of contaminated mindware is sometimes echoed in the scholarly literature as well. For example, some philosophers have argued that human irrationality is a conceptual impossibility, and other theorists have argued that evolution guarantees human rationality.

The latter argument is now widely recognized to be flawed.[9] Evolution guarantees that humans are genetic fitness optimizers in their local environments, not that they are *truth* or *utility* maximizers as rationality requires. Beliefs need not always track the world with maximum accuracy in order for fitness to increase. Thus, evolution does not guarantee perfect epistemic rationality. Neither does evolution ensure that optimum standards of instrumental rationality will be attained. Finally, the conceptual arguments of philosophers questioning the possibility of human irrationality are in some sense beside the point because literally hundreds of studies conducted by decision scientists, cognitive scientists, and behavioral economists over the last four decades have demonstrated that human action and belief acquisition violate even quite liberal rational strictures.[10]

Why is it so difficult for people to accept that humans can sometimes be systematically irrational—that they can believe things in the absence of evidence and behave in ways that thwart their interests? I suggest that it is because most of us share a folk theory of mindware acquisition that is faulty in one critical respect. The key to the error is suggested in the title of a paper written some years ago by psychologist Robert Abelson: "Beliefs Are Like Possessions." This phrase suggests why people find it difficult to understand why they (or anyone else) might hold beliefs (or other mindware) that do not serve their own interests. Current critiques of overconsumption aside, most of us feel that we have acquired our material possessions for reasons, and that among those reasons is the fact that our possessions serve our ends in some way. We feel the same about our beliefs. We feel that beliefs are something that we choose to acquire, just like the rest of our possessions.

In short, we tend to assume: (1) that we exercised agency in acquiring our mindware, and (2) that it serves our interests. The idea of contaminated mindware runs counter to both of these assumptions. If we consider the first assumption to be false—that sometimes we do not exercise agency when we acquire mindware—then the second becomes less likely, and the idea of contaminated mindware more plausible. This is precisely what an important theoretical position in the cognitive science of belief acquisition has asserted. A prominent set of thinkers has recently been exploring the implications of asking a startling question: What if you don't own your beliefs, but instead they own *you*?

Why Are People Infected by Contaminated Mindware?

Surely almost all of us feel that our beliefs must be serving *some* positive purpose. But what if that purpose isn't one of *our* purposes? Cultural replicator theory and the science of memetics have helped us come to terms with this possibility. The term *cultural replicator* refers to an element of a culture that may be passed on by non-genetic means. An alternative term for a cultural replicator—*meme*—was introduced by Richard Dawkins in his famous 1976 book *The Selfish Gene*.[11] The term *meme* is also sometimes used generically to refer to a so-called memeplex—a set of co-adapted memes that are copied together as a set of interlocking ideas (so, for example, the notion of democracy is a complex interconnected set of memes—a memeplex).

It is legitimate to ask why one should use this new term for a unit of culture when a variety of disciplines such as cultural anthropology already exist that deal with the diffusion of culture. The reason I think the term *meme* is useful is that the new and unfamiliar terminology serves a decentering function that makes understanding the concept of contaminated mindware easier. It can help somewhat to dislodge the "beliefs as possessions" metaphor that we see implicit in phrases such as "my belief" and "my idea." Because the usage "my meme" is less familiar, it does not signal ownership via an act of agency in the same way. The second reason the term is useful is that it suggests (by its analogy to the term *gene*) using the insights of Universal Darwinism to understand belief acquisition and change. Specifically, Universal Darwinism emphasizes that organisms are built to advance the interests of the genes (replication) rather than for any interests of the organism itself. This insight prompts, by analogy, the thought that memes may occasionally replicate at the expense of the interests of their hosts.

Thus, the fundamental insight triggered by the meme concept is that a belief may spread *without necessarily being true or helping the human being who holds the belief in any way*. Memetic theorists often use the example of a chain letter: "If you do not pass this message on to five people you will experience misfortune." This is an example of a meme—an idea unit. It is the instruction for a behavior that can be copied and stored in brains. It has been a reasonably successful meme. Yet there are two remarkable things about this meme. First, it is not true. The reader who does not pass on the message will not as a result experience misfortune. Second, the person who stores the meme and passes it on will receive no benefit—the person will be no richer or healthier or wiser for having passed it on. Yet the meme survives. It survives because of its *own* self-replicating properties (the essential logic of this meme is that basically it does nothing more than say "copy me—or else"). In short, memes do not necessarily exist in order to help the person in whom they are lodged. They exist because, through memetic evolution, they have displayed the best fecundity, longevity, and copying fidelity—the defining characteristics of successful replicators.

Memetic theory has profound effects on our reasoning about ideas because it inverts the way we think about beliefs. Social psychologists traditionally tend to ask what it is about particular individuals that leads them to have certain beliefs. The causal model is one where the person determines what beliefs to have. Memetic theory asks instead what it is about certain memes that leads them to collect many "hosts" for themselves. The question is not how people acquire beliefs (the tradition in social and cognitive psychology) but how beliefs acquire people!

If this inversion of our traditional way of thinking at first seems odd, consider that participation in political movements has been found to be more related to proximity to others believing the same thing rather than to any psychological factors that have been identified.[12] Likewise, religious affiliations are predicted best by geographic proximity as opposed to specific psychological characteristics.

Our commonsense view of why beliefs spread is the notion that "belief X spreads because it is true." This notion, however, has trouble accounting for ideas that are true but not popular, and ideas that are popular but not true. Memetic theory tells us to look to a third principle in such cases. Idea X spreads among people because it is a good replicator—it is good at acquiring hosts. Memetic theory focuses us on the properties of ideas as replicators rather than the qualities of people acquiring the ideas. This is the single distinctive function served by the meme concept and it is a critical one.

With this central insight from memetic theory in mind, we can now discuss a fuller classification of reasons why mindware survives and spreads. The first three classes of reasons are reflected in traditional assumptions in the behavioral and biological sciences. The last reflects the new perspective of memetic theory:

1. Mindware survives and spreads because it is helpful to the people that store it.

2. Certain mindware proliferates because it is a good fit to pre-existing genetic predispositions or domain-specific evolutionary modules.

3. Certain mindware spreads because it facilitates the replication of genes that make vehicles that are good hosts for that particular mindware (religious beliefs that urge people to have more children would be in this category).

4. Mindware survives and spreads because of the self-perpetuating properties of the mindware itself.

Categories 1, 2, and 3 are relatively uncontroversial. The first is standard fare in the discipline of cultural anthropology, which tends to stress the functionality of belief. Category 2 is emphasized by evolutionary psychologists. Category 3 is meant to capture the type of effects emphasized by theorists stressing gene/culture coevolution.[13] It is category 4 that introduces new ways of thinking about beliefs as symbolic instructions that are more or less good at colonizing brains. Of course, mindware may reside in more than one category. Mindware may spread because it is useful to its host *and* because it fits genetic predispositions *and* because of its self-perpetuating properties. Category 4 does, however, raise the possibility of truly contaminated mindware—mindware that is not good for the host because it supports irrational behavior.

Various theorists have discussed some of the types of mindware (defined by their self-replicative strategies) that are in category 4.[14] For example, there is parasitic mindware that mimics the structure of helpful ideas and deceives the host into thinking that the host will derive benefit from them. Advertisers are of course expert at constructing parasites—beliefs that ride on the backs of other beliefs and images. Creating unanalyzed conditional beliefs such as "if I buy this car I will get this beautiful model" is what advertisers try to do by the judicious juxtaposition of ideas and images. Other self-preservative memetic strategies involve changing the cognitive environment. Many religions, for example, prime the fear of death in order to make their promise of the afterlife more enticing.

More sinister are so-called adversative strategies that alter the cultural environment in ways that make it more hostile for competing memes or that influence their hosts to attack the hosts of alternate mindware. Many moderate residents of fundamentalist religious communities refrain from criticizing the extremist members of their communities because of fear that their neighbors are harboring mindware like that illustrated in the following excerpt:

From an April 5 interview with Omar Bakri Muhammad, head of Al Muhajiroun, a radical Islamic group based in London, conducted by Paulo Moura of *Publico*, a Portuguese daily newspaper:

Q: What could justify the deliberate killing of thousands of innocent civilians?

A: We don't make a distinction between civilians and non-civilians, innocents and non-innocents. Only between Muslims and nonbelievers. And the life of a nonbeliever has no value. There's no sanctity in it.

Q: But there were Muslims among the victims.

A: According to Islam, Muslims who die in attacks will be accepted immediately into paradise as martyrs. As for the others, it is their problem. (*Harper's Magazine*, July 2004, pp. 22–25)

Deal Breaker Memes

How can any person presume to know that this is the way the universe works? Because it says so in our holy books. How do we know that our holy books are free from error? Because the books themselves say so. Epistemological black holes of this sort are fast draining the light from our world.
—*Sam Harris*, The End of Faith, 2004

As the example that ended the last section shows, the normal calculus of behavioral cause and effect does not apply when contaminated mindware is involved. The default assumption that people always act in their own interests (or in the interests of those they care about) does not apply in the case of contaminated mindware, which acts in its own interests—replication. This insight, an outgrowth of modern Universal Darwinism, has only recently been fully absorbed by society.[15] Its parallel, the insight that genes do not necessarily serve the interests of their human hosts, was not brought to general public attention until Richard Dawkins synthesized a set of evolutionary insights in his famous 1976 book. The insight that cultural replicators (mind-ware) could likewise not serve the individual is even more recent, and it remains counterintuitive for some people.

The counterintuitive nature of the insight is reflected in the difficulty people have in dropping the default assumption of rationality in their attempts to explain behavior. One of the most salient events of the twenty-first century provides a glaring example. In the near aftermath of the destruction of the World Trade Center on September 11, 2001, the First Lady of the United States, Laura Bush, was asked to comment on the event and, in the course of her answer, she mentioned the importance of education in preventing such tragedies. Interestingly, in an interview around the same time, the wife of the prime minister of Great Britain, Cherie Blair, also mentioned education as a preventative for events like those of September 11. However, commentators at the time, and the more comprehensive 9/11 Report three years later, point out the disturbing fact that the hijackers of the airplanes on September 11 were by no means uneducated.[16] For example, Mohammed Atta, who piloted American Airlines Flight 11 after the hijacking and incinerated scores of people when he slammed the plane into the North Tower of the World Trade Center, had a degree in city engineering and planning.

People have a hard time accepting such behavior from fully educated and intelligent people. Because people are rational, the thinking goes, there must be some critical thing that they didn't know—some educational or informational gap that led to this behavior.[17] The concept of contaminated mindware opens up for us another possibility—perhaps the terrorists had not too little mindware but, instead, too much. Specifically, a variety of pernicious parasite memes had infected the terrorists—the martyrdom meme and the meme for extravagant rewards in the afterlife, for example. The destruction of the World Trade Center has, sadly, helped many people understand this horrific logic of the virus meme that will replicate itself at any cost to human life. It has spawned a more explicit discussion of the danger of memes that become weapons because they commandeer their hosts so completely.

Memeplexes like that exemplified in the Harper's excerpt that ended the last section are not serving any rational human ends. Instead, they might be called deal breaker memes—memes that brook no compromise with their replication strategies. The reason such a property facilitates idea propagation follows from the principles of Universal Darwinism. A replicator increases in frequency along with increases in its fecundity, longevity, and copying fidelity. A cultural replicator has much lower copying fidelity than a gene. Segments of cultural replicators are constantly being mixed and matched as they jump from brain to brain. By refusing to enter the bouillabaisse that is human culture, deal breaker memes assure themselves a clean replication into the future. On a frequency-dependent basis, there is probably a niche for deal breaker memes. The important point for the discussion here is that such mindware will not display the flexibility that is necessary to serve human interests in a changing world. Deal breaker memes thus become prime candidates for contaminated mindware.

Strategies for Avoiding Contaminated Mindware

The previous discussion suggests that we need strategies for avoiding contaminated mindware. The following are some rules for avoiding such mindware:

1. Avoid installing mindware that could be physically harmful to you, the host.
2. Regarding mindware that affects your goals, make sure the mindware does not preclude a wide choice of future goals.
3. Regarding mindware that relates to beliefs and models of the world, seek to install only mindware that is true—that is, that reflects the way the world actually is.
4. Avoid mindware that resists evaluation.

Rules 1 and 2 are similar in that they both seek to preserve flexibility for the person if his or her goals should change. We should avoid mindware harmful to the host because the host's ability to pursue any future goal will be impaired if it is injured or has expired. Likewise, mindware that precludes future goals that may be good for a person to acquire is problematic. For example, there is in fact some justification for our sense of distress when we see a young person adopt mindware that threatens to cut off the fulfillment of many future goal states (early pregnancy comes to mind, as do the cases of young people joining cults that short-circuit their educational progress and that require severing ties with friends and family).

Rule 3 serves as a mindware check in another way. The reason is that beliefs that are true are good for us because accurately tracking the world helps us achieve our goals. Almost regardless of what a person's future goals may be, these goals will be better served if accompanied by beliefs about the world which happen to be true. Obviously there are situations where not tracking truth may (often only temporarily) serve a particular goal. Nevertheless, other things being equal, the presence of the desire to have true beliefs will have the long-term effect of facilitating the achievement of many goals.

Parasitic mindware, rather than helping the host, finds tricks that will tend to increase its longevity.[18] Subverting evaluation attempts by the host is one of the most common ways that parasitic mindware gets installed in our cognitive architectures. Hence rule 4—avoid mindware that resists evaluation. Here we have a direct link to the discussion of falsifiability in the last chapter. In science, a theory must go out on a limb, so to speak. In telling us what should happen, the theory must also imply that certain things will not happen. If these latter things do happen, then we have a clear signal that something is wrong with the theory. An unfalsifiable theory, in contrast, precludes change by not specifying which observations should be interpreted as refutations. We might say that such unfalsifiable theories are evaluation disabling. By admitting no evaluation, they prevent us from replacing them, but at the cost of scientific progress.

It is likewise with all mindware. We need to be wary of all mindware that has evaluation-disabling properties. Instead, we should be asking what empirical and logical tests it has passed. The reason is that passing a logical or empirical test provides at least some assurance that the mindware is logically consistent or that the meme maps the world and thus is good for us (rule 3 above). Untestable mindware that avoids such critical evaluation provides us with no such assurance.

Of course, the classic example of unfalsifiable mindware is mindware that relies on blind faith.[19] The whole notion of blind faith is meant to disarm the hosts in which it resides from ever evaluating it. To have faith in mindware means that you do not constantly and reflectively question its origins and worth. The whole logic of faith-based mindware is to disable critique. For example, one of the tricks that faith-based mindware uses to avoid evaluation is to foster the notion that mystery itself is a virtue (a strategy meant to short-circuit the search for evidence that mindware evaluation entails). In the case of faith-based mindware, many of the adversative properties mentioned earlier come into play. Throughout history, many religions have encouraged their adherents to attack nonbelievers or at least to frighten nonbelievers into silence.

It is of course not necessarily the case that all faith-based memes are bad. Some may be good for the host; but a very stiff burden of proof is called for in such cases. One really should ask of any faith-based mindware why it is necessary to disable the very tools in our cognitive arsenal (logic, rationality, science) that have served us so well in other spheres. However, evaluation-disabling strategies are common components of parasitic memeplexes.

Another ground (in addition to falsifiability) for suspicion about our mindware occurs when the deck of costs and benefits seems stacked against the possibility of disposing of the mindware. Such situations have been called "belief traps."[20] For example, Gerry Mackie cites the following case:

> Women who practice infibulation [a form of female genital mutilation] are caught in a belief trap. The Bambara of Mali believe that the clitoris will kill a man if it comes in contact with the penis during intercourse. In Nigeria, some groups believe that if a baby's head touches the clitoris during delivery, the baby will die. I call these self-reinforcing beliefs: a belief that cannot be revised, because the believed costs of testing the belief are too high. (1996, p. 1009)

The case here is a little different from that of falsifiability. In principle, this belief could be tested. It is in principle falsifiable. But the actual costs of engaging in the test are just too high. Note that on an expected value basis, if you thought that there was only a .01 probability of the belief being true, you still would not test it because the risks are too high. Once installed as mindware, it will be difficult to dislodge.

In addition to falsifiability and excessive costs, another ground for suspicion about mindware occurs when it contains adversative properties. If an idea or strategy is true or good or helpful to the host, why should it need to fight off other mindware? Should not helpful mindware welcome comparative tests against other (presumably less useful) memes? So the presence of adversative properties (in addition to evaluation-disabling strategies) is another cue to the possible presence of contaminated mindware.

Dysrationalia Due to Contaminated Mindware

Smart people are uniquely capable of producing noxious ideas.
—*Steven Lagerfeld*, The Wilson Quarterly, 2004

Intelligence is no inoculation against irrational behavior generated by contaminated mindware. Pseudosciences provide many examples of contaminated mindware—and many pseudosciences are invented by and believed in by people of high intelligence. Additionally, participation in pseudoscientific belief systems is so widespread that it is a statistical certainty that many people participating are of high intelligence and thus displaying dysrationalia. For example, there are 20 times more astrologers in the United States than there are astronomers. A subcommittee of the U.S. Congress has estimated that $10 billion is spent annually on medical quackery, an amount that dwarfs the sum that is spent on legitimate medical research. The list of pseudosciences in which the participants number in the tens of thousands seems never-ending: astrological prediction, subliminal weight loss, biorhythms, the administration of laetrile, psychic surgery, pyramid schemes, Ponzi schemes, out-of-body experiences, firewalking.

The remarkable prevalence of pseudoscientific beliefs indicates that a considerable amount of inadequate belief formation is taking place—too much to blame solely on the members of our society with low intelligence. Purely on a quantitative basis, it must be the case that some people with fairly high IQs are thinking quite poorly. The 22 percent of our population who believe in Big Foot, the 25 percent who believe in astrology, the 16 percent who believe in the Loch Ness monster, the 46 percent who believe in faith healing, the 49 percent who believe in demonic possession, the 37 percent who believe in haunted houses, the 32 percent who believe in ghosts, the 26 percent who believe in clairvoyance, the 14 percent who have consulted a fortune-teller, and the 10 percent who feel that they have spoken with the Devil are not all individuals with intellectual disability. A large number of them, however, may be dysrationalic.

Actually, we do not have to speculate about the proportion of high-IQ people with these beliefs. Several years ago, a survey of paranormal beliefs was given to members of a Mensa club in Canada, and the results were instructive. Mensa is a club restricted to high-IQ individuals, and one must pass IQ-type tests to be admitted. Yet 44 percent of the members of this club believed in astrology, 51 percent believed in biorhythms, and 56 percent believed in the existence of extraterrestrial visitors—all beliefs for which there is not a shred of evidence.[21]

In this chapter, I have established that high-IQ individuals can easily be plagued by contaminated mindware. In the previous chapter, I discussed how high-IQ individuals are not immune from the mindware gaps in the domains of probabilistic thinking and scientific thinking that can lead to irrational beliefs and action. In Chapters 6 through 9 we saw that the tendency to display the characteristics of the cognitive miser (egocentric processing, framing, attribute substitution tendencies) is largely unassessed on intelligence tests.

It is beginning to become clear, I hope, why we should not be so surprised when we witness dysrationalia—smart people acting foolishly. But perhaps it is also beginning to seem puzzling that so much in the cognitive domain is missing from intelligence tests. A common criticism of intelligence tests is the argument that they do not tap important aspects of social and emotional functioning. But that has not been my argument here. I do not intend to cede the cognitive domain to the concept of intelligence, but instead wish to press the point that intelligence is a limited concept even *within* the cognitive domain. This chapter and the last illustrated that tests of intelligence do not assess for the presence of mindware critical to rational thought, or for disruptive mindware that impedes rational thought. Earlier chapters established that thinking dispositions relevant to rational thought also go unassessed. Many of these are related to the tendency to use (or avoid) strategies that trump Type 1 miserly processing with Type 2 cognition. In short, there are many more ways that thinking can go wrong than are assessed on intelligence tests. The next chapter presents a taxonomy of these thinking errors.

TWELVE

How Many Ways Can Thinking Go Wrong?
A Taxonomy of Irrational Thinking Tendencies
and Their Relation to Intelligence

Behavioral economics extends the paternalistically protected category of "idiots" to include most people, at predictable times. The challenge is figuring out what sorts of "idiotic" behaviors are likely to arise routinely and how to prevent them.

—*Colin Camerer and colleagues*, University of
Pennsylvania Law Review, 2003

For decades now, researchers have been searching for the small set of mental attributes that underlie intelligence. Over one hundred years ago, Charles Spearman proposed that a single underlying mental quality, so-called psychometric g, was the factor that accounted for the tendency of mental tests to correlate with each other.[1] Few now think that this is the best model of intelligence. Proponents of the Cattell/Horn/Carroll theory of intelligence, Gf/Gc theory, posit that tests of mental ability tap a small number of broad factors, of which two are dominant. Some theorists like to emphasize the two broad factors, fluid intelligence (Gf) and crystallized intelligence (Gc), because they reflect a long history of considering two aspects of intelligence (intelligence-as-process and intelligence-as-knowledge) and because we are beginning to understand the key mental operations— cognitive decoupling—that underlie Gf. Other theorists give more weight to several other group factors beyond Gf and Gc that can be identified.

Regardless of how these scientific debates are resolved, it is clear that a relatively few scientifically manageable cognitive features underlie intelligence, and they will eventually be understood. Rational thinking, in contrast, seems to be a much more unwieldy beast. Many different sources of irrational thinking and many different tasks on which subjects make fundamental thinking errors have been identified. I have detailed many of these in Chapters 6 through 11, but I have not covered them exhaustively. There are in fact many more than I have room here to discuss.[2] Recall my earlier argument that rational thinking errors are multifarious because there are many ways that people can fail to maximize their goal achievement (instrumental rationality) and many ways that beliefs can fail to reflect reality (epistemic rationality).

Rational thinking errors appear to arise from a variety of sources—it is unlikely that anyone will propose a psychometric g of rationality. Irrational thinking does not arise from a single cognitive problem, but the research literature does allow us to classify thinking into smaller sets of similar problems. Our discussion so far has set the stage for such a classification system, or taxonomy. First, though, I need to introduce one additional feature in the generic model of the mind outlined in Chapter 3.

Serial Associative Cognition with a Focal Bias

Figure 12.1 updates the preliminary model of the mind outlined in Chapter 3 with the addition of one new idea. Previous dual-process theories have emphasized the importance of the override function—the ability of Type 2 processing to take early response tendencies triggered by Type 1 processing offline and to substitute better responses. This override capacity is a property of the algorithmic mind, and it is indicated by the arrow labeled A in Figure 12.1. The higher-level cognitive function that initiates override is a dispositional property of the reflective mind that is related to rationality. In the model in Figure 12.1, it is shown by arrow B, which represents, in machine intelligence terms, the call to the algorithmic mind to override the Type 1 response by taking it offline. This is a different mental function from the override function itself (arrow A), and the two functions are indexed by different types of individual differences—the ability to sustain the inhibition of the Type 1 response is indexed by measures of fluid intelligence, and the ten-

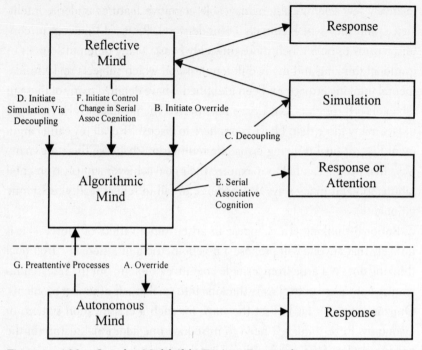

Figure 12.1. A More Complete Model of the Tripartite Framework

dency to initiate override operations is indexed by thinking dispositions such as reflectiveness and need for cognition.

The simulation process that computes the alternative response that makes the override worthwhile is represented in Figure 12.1 as well as the fact that the call to initiate simulation originates in the reflective mind. Specifically, the decoupling operation (indicated by arrow C) is carried out by the algorithmic mind and the call to initiate simulation (indicated by arrow D) by the reflective mind. Again, two different types of individual differences are associated with the initiation call and the decoupling operator—specifically, rational thinking dispositions with the former and fluid intelligence with the latter.

The model in Figure 12.1 defines a third critical function for the algorithmic mind in addition to Type 1 processing override and enabling simulation via decoupling. The third is a function that in the figure is termed serial associative cognition (arrow labeled E). This function is there to remind us that not all Type 2 processing involves strongly decoupled cognitive simulation. There are types of slow, serial cognition that do not involve simulating alternative worlds and exploring them exhaustively.

Recall that the category of Type 1 processes is composed of: affective responses, previously learned responses that have been practiced to automaticity, conditioned responses, adaptive modules that have been shaped by our evolutionary history. These cover many situations indeed, but modern life still creates many problems for which none of these mechanisms are suited. Consider Peter Wason's four-card selection task discussed previously:

Each of the cards has a letter on one side and a number on the other side. Here is a rule: If a card has a vowel on its letter side, then it has an even number on its number side. Two of the cards are letter-side up, and two of the cards are number-side up. Your task is to decide which card or cards must be turned over in order to find out whether the rule is true or false. Indicate which cards must be turned over. The four cards confronting the subject have the stimuli K, A, 8, and 5 showing.

The correct answer is A and 5 (the only two cards that could show the rule to be false) but the majority of subjects answer (incorrectly) A and 8. However, studies have been done which have subjects think aloud while solving the problem. When these think-aloud protocols are analyzed, it has seemed that most subjects were engaging in some slow, serial processing, but of a type that was simply incomplete. A typical protocol from a subject might go something like this: "Well, let's see, I'd turn the A to see if there is an even number on the back. Then I'd turn the 8 to make sure a vowel is in the back." Then the subject stops.

Several things are apparent here. First, it makes sense that subjects are engaging in some kind of Type 2 processing. Most Type 1 processes would be of no help on this problem. Affective processing is not engaged, so processes of emotional regulation are no help. Unless the subject is a logic major, there are no highly practiced procedures that have become automatized that would be of any help. Finally, the problem is evolutionarily unprecedented, so there will be no Darwinian modules that would be helpful.

The subject is left to rely on Type 2 processing, but I would argue that that processing is seriously incomplete in the example I have given. The subject has relied on serial associative cognition rather than exhaustive simulation of an alternative world—a world that includes situations in which the rule is false. The subject has not constructed the false case—a vowel with an odd number on the back. Nor has the subject gone systematically through the cards asking the question of whether that card could be a vowel/odd combination. Answer: K(no), A(yes), 8(no), 5(yes). Such a procedure yields the correct choice of A and 5. Instead the subject with this protocol started from the model given—the rule as true—and then just worked through implications of what would be expected if the rule were true. A fully simulated world with all the possibilities—including the possibility of a false rule—was never constructed. The subject starts with the focal rule as given and then just generates associates that follow from that. Hence my term for this type of processing: serial associative cognition.

Thus, it is correct to argue that Type 2 processing is occurring in this task, but it is not full-blown cognitive simulation of alternative world models. It is thinking of a shallower type—cognition that is inflexibly locked into an associative mode that takes as its starting point a model of the world that is given to the subject. In the selection task, subjects accept the rule as given, assume it is true, and simply describe how they would go about verifying it. They then reason from this single focal model—systematically generating associations from this focal model but never constructing another model of the situation. This is what I would term serial associative cognition with a focal bias.

One way in which to characterize serial associative cognition with a focal bias is as a second-stage strategy of the cognitive miser. Traditional dual-process theory has heretofore highlighted only Rule 1 of the Cognitive Miser: default to Type 1 processing whenever possible. But defaulting to Type 1 processing is not always possible—particularly in novel situations where there are no stimuli available to domain-specific evolutionary modules, nor perhaps any information with which to run overlearned and well-compiled procedures that have been acquired through practice. Type 2 processing will be necessary, but a cognitive miser default is operating even there. Rule 2 of the Cognitive Miser is: when Type 2 processing is necessary, default to serial associative cognition with a focal bias (not fully decoupled cognitive simulation).

My notion of focal bias conjoins several current ideas in cognitive science under the overarching theme that they all have in common—that humans will find any way they can to ease the cognitive load and process less information.[3] Focal bias is the basic idea that the information processor is strongly disposed to deal only with the most easily constructed cognitive model. The most easily constructed model tends to represent only one state of affairs; it accepts what is directly presented and models what is presented as true; it ignores moderating factors—probably because taking account of those factors would necessitate modeling several alternative worlds, and this is just what a focal processing allows us to avoid; and finally, given the voluminous literature in cognitive science on belief bias and the informal reasoning literature on myside bias, the easiest models to represent are those closest to what a person already believes in and has modeled previously (myside bias and belief bias).

With this discussion of serial associative cognition, we can now return to Figure 12.1 and identify a third function of the reflective mind—initiating an interrupt of serial associative cognition (arrow F). This interrupt signal alters the next step in a serial associative sequence that would otherwise direct thought. This interrupt signal might have a variety of outcomes. It might stop serial associative cognition altogether in order to initiate a comprehensive simulation (arrow C). Alternatively, it might start a new serial associative chain (arrow E) from a different starting point by altering the temporary focal model that is the source of a new associative chain. Finally, the algorithmic mind often receives inputs from the computations of the autonomous mind via so-called preattentive processes (arrow G).[4]

A Preliminary Taxonomy of Rational Thinking Problems

With a more complete generic model of the mind in place, in Figure 12.2 I present an initial attempt at a taxonomy of rational thinking problems. At the top of the figure are three characteristics of the cognitive miser listed in order of relative cognitive engagement. The characteristic presented first is defaulting to the response options primed by the autonomous mind. It represents the shallowest kind of processing because no Type 2 processing is done at all. The second type of processing tendency of the cognitive miser is to engage in serial associative cognition with a focal bias. This characteristic represents a tendency to over-economize during Type 2 processing—specifi-

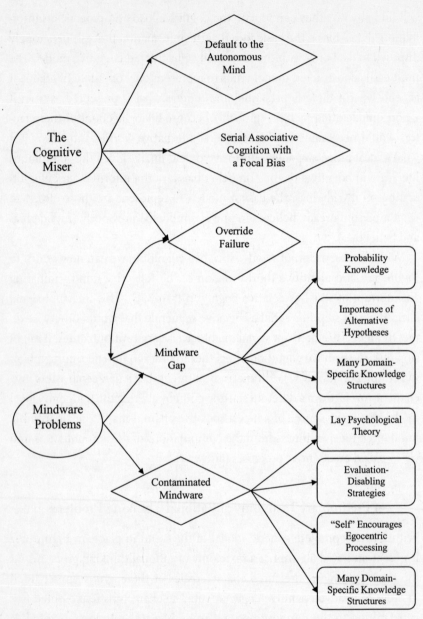

Figure 12.2. A Basic Taxonomy of Thinking Errors

cally, to fail to engage in the full-blown simulation of alternative worlds or to engage in fully disjunctive reasoning (see Chapter 6).

The third category is that of override failure, which represents the least miserly tendency because, here, Type 2 cognitive decoupling is engaged. Inhibitory Type 2 processes try to take the Type 1 processing of the autonomous mind offline in these cases, but they fail. So in override failure, cognitive decoupling does take place, but it fails to suppress the Type 1 processing of the autonomous mind.

In Figure 12.2 mindware problems are divided into mindware gaps and contaminated mindware. In the category of mindware gaps, the curved rectangles in the figure are meant to represent missing knowledge bases. I have not represented an exhaustive set of knowledge partitionings—to the contrary, the figure shows only a minimal sampling of a potentially large set of coherent knowledge bases in the domains of probabilistic reasoning, causal reasoning, logic, and scientific thinking, the absence of which could result in irrational thought or behavior. The two I have represented are mindware categories that have been implicated in research in the heuristics and biases tradition: missing knowledge about probability and probabilistic reasoning strategies; and ignoring alternative hypotheses when evaluating hypotheses. These are just a few of many mindware gaps that have been suggested in the literature on behavioral decision making. There are many others, and the box labeled "Many Domain-Specific Knowledge Structures" indicates this.

Finally, at the bottom of the figure is the category of contaminated mindware. Again, the curved rectangles represent problematic knowledge and strategies. They do not represent an exhaustive partitioning (the mindware-related categories are too diverse for that), but instead indicate some of the mechanisms that have received some discussion in the literature. First is a subcategory of contaminated mindware that is much discussed—mindware that contains evaluation-disabling properties. Some of the evaluation-disabling properties that help keep some mindware lodged in a host are: the promise of punishment if the mindware is questioned; the promise of rewards for unquestioning faith in the mindware; or the thwarting of evaluation attempts by rendering the mindware unfalsifiable.

The second subcategory of contaminated mindware that has been discussed by several theorists is a concept of "self" that serves to encourage egocentric thinking.[5] The self, according to these theorists, is a mechanism that fosters one characteristic of focal bias: that we tend to build models of the world from a single myside perspective. The egocentrism of the self was of course evolutionarily adaptive. Nonetheless, it is sometimes nonoptimal in an environment different from the environment of evolutionary adaptation because myside processing makes difficult such modern demands as: unbiasedness; sanctioning of nepotism; and discouragement of familial, racial, and religious discrimination. Finally, the last subcategory of contaminated mindware pictured in the figure is meant to represent what is actually a whole set of categories: mindware representing specific categories of information or maladaptive memeplexes. As with the mindware gap category, there may be a large number of instances of misinformation-filled mindware that would support irrational thought and behavior.[6]

Lay psychological theory is represented as both contaminated mindware and a mindware gap in Figure 12.2. Lay psychological theories are the theories that people have about their own minds. Mindware gaps are the many things about our own minds that we do not know; for example, how quickly we will adapt to both fortunate and unfortunate events. Other things we think we know about our own minds are wrong. These misconceptions represent contaminated mindware. An example would be the folk belief that we accurately know our own minds. This contaminated mindware accounts for the incorrect belief that we always know the causes of our own actions and think that although others display myside and other thinking biases, we ourselves have special immunity from the very same biases.[7]

Finally, note the curved, double-headed arrow in this figure indicating an important relationship between the override failure category and the mindware gap category. In a case of override failure, an attempt must be made to trump a response primed by the autonomous mind with alternative conflicting information or a learned rule. For an error to be classified as an override failure, one must have previously learned the alternative information or an alternative rule different from the Type 1 response. If, in fact, the relevant mindware is not available because it has not been learned (or at least not learned to the requisite level to sustain override) then we have a case of a mindware gap rather than override failure.

Note one interesting implication of the relation between override failure and mindware gaps—the fewer gaps one has, the more likely that an error may be attributable to override failure. Errors made by someone with considerable mindware installed are more likely to be due to override failure than to mindware gaps. Of course, the two categories trade off in a continuous manner with a fuzzy boundary between them. A well-learned rule not appropriately applied is a case of override failure. As the rule is less and less well instantiated, at some point it is so poorly compiled that it is not a candidate to override the Type 1 response, and thus the processing error becomes a mindware gap. Consider the example of the John F. Kennedy Jr. aircraft crash presented at the opening of Chapter 9. Presumably, Kennedy knew the rules of night flying but failed to use them to override natural physiological and motor responses in an emergency. We thus classify his actions as an override failure. Had Kennedy not known the night flying rules at all, his ineffectual actions would no longer be classified as an override failure but would be, instead, a mindware gap.

In Table 12.1 I have classified many of the processing styles and thinking errors discussed in the book so far in terms of the taxonomy in Figure 12.2.[8] For example, the three Xs in the first column signify defaults to the autonomous mind: vividness effects, affect substitution, and impulsively associative thinking. Recall that defaulting to the most vivid stimulus is a common way that the cognitive miser avoids Type 2 processing. Likewise defaulting to affective valence is often used in situations with emotional salience. And affect substitution is a specific form of a more generic trick of the cognitive miser, attribute substitution—substituting an easier question for a harder one.[9] Recall from Chapter 6 the bat and ball problem (A bat and a ball cost $1.10 in total. The bat costs $1 more than the ball. How much does the ball cost?) and the Levesque problem ("Jack is looking at Anne but Anne is looking at George"). Failure on problems of this type is an example of the miserly tendency termed impulsively associative thinking. Here, subjects look for any simple association that will prevent them from having to engage in Type 2 thought (in this case associating Anne's unknown status with the response "cannot be determined").

The second category of thinking error presented in Table 12.1 is over-reliance on serial associative cognition with a focal bias (a bias toward the most easily constructed model). This error often occurs in novel situations

Table 12.1. A Basic Taxonomy of Thinking Errors

Tasks, Effects, and Processing Styles	The Cognitive Miser			Mindware Gaps (MG)		MG & CM	Contaminated Mindware (CM)	
	Default to the Autonomous Mind	Focal Bias	Override Failure	Probability Knowledge	Alternative Thinking	Lay Psychological Theory	Evaluation-Disabling Strategies	Self and Egocentric Processing
Vividness effects	X							
Affect substitution	X							
Impulsively associative thinking	X							
Framing effects		X						
Belief bias			X					
Denominator neglect			X					
Self-control problems			X					
Conjunction errors				X				
Noncausal base rates				X				
Bias blind spot						X		
Four-card selection task		X			X			
Myside processing		X				X		X
Affective forecasting errors		X				X		
Confirmation bias		X			X		X	

where some Type 2 processing will be necessary. Framing effects are the example here ("the basic principle of framing is the passive acceptance of the formulation given": Kahneman, 2003a, p. 703). The frame presented to the subject is taken as focal, and all subsequent thought derives from it rather than from alternative framings because the latter would require more thought.

Pure override failure—the third category of thinking errors presented in Table 12.1—is illustrated by the three effects that were discussed in Chapter 9: belief bias effects ("roses are living things"), denominator neglect (the Epstein jelly bean task), and self-control problems such as the inability to delay gratification. It is also involved in the failure of moral judgment override such as that displayed in the trolley problem.

Table 12.1 also portrays two examples of mindware gaps that are due to missing probability knowledge: conjunction errors and noncausal base-rate usage. Listed next is the bias blind spot—the fact that people view other people as more biased than themselves. The bias blind spot is thought to arise because people have incorrect lay psychological theories. They think, incorrectly, that biased thinking on their part would be detectable by conscious introspection. In fact, most social and cognitive biases operate unconsciously.

Multiply Determined Problems of Rational Thought

Several of the remaining tasks illustrated in Table 12.1 represent irrational thought problems that are hybrids. That is, they are co-determined by several different cognitive difficulties. For example, I speculate that problems with the Wason four-card selection task are multiply determined. It is possible that people have trouble with that task because they have not well instantiated the mindware of alternative thinking—the learned rule that thinking of the false situation or thinking about a hypothesis other than the one you have might be useful. Alternatively, people might have trouble with the task because of a focal bias: they focus on the single model given in the rule (vowel must have even) and do all of their reasoning from only this assumption without fleshing out other possibilities. Table 12.1 represents both of these possibilities.

Another thinking error with multiple determinants is myside processing, which is no doubt fostered by contaminated mindware (our notion of "self" that makes us egocentrically think that the world revolves around ourselves). But a form of focal bias may be contributing to that error as well—the bias to base processing on the mental model that is the easiest to construct. What easier model is there to construct than a model based on our own previous beliefs and experiences? Such a focal bias is different from the egocentric mindware of the self. The focal bias is not egocentric in the motivational sense that we want to build our self-esteem or sense of self-worth. The focal bias is simply concerned with conserving computational capacity, and it does so in most cases by encouraging reliance on a model from a myside perspective. Both motivationally driven "self" mindware and computationally driven focal biases may be contributing to myside processing, making it another multiply determined bias.

Errors in affective forecasting are likewise multiply determined. Affective forecasting refers to our ability to predict what will make us happy in the future. Research in the last decade has indicated that people are surprisingly poor at affective forecasting.[10] We often make choices that reduce our happiness because we find it hard to predict what will make us happy. People underestimate how quickly they will adapt to both fortunate and unfortunate events. One reason that people overestimate how unhappy they will be after a negative event is that they have something missing from their lay psychological theories (the personal theories they use to explain their own behavior). They fail to take into account the rationalization and emotion-dampening protective thought they will engage in after the negative event ("I really didn't want the job anyway," "colleagues told me he was biased against older employees"). People's lay theories of their own psychology do not give enough weight to these factors and thus they fail to predict how much their own psychological mechanisms will damp down any unhappiness about the negative event.

Another, and even more important, source of affective forecasting errors is focal bias. Researchers in the affective forecasting literature have theorized specifically about focalism interfering with hedonic predictions. For example, a sports fan overestimates how happy the victory of the home team will make him two days after the event. When making the prediction, he fixates on the salient focal event—winning the game—simulates the emotion he will feel in response to the event, and projects that same emotion two days into the future. What does not enter into his model—because such models are not easy to construct in imagination (hence too effortful for the cognitive miser)—are the myriad other events that will be happening two days after the game and that will then impinge on his happiness in various ways (it is the case that most of these other events will not be as happiness-inducing as was winning the game). In a much-cited study, David Schkade and Daniel Kahneman found that subjects from Michigan and California were about equal in life satisfaction. However, when predicting the satisfaction of the other, both Michigan and California subjects thought that California subjects would be more satisfied with life. The *comparative* judgment made focal an aspect of life, the weather, that in fact was not one of the most important dimensions in life satisfaction (job prospects, financial considerations, social life, and five other factors ranked higher). As Schkade and Kahneman have argued, "Nothing that you focus on will make as much difference as you think" (1998, p. 345). Thus, as Table 12.1 indicates, errors in affective forecasting are a complex mix of focal bias and gaps in lay psychological theories.

In the remainder of this chapter, I will discuss the linkage between each of the major categories of rational thinking error in Figure 12.2 and intelligence. However, before I do, I need to define a sixth category of irrational thinking, one whose characteristics I did not discuss in earlier chapters because it is not a fully *cognitive* category. I include this category here for completeness—it fills in a fuller taxonomy of the sources of irrational thought and action.

The Mr. Spock Problem:
Missing Input from the Autonomous Mind

In his book *Descartes' Error*, neurologist Antonio Damasio describes one of his most famous patients, Elliot. Elliot had had a successful job in a business firm, and served as a role model for younger colleagues. He had a good marriage and was a good father. Elliot's life was a total success story until one day, Damasio tells us, it began to unravel. Elliot began to have headaches and he lost his focus at work. It was discovered that the headaches had been caused by a brain tumor, which was then surgically removed. Subsequent to the surgery, it was determined that Elliot had sustained substantial damage to the ventromedial area of the prefrontal cortex.

That was the bad news. The good news was that on an intelligence test given subsequent to the surgery, Elliot scored in the superior range. Further good news came from many other neuropsychological tests on which Elliot scored at least in the normal range. In short, there were numerous indications that Elliot's algorithmic mind was functioning fine. There was just one little problem here—one little remaining piece of bad news: Elliot's life was a mess.

At work subsequent to the surgery Elliot was unable to allocate his time efficiently. He could not prioritize his tasks and received numerous admonitions from supervisors. When he failed to change his work behavior in the face of this feedback, he was fired. Elliot then charged into a variety of business ventures, all of which failed. One of these ventures ended in bankruptcy because Elliot had invested all of his savings in it. His wife divorced him. After this, he had a brief relationship with an inappropriate woman, married her quickly, and then, just as quickly, divorced her. Elliot had just been denied social security disability benefits when he landed in Dr. Damasio's office.

Damasio described why it took so long and so much testing to reveal the nature of Elliot's problem: "I realized I had been overly concerned with the state of Elliot's intelligence" (p. 44). It was in the realm of emotion rather than intelligence that Elliot was lacking: "He had the requisite knowledge, attention, and memory; his language was flawless; he could perform calculations; he could tackle the logic of an abstract problem. There was only one significant accompaniment of his decision-making failure: a marked alteration of the ability to experience feelings" (p. xii). Elliot was a relatively pure case of what we will call here the Mr. Spock problem, naming it after the *Star Trek* character depicted as having attenuated emotions. Elliot had a problem in decision making because of a lack of regulatory signals from emotion modules in the autonomous mind. Because Elliot was an individual of high intelligence, his lack of rationality represents a type of dysrationalia, but different from any of the categories we have considered before.

Antoine Bechara, Damasio, and colleagues developed a laboratory marker for the type of problem that Damasio had observed in Elliot—the Iowa Gambling Task.[11] The task mirrors real-life situations where ventromedial prefrontal damage patients like Elliot have difficulty because it requires real-time decision making, involves rewards and punishments, is full of uncertainty, and requires estimates of probabilities in a situation where precise calculation is not possible.

Damasio argued that individuals with ventromedial prefrontal damage seem to lack emotional systems that mark positive and negative outcomes with evaluative valence and that regenerate these valences the next time a similar situation arises. The key insight here is that there are two ways in which the rational regulation involving the autonomous mind can go wrong. The override failures discussed previously are one way. In these situations, the signals shaping behavior from the autonomous mind are too pervasive and are not trumped by Type 2 processing. The second way that behavioral regulation involving the autonomous mind can go awry has the opposite properties. In this case, the automatic and rapid regulation of goals is absent and Type 2 processing is faced with a combinatorial explosion of possibilities because the constraining function of autonomous modules such as emotions is missing. Behavioral regulation is not aided by crude but effective autonomous signals that help to prioritize goals for subsequent action. A module failure of this type represents a case where there is not too much regulation from the autonomous mind but instead too little.[12]

The problem manifest in the case of Elliot, the Mr. Spock problem, represents a relatively pure case of dysrationalia. Does the Mr. Spock problem occur in individuals who have no overt and identified brain damage caused by tumor or sudden insult? There is increasing evidence that the Mr. Spock form of dysrationalia may extend beyond extreme clinical cases such as that of Elliot (with measurable ventromedial prefrontal damage). Several groups of people with problems of behavioral regulation perform poorly on the Iowa Gambling Task despite having near-normal intelligence. For example, it has been found that heroin addicts also displayed more disadvantageous choices in the Iowa Gambling Task than controls of equal intelligence. My own research group examined the performance of a nonclinical sample of adolescents who were experiencing problems of behavioral adjustment (multiple school suspensions) on the Iowa Gambling Task. Like Damasio's patients, our participants with suspensions did not differ from their controls in general intelligence. The students with multiple suspensions in our study made significantly poorer choices. Other studies of subjects without overt brain damage have also shown subpar performance on the Iowa Gambling Task, for example, pathological gamblers. Likewise, neuropsychological research has demonstrated a variety of mental disabilities—for example, alexithymia (difficulty in identifying feelings) and schizophrenia—that implicate defects in various types of autonomous monitoring activities that are independent of intelligence.[13]

The Taxonomy in Terms of Intelligence/Rationality Correlations

With the introduction of the Mr. Spock problem, we can now present a fuller taxonomy of the categories of rational thinking error, and it is illustrated in Figure 12.3. Each of the six categories represents a separate explanation of why human thought and action are sometimes irrational. Each category dissociates from intelligence to some extent and thus is a source of dysrationalia. In this section, I will discuss the empirical evidence and theoretical arguments regarding the extent to which the thinking error represented by each category is dissociated from intelligence.

The Mr. Spock problem represents the most clear-cut category because it is likely to be as prevalent in high-IQ individuals as in low-IQ individuals. The reason is that these problems result from inadequate (or incorrect) input from the autonomous mind (for example, from modules of emotional regulation). Variation in the subprocesses of the autonomous mind is largely independent of intelligence.

The next category (defaulting to the autonomous mind and not engaging at all in Type 2 processing) is the most shallow processing tendency of the cognitive miser. The ability to sustain Type 2 processing is of course related to intelligence. But the *tendency* to engage in such processing or to default to autonomous processes is a property of the reflective mind that is not assessed on IQ tests. Consider the Levesque problem ("Jack is looking at Anne but Anne is looking at George") as an example of avoiding Type 2 processing. The subjects who answer this problem correctly are no higher in intelligence than those who do not, at least in a sample of university students studied by Maggie Toplak in my own laboratory.

Disjunctive reasoning problems such as Levesque's Anne problem require the decoupling of cognitive representations and the computation of possible

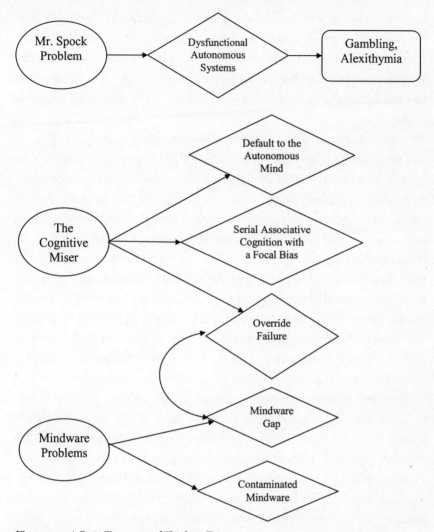

Figure 12.3. A Basic Taxonomy of Thinking Errors

worlds with the decoupled representations—one of the central operations of the algorithmic mind (and one of the processes at the heart of measured intelligence). But clearly one has to discern the necessity of disjunctive reasoning in this situation in order to answer correctly. One has to avoid the heuristic reaction: "Oh, since we don't know whether Anne is married or not we cannot determine anything." And with respect at least to these particular problems, individuals of high intelligence are no more likely to do so. Goal directions to engage in decoupling operations are not sent from higher-level systems of strategic control in the reflective mind to the algorithmic mind. No doubt, were they sent, the decoupled operations would be more reliably sustained by people of higher intelligence. But intelligence is of no use in this task unless the instruction is sent to engage in the modeling of possible worlds.

Theoretically, one might expect a positive correlation between intelligence and the tendency of the reflective mind to initiate Type 2 processing because it might be assumed that those of high intelligence would be more optimistic about the potential efficacy of Type 2 processing and thus be more likely to engage in it. Indeed, some insight tasks do show a positive correlation with intelligence, one in particular being the task studied by Shane Frederick and mentioned in Chapter 6: A bat and a ball cost $1.10 in total. The bat costs $1 more than the ball. How much does the ball cost? Nevertheless, the correlation between intelligence and a set of similar items is quite modest, .43–.46, leaving plenty of room for performance dissociations of the type that define dysrationalia.[14] Frederick has found that large numbers of high-achieving students at MIT, Princeton, and Harvard when given this and other similar problems rely on this most primitive of cognitive miser strategies.

A somewhat more demanding strategy of the cognitive miser is to rely on serial associative processing with a focal bias. It is a more demanding strategy in that it does involve Type 2 processing. It is still a strategy of the miser, though, in that it does not involve fully fleshed-out mental simulation. Framing effects provide examples of the focal bias in the processing of the cognitive miser. When between-subjects framing effects are examined, the tendency to display this type of bias is virtually independent of intelligence. When examined within subjects, the tendency to avoid framing does show a very small correlation with intelligence.[15] Individuals of high intelligence are almost as likely to display irrational framing effects as those of lower intelligence. Thus, dysrationalia due to framing will be common.

In the next category of thinking error, override failure, inhibitory Type 2 processes try to take the Type 1 processing of the autonomous mind offline in order to substitute an alternative response, but the decoupling operations fail to suppress the Type 1 response. We would expect that this category of cognitive failure would have the highest (negative) correlation with intelligence. This is because intelligence indexes the computational power of the algorithmic mind that can be used for the decoupling operation. Theoretically, though, we should still expect the correlation to be somewhat less than perfect. The reflective mind must first trigger override operations before any individual differences in decoupling could become apparent. The tendency to trigger override could be less than perfectly correlated with the capacity to sustain override.

That is the theory. What does the evidence say? We might begin by distinguishing so-called hot override from so-called cold override. The former refers to the override of emotions, visceral drives, or short-term temptations (by analogy to what has been called "hot" cognition in the literature). The latter refers to the override of overpracticed rules, Darwinian modules, or Type 1 tendencies which are not necessarily linked to visceral systems (by analogy to what has been called "cold" cognition in the literature).

In the domain of hot override, we know most about delay of gratification situations. Psychologist Walter Mischel pioneered the study of the delay of gratification paradigm with children. The paradigm has many variants, but the essence of the procedure is as follows. Age appropriate rewards (toys, desirable snacks) are established, and the child is told that he or she will receive a small reward (one marshmallow) or a larger reward (two marshmallows). The child will get the larger reward if, after the experimenter leaves the room, the child waits until the experimenter returns and does not recall the experimenter by ringing a bell. If the bell is rung before the experimenter returns, the child will get only the smaller reward. The dependent variable is the amount of time the child waits before ringing the bell.[16]

Rodriguez, Mischel, and colleagues observed a correlation of just .39 between measured intelligence and delay in this paradigm. Likewise, in a similar study of young children, David Funder and Jack Block observed a correlation of .34 between intelligence and delay (consistent with the idea that this paradigm involves the reflective mind as well as the algorithmic mind, personality measures predicted delay after the variance due to intelligence had been partialled out). Data from adults converge with these findings.

Real-life override failures correlate with intelligence too, but the correlations are modest. For example, the control of addictive behaviors such as smoking, gambling, and drug use is often analyzed in terms of override failure. Thus, it is interesting that Elizabeth Austin and Ian Deary report analyses of the longitudinal Edinburgh Artery Study looking at whether intelligence might be a long-term protective factor against both smoking and drinking (presumably through the greater ability to sustain inhibition of the autonomous mind). In this study, they found no evidence at all that, longitudinally, intelligence served as a protective against problem drinking. There was a very small but significant longitudinal link between intelligence and smoking.[17]

The correlations in the studies I have been discussing were statistically significant, but they are, by all estimates, moderate in absolute magnitude. They leave plenty of room for dissociations between intelligence and successful override of autonomous systems. A very similar story plays out when we look at the relationship between intelligence and "cold" override failure. Two cold override tasks discussed in Chapter 9—belief bias tasks ("roses are living things") and the Epstein jelly bean task (pick from a bowl with 1 of 10 red versus one with 8 of 100 red)—provide examples. Successful override correlates with intelligence in the range of .35–.45 for belief bias tasks and in the range of .25–.30 for the Epstein task.[18] Again, these are significant but modest associations—ones that leave plenty of room for the dissociation that defines dysrationalia.

Continuing down in the taxonomy in Figure 12.3, we see that irrational behavior can occur for a fifth reason: the right mindware (cognitive rules, strategies, knowledge, and belief systems) is not available to use in decision making. We would expect to see a correlation with intelligence here because mindware gaps most often arise because of lack of education or experience. Nevertheless, while it is true that more intelligent individuals learn more things than less intelligent individuals, much knowledge (and many thinking dispositions) relevant to rationality is picked up rather late in life. Explicit teaching of this mindware is not uniform in the school curriculum at any level. That such principles are taught very inconsistently means that some intelligent people may fail to learn these important aspects of critical thinking. Correlations with cognitive ability have been found to be roughly (in absolute magnitude) in the range of .25–.35 for various probabilistic reasoning tasks, in the range of .20–.25 for various covariation detection and hypothesis testing tasks, and in the range of .05–.20 for various indices of Bayesian reasoning—again, relationships allowing for substantial discrepancies between intelligence and the presence of the mindware necessary for rational thought.[19]

Regarding the sixth category in Figure 12.3—contaminated mindware—we would of course expect more intelligent individuals to acquire more mindware of all types based on their superior learning abilities. This would result in their acquiring more mindware that fosters rational thought. However, this superior learning ability would not preclude more intelligent individuals from acquiring contaminated mindware—that is, mindware that literally causes irrationality. Many parasitic belief systems are conceptually somewhat complex. Examples of complex parasitic mindware would be Holocaust denial and many financial get-rich-quick schemes as well as bogus tax evasion schemes. Such complex mindware might even require a certain level of intelligence in order to be enticing to the host. This conjecture is supported by research on the characteristics of financial fraud victims.[20] Pseudoscientific beliefs are also prevalent even among those of high intelligence.

Conclusion: Dysrationalia Will Be Ubiquitous

As the discussion in the last section indicated, intelligence is no inoculation against any of the sources of irrational thought presented in Figure 12.3. As we have gone through the categories looking at the intelligence/rationality correlations, even categories where there does appear to be a significant correlation leave enough room for a substantial number of dissociations. There is thus no reason to expect dysrationalia to be rare. We should not be surprised at smart people acting foolishly.

Not one of the six categories of cognitive error we have just considered is prevented (very much) by having a high IQ, and that should not be surprising. Rationality is a multifarious concept—not a single mental quality. It requires various thinking dispositions that act to trump a variety of miserly information-processing tendencies. It depends on the presence of various knowledge bases related to probabilistic thinking and scientific thinking. It depends on avoiding contaminated mindware that fosters irrational thought and behavior for its own ends. None of these factors are assessed on popular intelligence tests (or their proxies like the SAT). Intelligence tests do not assess the *propensity* to override responses primed by the autonomous mind or to engage in full cognitive simulation. The crystallized abilities assessed on intelligence tests do not probe for the presence of the specific mindware that is critical for rational thought. And finally, there are no probes on intelligence tests for the presence of contaminated mindware. Thus, we should not be surprised when smart people act foolishly. That we in fact *are* sometimes surprised indicates that we are overvaluing and overconceptualizing the term *intelligence*—we are attributing to it qualities that intelligence tests do not measure.

THIRTEEN

The Social Benefits of Increasing Human Rationality—and Meliorating Irrationality

In saying that a person is irrational, we are not accusing him of any irreme-diable flaw, but, rather, just urging him and people who think like him to reform.

—*Jonathan Baron*, Rationality and Intelligence, 1985

The tendency for our society to focus on intelligence and undervalue rational thinking is ironic and exasperating to a cognitive scientist like myself. Throughout this book, I have illustrated how several different rational thinking strategies and knowledge bases affect people's lives. Yet we fail to teach these tools in schools and refuse to focus our attention on them as a society. Instead, we keep using intelligence proxies as selection devices in a range of educational institutions from exclusive preschools to graduate schools. Corporations and the military are likewise excessively focused on IQ measures.[1]

Consider the example of Ivy League universities in the United States. These institutions are selecting society's future elite. What societal goals are served by the selection mechanisms (for example, SAT tests) that they use? Social critics have argued that the tests serve only to maintain an eco-nomic elite. But the social critics seem to have missed a golden opportunity to critique current selection mechanisms by failing to ask the question "Why select for intelligence only and ignore rationality completely?"

In short, we have been valuing only the algorithmic mind and not the reflective mind. This is in part the result of historical accident. We had measures of algorithmic-level processing efficiency long before we had measures of rational thought and the operation of the reflective mind. The dominance and ubiquitousness of early IQ tests served to divert attention from any aspect of cognition except algorithmic-level efficiency. And then, because of this historical accident, we have been trying to back out of this mistake (overvaluing the algorithmic part of the mind) ever since.

In order to illustrate the oddly dysfunctional ways that rationality is devalued in comparison to intelligence, I would like to embellish on a thought experiment first imagined by cognitive psychologist Jonathan Baron in a 1985 book. Baron asks us to imagine what would happen if we were able to give everyone an otherwise harmless drug that increased their algorithmic-level cognitive capacities (for example, discrimination speed, working memory capacity, decoupling ability)—in short, that increased their intelligence as I have defined it in this book. Imagine that everyone in North America took the pill before retiring and then woke up the next morning with more memory capacity and processing speed. Both Baron and I believe that there is little likelihood that much would change the next day in terms of human happiness. It is very unlikely that people would be better able to fulfill their wishes and desires the day after taking the pill. In fact, it is quite likely that people would simply go about their usual business—only more efficiently. If given more memory capacity and processing speed, people would, I believe: carry on using the same ineffective medical treatments because of failure to think of alternative causes (Chapter 10); keep making the same poor financial decisions because of overconfidence (Chapter 8); keep misjudging environmental risks because of vividness (Chapter 6); play host to the contaminated mindware of Ponzi and pyramid schemes (Chapter 11); be wrongly influenced in their jury decisions by incorrect testimony about probabilities (Chapter 10); and continue making many other of the suboptimal decisions described in earlier chapters. The only difference would be that they would be able to do all of these things much more quickly!

Of course, I use this thought experiment as an intuition pump to provoke thought and discussion about what society loses by the particular way we value cognitive attributes. The thought experiment has obvious caveats. More cognitive capacity *would* help to increase rational responding in the cases discussed in Chapter 9—where the algorithmic mind fails to override the processing tendencies of the autonomous mind. But it would do nothing to help in the many situations in which suboptimal rational thinking dispositions were at fault.

Another aspect of the "IQ debate" that is exasperating for cognitive scientists who study reasoning and rational thought is the endless argument about whether intelligence is malleable.[2] No one denies that this is an important question that needs to be resolved, but it has totally overshadowed cognitive skills that are just as useful as intelligence and that may well be more teachable. Likewise, we have failed to ameliorate the suboptimal consequences of difficulties in rational thinking that can be avoided by restructuring the environment so that it does not expose human fallibility. None of this will be possible if we continue to focus on intelligence at the expense of other cognitive skills. We will miss opportunities to teach people to think more rationally in their day-to-day life, and we will miss opportunities to restructure the environment so that people's mindware problems and cognitive miser tendencies will be less costly (either for themselves or for society as a whole).

The lavish attention devoted to intelligence (raising it, praising it, worrying when it is low, etc.) seems wasteful in light of the fact that we choose to virtually ignore another set of mental skills with just as much social consequence—rational thinking mindware and procedures. Popular books tell parents how to raise more intelligent children, educational psychology textbooks discuss the raising of students' intelligence, and we feel reassured when hearing that a particular disability does not impair intelligence. There is no corresponding concern on the part of parents that their children grow into rational beings, no corresponding concern on the part of schools that their students reason judiciously, and no corresponding recognition that intelligence is useless to a child unable to adapt to the world.

I simply do not think that society has weighed the consequences of its failure to focus on irrationality as a real social problem. These skills and dispositions profoundly affect the world in which we live. Because of inadequately developed rational thinking abilities—because of the processing biases and mindware problems discussed in this book—physicians choose less effective medical treatments; people fail to accurately assess risks in their environment; information is misused in legal proceedings; millions of dollars are spent on unneeded projects by government and private industry; parents fail to vaccinate their children; unnecessary surgery is performed; animals are hunted to extinction; billions of dollars are wasted on quack medical remedies; and costly financial misjudgments are made.[3] Distorted processes of belief formation are also implicated in various forms of ethnocentric, racist, sexist, and homophobic hatred.

It is thus clear that widespread societal effects result from inadequately developed rational thinking dispositions and knowledge. In the modern world, the impact of localized irrational thoughts and decisions can be propagated and magnified through globalized information technologies, thus affecting large numbers of people. That is, you may be affected by the irrational thinking of others even if you do not take irrational actions yourself. This is why, for example, the spread of pseudoscientific beliefs is everyone's concern. For example, police departments hire psychics to help with investigations even though research has shown that their use is not efficacious. Jurors have been caught making their decisions based on astrology. Major banks and several Fortune 500 companies employ graphologists for personnel decisions even though voluminous evidence indicates that graphology is useless for this purpose.[4] To the extent that pseudodiagnostic graphological cues lead employers to ignore more valid criteria, both economic inefficiency and personal injustice are the result. How would you like to lose your chance for a job that you really wanted because you have a particular little "loop" in your handwriting? How would you like to be convicted of a crime because of an astrological "reading"?

Unfortunately, these examples are not rare. We are all affected in numerous ways when such contaminated mindware permeates society—even if we avoid this contaminated mindware ourselves. Pseudosciences such as astrology are now large industries, involving newspaper columns, radio shows, book publishing, the Internet, magazine articles, and other means of dissemination. The House of Representatives Select Committee on Aging has estimated that the amount wasted on medical quackery nationally reaches into the billions. Physicians are increasingly concerned about the spread of medical quackery on the Internet and its real health costs.

Pseudoscientific beliefs appear to arise from a complex combination of thinking dispositions, mindware gaps, and contaminated mindware. Pseudoscientific beliefs are related to the tendency to display confirmation bias, failure to consider alternative hypotheses, ignoring chance as an explanation of an outcome, identifying with beliefs and not critiquing them, and various fallacies in probabilistic thinking.[5] Throughout this book I have argued that these rational thinking attributes are very imperfectly correlated with intelligence. But can we do anything about these attributes? Putting the decades-old debate about the malleability of intelligence aside, what do we know about the malleability of rational thinking tendencies?

The Good News: Rationality Can Be Learned

Regardless of the eventual outcome of the long-standing debate about the malleability of intelligence, it is striking that the field of psychology has not displayed an anywhere comparable concern about the malleability of rationality. This lack of concern is ironic given that there are at least preliminary indications that rationality may be more malleable than intelligence.

Irrationality caused by mindware gaps is most easily remediable as it is entirely due to missing strategies and declarative knowledge that can be taught.[6] Overriding the tendencies of the autonomous mind is most often done with learned mindware, and sometimes override fails because of inadequately instantiated mindware. In such a case, inadequately learned mindware is the source of the problem. For example, disjunctive reasoning is the tendency to consider all possible states of the world when deciding among options or when choosing a problem solution in a reasoning task. It is a rational thinking strategy with a high degree of generality. People make many suboptimal decisions because of the failure to flesh out all the possible options in a situation, yet the disjunctive mental tendency is not computationally expensive. This is consistent with the finding that there are not strong intelligence-related limitations on the ability to think disjunctively and with evidence indicating that disjunctive reasoning is a rational thinking strategy that can be taught.[7]

The tendency to consider alternative hypotheses is, like disjunctive reasoning, strategic mindware of great generality. Also, it can be implemented in very simple ways. Many studies have attempted to teach the technical issue of thinking of $P(D/\sim H)$ (the probability of the observed data given the alternative hypothesis) or thinking of the alternative hypothesis by instructing people in a simple habit. People are given extensive practice at saying to themselves the phrase "think of the opposite" in relevant situations. This strategic mindware does not stress computational capacity and thus is probably easily learnable by many individuals. Several studies have shown that practice at the simple strategy of triggering the thought "think of the opposite" can help to prevent a host of the thinking errors studied in the heuristics and biases literature, including but not limited to: anchoring biases, overconfidence effects, hindsight bias, confirmation bias, and self-serving biases.[8]

Various aspects of probabilistic thinking represent mindware of great generality and potency. However, as any person who has ever taught a statistics course can attest (your present author included), some of these insights are counterintuitive and unnatural for people—particularly in their application. There is nevertheless still some evidence that they are indeed teachable—albeit with somewhat more effort and difficulty than strategies such as disjunctive reasoning or considering alternative hypotheses. Aspects of scientific thinking necessary to infer a causal relationship are also definitely teachable.[9] Other strategies of great generality may be easier to learn—particularly by those of lower intelligence. For example, psychologist Peter Gollwitzer has discussed an action strategy of extremely wide generality—the use of implementation intentions.[10] An implementation intention is formed when the individual marks the cue-action sequence with the conscious, verbal declaration: "when X occurs, I will do Y." Often with the aid of the context-fixing properties of language,[11] the triggering of this cue-action sequence on just a few occasions is enough to establish it in the autonomous mind. Finally, research has shown that an even more minimalist cognitive strategy of forming mental goals (whether or not they have implementation intentions) can be efficacious. For example, people perform better in a task when they are told to form a mental goal ("set a specific, challenging goal for yourself") for their performance as opposed to being given the generic motivational instructions ("do your best").[12]

We are often making choices that reduce our happiness because we find it hard to predict what will make us happy. For example, people often underestimate how quickly they will adapt to both fortunate and unfortunate events. Our imaginations fail at projecting the future. Psychologist Dan Gilbert cites evidence indicating that a remediating strategy in such situations might be to use a surrogate—someone who is presently undergoing the event whose happiness (or unhappiness) you are trying to simulate. For example, if you are wondering how you will react to "empty nest" syndrome, ask someone who has just had their last child leave for college rather than trying to imagine yourself in that situation. If you want to know how you will feel if your team is knocked out in the first round of the tournament, ask someone whose team has just been knocked out rather than trying to imagine it yourself. People tend not to want to use this mechanism because they think that their own uniqueness makes their guesses from introspection more accurate than the actual experiences of the people undergoing the event. People are simply skeptical about whether other people's experiences apply to them. This is a form of egocentrism akin to the myside processing which I have discussed. Gilbert captures the irony of people's reluctance to adopt the surrogate strategy by telling his readers: "If you are like most people, then like most people, you don't know you're like most people" (2006, p. 229).

Much of the strategic mindware discussed so far represents learnable strategies in the domain of instrumental rationality (achieving one's goals). Epistemic rationality (having beliefs well calibrated to the world) is often dis-rupted by contaminated mindware. However, even here, there are teachable macro-strategies that can reduce the probability of acquiring mindware that is harmful to its host. For example, the principle of falsifiability provides a wonderful inoculation against many kinds of nonfunctional beliefs. It is a tool of immense generality. It is taught in low-level methodology and philosophy of science courses, but could be taught much more broadly than this.[13] Many pseudoscientific beliefs represent the presence of contaminated mindware. The critical thinking skills that help individuals to recognize pseudoscientific belief systems can be taught in high school courses.

Finally, the language of memetics itself is therapeutic—a learnable men-tal tool that can help us become more conscious of the possibility that we are hosting contaminated mindware. One way the meme concept will aid in cognitive self-improvement is that by emphasizing the epidemiology of belief it will indirectly suggest to many (for whom it will be a new insight) the *contingency* of belief. By providing a common term for all cultural units, memetic science provides a neutral context for evaluating whether any belief serves our interests as humans. The very concept of the meme will suggest to more and more people that they need to engage in mindware examination.

In this section, I have presented just a few examples of the many components of the multifarious concept of rationality that can be taught. There are learnable macro-strategies for avoiding contaminated mindware. The forming of implementation intentions, mental bundling, and goal formation represent very learnable strategies in the domain of instrumental rationality (achieving one's goals). These strategies complement nicely the learnable mindware that facilitates the optimal calibration and interpretation of evidence (probabilistic and scientific reasoning skills). Although there are no precise quantitative studies of the issue, it would appear that the propensity for rational thinking is at least as malleable as intelligence.

It's the Portions, Stupid! Changing the Environment to Help the Cognitive Miser

Perhaps ridding ourselves of our humanity is not in the works; we need tricks, not some grandiose moralizing help.
—*Nassim Nicholas Taleb*, Fooled by Randomness, 2001

In previous chapters, I argued how our tendencies to process information as cognitive misers are a threat to our autonomy. If the cognitive miser is easily framed, responds to the most vivid stimulus present, and accepts defaults as given, then the behavior of misers will be shaped by whoever in their world has the power to determine these things. Phrased in this manner, the state of affairs seems somewhat ominous. But maybe there is an upside here. Yes, a malicious controller of our environment might choose to exploit us. But perhaps a benevolent controller of our environment could help us—could save us from our irrational acts without our having to change basic aspects of our cognition. The upside is that for certain cognitive problems it might be easier to change the environment than to change people. Because in a democracy we in part control our own environment, as a society we could decide to restructure the world so that it helped people to be more rational.

For example, in a cross-national study of organ donation rates, Eric Johnson and Daniel Goldstein found that 85.9 percent of individuals in Sweden had agreed to be organ donors. However, the rate in the United Kingdom was only 17.2 percent.[14] What is the difference between the Swedes and the British that accounts for such a large gap in their attitudes about organ donation? Is it that Sweden is a more collectivist society and the United Kingdom a more individualistic one? Are Swedes more altruistic than people from the United Kingdom? Perhaps a clue to the difference might be obtained by looking at the organ donor rate in the United States. It is roughly 28 percent, more similar to that in the United Kingdom than to that in Sweden. Could the difference be one between Anglophone nations and non-Anglophone nations?

You no doubt have guessed the answer to this puzzle by now. The difference in organ donorship among these countries has nothing to do with internal psychological differences between their citizens. The differences among Sweden, the United Kingdom, and the United States have nothing to do with *attitudes* toward organ donation. The differences are due to a contrast in the public policy about becoming an organ donor in these different countries. In Sweden — like Belgium, France, Poland, and Hungary, where agreement to organ donorship is over 95 percent — the default value on organ donorship is presumed consent. In countries with this public policy, people are assumed to have allowed their organs to be harvested, but can opt out by taking an action (usually by getting a notation on their driver's licenses). In contrast, in the United States and United Kingdom — like Germany, Denmark, and the Netherlands, where agreement to organ donorship is less than 30 percent — the default value is no donation, with explicit action required to opt *for* organ donation.

In short, the difference between Sweden and the United Kingdom is not in the people. The citizens of both countries are cognitive misers and probably to a roughly equal extent. The great difference is in the form of a particular public policy. As misers, the citizens of both countries are strongly affected by the default heuristic. The option offered as the default is "sticky" in that it is overly influential. Johnson and Goldstein determined that when people really think about this issue without a default being given to them, roughly 80 percent (much closer to the percentage in Sweden and other opt-out countries) prefer to be organ donors. Since 1995, over 45,000 people have died while on waiting lists for an organ in the United States. A very small change in the donor decision-making environment that hurts no one (since an opt-out procedure is allowed in all countries with presumed consent) could save the lives of thousands of people. The tendencies of the cognitive miser have cost thousands of people their lives. But these tragic consequences are preventable. The best prevention in this case, though, is a change in the environment rather than a change in people because the former is so much easier to implement.

Examples such as organ donation are what led legal theorist Cass Sunstein and economist Richard Thaler to advocate a policy of what they call libertarian paternalism.[15] The paternalistic part of their philosophy is the acknowledgment that government should try to steer the choices of people toward actions that will be good for them. The libertarian part of their philosophy is the guarantee that any policy changes preserve complete freedom of choice. How is it possible to steer people's choices without interfering with freedom of choice? The answer is: exploit the tendencies of the cognitive miser. Specifically, this often means controlling the aspects of the environment that control the behavior of the cognitive miser—default values and framings.

Consider an example from a domain in which libertarian paternalism has actually been implemented. Financially, Americans are massively underprepared for their retirement. They have not saved enough. Many people are not participating in the 401(k)s and other retirement savings options that they have available to them. Thaler and colleague Shlomo Benartzi have popularized a series of pension-plan enrollment reforms that could literally rescue the retirement years of millions of workers—years that would have been ruined due to dysrationalic decisions earlier in life. Their reforms are making their way into legislation, and many corporations are beginning to adopt them.[16]

Thaler and Benartzi's reforms involve several steps, each involving a way of circumventing a well-known thinking error that is implicated when people make 401(k) decisions. The first step comes at the point when employees of most large companies must first choose to enroll. If they do nothing (do not fill out the relevant form) they are not enrolled. Here is where things first go wrong. Many employees do not enroll. In the Thaler/Benartzi program, employees are automatically signed up for the 401(k) and must choose (by filling out a form) to opt out of the system. Thus, their program exploits the default bias of the cognitive miser.

The second place where employees trip up when making 401(k) decisions is in the allocation of their (and their employer's) contributions. The Thaler/Benartzi program makes additional use of the default bias by automatically allocating the employee's contribution equally among a small set of mutual funds to ensure that the initial allocation is diversified. Another of Thaler and Benartzi's suggested reforms involves getting employees to increase their 401(k) contributions by asking them to commit in advance to having a proportion of their future *raises* allocated to additional 401(k) contributions. This strategy ensures that the employee will never experience the additional contribution as a loss, because the employee never sees a decrease in the paycheck. Of course, the contribution is the same in either case, but such a procedure encourages the employee to frame it in a way that, according to prospect theory, makes it less aversive.

Thaler and Benartzi have developed a savings program called Save More Tomorrow™ (SMarT), which puts into practice many of the reforms discussed here. It has been used by major corporations such as Hewlett Packard and Philips Electronics. The important point for our discussion here is that it represents an example of inoculation against irrational behavior by changing the environment rather than people. The SMarT program demonstrates that some of the difficulties that arise because of miser tendencies can be dealt with by changes in the environment.

Even in the case of missing mindware, we can sometimes make the environment less onerous for those with critical mindware gaps. For example, cognitive psychologist Gerd Gigerenzer has demonstrated that many people have trouble dealing with single-event probabilities (for example, there is a 40 percent probability that the economy will go into a recession). In a survey, Gigerenzer and colleagues found that over 25 percent of survey participants in New York misunderstood the phrase "there will be a 30 percent chance of rain tomorrow." This minority did not understand the statement to mean that on 30 percent of the days like tomorrow it will rain. They had alternative interpretations such as that it will rain tomorrow 30 percent of the time, or that it will rain over 30 percent of the region tomorrow.

Such misunderstandings of probability terminology are widespread in the domain of medicine. Physician Richard Friedman described the reaction of one patient on being told that the chances were 60 percent that an anti-depressant prescribed for her would work. The patient said, "That means that 60 percent of the time I will feel better on this, right?"—displaying one of the classic misunderstandings revealed in the study by Gigerenzer and colleagues. Of course, people should be taught the use of this mindware of probability terminology. But it would be easy to supplement the communication of single-event probabilities with their correct interpretation ("there is a 30 percent chance of rain tomorrow, which means that that if there are 100 days like tomorrow it will rain on 30 of them"). This simple environmental change would prevent people without the relevant mindware from mis-interpretation, and it would help them to acquire the mindware. Gigerenzer and other investigators have shown that the processing of probabilistic in-formation, not only by laboratory subjects but also by practicing physicians, is facilitated by clarifying the point that probabilistic information refers to instances of classes.[17]

All of these examples show how simple environmental changes can prevent rational thinking problems. An even larger category of problems where people need help from their environments is problems of self-control. People over-eat, they over-spend, they procrastinate, they smoke, and they drink too much. Solutions to these problems with self-control are of two forms—corresponding to changes in the individual and changes in the environment. People try to bolster their "willpower"—that is, their internal powers of self-control. Alternatively, they try to rearrange their environments so that less exercise of willpower (autonomous system override) will be necessary. A common strategy here is to use pre-commitment devices. People enroll in automatic savings plans so that they will not over-spend. They prepackage meals so they will not over-eat. They commit themselves to deadlines so they will not procrastinate. Pre-commitments represent our deliberate attempts to restructure our environments so that they will be more conducive to our self-control attempts.

There is some evidence that these pre-commitment devices are success-ful—producing outcomes that people view as more rational when they are in a reflective state. There is massive evidence that pre-commitment to saving money is efficacious. In other domains there is also suggestive evidence.[18]

Dan Ariely and Klaus Wertenbroch found that students using self-imposed deadlines in academic settings performed better than students not using self-imposed deadlines. Interestingly, however, the self-imposed deadlines were not as good at boosting performance as *externally* imposed deadlines.

One of the reasons why the domain of weight control remains so intractable is that people have found myriad ways not to pre-commit themselves to one of only two things that will bring their weight down—consuming fewer calories (the other being exercise, of course). The diet industry encourages this tendency by continually implying that there is a way around the prescription to eat less. There are numerous variants: eat only protein and avoid carbohydrates; eat the right carbs, not the wrong carbs; avoid high glycemic-index foods; eat the Top Ten Sonoma Diet Power Foods; eat only sushi; eat all the spaghetti you want as long as you don't—fill in the blank; the list is endless. All of these prescriptions are ways of avoiding the real point: It's the portions, stupid! As *Consumer Reports* (June 2007) advises: "The basic formula for losing weight has not changed: consume fewer calories than you burn" (p. 12).

We are getting no paternalistic help (libertarian or not) in the domain of eating. Our environment is literally making us ill. This is what the work of Paul Rozin and colleagues strongly suggested when they attempted to study the so-called French paradox.[19] The mortality rate from heart disease in France is much lower than that in the United States despite the fact that the French have higher blood cholesterol levels and they have more fats (both saturated and unsaturated) in their diets. One reason for the higher heart disease mortality rates in the United States may be that Americans are more obese. Indeed, despite French people eating a higher-fat diet than Americans, the obesity rate in France is only 7.4 percent compared with 22.3 percent in the United States. Rozin and colleagues posited that one reason that Americans were heavier despite eating less fat was because they were routinely exposed to larger portion sizes.

Rozin and colleagues found evidence from a variety of sources indicating that this was in fact the case. They studied portion sizes in chain restaurants that exist in both countries and found that, for example, portion sizes were 28 percent larger in McDonald's restaurants in the United States than in France. Portion sizes at Pizza Huts in the United States were 42 percent larger. Across eleven comparisons, the United States portion size was 25 percent larger than that in France. Rozin and colleagues examined equivalent recipes from *The Joy of Cooking* and *Je sais cuisiner* for seven meat dishes. The mean recipe size was 53 percent larger in *The Joy of Cooking*. Individual-portion foods were examined, and it was found that, for example, a lasagna dinner was 19 percent larger in the United States. A Nestle Crunch bar in the United States was 41 percent larger, and a yoghurt was 82 percent larger. Over a varied selection of such items, the individual portion in the United States was 37 percent larger. Clearly, in the United States it would be possible to provide much more environmental help than we are getting in the domain of weight control.

Rozin and colleagues have studied the so-called unit bias: that people will tend to eat one portion of something, regardless of the size of that portion, or will tend to eat a unit of something regardless of the size of that unit. In several different studies, the researchers left snacks (M&M's, Tootsie Rolls, pretzels) in public places. When the size of the snacks was doubled or quadrupled, people did not cut their consumption proportionately. Instead, people consumed much more when the unit sizes were larger. A simple environmental fix—smaller portion sizes—could do a great deal in helping us with the obesity epidemic in the United States.

Society's Selection Mechanisms

As the brief review in this chapter suggests, many suboptimal outcomes that result from thinking that is less than rational can be prevented. Interestingly, even if intelligence is malleable (as I think it is), the methods needed to increase it will almost certainly involve more long-term training than those involved in teaching most well-known skills of rational thinking.[20] It is no wonder that our culture is so full of dysrationalic behavior, when we fail to maximize the use of known mental tools in one domain (rational thinking) while we go in desperate search of ways to facilitate another (intelligence) that, although not unimportant, is no *more* important.

Given the social consequences of rational versus irrational thinking, the practical relevance of this domain of skills cannot be questioned. Why then, do the selection mechanisms used by society tap only algorithmic-level cognitive capacities and ignore rationality? It makes little sense to test for the narrow concept of intelligence and then confer rewards as if someone had been vetted on the larger, broader concept.

In fact, the issue of the differential privileging of some cognitive skills over others deserves more explicit public discussion. For example, some philosophers have found demonstrations of irrationality in the cognitive science literature implausible because, they say, the subjects—mostly college students—"will go on to become leading scientists, jurists, and civil servants" (Stich, 1990, p. 17). I do think that these philosophers have drawn our attention to something startling, but I derive a completely different moral from it. Most jurists and civil servants, in my experience, do seem to have adequate algorithmic-level cognitive capacities. However, despite this, their actions are often decidedly suboptimal. Their performance often fails to measure up, not because they lack working memory capacity or memory retrieval speed, but because their dispositions toward rationality are sometimes low. They may not lack intelligence, but they *do* lack some rational thinking skills.

The poor performance of the college students in the experiments in the literature on reasoning and decision making is not in the least paradoxical. The college students who fail laboratory tests of decision making and probabilistic reasoning are indeed the future jurists who, despite decent cognitive capacities, will reason badly. These students have never been specifically screened for rationality before entering the laboratory. And they will not be so assessed at any other time. If they are at elite state universities or elite private schools, they will continue up the academic, corporate, political, and economic ladders by passing SATs, GREs, placement tests, and performance simulations that assess primarily the algorithmic mind. Rationality assessment will never take place.

But what if it did? It is an interestingly open question, for example, whether race and social class differences on measures of rationality would be found to be as large as those displayed on intelligence tests. Suggestively, Robert Sternberg finds that race and class differences on measures of practical intelligence (the aspect of his broad view of intelligence that is closest to rationality) are less than they are on IQ tests.[21] The framework that I have outlined would at least predict that rankings of individuals on assessments of rational thinking would be different from rankings on intelligence. The reason is that rationality involves thinking dispositions of the reflective mind not assessed on intelligence tests.

Indeed, perhaps assessing rationality more explicitly is what is needed in order both to draw more attention toward rational thinking skills and to highlight the limitations of what intelligence tests assess. At present, of course, there is no IQ-type test for rationality—that is, a test of one's RQ (rationality quotient). But it may be that it would at least help the debate to start talking about such a thing. I am not saying that an RQ test could be constructed tomorrow. Such instruments are not constructed on the back of an envelope. It would of course take an ETS-like effort costing millions of dollars. But the point is that, practically, in terms of the cognitive technology now in place, it is doable. Only issues of demand and cost prevent it.

Rather than debate the logistics of such an endeavor, the main point I wish to emphasize here is that there is nothing *conceptually* or *theoretically* preventing us from developing such a test. We know the types of thinking processes that would be assessed in such an instrument, and we have in hand prototypes of the kinds of tasks that would be used in the domains of both instrumental rationality and epistemic rationality. There is no limitation on constructing an RQ test that comes from the technology of ability assessment surrounding rational thought.[22] Nor is there a conceptual limitation.

In this book, I have discussed several ways that cognitive scientists test both epistemic rationality and instrumental rationality. There are many more such tests described in the references that I have cited, but that I have not discussed here for a variety of reasons (most often because the task involved was technical, difficult to explain, or somewhat redundant with examples I have given). This book provides a selective survey, not an exhaustive handbook of rational thinking tasks. Nevertheless, I have been able to show how psychologists study aspects of epistemic rationality and irrationality, such as: the tendency to show incoherent probability assessments; the tendency toward overconfidence in knowledge judgments; the tendency to ignore base rates; the tendency not to seek to falsify hypotheses; the tendency to try to explain chance events; the tendency toward self-serving personal judgments; the tendency to evaluate evidence with a myside bias; and the tendency to ignore the alternative hypothesis.

Additionally, I have been able to show how psychologists study aspects of instrumental rationality and irrationality, such as: the ability to display disjunctive reasoning in decision making; the tendency to show inconsistent preferences because of framing effects; the tendency to show a default bias; the tendency to substitute affect for difficult evaluations; the tendency to over-weight short-term rewards at the expense of long-term well-being; the tendency to have choices affected by vivid stimuli; and the tendency for decisions to be affected by irrelevant context.

Finally, there are numerous examples of our knowledge of rational and irrational thinking being used to help people live fuller lives. In studies cited in this book, it has been shown that:

- Psychologists have found ways of presenting statistical information so that we can make more rational decisions related to medical matters and in any situation where statistics are involved.
- Cognitive psychologists have shown that a few simple changes in presenting information in accord with default biases could vastly increase the frequency of organ donations, thus saving thousands of lives.
- Americans annually pay millions of dollars for advice on how to invest their money in the stock market, when following a few simple principles from decision theory would lead to returns on their investments superior to any of this advice. These principles would help people avoid the cognitive biases that lead them to reduce their returns — over-reacting to chance events, overconfidence, wishful thinking, hindsight bias, misunderstanding of probability.
- Decision scientists have found that people are extremely poor at assessing environmental risks. This is mainly because vividness biases dominate people's judgment to an inordinate extent. People could improve, and this would make a huge difference because these poor assessments come to affect public policy (causing policy makers to implement policy A, which saves one life for each $3.2 million spent, instead of policy B, which would have saved one life for every $220,000 spent, for example).
- Psychologists from various specialty areas are beginning to pinpoint the cognitive illusions that sustain pathological gambling behavior — pseudodiagnosticity, belief perseverance, over-reacting to chance

events, cognitive impulsivity, misunderstanding of probability—behavior that destroys thousands of lives each year.

- Cognitive psychologists have studied the overconfidence effect in human judgment—that people miscalibrate their future performance, usually by making overoptimistic predictions. Psychologists have studied ways to help people avoid these problems in self-monitoring, making it easier for people to plan for the future (overconfident people get more unpleasant surprises).
- Social psychological research has found that controlling the explosion of choices in our lives is one of the keys to happiness—that constraining choice often makes people happier.
- Simple changes in the way pension plans are organized and administered could make retirement more comfortable for millions of people.
- Probabilistic reasoning is perhaps the most studied topic in the decision-making field, and many of the cognitive reforms that have been examined—for example, eliminating base-rate neglect—could improve practices in courtrooms, where poor thinking about probabilities has been shown to impede justice.

These are just a small sampling of the teachable reasoning strategies and environmental fixes that could make a difference in people's lives, and they are more related to rationality than intelligence. They are examples of the types of outcomes that would result if we all became more rational thinkers and decision makers. They are the types of outcomes that would be multiplied if schools, businesses, and government focused on the parts of cognition that intelligence tests miss. Instead, we continue to pay far more attention to intelligence than to rational thinking. It is as if intelligence has become totemic in our culture, and we choose to pursue it rather than the reasoning strategies that could transform our world.

1 Inside George W. Bush's Mind

1. On George W. Bush's IQ, see: Simonton (2006); Immelman (2001); Sailer (2004); Kessler (2004, pp. 23–28); http://www.sq.4mg.com/Presidents.htm (retrieved July 16, 2007).
2. On the SAT as a measure of general intelligence, see Frey and Detterman (2004), Lemann (1999), and Unsworth and Engle (2007).
3. The NFL gives quarterbacks the Wonderlic Test (Wonderlic Personnel Test, 2002).
4. On the changes in the incidence of various disabilities and their causes see Barbaresi, Katusic, Colligan, Weaver, and Jacobsen (2005); Friend (2005); Gernsbacher, Dawson, and Goldsmith (2005); Gordon, Lewandowski, and Keiser (1999); Kelman and Lester (1997); and Parsell (2004).

2 Dysrationalia

1. See Sternberg (2002a) and Perkins (1995, 2002).
2. On intelligence as adaptation, there are many different discussions (see Matthews, Zeidner, and Roberts, 2002; Neisser et al., 1996; Sternberg, 2000b; Sternberg and Detterman, 1986). The distinction between broad and narrow theories of intelligence is also discussed in a variety of sources (Baron, 1985; Gardner, 1983, 1999; 2006a, 2006b; Perkins, 1995, 2002; Sternberg, 1997a, 1997b, 2000b, 2003b; Sternberg and Detterman, 1986; Sternberg and Kaufman, 1998; Visser, Ashton, and Vernon, 2006).
3. An important caveat is that the behavioral phenomenon that folk psychology marks as surprising is not a single, isolated instance of injudicious behavior, but when ostensibly smart people repeatedly act injudiciously.
4. The theory of fluid and crystallized intelligence has generated a substantial literature (Carroll, 1993; Cattell, 1963, 1998; Daniel, 2000; Geary, 2005; Horn and

Cattell, 1967; Horn and Noll, 1997; Kaufman, 2001; McGrew, 1997; McGrew and Woodcock, 2001; Taub and McGrew, 2004). On fluid intelligence in particular see Kane and Engle (2002) and Unsworth and Engle (2005). Some theories define a general factor (g) from the nonzero correlation between Gf and Gc (see Carroll, 1993). This factor may result from the investment of fluid intelligence in the acquisition of knowledge, as in Cattell's (1971) investment theory (see Ackerman and Kanfer, 2004; Hambrick, 2003). On intelligence-as-process and intelligence-as-knowledge, see Ackerman (1996).

5. Sternberg has conducted numerous studies of folk theories of intelligence (Sternberg, 2000b; Sternberg, Conway, Ketron, and Bernstein, 1981; Sternberg and Grigorenko, 2004; see also Cornelius, Kenny, and Caspi, 1989).

6. There is an extensive empirical literature in cognitive science on people's tendencies to think rationally (see Baron, 2000; Camerer, Loewenstein, and Rabin, 2004; Evans, 2002a, 2002b, 2004, 2007; Evans and Over, 1996; Gilovich, Griffin, and Kahneman, 2002; Johnson-Laird, 2006; Kahneman, 2003a, 2003b; Kahneman and Tversky, 2000; Koehler and Harvey, 2004; LeBoeuf and Shafir, 2005; Loewenstein, Read, and Baumeister, 2003; Manktelow and Chung, 2004; Nickerson, 2004; Samuels and Stich, 2004; Shafir and LeBoeuf 2002; Stanovich, 1999, 2004; Stanovich and West, 1998c, 1999, 2000, 2008a, 2008b).

7. The technicalities of the axioms of expected utility theory are beyond our scope here (see Allingham, 2002; Dawes, 1998; Edwards, 1954; Jeffrey, 1983; Luce and Raiffa, 1957; Savage, 1954; von Neumann and Morgenstern, 1944; Wu, Zhang, and Gonzalez, 2004). Suffice it to say that when people's choices follow certain patterns (the so-called axioms of choice—things like transitivity and freedom from certain kinds of context effects), then they are behaving as if they are maximizing utility.

8. Epistemic rationality is sometimes called theoretical rationality or evidential rationality (see Audi, 1993, 2001; Foley, 1987; Harman, 1995; Manktelow, 2004). On instrumental and epistemic rationality, see Manktelow (2004), Mele and Rawling (2004), Millgram (2001), and Over (2004).

9. For my earliest discussion of dysrationalia, see Stanovich (1993a, 1994a). The discrepancy notion is also at work in definitions that excluded from the learning disability classification children of low intelligence (e.g., the landmark Education for All Handicapped Children Act [PL 94–142]; the National Joint Committee on Learning Disabilities, Hammill, 1990). It is now known that the whole notion of discrepancy measurement in the domain of reading disability was a mistake (Fletcher et al., 1994; Stanovich, 2000, 2005; Stanovich and Siegel, 1994; Stuebing et al., 2002; Vellutino et al., 2004). The proximal cause of most cases of reading difficulty—problems in phonological processing—is the same for individuals of high and low IQ (Stanovich, 2000; Vellutino et al., 2004). Phonological processing is only modestly correlated with intelligence, so that cases of reading difficulty in the face of high IQ are in no way surprising and do not need a special explanation.

3 The Reflective Mind, the Algorithmic Mind, and the Autonomous Mind

1. The consensus on the basic issues surrounding intelligence, particularly fluid intelligence, is a discernible trend in the literature on cognitive abilities (Bouchard, 2004; Carroll, 1993; Deary, 2001; Engle et al., 1999; Flynn, 2007; Geary, 2005; Lubinski, 2004; Neisser et al., 1996; Plomin and Spinath, 2004; Sternberg, 2000a; Unsworth and Engle, 2005).

2. Schmidt and Hunter (1992, 1998, 2004) have done the most sustained and comprehensive research on this issue (see also Deary et al., 2004; Geary, 2005; Kuncel, Hezlett, and Ones, 2004; Ones, Viswesvaran, and Dilchert, 2005).

3. For over two decades Jonathan Evans has contributed to dual-process theory, and his work has influenced my approach considerably (Evans, 1984, 1989, 2003, 2004, 2006a, 2006b, 2008a, 2008b; Evans and Over, 1996, 2004; Evans and Wason, 1976). A dual-process view was implicit within the early writings in the groundbreaking heuristics and biases research program (Kahneman, 2000, 2003a; Kahneman and Frederick, 2002, 2005; Kahneman and Tversky, 1982a, 1996; Tversky and Kahneman, 1974, 1983). Dual-process theories have been developed in numerous subfields within psychology (Brainerd and Reyna, 2001; Epstein, 1994; Feldman Barrett, Tugade, and Engle, 2004; Haidt, 2001; Johnson-Laird, 1983; Metcalfe and Mischel, 1999; Sloman, 1996, 2002; Smith and Decoster, 2000; Stanovich, 1999; Stanovich and West, 2000). A list of over 23 dual-process models is presented in a table in Stanovich (2004). The details and terminology of the various dual-process theories differ, but they all share a family resemblance. Neurophysiological work supporting a dual-process conception continues to grow (Bechara, 2005; DeMartino, Kumaran, Seymour and Dolan, 2006; Goel and Dolan, 2003; Greene, Nystrom, Engell, Darley, and Cohen, 2004; Lieberman, 2003; McClure, Laibson, Loewenstein and Cohen, 2004; Prado and Noveck, 2007; Westen, Blagov, Kilts, and Hamann, 2006).

4. There has been much research on each of the different kinds of Type 1 processing (e.g., Atran, 1998; Buss, 2005; Evans, 2003, 2006a; Fodor, 1983; Lieberman, 2000, 2003; Ohman and Mineka, 2001; Pinker, 1997; Smith, Patalino, and Jonides, 1998; Willingham, 1998, 1999). Type 1 processes conjoin the properties of automaticity, quasi-modularity, and heuristic processing as these constructs have been variously discussed in cognitive science (e.g., Bargh and Chartrand, 1999; Barrett and Kurzban, 2006; Carruthers, 2006; Coltheart, 1999; Evans, 1984, 2006b, 2008a, 2008b; Samuels, 2005, 2008; Shiffrin and Schneider, 1977; Sperber, 1994). See Wilson (2002) on the adaptive unconscious.

5. E.g., Dempster and Corkill (1999); Hasher, Lustig, and Zacks (2007); Miyake et al. (2000); Zelazo (2004).

6. Hypothetical reasoning and cognitive simulation are central topics in cognitive science (see Barrett, Henzi, and Dunbar, 2003; Buckner and Carroll, 2007; Byrne, 2005; Currie and Ravenscroft, 2002; Decety and Grezes, 2006; Dougherty, Gettys, and Thomas, 1997; Evans, 2007; Evans and Over, 2004; Kahneman and Tversky,

1982b; Nichols and Stich, 2003; Oatley, 1999; Roese, 1997; Sterelny, 2001; Suddendorf and Corballis, 2007; Suddendorf and Whiten, 2001).

7. Leslie's (1987) model can best be understood by adopting the primary/secondary terminology later used by Perner (1991), and I have done so here. Subsequent to Leslie (1987), cognitive decoupling has been discussed in related and somewhat differing ways by a large number of different investigators coming from a variety of different perspectives, not limited to: developmental psychology, evolutionary psychology, artificial intelligence, and philosophy of mind (Atance and O'Neill, 2001; Carruthers, 2000, 2002; Clark and Karmiloff-Smith, 1993; Corballis, 2003; Cosmides and Tooby, 2000; Dennett, 1984; Dienes and Perner, 1999; Evans and Over, 1999; Jackendoff, 1996; Lillard, 2001; Perner, 1991, 1998; Sperber, 2000; Sterelny, 2001; Suddendorf, 1999; Suddendorf and Whiten, 2001; Tomasello, 1999). See Glenberg (1997) on the difficulty of decoupling and Nichols and Stich (2003) on the "possible world box."

8. These domains do indeed show greatly restricted variance among people (e.g., Anderson, 2005; Baron-Cohen, 1995; Reber, 1992, 1993; Reber, Walkenfeld, and Hernstadt, 1991; Saffran, Aslin, and Newport, 1996; Vinter and Detable, 2003; Vinter and Perruchet, 2000; Zacks, Hasher, and Sanft, 1982); however, this not just true of the Darwinian modules. It can be equally true of processes that have become highly overlearned with practice. Ackerman (1988) has demonstrated how the correlation with intelligence drops as a task becomes more thoroughly learned.

9. There may be a few select domains such as behavioral prediction (so-called theory of mind) in which decoupling is not so cognitively demanding because it has been built in by evolution. The speculation that the raw ability to sustain mental simulations while keeping the relevant representations decoupled is likely the key aspect of the brain's computational power that is being assessed by measures of fluid intelligence (see Stanovich, 2001a, 2004) is suggested because the correlation between fluid intelligence and executive functioning is substantial (Baddeley, 1992; Baddeley, Chincotta, and Adlam, 2001; Duncan, et al., 2000; Fuster, 1990; Gernsbacher and Faust, 1991; Goldman-Rakic, 1992; Gray, Chabris, and Braver, 2003; Hasher, Zacks, and May, 1999; Kane, 2003; Kane and Engle, 2002; Salthouse, Atkinson, and Berish, 2003), as is the correlation between intelligence and working memory (Colom, Rebollo, Palacios, Juan-Espinosa, and Kyllonen, 2004; Conway, Cowan, Bunting, Therriault, and Minkoff, 2002; Conway, Kane, and Engle, 2003; Engle, 2002; Engle, Tuholski, Laughlin, and Conway, 1999; Geary, 2005; Kane, Bleckley, Conway, and Engle, 2001; Kane and Engle, 2003; Kane, Hambrick, and Conway, 2005; Kane, Hambrick, Tuholski, Wilhelm, Payne, and Engle, 2004; Lepine, Barrouillet, and Camos, 2005; Sub, Oberauer, Wittmann, Wilhelm, and Schulze, 2002).

10. My view of individual differences in cognitive decoupling as the key operation assessed by measures of fluid intelligence was anticipated by Thurstone (1927), who

also stressed the idea that intelligence was related to inhibition of automatic responses: "Intelligence is therefore the capacity of abstraction, which is an inhibitory process. In the intelligent moment the impulse is inhibited while it is still only partially specified, while it is still only loosely organized. . . . The trial-and-error choice and elimination, in intelligent conduct, is carried out with alternatives that are so incomplete and so loosely organized that they point only toward types of behaviour without specifying the behaviour in detail" (p. 159).

11. On levels of analysis in cognitive science, see Anderson (1990, 1991), Bermudez (2001), Dennett (1978, 1987), Levelt (1995), Marr (1982), Newell (1982, 1990), Oaksford and Chater (1995), Pollock (1995), Pylyshyn (1984), Sloman (1993), Sloman and Chrisley (2003), and Sterelny (1990). The terms for the levels of analysis are diverse. For a discussion of this and the arguments behind my choice of the term *algorithmic*, see Stanovich (1999, 2004).

12. On the typical versus optimal/maximal distinction, see Ackerman (1994, 1996; Ackerman and Heggestad, 1997; Ackerman and Kanfer, 2004); see also Cronbach (1949); Matthews, Zeidner, and Roberts (2002).

13. Various authors discuss thinking dispositions (e.g., Ackerman and Heggestad, 1997; Baron, 1985, 2000; Cacioppo et al., 1996; Dole and Sinatra, 1998; Kruglanski and Webster, 1996; Norris and Ennis, 1989; Perkins, 1995; Schommer, 1990; Stanovich, 1999; Sternberg, 1997c, 2003b; Sternberg and Grigorenko, 1997; Strathman et al., 1994).

14. One reason for endorsing a tripartite structure is that breakdowns in cognitive functioning in the three kinds of minds manifest very differently. For example, disruptions in algorithmic-level functioning are apparent in general impairments in intellectual ability of the type that cause intellectual disability (what used to be called mental retardation). And these disruptions vary quite continuously. Disruptions to the autonomous mind often reflect damage to cognitive modules that result in very discontinuous cognitive dysfunction such as autism or the agnosias and alexias. They often concern so-called subpersonal functions—micro-processing operations rather than the beliefs and goals of the whole person. In contrast, disorders of the reflective mind concern just that—the goals and large-scale actions of the whole person. Difficulties of the reflective mind are present in many psychiatric disorders (particularly those such as delusions) which involve impairments of rationality (see Bermudez, 2001).

15. These correlations are summarized in a variety of publications (e.g., Ackerman and Heggestad, 1997; Austin and Deary, 2002; Baron, 1982; Bates and Shieles, 2003; Cacioppo et al., 1996; Eysenck, 1994; Goff and Ackerman, 1992; Kanazawa, 2004; Kokis, Macpherson, Toplak, West, and Stanovich, 2002; Noftle and Robins, 2007; Reiss and Reiss, 2004; Zeidner and Matthews, 2000). Furthermore, the correlations that do occur are more often with Gc than with Gf (Ackerman and Heggestad, 1997; Matthews et al., 2002)

16. On thinking dispositions and the calibration of ambiguous evidence, see Kardash and Scholes (1996) and Schommer (1990). Our argument evaluation task is described in several publications (Stanovich and West, 1997, 1998c; Sá, West, and Stanovich, 1999).

17. One type of problem in this genre of research involves having subjects choose between contradictory car purchase recommendations—one from a large-sample survey of car buyers and the other the heartfelt and emotional testimony of a single friend. For other problems using this type of paradigm, see Fong, Krantz, and Nisbett (1986). For individual differences results using this paradigm, see Kokis et al. (2002) and Stanovich and West (1998c).

18. See Sá and Stanovich (2001), Stanovich (1999), Stanovich and West (2000), and Toplak and Stanovich (2002). See also research from other laboratories (Bruine de Bruin, Parker, and Fischhoff, 2007; Parker and Fischhoff, 2005).

19. On the study of self-discipline, see Duckworth and Seligman (2005). There have been many studies linking conscientiousness to important outcome variables (Goff and Ackerman, 1992; Higgins et al., 2007; Ozer and Benet-Martinez, 2006). Tetlock's work is described in his book *Expert Political Judgment* (2005). On the study of poor decision-making outcomes, see Bruine de Bruin et al. (2007).

20. However, working in the other direction (to *attenuate* the magnitude of the correlations observed in the literature) is the fact that most studies had a restricted range of intelligence in their samples.

21. See studies by Klaczynski (1997; Klaczynski and Gordon, 1996; Klaczynski, Gordon, and Fauth, 1997; Klaczynski and Lavallee, 2005; Klaczynski and Robinson, 2000). The studies from my lab are reported in several papers (Macpherson and Stanovich, 2007; Sá, Kelley, Ho, and Stanovich, 2005; Toplak and Stanovich, 2003). On informal reasoning more generally, see the work of Kuhn (1991, 2005) and Perkins (1985; Perkins et al., 1991).

22. For a discussion of the term *mindware* see Perkins (1995).

23. There are many sources (many written by conservative commentators) that converge in their characterization of Bush's mental tendencies (Barnes, 2006; Draper, 2007; Frum, 2003; Kessler, 2004; Suskind, 2006; Thomas and Wolffe, 2005; Will, 2005; Woodward, 2006). The consistency in these reports is overwhelming. For example, David Kay, one of the world's leading experts on weapons inspections, gave a briefing to Bush at the height of the controversy about whether there were weapons of mass destruction in Iraq. Reporter Bob Woodward relates that "Kay left the meeting almost shocked at Bush's lack of inquisitiveness" (p. 237). Ron Suskind, in his book on America's security concerns after September 11, reports senior White House staff members worrying *"was he reading the materials, was he thinking things through?* [italics in original]. . . . Left unfettered, and unchallenged, were his instincts, his 'gut,' as he often says, and an unwieldy aggressiveness that he'd long been cautioned to contain" (pp. 72–73). This reliance on instincts and gut feelings over knowledge,

information, and thought is a recurring theme among those who know Bush, even among his stoutest defenders. For example, Bob Woodward relates that in an August 20, 2002, interview, Bush himself mentioned instincts as his guides to decision making literally dozens of times. At one point, Bush said to Woodward, "I'm not a textbook player, I'm a gut player" (p. 11).

Bush is famously incapable of self-criticism. In an April 13, 2004, presidential press conference, a questioner asked him: "In the last campaign, you were asked a question about the biggest mistake you'd made in your life, and you used to like to joke that it was trading Sammy Sosa. You've looked back before 9-11 for what mistakes might have been made. After 9-11, what would your biggest mistake be, would you say, and what lessons have [you] learned from it?" Bush's reply betrayed his problems with counterfactual thinking, his overconfidence, and his reluctance to self-examine. He told the questioner, "I wish you'd have given me this written question ahead of time so I could plan for it. John, I'm sure historians will look back and say, gosh, he could've done it better this way or that way. You know, I just—I'm sure something will pop into my head here in the midst of this press conference, with all the pressure of trying to come up with answer, but it hasn't yet."

There is also consensus among commentators that Bush hates doubt and encourages certainty. General Richard B. Myers, chairman of the Joint Chiefs of Staff during the opening of the Iraq war, reported that "when any doubt started to creep into the small, windowless Situation Room, the president almost stomped it out" (Woodward, 2006, p. 371).

24. The situation regarding crystallized intelligence—Gc—is probably complex in this case. Generally, Gc is related to Gf (see Schweizer and Koch, 2002). However, Gc is also related to the thinking disposition openness to experience (Ackerman and Heggestad, 1997; Bates and Shieles, 2003), in which clearly, given the commentaries I have just reviewed, Bush would be quite low. It is thought that this disposition toward openness leads people to read and to collect the type of information that makes for high Gc. Bush is low on openness and, consistent with what is known about the correlates of that thinking disposition, he does not read nor is he a compulsive information collector. Quite the opposite. All of this would depress his score on a measure of crystallized intelligence below what would be expected from someone with his fluid intelligence, age, social class, and educational peers. Nonetheless, given his university education and social position, compared to a nationally representative sample that forms the norming group for an IQ test, he might well still be average or slightly above on Gc. *Most* Americans are quite ill informed (Jacoby, 2008; Whittington, 1991).

25. Interestingly, biographers of Bush's father, George H. W. Bush, indicate that he by no means shared the extreme cognitive inflexibility of his son. Unlike his son, George H. W. Bush assembled foreign policy advisers of mixed views and listened to opposing ideas before making decisions (Naftali, 2007). Famously, he did not

proceed to Baghdad and occupy Iraq after Operation Desert Storm in 1991. He reversed himself and broke a pledge not to raise taxes when economic conditions changed (which perhaps cost him the subsequent election). His nuanced and restrained behavior during the collapse of the Soviet Union and the eastern bloc is viewed by historians as aiding international relations (Naftali, 2007).

4 Cutting Intelligence Down to Size

1. Broad theories include aspects of functioning that are captured by the vernacular term *intelligence* whether or not these aspects are actually measured by existing tests of intelligence (Ceci, 1996; Gardner, 1983, 1999, 2006a; Perkins, 1995; Sternberg, 1985, 1988, 1997a, 2003b). Narrow theories, in contrast, confine the concept of intelligence to the set of mental abilities actually tested on existing IQ tests. It is important to note that the issue should not be framed dichotomously as broad theories of intelligence versus narrow theories. This is because, significantly, broad theorists do not agree among themselves. For example, Gardner (1999) warns that "Sternberg and I agree more on our criticism of standard intelligence theory than on the direction that new theoretical work should follow" (p. 101).

2. For example, I am not averse to Sternberg's (1988, 1997a, 2003b) concern for disrupting the obsessive societal focus on MAMBIT. We do, however, differ on strategies—he being an advocate of stretching the term *intelligence* to de-emphasize MAMBIT and my preference being to *limit* the concept *intelligence* to MAMBIT in order to highlight other terms already in folk psychology that have languished unnecessarily (*rationality*). This difference in strategy explains why we have disagreed about the appropriate terminology in which to couch our arguments (Stanovich, 1993a, 1993b, 1994a, 1994b; Sternberg, 1993, 1994). Nevertheless, his concepts of practical intelligence, creative intelligence, and wisdom encompass some of the mental properties that I wish to highlight by my emphasis on rationality (see Stanovich, 2001b; Sternberg, 2001, 2003b). Cognitive psychology has been almost exclusively focused on the algorithmic mind and, until quite recently, has given short shrift to the reflective mind. However, Sternberg has been among a handful of investigators (e.g., Ackerman and Heggestad, 1997; Baron, 1982, 1985; Keating, 1990; Moshman, 1994, 2004; Perkins, 1995; Perkins, Jay, and Tishman, 1993; Perkins and Ritchhart, 2004; Stanovich, 1999) who have emphasized concepts such as thinking dispositions (see Sternberg, 1997c; Sternberg and Grigorenko, 1997; Sternberg and Ruzgis, 1994). By and large, psychometric instruments such as IQ tests have tapped cognitive capacities almost exclusively and have ignored cognitive styles, thinking dispositions, and wisdom. Importantly, Baron (1988) argues that, in ignoring dispositions, the IQ concept "has distorted our understanding of thinking. It has encouraged us to believe that the only general determinants of good thinking are capacities, and this attitude has led to the neglect of general dispositions" (p. 122)—a point Sternberg has emphasized in many of his own writings (e.g., Sternberg, 1997c, 2001, 2003b).

3. On the use of the intelligence term as a motivational tool see Bereiter (2002), Klein (1997), and Willingham (2004). The conceptual coherence of concepts such as social intelligence, emotional intelligence, and practical intelligence continues to be debated in the literature (Brody, 2003, 2004; Cherness, Extein, Goleman, and Weissberg, 2006; Gardner and Moran, 2006; Goleman, 1995, 2006; Keating, 1978; Kihlstrom and Cantor, 2000; Klein, 1997, 2003; Matthews et al., 2002; Sternberg, 2003a, 2006; Visser, Ashton, and Vernon, 2006; Waterhouse, 2006).

4. Of course, Gardner (1983, 1999) stresses exactly the opposite and emphasizes the independence of his different "intelligences"—that someone high in logical-mathematical intelligence is not necessarily high in musical intelligence. Gardner (1999) also correctly emphasizes the nonfungibility of the intelligences—that one cannot substitute for the other. However, Willingham (2004) has argued that Gardner's use of the "intelligence" terminology has encouraged just the opposite view among teachers: "It is also understandable that readers believed that some of the intelligences must be at least partially interchangeable. No one would think that the musically talented child would necessarily be good at math. But refer to the child as possessing 'high musical intelligence,' and it's a short step to the upbeat idea that the mathematics deficit can be circumvented by the intelligence in another area—after all, both are intelligences" (Willingham, 2004, p. 24).

5. I reiterate here the warning that all broad theories of intelligence are not compatible with each other. For example, Gardner (1999) rejects the concepts of creative intelligence, moral intelligence, and emotional intelligence—types of "intelligences" that are quite popular with some other broad theorists. He goes on to warn that "we cannot hijack the word intelligence so that it becomes all things to all people—the psychometric equivalent of the Holy Grail" (p. 210). But in fact, if we concatenate all of the broad theories that have been proposed by various theorists—with all of their different "intelligences"—under the umbrella term *intelligence*, we will have encompassed virtually all of mental life. Intelligence will be "everything the brain does"—a vacuous concept.

6. Broad theorists might argue that there are higher correlations among the features of automobiles than there are among the intelligences they propose. I think the data on this conjecture are not in yet (Klein, 1997; Willingham, 2004), and even if a quantitative difference were obtained, I doubt that it would substantially reduce the force of the thought experiment. The point is that when Gardner (1999) states, "I put forth the intelligences as a new definition of human nature, cognitively speaking" (p. 44), he is adding positive valence to the term *intelligence* and to its closest associates: MAMBIT and the IQ tests themselves.

7. I cannot resist an "inside baseball" professional remark here. The field of psychology has for decades been plagued by clinical training programs that have had to be dragged kicking and screaming into the scientific world (Dawes, 1994; Lilienfeld, 2007). I would ask advocates of broad definitions of intelligence if they can *really* imagine, in the near future, thousands of clinical instructors in hundreds of pro-

grams vigorously admonishing their students, who are being taught to administer the Wechsler, in the following words: "Now remember, *never ever* call this assessment intelligence—instead call it analytic capacity or logical-verbal ability, but never *just* call it intelligence!" Of course, my point is that hell will freeze over before clinical psychology stops calling MAMBIT intelligence, and this must be understood as another huge inertial force in our profession in addition to the psychometric test industry.

8. To say that "there is every indication that work in the traditional paradigm is carving nature at its joints" is not to deny Gardner's (1983, 1999) point that there may be additional ways of carving nature that we have been missing; it is only to stress the progress that has been made within the traditional paradigm. Also, because I am focusing here on progress on the psychometric study of intelligence—individual differences—another caveat is in order. Whereas a cognitive scientist might focus on a host of processes when analyzing performance on a particular task, the focus of the psychometrician will be on the (often) much smaller set of information process-ing operations where large individual differences arise. So when a psychometrician says that process X is the key process in task Z, he or she means that process X is where most of the individual differences arise from, *not* that process X is all we need to know to understand how task Z is accomplished. Task Z may require many more information processing operations, but these are of less interest to the psychometri-cian if they are not sources of individual differences.

9. The overlap is not 100 percent, but regression weights in structural equation models are on the order of .7–.8 (Kane, Hambrick, and Conway, 2005).

10. This conclusion is often obscured in introductory presentations of intelligence research to beginning students. Introductory psychology textbooks often present to students the broad versus narrow theory of intelligence controversy—usually with a bias toward the former, because it is easier to present nontechnically. Later in the same chapter, the textbook will often make reference to "how difficult it is to mea-sure something as complex as intelligence." But, of course, there is an inconsistency here. Intelligence is *not* difficult to measure on the narrow view—it is the broad view that causes the measurement problems. We have not only tests, but laboratory measures as well that index MAMBIT pretty precisely in terms of information pro-cessing capabilities. It is a point in favor of the narrow concept that we have a reason-ably stable construct of it and ways to reliably measure it.

11. On the Flynn effect, see Flynn (1984, 1987, 2007) and Neisser (1998). My own view of the Flynn effect is that schooling and modernity in general have increased decon-textualizing thinking styles and also the use of language as a decoupling tool (Evans and Over, 2004). These mechanisms represent mindware (like rehearsal strategies in short-term memory) that can increase algorithmic-level functioning—particularly the decoupling operation—by making it less capacity demanding and unnatural. Schooler (1998) explores a similar hypothesis in the Neisser volume (see also Green-

field, 1998; Williams, 1998). Interestingly, in a recent book, Flynn (2007) has altered his earlier position and now views the IQ gains as real—the result of the spread of scientific thinking making hypothetical thought more habitual.

12. Issues surrounding issues of prevalence can be complex (see Barbaresi et al., 2005; Friend, 2005; Parsell, 2004; Gernsbacher, Dawson, and Goldsmith, 2005; Gordon, Lewandowski, and Keiser, 1999; Kelman and Lester, 1997; Lilienfeld and Arkowitz, 2007). I would, however, insert a couple of additional caveats here. First, studies have indicated that ADHD is in fact associated with somewhat lower than normal intelligence (Barkley, 1998), but this empirical finding is not stressed at all on websites and informational packets directed to parents. Second, the tendency for information directed to the public to stress the high intelligence of individuals with learning disabilities is scientifically unjustified, because if learning disabilities were properly diagnosed, they would be just as prevalent in low-IQ as in high-IQ individuals (Stanovich, 2005; Stuebing et al., 2002).

5 Why Intelligent People Doing Foolish Things Is No Surprise

1. The figures used here are from Zweig (2002).

2. It appears that loss aversion (see Kahneman and Tversky, 1979) is an affective forecasting error—when the events actually occur, the aversive valence of the loss is in fact not twice that of the gain (Kermer, Driver-Linn, Wilson, and Gilbert, 2006). On myopic loss aversion see Thaler, Tversky, Kahneman, and Schwartz (1997). On the tendency to explain chance events, particularly those that occur in markets, see Malkiel (2004), Nickerson (2004), and Taleb (2001, 2007).

3. Several classic papers in psychology established the idea of humans as cognitive misers (Dawes, 1976; Simon, 1955, 1956; Taylor, 1981; Tversky and Kahneman, 1974).

4. Of course, evolution guarantees rationality in the dictionary sense of "the quality or state of being able to reason" because evolution built the human brain. What I mean here is that evolution does not guarantee rationality in the sense the term is used throughout cognitive science—as maximizing subjective expected utility (Gauthier, 1975). There is a literature on the nature of human long-term interests and their possible divergence from the short-term strategies of evolutionary adaptation (Ainslie, 2001; de Sousa, 2007; Haslam and Baron, 1994; Loewenstein, 1996; Nozick, 1993; Oatley, 1992; Parfit, 1984; Pinker, 1997; Sabini and Silver, 1998; Stanovich, 2004). On natural selection as a "better than" mechanism, see Cosmides and Tooby (1996, p. 11). Ridley (2000) spins this point another way, calling evolution "short-termish" because it is concerned with immediate advantage rather than long-term strategy. Human rationality, in contrast, must incorporate the long-term interests of the individual.

5. On affective forecasting, see Gilbert (2006), Kahneman, Diener, and Schwarz (1999), and Wilson and Gilbert (2005).

6. On the culturally derived nature of rational standards, see Jepson, Krantz, and Nisbett (1983), Krantz (1981), and Thagard and Nisbett (1983). On changes in the environment and their implications for fitness and human goals, see Richerson and Boyd (2005) and Stanovich (2004).

7. Being a cognitive miser is the universal default in naturalistic situations. When cued that more intense cognitive effort is necessary, those of higher intelligence will have an advantage due to their greater computational ability.

8. Two critical caveats are in order here. Most (but not all) of the studies that I cite in this book employed university students as subjects. The higher and lower intelligence groups that I am discussing are, in most instances, partitionings of the upper half and lower half of the subject sample. Thus, the lower-IQ individuals are not low-IQ in an absolute sense. They simply are of lower intelligence relative to their counterparts in the particular study. The second point is related to the first. The magnitude of the correlations involving intelligence obtained in these investigations is undoubtedly attenuated because of restriction of range. Again, this is because most investigations employed university students as subjects. Nevertheless, this caveat about attenuation itself needs contextualization. Certainly, it is true that individuals with average and above average cognitive ability are over-represented in samples composed entirely of university students. Nevertheless, the actual range in cognitive ability found among college students in the United States is quite large. In the past 30 years, the percentage of 25- to-29-years-olds in the United States who have attended college has increased by 50 percent. By 2002, 58 percent of these young adults had completed at least one or more years of college, and 29 percent had received at least a bachelor's degree (Trends, 2003). Finally, the fact that the range of the samples studied is somewhat restricted makes many of the findings (of near zero correlations between intelligence and rational thought) no less startling. It is quite unexpected that, across even the upper two thirds of cognitive ability, there would be little relation between rational thought and intelligence.

9. See Postman (1988, pp. 86–87).

6 The Cognitive Miser

1. The Anne problem, and others like it, are discussed in Levesque (1986, 1989), and our work on these types of problem is discussed in Toplak and Stanovich (2002). On disjunctive reasoning, see Johnson-Laird (2006), Shafir (1994), and Toplak and Stanovich (2002). The tendency toward default processing that is computationally simple is not restricted to problems that are themselves simple. It is displayed in more complex problems as well (see Evans, 2007; Kahneman, 2003a; Stanovich, 1999, 2004; Taleb, 2007).

2. The bat and ball problem is described in Kahneman and Frederick (2002) and the studies of MIT, Princeton, and Harvard students in Frederick (2005).

3. See Kahneman (2003a) on accessibility and how it is substituted for more complex

judgments of probability. On the California earthquake example, see Kahneman and Frederick (2002), and Tversky and Kahneman (1983).

4. The literature on affective valuation is extensive (e.g., Forgas, 1995; Frederick, 2002; Loewenstein, Weber, Hsee, and Welch, 2001; Oatley, 1992, 2004; Rottenstreich and Hsee, 2001; Schwarz and Clore, 2003; Slovic, Finucane, Peters, and MacGregor, 2002; Slovic and Peters, 2006). On the shock study, see Rottenstreich and Hsee (2001). On public valuation studies, see Kahneman and Frederick (2002). The panda study is from Hsee and Rottenstreich (2004).

5. There are numerous ways to calculate travel risk, but driving consistently looks extremely dangerous across various metrics (Galovski, Malta, and Blanchard, 2006; National Safety Council, 1990, 2001; Sivak, 2002; Sivak and Flannagan, 2003; Sunstein, 2002). The post–September 11, 2001, travel statistics are from Gigerenzer (2004) and Sivak and Flanagan (2003). On diabetes versus staph infections, see Fountain (2006).

6. Yamagishi (1997). On the effect of vividness, see Slovic (2007).

7. On the money illusion, see Kahneman, Knetsch, and Thaler (1986) and Shafir, Diamond, and Tversky (1997). Raghubir and Srivastava (2002) reported the foreign currency study. Wertenbroch, Soman, and Chattopadhyay (2007) have shown that the face value effect can be dependent on budgetary limitations that people use as reference points. Their findings complexify our understanding of the money illusion but do not change my point here—that the money illusion is an example of cognitive miser tendencies in human information processing.

8. On the usefulness of heuristic processing, see Gigerenzer (2007); Gladwell (2005); Klein (1998); McKenzie (1994); Pinker (1997); Todd and Gigerenzer (2007).

9. Classic work in the psychology of anchoring is described in Tversky and Kahneman (1974). As always in cognitive psychology, after the initial discovery of an important phenomenon, our understanding of the phenomenon quickly "complexifies." For example, sometimes anchoring appears to derive from insufficient adjustment from an anchor, and other times it is due to the increased accessibility of anchor-consistent information (the former when the anchor is self-generated and the latter in the standard paradigm; see Epley and Gilovich, 2006). A more fine-grained view of how anchoring and adjustment works is provided in many other publications (see Brewer and Chapman, 2002; Epley and Gilovich, 2004, 2006; Jacowitz and Kahneman, 1995; Jasper and Chirstman, 2005; LeBoeuf and Shafir, 2006; Mussweiler and Englich, 2005; Mussweiler, Englich, and Strack, 2004; Wilson, Houston, Etling, and Brekke, 1996). The nuances surrounding our current understanding of anchoring effects have no bearing on the very basic points I make about anchoring in this book. The study of the real estate agents is reported in Northcraft and Neale (1987). For the study of actual judges being affected by anchoring, see Englich, Mussweiler, and Strack (2006).

10. Several studies have shown the less-is-more context effect (Bartels, 2006; Slovic

et al., 2002; Slovic and Peters, 2006). On evaluability, see Hsee (1996); Hsee, Loewenstein, Blount, and Bazerman (1999); and Hsee and Zhang (2004).

11. Todd and Gigerenzer (2007) use the term *default heuristic*. Several important papers discuss work on the status quo bias (Frederick, 2002; Hartman, Doane, and Woo, 1991; Kahneman, Knetsch, and Thaler, 1991; Samuelson and Zeckhauser, 1988; Thaler, 1980). It should be emphasized that it is an unthinking overuse of the default heuristic that is irrational. Many theorists have pointed out that in some situations it is rational to view defaults as the recommendations of a policy maker (Johnson and Goldstein, 2006; McKenzie, Liersch, and Finkelstein, 2006; Sunstein and Thaler, 2003).

12. Gigerenzer (2002, 2007; Brandstatter, Gigerenzer, and Hertwig, 2006; Gigerenzer and Goldstein, 1996; Todd and Gigerenzer, 2000, 2007) is an influential champion of this view (in rebuttal, see Evans, 2007; Kahneman and Tversky, 1996; Over, 2000; Stanovich, 2004). However, whether the heuristics studied by the Gigerenzer group fit the category of Type 1 processes is very doubtful (see Evans, 2007, and Kahneman and Frederick, 2002, for a discussion). Sterelny (2003) has written perceptively about the evolutionary significance of hostile environments. Writer Louis Menand (2004), in discussing work on the heuristics people use for voting decisions, contextualizes the use of heuristics in the manner that I do here: "Any time information is lacking or uncertain, a shortcut is generally better than nothing. But the shortcut itself is not a faster way of doing the math; it's a way of skipping the math altogether. My hunch that the coolest-looking stereo component is the best value simply does not reflect an intuitive grasp of electronics. My interest in a stereo is best served if I choose the finest sound for the money, as my interest in an election is best served if I choose the candidate whose policies are most likely to benefit me or the people I care about" (p. 95).

13. The chapter subtitled "How Ignorance Makes Us Smart" is in Gigerenzer and Todd (1999). The Wimbledon study is described in Todd and Gigerenzer (2007). See also Goldstein and Gigerenzer (1999, 2002). Bazerman (2001) discusses proper personal finance strategies, and the British bank example is in MacErlean (2002, p. 2).

14. Here is an example of how advocates of rational thinking often get caricatured. By the phrase "think through the alternatives" I obviously do not mean an exhaustive comparison and contrast of each of the thousands of mutual funds on offer. Instead, I mean thinking through each of the major *classes* of decision in this domain: load versus no-load funds; index funds versus managed funds; bond, stock, and cash allocation; the amount of foreign exposure; the amount of real estate and commodities exposure; etc. It is a common strategy to denigrate explicit rational thought by showing that a particular decision situation involves a combinatorial explosion beyond even what the largest computer could handle (pairwise comparison of 6000 mutual funds on X dimensions from Y different perspectives on Z different personal financial goals). But the advocates of rational strategies have no such ludicrous mechanical procedure in mind. Just because the comparison of thousands of funds is unfea-

sible does not mean that we should rely on a quick and dirty heuristic response in this important domain of personal finance. Between the exhaustive comparison and the quick and dirty heuristic is a middle ground where, in this domain for example, we would engage in extended explicit thought about a few key variables: tolerance for risk, age, current assets and debts, income needed in retirement, and a few other key factors.

15. Sinaceur, Heath, and Cole (2005).

7 Framing and the Cognitive Miser

1. See McCaffery and Baron (2004, 2006a, 2006b, especially 2006b) for discussions of their studies. My example is a simplified variant of the type of problem that appeared in their experiments. The child deduction example was originally discussed in Schelling (1984, pp. 18–20).

2. The rule of descriptive invariance is, according to Tversky and Kahneman (1986), that "variations of form that do not affect the actual outcomes should not affect the choice" (p. 253). For further discussions of descriptive invariance see Kahneman and Tversky (1984, 2000) and Tversky and Kahneman (1981). Beyond descriptive invariance, utility maximization requires adherence to a set of further axioms of choice (see Allingham, 2002; Dawes, 1998; Edwards, 1954; Jeffrey, 1983; Luce and Raiffa, 1957; Savage, 1954; von Neumann and Morgenstern, 1944; see Wu et al., 2004, for a review).

3. There have been several important papers on the equality heuristic (e.g., Frederick, 2002; Harris and Joyce, 1980; Messick, 1999; Messick and Schell, 1992).

4. The transplant study is discussed in Ubel (2000).

5. On the cognitive miser tendency to take a problem representation as "given," and on other aspects of framing effects discussed in this chapter, see the voluminous literature on framing effects in decision science (Kahneman and Tversky, 1984, 2000; Kuhberger, 1998; LeBoeuf and Shafir, 2003; Levin et al., 2002; Maule and Ville-joubert, 2007; McElroy and Seta, 2003; Simon, Fagley, and Halleran, 2004; Slovic, 1995; Tversky and Kahneman, 1981, 1986). This literature describes many paradigms not involving gambling at all and several involving real-world content (Epley, Mak, and Chen Idson, 2006; Friedrich, Lucas, and Hodell, 2005; McNeil, Pauker, Sox, and Tversky, 1982; Schneider, Burke, Solomonson, and Laurion, 2005). Decisions 1 and 2 are from Tversky and Kahneman (1986).

6. On coding options from a zero reference point, see also Markowitz (1952), and on the valuation of good and bad outcomes see Baumeister, Bratslavsky, Finkenauer, and Vohs (2001). Other key features of prospect theory are covered in Kahneman and Tversky (1979) and Tversky and Kahneman (1986, 1992).

7. Epley, Mak, and Chen Idson (2006). See also Epley (2008).

8. Thaler (1980). The operation of the default heuristic in insurance decisions is described in Johnson, Hershey, Meszaros, and Kunreuther (2000).

9. Friedrich, Lucas, and Hodell (2005).

10. Individual differences work on framing using both types of designs is not extensive, but the literature is growing (see Bruine de Bruin et al., 2007; Frederick, 2005; Le-Boeuf and Shafir, 2003; Parker and Fischhoff, 2005; Stanovich and West, 1998b, 1999, 2008b).

11. I will repeat here the caveat that the higher- and lower-intelligence groups that I am often discussing are, in most instances, partitionings of the upper half and lower half of a university sample. Thus, the lower-IQ individuals are not low-IQ in an absolute sense. Also, the magnitude of the correlations involving intelligence obtained in these investigations is undoubtedly attenuated because of restriction of range. Nonetheless, it is still quite striking that, across even the upper two-thirds of cognitive ability, there would be so little relation between crucial aspects of rational thought and intelligence.

12. See Bruine de Bruin et al. (2007); Parker and Fischhoff (2005); Stanovich and West (1999; 2008b); Toplak and Stanovich (2002).

8 Myside Processing

1. For the relevant crash statistics at the time the study was conducted, see NHTSA (2000), *Vehicle design versus aggressivity*, National Highway Traffic Safety Administration, U.S. Department of Transportation (DOT HS 809 194), Retrieved February 23, 2002, from NHTSAwebsite http://www-nrd.nhtsa.dot.gov/pdf/nrd-11/DOT_HS_809194.pdf.

2. Our study is reported in Stanovich and West (2008a). The Westen study is reported in Westen, Blagov, Kilts, and Hamann (2006). Related paradigms have been studied by our lab (Stanovich and West, 2007) and are discussed in a variety of sources (Kunda, 1990, 1999; Mele, 2003; Molden and Higgins, 2005; Perkins, Farady, and Bushey, 1991; Thagard, 2006). On the argument generation paradigm described in this chapter, see Baron (1995), Macpherson and Stanovich (2007), Perkins (1985), Toplak and Stanovich (2003).

3. The experiment evaluation paradigm has generated a small literature (Klaczynski, 1997; Klaczynski and Gordon, 1996; Klaczynski, Gordon, and Fauth, 1997; Klaczynski and Lavallee, 2005; Klaczynski and Robinson, 2000; Macpherson and Stanovich, 2007). Educational psychologist Deanna Kuhn has developed a structured interview to study myside bias in informal reasoning (Kuhn, 1991, 1992, 1993). Our study using the Kuhnian interview is reported in Sá et al. (2005).

4. On otherside processing being demanding, see Gilbert, Pelham, and Krull (1988). Taber and Lodge (2006) report one of the more comprehensive studies of various aspects of myside processing.

5. The knowledge calibration paradigm specifically, and belief calibration in general, have undergone three decades of research (e.g., Fischhoff, Slovic, and Lichtenstein, 1977; Griffin and Tversky, 1992; Koriat, Lichtenstein, and Fischhoff, 1980; Lichtenstein and Fischhoff, 1977; Schaefer, Williams, Goodie, and Campbell, 2004; Sieck and Arkes, 2005; Tetlock, 2005; Yates, Lee, and Bush, 1997). This literature and its

methodological complexities have been reviewed in several sources (Baron, 2000; Fischhoff, 1988; Griffin and Varey, 1996; Lichtenstein, Fischhoff, and Phillips, 1982).

6. These five questions were taken from Plous (1993) and Russo and Schoemaker (1989).

7. Overconfidence effects have been found in perceptual and motor domains (Baranski and Petrusic, 1994, 1995; West and Stanovich, 1997; Wright and Ayton, 1994), sports outcomes (Ronis and Yates, 1987), reading comprehension monitoring (Pressley and Ghatala, 1990), judging the sex of handwriting samples (Schneider, 1995), prediction of one's own behavior or life outcomes (Hoch, 1985; Vallone, Griffin, Lin, and Ross, 1990), and economic forecasts and political predictions (Åstebro, Jeffrey, and Adomdza, 2007; Braun and Yaniv, 1992; Tetlock, 2005). On the planning fallacy, see Buehler, Griffin, and Ross (2002). The Kahneman anecdote is from "A Short Course in Thinking About Thinking" by Daniel Kahneman, retrieved on 9/27/07 from http://www.edge.org/3rd_culture/kahneman07/kahneman07_index .html.

8. Cell phone use—even the use of hands-free phones—impairs driving ability to an extent that substantially increases the probability of an accident (McEvoy et al., 2005; Strayer and Drews, 2007; Strayer and Johnston, 2001). The Canada Safety Council study is discussed in Perreaux (2001). On most drivers thinking they are above average, see Svenson (1981). Groopman (2007) discusses overconfidence among physicians.

9. The study of the 800,000 students is described by Friedrich (1996). See Kruger and Dunning (1999) for the study of the test takers. Biased self-assessment research has many methodological and statistical complexities that are well discussed by Moore (2007) and by Larrick, Burson, and Soll (2007). Many of the earlier interpretations of this research are undergoing renewed debate. Nonetheless, for a sampling of the research that I am drawing from, see: Dunning, Heath, and Suls (2004); Dunning, Johnson, Ehrlinger and Kruger (2003); Friedrich (1996); Kruger and Dunning (1999); Larrick et al. (2007); Moore and Small (2007); and Myers (1990). Larrick et al. (2007) and Moore and Small (2007) discuss the complex issue of how overestimates of one's own performance are related to overestimates of one's own performance relative to others. Regardless of the outcome of these theoretical disputes, both phenomena seem to result from myside processing that always makes one's own beliefs the focal model for subsequent processing.

10. Much research on the so-called bias blind spot is quite recent (Ehrlinger, Gilovich, and Ross, 2005; Pronin, 2006; Pronin, Lin, and Ross, 2002).

11. The illusion of control is described in Langer (1975). The study of the traders is reported by Fenton-O'Creevy, Nicholson, Soane, and Willman (2003).

12. The e-mail communication studies were conducted by Kruger, Epley, Parker, and Ng (2005).

13. On feature creep and feature fatigue, see Rae-Dupree (2007) and Surowiecki (2007).

14. But the designers are not solely to blame here. As in many areas of human affairs (see Gilbert, 2006), at the time they are choosing an electronic device, people do not know what will make them happy when they use it. Surowiecki (2007) discusses research indicating that people often think that more features will make them happier and thus prefer feature-laden products only to get the product home and find out that what they really wanted was simplicity. That many people really do want simplicity at the time of use is indicated by a study in which it was found that individuals returning an electronic device because it was too complicated spent just twenty minutes with it before giving up!

15. Several sources review aspects of the myside processing literature (Baron, 1995, 2000; Kunda, 1990, 1999; Mele, 2001; Molden and Higgins, 2005; Perkins et al., 1991; Thagard, 2006).

16. To summarize the individual differences research, intelligence differences in myside bias in the Ford Explorer–type problem are virtually nonexistent (Stanovich and West, 2007, 2008a). In the argument generation paradigms, they are also nonexistent (Macpherson and Stanovich, 2007; Toplak and Stanovich, 2003). Very low correlations between intelligence and myside bias are obtained in experiment evaluation paradigms (Klaczynski and Lavallee, 2005; Klaczynski and Robinson, 2000; Macpherson and Stanovich, 2007). Certain aspects of myside processing in the Kuhnian interview paradigm show modest relations with intelligence, but many others do not (Sá et al., 2005). Moderate (negative) correlations have been found between overconfidence effects and intelligence (Bruine de Bruin et al., 2007; Pallier, Wilkinson, Danthiir, Kleitman, Knezevic, Stankov, and Roberts, et al., 2002; Parker and Fischhoff, 2005; Stanovich and West, 1998c).

9 A Different Pitfall of the Cognitive Miser

1. See Gladwell (2000).

2. On multiple-minds views of cognition and the concept of cognitive override, see Chapter 3, Evans (2003, 2007), and Stanovich (2004).

3. There are discussions of the trolley problem and its philosophical and psychological implications in Foot (1967); Hauser (2006); Mikhail (2007); Petrinovich et al. (1993); Thompson (1976, 1985, 1990); Unger (1996); and Waldmann and Dietrich (2007). Greene's work is described in several sources (Greene, 2005; Greene, Nystrom, Engell, Darley, and Cohen, 2004; Greene, Sommerville, Nystrom, Darley, and Cohen, 2001).

4. The confabulatory tendencies of the conscious mind, as well as its tendency toward egocentric attribution, are discussed in, e.g., Calvin (1990); Dennett (1991, 1996); Evans and Wason (1976); Gazzaniga (1998); Johnson (1991); Moscovitch (1989); Nisbett and Ross (1980); Wegner (2002); T. Wilson (2002); Wolford, Miller, and Gazzaniga (2000); and Zajonc (2001); Zajonc and Markus (1982).

5. The use of the term *hot cognition* for affect-laden cognition was the idea of psychologist Robert Abelson (Abelson, 1963; Roseman and Read, 2007). When the

term *cold cognition* is used to label a task it does not mean that emotion is *totally* absent, only that affect is much less involved than it is in situations characterized as involving hot cognition.

6. Epstein has conducted several studies using the task (Denes-Raj and Epstein, 1994; Kirkpatrick and Epstein, 1992; Pacini and Epstein, 1999). For information on children's responses to the task, see Kokis et al. (2002).

7. There has been a substantial amount of work on syllogisms where the validity of the syllogism conflicts with the believability of the conclusion (see, e.g., De Neys, 2006; Dias, Roazzi, and Harris, 2005; Evans, 2002b, 2007; Evans, Barston, and Pollard, 1983; Evans and Curtis-Holmes, 2005; Evans and Feeney, 2004; Goel and Dolan, 2003; Markovits and Nantel, 1989; Sá et al., 1999; Simoneau and Markovits, 2003; Stanovich and West, 1998c).

8. Several studies on individual differences in conflict-type syllogisms have been conducted in my laboratory (Kokis et al., 2002; Sá et al., 1999; Macpherson and Stanovich, 2007; Stanovich and West, 1998c, 2008a).

9. See Ainslie (2001, 2005), Baumeister and Vohs (2003, 2007), Loewenstein, Read, and Baumeister (2003), Rachlin (2000), and Stanovich (2004).

10. Delayed-reward paradigms have been much investigated in psychology (Ainslie, 2001; Green and Myerson, 2004; Kirby and Herrnstein, 1995; Kirby, Winston, and Santiesteban, 2005; Loewenstein et al., 2003; McClure, Laibson, Loewenstein, and Cohen, 2004; Rachlin, 1995, 2000). The example is from Herrnstein (1990). There is a large literature on so-called akrasia (weakness of the will) in philosophy (Charlton, 1988; Davidson, 1980; Stroud and Tappolet, 2003) and an equally large literature on problems of self-control in psychology, economics, and neurophysiology (Ainslie, 1992, 2001; Baumeister and Vohs, 2003, 2007; Berridge, 2003; Elster, 1979; Loewenstein et al., 2003; Mischel, Shoda, and Rodriguez, 1989; O'Donoghue and Rabin, 2000; Rachlin, 1995, 2000). Problems of behavioral regulation that characterize various clinical syndromes are also the subject of intense investigation (Barkley, 1998; Castellanos, Sonuga-Barke, Milham, and Tannock, 2006; Tannock, 1998).

11. There are many versions of the bundling idea in the literature (Ainslie, 2001; Loewenstein and Prelec, 1991; Prelec and Bodner, 2003; Read, Loewenstein, and Rabin, 1999; Rachlin, 2000; but see Khan and Dhar, 2007).

10 Mindware Gaps

1. There is a substantial literature on the history of facilitated communication (Dillon 1993; Gardner, 2001; Jacobson, Mulick, and Schwartz, 1995; Spitz, 1997; Twachtman-Cullen, 1997) and, by now, a number of studies showing it to be a pseudoscientific therapy (Burgess, Kirsch, Shane, Niederauer, Graham, and Bacon, 1998; Cummins and Prior, 1992; Hudson, Melita, and Arnold, 1993; Jacobson, Foxx, and Mulick, 2004; Mostert, 2001; Wegner, Fuller, and Sparrow, 2003). On autism, see Baron-Cohen (2005) and Frith (2003).

2. My account of these two cases is taken from *The Economist* (January 24, 2004,

p. 49), *The Daily Telegraph* (London) (June 12, 2003), *The Times* (London) (June 12, 2003), and Watkins (2000). On sudden infant death syndrome, see Hunt (2001) and Lipsitt (2003).

3. The literature on heuristics and biases contains many such examples (e.g., Baron, 2000; Evans, 2007; Gilovich et al., 2002; Johnson-Laird, 2006; Kahneman and Tversky, 2000; Koehler and Harvey, 2004; Nickerson, 2004; Shafir, 2003; Sunstein, 2002; Tversky and Kahneman, 1974, 1983).

4. On Thomas Bayes, see Stigler (1983, 1986). On the Bayesian formulas as commonly used in psychology, see Fischhoff and Beyth-Marom (1983).

5. It is important to emphasize here a point that will become clear in later chapters. It is that the problems in probabilistic reasoning discussed in this chapter are not merely confined to the laboratory or to story problems of the type I will be presenting. They are not just errors in a parlor game. We will see in other examples throughout this book that the errors crop up in such important domains as financial planning, medical decision making, career decisions, family planning, resource allocation, tax policy, and insurance purchases. The extensive literature on the practical importance of these reasoning errors is discussed in a variety of sources (Åstebro, Jeffrey, and Adomdza, 2007; Baron, 1998, 2000; Belsky and Gilovich, 1999; Camerer, 2000; Chapman and Elstein, 2000; Dawes, 2001; Fridson, 1993; Gilovich, 1991; Groopman, 2007; Hastie and Dawes, 2001; Hilton, 2003; Holyoak and Morrison, 2005; Kahneman and Tversky, 2000; Koehler and Harvey, 2004; Lichtenstein and Slovic, 2006; Margolis, 1996; Myers, 2002; Prentice, 2003; Schneider and Shanteau, 2003; Sunstein, 2002, 2005; Taleb, 2001, 2007; Ubel, 2000).

6. This probability is calculated using an alternative form of the Bayesian formula:

$$P(H/D) = P(H)P(D/H)/[P(H)P(D/H) + P(\sim H)P(D/\sim H)]$$
$$P(H/D) = (.5)(.99)/[(.5)(.99) + (.5)(.90)] = .5238$$

7. Doherty and Mynatt (1990).

8. The covariation detection paradigm is described in a number of publications (e.g., Levin et al., 1993; Shanks, 1995; Stanovich and West, 1998d; Wasserman, Dorner, and Kao, 1990). Such errors have been found among medical personnel (Chapman and Elstein, 2000; Groopman, 2007; Kern and Doherty, 1982; Wolf, Gruppen, and Billi, 1985).

9. The literature on the four-card selection task (Wason, 1966, 1968) has been reviewed in several sources (e.g., Evans, Newstead, and Byrne, 1993; Evans and Over, 2004; Manktelow, 1999; Newstead and Evans, 1995; Stanovich, 1999). There have been many theories proposed to explain why subjects respond to it as they do (Evans, 1972, 1996, 1998, 2006b, 2007; Hardman, 1998; Johnson-Laird, 1999, 2006; Klauer, Stahl, and Erdfelder, 2007; Liberman and Klar, 1996; Margolis, 1987; Oaksford and Chater, 1994, 2007; Sperber, Cara and Girotto, 1995; Stenning and van Lambalgen, 2004). On confirmation bias in general, see Nickerson (1998).

10. The task was originally presented in Wason (1960). As with the four-card selection task, there are alternative theories about why subjects perform poorly in the 2-4-6 task (Evans, 1989, 2007; Evans and Over, 1996; Gale and Ball, 2006; Klayman and Ha, 1987; Poletiek, 2001). As with the four-card selection task, though, regardless of which of these descriptive theories explains the poor performance on the task, it is clear from research that a concern for falsifiability would facilitate performance. The DAX/MED experiment is reported by Tweney, Doherty, Warner, and Pliske (1980).

11. Versions of the problem are investigated in Casscells, Schoenberger, and Graboys (1978); Cosmides and Tooby (1996); Sloman, Over, Slovak, and Stibel (2003); and Stanovich and West (1999).

12. Dawkins (1976) emphasizes the point I am stressing here: "Just as we may use a slide rule without appreciating that we are, in effect, using logarithms, so an animal may be pre-programmed in such a way that it behaves as if it had made a complicated calculation. . . . When a man throws a ball high in the air and catches it again, he behaves as if he had solved a set of differential equations in predicting the trajectory of the ball. He may neither know nor care what a differential equation is, but this does not affect his skill with the ball. At some subconscious level, something functionally equivalent to the mathematical calculations is going" (p. 96).

13. The Linda problem was first investigated by Tversky and Kahneman (1983). As with most of the tasks discussed in this book, the literature on it is voluminous (e.g., Dulany and Hilton, 1991; Girotto, 2004; Mellers, Hertwig, and Kahneman, 2001; Politzer and Macchi, 2000; Politzer and Noveck, 1991; Slugoski and Wilson, 1998). On inverting conditional probabilities, see Dawes (1988).

14. On need for cognition, see Cacioppo et al. (1996). Our belief identification scale is described in Sá et al. (1999). The Matching Familiar Figures Test was developed by Kagan, Rosman, Day, Albert, and Phillips (1964).

15. See the growing literature on the small but significant correlations between rational thinking mindware and intelligence (Bruine de Bruin et al., 2007; Kokis et al., 2002; Parker and Fischhoff, 2005; Sá et al., 1999; Stanovich and West, 1997, 1998c, 1998d, 1999, 2000, 2008b; Toplak et al., 2007; Toplak and Stanovich, 2002; West and Stanovich, 2003).

16. In many situations, high-IQ people actually do *not* learn faster — or at least not uniformly so. Often, a better predictor of learning is what people already know in the relevant domain rather than how intelligent they are (Ceci, 1996; Hambrick, 2003).

11 Contaminated Mindware

1. My description of Ponzi schemes and the crisis in Albania is drawn from Bezemer (2001), Jarvis (2000), and Valentine (1998).

2. Of course, such situations occur for a variety of reasons — many of them going beyond factors of individual cognition. Bezemer (2001) discusses many of the macroeconomic factors that contributed to the situation in Albania. To illustrate my point

in this chapter, it is only necessary to acknowledge that irrational economic beliefs were one contributing factor in the Albania crisis.

3. For my account of the recovered memory phenomenon, multiple personality disorder, and satanic ritual abuse, I have drawn on many sources (Brainerd and Reyna, 2005; Clancy, 2005; Hacking, 1995, Lilienfeld, 2007; Loftus and Guyer, 2002; Loftus and Ketcham, 1994; McNally, 2003; Nathan and Snedeker, 1995; Piper, 1998; Showalter, 1997). Multiple personality disorder is now termed dissociative identity disorder.

4. The study is reported in Consumer Fraud Research Group (2006).

5. These examples come from a variety of sources (e.g., Bensley, 2006; Brandon, 1983; Bulgatz, 1992; Dawes, 1988; Farias, 1989; Lehman, 1991; Lipstadt, 1994; Moore, 1977; Muller, 1991; Randi, 1980; Shermer, 1997; Stenger, 1990; Torrey, 1984).

6. On the Nazi war criminals, see Lagerfeld (2004). On the doctoral degrees, see Gardner (1999, p. 205). On Holocaust deniers, see Lipstadt (1994).

7. Stanovich (1999) used the term *knowledge projection* to classify an argument that recurs throughout many different areas of cognitive science (e.g., Dawes, 1989; Edwards and Smith, 1996; Koehler, 1993; Kornblith, 1993; Krueger and Zeiger, 1993; Mitchell, Robinson, Isaacs, and Nye, 1996). Evans, Over, and Manktelow (1993) use this argument to explain the presence of the belief bias effect in syllogistic reasoning. On knowledge assimilation, see Hambrick (2003).

8. Rationalization tendencies have been discussed by many researchers (see Evans, 1996; Evans and Wason, 1976; Margolis, 1987; Nickerson, 1998; Nisbett and Wilson, 1977; Wason, 1969).

9. A number of reasons why evolution does not guarantee human rationality have been discussed in the literature (Kitcher, 1993; Nozick, 1993; Over, 2002, 2004; Skyrms, 1996; Stanovich, 1999, 2004; Stein, 1996; Stich, 1990). Stich (1990), for example, discusses why epistemic rationality is not guaranteed. Regarding practical rationality, Skyrms (1996) devotes an entire book on evolutionary game theory to showing that the idea that "natural selection will weed out irrationality" (p. x) in the instrumental sense is false.

10. I can only begin to cite this enormous literature (Ainslie, 2001; Baron, 2000; Brocas and Carrillo, 2003; Camerer, 1995, 2000; Camerer, Loewenstein, and Rabin, 2004; Dawes, 1998, 2001; Evans, 1989, 2007; Evans and Over, 1996, 2004; Gilovich, Griffin, and Kahneman, 2002; Johnson-Laird, 1999, 2006; Kahneman, 2003a, 2003b; Kahneman and Tversky, 1984, 2000; Koehler and Harvey, 2004; Lichtenstein and Slovic, 2006; Loewenstein et al., 2003; McFadden, 1999; Pohl, 2004; Shafir, 2003; Shafir and LeBoeuf, 2002; Stanovich, 1999, 2004; Tversky and Kahneman, 1983, 1986)

11. The contributors in a volume edited by Aunger (2000) discuss these and other related definitions (see also Blackmore, 1999; Dennett, 1991, 1995, 2006; Distin, 2005; Gil-White, 2005; Hull, 2000; Laland and Brown, 2002; Lynch, 1996;

Mesoudi, Whiten, and Laland, 2006). I prefer to view a meme as a brain control (or informational) state that can potentially cause fundamentally new behaviors and/or thoughts when replicated in another brain. Meme replication has taken place when control states that are causally similar to the source are replicated in the brain host of the copy. Although my definition of the meme follows from Aunger's (2002) discussion, precision of definition is not necessary for my purposes here. A meme can simply be used to refer to an idea unit or a unit of cultural information.

There are numerous other controversial issues surrounding memetic theory, for example: the falsifiability of the meme concept in particular applications, the extent of the meme/gene analogy, how the meme concept differs from concepts of culture already extant in the social sciences. These debates in the science of memes are interesting, but they are tangential to the role that the meme concept plays in my argument. That role is simply and only to force on us one central insight: that some ideas spread because of properties of the ideas themselves. It is uncontroversial that this central insight has a different emphasis from the traditional default position in the social and behavioral sciences. In those sciences, it is usually assumed that to understand the beliefs held by particular individuals one should inquire into the psychological makeup of the individuals involved. It should also be noted that the term *meme*, for some scholars, carries with it connotations that are much stronger than my use of the term here. For example, Sperber (2000) uses the term *meme* not as a synonym for a cultural replicator in general, but as a cultural replicator "standing to be selected not because they benefit their human carriers, but because they benefit themselves" (p. 163). That is, he reserves the term for category 4 discussed later in this chapter. In contrast, my use of the term is more generic (as a synonym for cultural replicator) and encompasses all four categories listed below.

12. On proximity and belief, see Snow, Zurcher, and Ekland-Olson (1980).

13. In the literature, there are many discussions of evolutionary psychology (see Atran, 1998; Sperber, 1996; Tooby and Cosmides, 1992) and gene/culture coevolution (Cavalli-Sforza and Feldman, 1981; Durham, 1991; Gintis, 2007; Lumsden and Wilson, 1981; Richerson and Boyd, 2005).

14. See Blackmore (1999) and Lynch (1996).

15. On the implications of Universal Darwinism, see Aunger (2002), Dennett (1995), Hamilton (1996), and Stanovich (2004).

16. Numerous sources have documented the education of the terrorists (Benjamin and Simon, 2005; Caryl, 2005; Dingfalter, 2004; Krueger, 2007; Laqueur, 2004; McDermott, 2005).

17. The argument is not of course that the memeplex supporting this particular terrorist act is solely in category 4 discussed above. Most memeplexes combine properties of several categories. The point only is that there are some strong self-propagating properties in this memeplex, and that this fact forces us to look to the history and logic of these self-propagating properties rather than to a rational calculus based

on the assumption that it serves only the interests of the host. The issue here is one that I have previously termed "leveling the epistemic playing field" (Stanovich, 2004). It is a matter of establishing that the assumption that this memeplex is solely self-propagating is no less extreme than the assumption that it must be serving the interests of the host. Many memeplexes combine the two, and I am simply suggesting that the properties of this memeplex suggest that it is balanced in favor of the former.

18. It should be understood that anthropomorphic descriptions of replicator activity are merely a shorthand that is commonly used in biological writings. So for example the statement "replicators developed protective coatings of protein to ward off attacks" could be more awkwardly stated as "replicators that built vehicles with coatings became more frequent in the population." I will continue the practice here of using the metaphorical language about replicators having "goals" or "interests" in confidence that the reader understands that this is a shorthand only. Thus, I will follow Dawkins (1976/1989) in "allowing ourselves the licence of talking about genes as if they had conscious aims, always reassuring ourselves that we could translate our sloppy language back into respectable terms if we wanted to" (p. 88). The same is true for memes: memes that make more copies of themselves, copy with greater fidelity, or have greater longevity will leave more copies in future generations.

19. Of course, it is well known that President George W. Bush is strongly reliant on faith-based mindware (e.g., Woodward, 2006).

20. On belief traps, see Elster (1999) and Mackie (1996).

21. I have drawn the information on the prevalence of pseudoscientific beliefs in this section from a variety of sources (Druckman, and Swets, 1988; Eisenberg et al., 1993; Farha and Steward, 2006; Frazier, 1989; Gallup and Newport, 1991; Gilovich, 1991, p. 2; Hines, 2003; Musella, 2005; U.S. Congress, 1984). Percentages vary from survey to survey, but they are substantial in all studies. The study of the Mensa members is reported in Chatillon (1989).

12 How Many Ways Can Thinking Go Wrong?

1. See Spearman (1904). On Gf/Gc theory see Geary (2005) and Horn and Noll (1997); and on group factors beyond Gf and Gc, see Carroll (1993).

2. For lists and taxonomies of heuristics and/or rational thinking errors see Arkes (1991), Baron (2000), Harvey (2007), Larrick (2004), McFadden (1999), and Reyna, Lloyd, and Brainerd (2003).

3. The closely related ideas that the notion of a focal bias conjoins include Evans, Over, and Handley's (2003) singularity principle, Johnson-Laird's (1999, 2005) principle of truth, focusing (Legrenzi, Girotto, and Johnson-Laird, 1993), the effect/effort issues discussed by Sperber, Cara, and Girotto (1995), belief acceptance (Gilbert, 1991), and finally, the focalism issues that have been prominent in the literature on affective forecasting (Kahneman et al., 2006; Schkade and Kahneman, 1998; Wilson et al., 2000).

4. In short, three different types of "start decoupling" calls go out from the reflective mind: decouple the response primed by the autonomous mind so that it can be overridden; copy and decouple a secondary representation in order to carry out simulation; and decouple serial associative cognition in order to start a new serial chain of associations. The three different decoupling operations carried out by the algorithmic mind map suggestively into the components of executive functioning that have been discussed by Miyake et al. (2000): inhibition of prepotent responses, information updating, and set shifting, respectively.

5. On the "self" as problematic mindware, see Blackmore (1999) and Dennett (1991, 1995).

6. Among these might be the gambler's fallacy (Ayton and Fischer, 2004; Burns and Corpus, 2004; Croson and Sundali, 2005; Nickerson, 2004) and many of the other misunderstandings of probability that have been studied in the heuristics and biases literature. Of course, this example highlights the fact that the line between missing mindware and contaminated mindware may get fuzzy in some cases, and the domain of probabilistic thinking is probably one such case.

7. See Nisbett and Wilson (1977) and the work on the bias blindspot (Ehrlinger, Gilovich, and Ross, 2005; Pronin, 2006).

8. I have presented a more exhaustive classification of heuristics and biases tasks in other more technical publications (Stanovich, 2008, 2009).

9. On attribute substitution, see Kahneman and Frederick (2002).

10. This burgeoning area of research has been the focus of much creative work in the last decade (Ayton, Pott, and Elwakili, 2007; Gilbert, 2006; Gilbert, Pinel, Wilson, Blumberg, and Wheatley, 2002; Hsee and Hastie, 2006; Kahneman, 1999; Kahneman et al., 2006; Kahneman, Diener, and Schwarz, 1999; Schkade and Kahneman, 1998; Wilson and Gilbert, 2005). Hsee and Hastie (2006) describe focalism in hedonic prediction: "predictors pay too much attention to the central event and overlook context events" (p. 31).

11. There has been much work on the Iowa Gambling Task (Bechara, Damasio, Damasio, and Anderson, 1994; Bechara, Damasio, Tranel, and Damasio, 2005).

12. There is empirical evidence for rationality failures of the two different types. Dorsolateral prefrontal damage has been associated with executive functioning difficulties (and/or working memory difficulties) that can be interpreted as the failure to override automatized processes (Dempster and Corkill, 1999; Duncan et al., 1996; Harnishfeger and Bjorklund, 1994; Kane and Engle, 2002; Kimberg, D'Esposito, and Farah, 1998; Shallice, 1988). In contrast, ventromedial damage to the prefrontal cortex has been associated with problems in behavioral regulation that are accompanied by affective disruption. Difficulties of the former but not the latter kind are associated with lowered intelligence (see Bechara, Damasio, Tranel, and Anderson, 1998; Damasio, 1994; Duncan et al., 1996).

13. On the heroin addicts, see Petry, Bickel, and Arnett (1998). Our research is reported in Stanovich, Grunewald, and West (2003). There have been several studies of

pathological gamblers (Cavedini et al., 2002; Toplak et al., 2007). There is a burgeoning literature on alexithymia and schizophrenia (Bermudez, 2001; Coltheart and Davies, 2000; Mealey, 1995; Murphy and Stich, 2000; Nichols and Stich, 2003).

It is important to emphasize that the Iowa Gambling Task is deliberately designed so that the large rewards in decks A and B will be overwhelmed by penalties (thus resulting in negative expected value). As Loewenstein et al. (2001) point out, it would be easy to design an experiment with the opposite payoff structure—where the risky choices had a higher payoff (Shiv, Loewenstein, Bechara, Damasio, and Damasio, 2005). Indeed, there are real-world examples of just this structure. If one is investing for the long term, stocks—riskier on a short-term basis—tend to outperform bonds. It is an open question which structure (positive expected value being associated with large variance or negative expected value being associated with large variance) is more common in the real world.

14. See Frederick (2005). Gilhooly and Murphy (2005) have likewise found modest correlations between intelligence and performance on insight problems of this type (see also Toplak and Stanovich, 2002). Of course, the correlations observed in all of these investigations are attenuated somewhat by restriction of range in the university samples.

15. For individual differences work on framing using both types of designs see Bruine de Bruin et al. (2007) and Stanovich and West (1998b, 1999, 2008b).

16. There have been many studies of the Mischel paradigm (Ayduk and Mischel, 2002; Funder and Block, 1989; Mischel and Ebbesen, 1970; Mischel, Shoda, and Rodriguez, 1989; Rodriguez, Mischel, and Shoda, 1989). On data from adults, see Kirby, Winston, and Santiesteban (2005). It should be noted that other investigators interpret the failure to delay in the Mischel paradigm not as a failure of the override function but instead as indicating flawed reward and reward discounting mechanisms in the autonomous mind (e.g., Sonuga-Barke, 2002, 2003). If this alternative interpretation is correct, it reclassifies failure in the Mischel paradigm as an instance of the Mr. Spock problem rather than failure of override.

17. Austin and Deary (2002).

18. These correlations are derived from a small set of studies (Kokis et al., 2002; Macpherson and Stanovich, 2007; Stanovich and West, 1998c, 2008b).

19. These mindware gap correlations are derived from a variety of investigations (Bruine de Bruin et al., 2007; Kokis et al., 2002; Parker and Fischhoff, 2005; Sá et al., 1999; Stanovich and West, 1998c, 1998d, 1999, 2000; Toplak and Stanovich, 2002; West and Stanovich, 2003). Some of these data are from studies of children spanning a wide range of ability. The adult samples employ mostly range-restricted university samples.

20. On research on financial fraud, see Consumer Fraud Research Group (2006).

13 **The Social Benefits of Increasing Human Rationality—and Meliorating Irrationality**

1. It is true that in the last decade many corporations have tried to broaden their assessment efforts. But they have turned to instruments such as personality tests and so-called honesty tests—most of which are of questionable reliability and validity (Paul, 2005).

2. Not surprisingly for a psychological attribute that is roughly 50 percent heritable, intelligence is certainly malleable but not to an unlimited extent (Ceci, 1996; Hunt and Carlson, 2007; Neisser, 1998; Neisser et al., 1996; Nickerson, 2004).

3. These examples are drawn from a variety of sources (Arkes and Ayton, 1999; Baron, 1998, 2000; Bazerman, Baron, and Shonk, 2001; Camerer, 2000; Chapman and Elstein, 2000; Gigerenzer, 2002; Gilovich, 1991; Groopman, 2007; Hastie and Dawes, 2001; Hilton, 2003; Kahneman and Tversky, 2000; Lichtenstein and Slovic, 2006; Margolis, 1996; Myers, 2002; Reyna and Lloyd, 2006; Sunstein, 2002, 2005; Sunstein and Thaler, 2003; Taleb, 2001, 2007). On the study of hatred, see Sternberg (2005).

4. See the citations here on police psychics (Hines, 2003; Reiser, Ludwig, Saxe, Wagner, 1979), graphology (Ben-Shakhar, Bar-Hillel, Blui, Ben-Abba, and Flug, 1989; Neter and Ben-Shakhar, 1989), and examples of pseudoscientific beliefs on juries and in financial management (Krantz, 2000; Wilkinson, 1998). Many other publications detail further examples (Shermer, 1997; Stanovich, 2004; Sternberg, 2002b).

5. On the connection between pseudoscientific beliefs and these thinking attributes there is some evidence, but much of it is indirect (Macpherson and Stanovich, 2007; Nickerson, 1998; Shafir, 1994; Stanovich and West, 1997; Toplak et al., 2007; Waganaar, 1988).

6. In the perennial war in education between teaching declarative knowledge and teaching strategies, the mindware of rationality declares a truce because it comes from both categories. The tendency toward disjunctive thinking is more of a reasoning strategy, whereas many principles of probabilistic reasoning are more akin to declarative knowledge.

7. There are several sources on the issue of teaching strategies such as disjunctive reasoning as well as more global critical thinking skills (Adams, 1989; Baron and Brown, 1991; Feehrer and Adams, 1986; Kuhn, 2005; Nickerson, 1988, 2004; Reyna and Farley, 2006; Ritchhart and Perkins, 2005; Swartz and Perkins, 1989).

8. These studies include Arkes et al. (1988); Koehler (1994); Koriat, Lichtenstein, and Fischhoff (1980); Larrick (2004); Mussweiler, Strack, and Pfeiffer (2000); and Tweney et al. (1980). For complications in the implementation of this strategy, see Sanna and Schwarz (2004, 2006).

9. The work of Nisbett (1993; Fong et al., 1986; Lehman and Nisbett, 1990), Sedlmeier (1999; Sedlmeier and Gigerenzer, 2001), Leshowitz (Leshowitz, DiCerbo, and

Okun, 2002; Leshowitz, Jenkens, Heaton, and Bough, 1993; see also Larrick, 2004; Zimmerman, 2007), and Kuhn (2005, 2007) is relevant here.

10. See the work of Gollwitzer (1999; Gollwitzer and Schaal, 1998).

11. Language input can serve a rapid, so-called context-fixing function (Clark, 1996) in a connectionist network (see Rumelhart, Smolensky, McClelland, and Hinton, 1986). Where it might take an associationist network dozens of trials and a considerable length of time to abstract a prototype, a linguistic exchange can activate a pre-existing prototype in a single discrete communication. Clark (1996) calls this the context-fixing function of recurrent linguistic inputs into a connectionist network. Context fixers are "additional inputs that are given alongside the regular input and that may cause an input that (alone) could not activate an existing prototype to in fact do so" (p. 117). Clark (1996) argues that "linguistic exchanges can be seen as a means of providing fast, highly focused, context-fixing information" (p. 117).

12. There has been a considerable amount of work on forming mental goals (Heath, Larrick, and Wu, 1999; Locke and Latham, 1991) and on affective forecasting (Gilbert, 2006; Kahneman et al., 2006).

13. On teaching falsifiability at a low level, see Stanovich (2007). The critical thinking skills necessary to avoid pseudoscience have been much discussed (Lilienfeld et al., 2001; Marek et al., 1998).

14. Organ donation is discussed in Johnson and Goldstein (2006; see also Sunstein and Thaler, 2003).

15. See Sunstein and Thaler (2003).

16. Much has been written recently on the legislative and corporate impact of these reforms (Benartzi and Thaler, 2001; Camerer et al., 2003; The Economist, 2006; Quinn, 2008: Sunstein and Thaler, 2003; Thaler and Benartzi, 2004; Wang, 2006). On the negative effects of too much choice, see Schwartz (2004).

17. Gigerenzer's work is described in numerous sources (Gigerenzer, 2002; Gigerenzer et al., 2005; Todd and Gigerenzer, 2000, 2007). Several studies have demonstrated a variety of ways of presenting probabilistic information so that the relationship between instance and class is clarified in ways that make processing the information easier (Cosmides and Tooby, 1996; Evans et al., 2000; Gigerenzer, 1996, 2002; Girotto and Gonzalez, 2001; Macchi and Mosconi, 1998; Reyna, 2004; Sloman and Over, 2003; Sloman et al., 2003). The physician example is from Friedman (2005).

18. There has been work on pre-commitment in the domain of saving money (Thaler and Benartzi, 2004) and in other domains (Ariely and Wertenbroch, 2002).

19. Rozin has done work on the French paradox (Rozin, Kabnick, Pete, Fischler, and Shields, 2003) and the unit bias (Geier, Rozin, and Doros, 2006).

20. Of course, the argument about whether intelligence is malleable is vexed by the confusion about whether investigators are assuming a broad or narrow definition—whether it is the malleability of MAMBIT or some broader conception that is being debated. Definitional issues plague the entire debate. Nonetheless, I take it that the

malleability of MAMBIT is pretty well demonstrated by the existence of the Flynn effect (1984, 1987, 2007; Neisser, 1998). The rise in intelligence over time is greatest for tests like the Raven which are good measures of one of the fundamental cognitive operations underlying MAMBIT—the ability to decouple representations while ongoing mental activity takes place. On teaching rational thought, see Baron (2000) and Nickerson (2004).

21. Sternberg (2004).

22. The many universities that are trying to infuse tests of critical thinking into their institutional assessment might be viewed as trying to construct just such an instrument. However, their attempts to measure critical thinking are often theoretically confused by the failure to relate their critical thinking concept to the literature in cognitive science covered in this book—in short, the failure to situate their critical thinking concept in terms of what is known about both intelligence and rational thought.

Abelson, R. P. (1963). Computer simulation of "hot cognition." In S. Tomkins & S. Messick (Eds.), *Computer simulation of personality: Frontier of psychological theory* (277–298). New York: John Wiley.

Abelson, R. P. (1986). Beliefs are like possessions. *Journal of the Theory of Social Behaviour, 16,* 223–250.

Ackerman, P. L. (1988). Determinants of individual differences during skill acquisition: Cognitive abilities and information processing. *Journal of Experimental Psychology: General, 3,* 288–318.

Ackerman, P. L. (1994). Intelligence, attention, and learning: Maximal and typical performance. In D. K. Detterman (Ed.), *Current topics in human intelligence (Vol. 4)* (1–27). Norwood, NJ: Ablex.

Ackerman, P. L. (1996). A theory of adult development: Process, personality, interests, and knowledge. *Intelligence, 22,* 227–257.

Ackerman, P. L., & Heggestad, E. D. (1997). Intelligence, personality, and interests: Evidence for overlapping traits. *Psychological Bulletin, 121,* 219–245.

Ackerman, P. L., & Kanfer, R. (2004). Cognitive, affective, and conative aspects of adult intellect within a typical and maximal performance framework. In D. Y. Dai & R. J. Sternberg (Eds.), *Motivation, emotion, and cognition: Integrative perspectives on intellectual functioning and development* (119–141). Mahwah, NJ: Erlbaum.

Adams, M. J. (1989). Thinking skills curricula: Their promise and progress. *Educational Psychologist, 24,* 25–77.

Ainslie, G. (1992). *Picoeconomics.* Cambridge: Cambridge University Press.

Ainslie, G. (2001). *Breakdown of will.* Cambridge: Cambridge University Press.

Ainslie, G. (2005). Precis of Breakdown of will. *Behavioral and Brain Sciences,* 28, 635–673.

Allingham, M. (2002). *Choice theory.* New York: Oxford University Press.

American Psychiatric Association (1994). *Diagnostic and statistical manual of mental disorders* (IV). Washington, DC: Author.

Anderson, J. R. (1990). *The adaptive character of thought.* Hillsdale, NJ: Erlbaum.

Anderson, J. R. (1991). Is human cognition adaptive? *Behavioral and Brain Sciences,* 14, 471–517.

Anderson, M. (2005). Marrying intelligence and cognition: A developmental view. In R. J. Sternberg & J. E. Pretz (Eds.), *Cognition and intelligence* (268–287). New York: Cambridge University Press.

Ariely, D., & Wertenbroch, K. (2002). Procrastination, deadlines, and performance: Self-control by precommitment. *Psychological Science,* 13, 219–224.

Arkes, H. R. (1991). Costs and benefits of judgment errors: Implications for debiasing. *Psychological Bulletin,* 110, 486–498.

Arkes, H. R., & Ayton, P. (1999). The sunk cost and Concorde effects: Are humans less rational than lower animals? *Psychological Bulletin,* 125, 591–600.

Arkes, H., Faust, D., Guilmette, T., & Hart, K. (1988). Eliminating the hindsight bias. *Journal of Applied Psychology,* 73, 305–307.

Åstebro, T., Jeffrey, S. A., & Adomdza, G. K. (2007). Inventor perseverance after being told to quit: The role of cognitive biases. *Journal of Behavioral Decision Making,* 20, 253–272.

Atance, C. M., & O'Neill, D. K. (2001). Episodic future thinking. *Trends in Cognitive Sciences,* 5, 533–539.

Atran, S. (1998). Folk biology and the anthropology of science: Cognitive universals and cultural particulars. *Behavioral and Brain Sciences,* 21, 547–609.

Audi, R. (1993). *The structure of justification.* Cambridge: Cambridge University Press.

Audi, R. (2001). *The architecture of reason: The structure and substance of rationality.* Oxford: Oxford University Press.

Aunger, R. (Ed.) (2000). *Darwinizing culture: The status of memetics as a science.* Oxford: Oxford University Press.

Aunger, R. (2002). *The electric meme: A new theory of how we think.* New York: Free Press.

Austin, E. J., & Deary, I. J. (2002). Personality dispositions. In R. J. Sternberg

(Ed.), *Why smart people can be so stupid* (187–211). New Haven, CT: Yale University Press.

Ayduk, O., & Mischel, W. (2002). When smart people behave stupidly: Reconciling inconsistencies in social-emotional intelligence. In R. J. Sternberg (Ed.), *Why smart people can be so stupid* (86–105). New Haven, CT: Yale University Press.

Ayton, P., & Fischer, I. (2004). The hot hand fallacy and the gambler's fallacy: Two faces of subjective randomness? *Memory & Cognition, 32,* 1369–1378.

Ayton, P., Pott, A., & Elwakili, N. (2007). Affective forecasting: Why can't people predict their emotions? *Thinking and Reasoning, 13,* 62–80.

Baranski, J. V., & Petrusic, W. M. (1994). The calibration and resolution of confidence in perceptual judgments. *Perception & Psychophysics, 55,* 412–428.

Baranski, J. V., & Petrusic, W. M. (1995). On the calibration of knowledge and perception. *Canadian Journal of Experimental Psychology, 49,* 397–407.

Baddeley, A. D. (1992). Working memory. *Science, 255,* 556–559.

Baddeley, A., Chincotta, D., & Adlam, A. (2001). Working memory and the control of action: Evidence from task switching. *Journal of Experimental Psychology: General, 130,* 641–657.

Barbaresi, W., Katusic, S., Colligan, R., Weaver, A., & Jacobsen, S. (2005). The incidence of autism in Olmsted County, Minnesota, 1976–1997. *Archives of Pediatric and Adolescent Medicine, 159,* 37–44.

Bargh, J. A., & Chartrand, T. L. (1999). The unbearable automaticity of being. *American Psychologist, 54,* 462–479.

Barkley, R. A. (1998). *Attention-deficit hyperactivity disorder: A handbook for diagnosis and treatment* (2nd ed.). New York: Guilford Press.

Barnes, F. (2006). *Rebel-in-chief.* New York: Crown Forum.

Baron, J. (1982). Personality and intelligence. In R. J. Sternberg (Ed.), *Handbook of human intelligence* (308–351). Cambridge: Cambridge University Press.

Baron, J. (1985). *Rationality and intelligence.* Cambridge: Cambridge University Press.

Baron, J. (1988). *Thinking and deciding.* Cambridge: Cambridge University Press.

Baron, J. (1995). Myside bias in thinking about abortion. *Thinking and Reasoning, 1,* 221–235.

Baron, J. (1998). *Judgment misguided: Intuition and error in public decision making.* New York: Oxford University Press.

Baron, J. (2000). *Thinking and deciding* (3rd ed.). Cambridge, MA: Cambridge University Press.

Baron, J., & Brown, R. V. (Eds.) (1991). *Teaching decision making to adolescents*. Hillsdale, NJ: Erlbaum.

Baron-Cohen, S. (1995). *Mindblindness: An essay on autism and theory of mind*. Cambridge, MA: MIT Press.

Baron-Cohen, S. (2005). *Autism: The facts*. Oxford: Oxford University Press.

Barrett, H. C., & Kurzban, R. (2006). Modularity in cognition: Framing the debate. *Psychological Review, 113,* 628–647.

Barrett, L., Henzi, P., & Dunbar, R. (2003). Primate cognition: From "what now?" to "what if?". *Trends in Cognitive Sciences, 7,* 494–497.

Bartels, D. M. (2006). Proportion dominance: The generality and variability of favouring relative savings over absolute savings. *Organizational Behavior and Human Decision Processes, 100,* 76–95.

Bates, T. C., & Shieles, A. (2003). Crystallized intelligence as a product of speed and drive for experience: The relationship of inspection time and openness to g and Gc. *Intelligence, 31,* 275–287.

Baumeister, R. F., Bratslavsky, E., Finkenauer, C., & Vohs, K. D. (2001). Bad is stronger than good. *Review of General Psychology, 5,* 323–370.

Baumeister, R. F., & Vohs, K. D. (2003). Willpower, choice and self-control. In G. Loewenstein, D. Read, & R. Baumeister (Eds.), *Time and decision: Economic and psychological perspectives on intertemporal choice* (201–216). New York: Russell Sage Foundation.

Baumeister, R. F., & Vohs, K. D. (Eds.) (2007). *Handbook of self-regulation: Research, theory, and applications*. New York: Guilford Press.

Bazerman, M. (2001). Consumer research for consumers. *Journal of Consumer Research, 27,* 499–504.

Bazerman, M., Baron, J., & Shonk, K. (2001). *"You can't enlarge the pie": Six barriers to effective government*. New York: Basic Books.

Bechara, A. (2005). Decision making, impulse control and loss of willpower to resist drugs: A neurocognitive perspective. *Nature Neuroscience, 8,* 1458–1463.

Bechara, A., Damasio, A. R., Damasio, H., & Anderson, S. (1994). Insensitivity to future consequences following damage to human prefrontal cortex. *Cognition, 50,* 7–15.

Bechara, A., Damasio, H., Tranel, D., & Anderson, S. (1998). Dissociation of working memory from decision making within the human prefrontal cortex. *Journal of Neuroscience, 18,* 428–437.

Bechara, A., Damasio, H., Tranel, D., & Damasio, A. R. (2005). The Iowa Gambling Task and the somatic marker hypothesis: Some questions and answers. *Trends in Cognitive Sciences, 9,* 159–162.

Bechara, A., Tranel, D., & Damasio, A. R. (2000). Poor judgment in spite of high intellect: Neurological evidence for emotional intelligence. In R. Bar-On & J. Parker (Eds.), *Handbook of emotional intelligence* (192–214). San Francisco: Jossey-Bass.

Belsky, G., & Gilovich, T. (1999). *Why smart people make big money mistakes — and how to correct them: Lessons from the new science of behavioral economics.* New York: Simon & Schuster.

Benartzi, S., & Thaler, R. H. (2001). Naive diversification strategies in defined contribution saving plans. *American Economic Review, 91,* 79–98.

Benjamin, D., & Simon, S. (2005). *The next attack: The failure of the war on terror and a strategy to get it right.* New York: Times Books.

Ben-Shakhar, G., Bar-Hillel, M., Blui, Y., Ben-Abba, E., & Flug, A. (1989). Can graphological analysis predict occupational success? *Journal of Applied Psychology, 71,* 645–653.

Bensley, D. A. (2006, July/August). Why great thinkers sometimes fail to think critically. *Skeptical Inquirer, 27,* 47–52.

Bereiter, C. (2002). *Education and mind in the knowledge age.* Mahwah, NJ: Erlbaum.

Bermudez, J. L. (2001). Normativity and rationality in delusional psychiatric disorders. *Mind & Language, 16,* 457–493.

Berridge, K. C. (2003). Irrational pursuits: Hyper-incentives from a visceral brain. In I. Brocas & J. D. Carrillo (Eds.), *The psychology of economic decisions (Vol. 1): Rationality and well-being* (17–40). Oxford: Oxford University Press.

Beyth-Marom, R., & Fischhoff, B. (1983). Diagnosticity and pseudodiagnosticity. *Journal of Personality and Social Psychology, 45,* 1185–1195.

Bezemer, D. J. (2001). Post-socialist financial fragility: The case of Albania. *Cambridge Journal of Economics, 25,* 1–23.

Blackmore, S. (1999). *The meme machine.* New York: Oxford University Press.

Boring, E. G. (1923). Intelligence as the tests test it. *New Republic, 35,* 35–37.

Bouchard, T. J. (2004). Genetic influences on human psychological traits: A survey. *Current Directions in Psychological Science, 13,* 148–151.

Brainerd, C. J., & Reyna, V. F. (2001). Fuzzy-trace theory: Dual processes in memory, reasoning, and cognitive neuroscience. In H. W. Reese & R. Kail (Eds.), *Advances in child development and behavior (Vol. 28)* (41–100). San Diego: Academic Press.

Brainerd, C. J., & Reyna, V. F. (2005). *The science of false memory.* Oxford: Oxford University Press.

Brandon, R. (1983). *The spiritualists.* London: Weidenfeld & Nicolson.

Brandstatter, E., Gigerenzer, G., & Hertwig, R. (2006). The priority heuristic: Making choices without trade-offs. *Psychological Review, 113,* 409–432.

Braun, P. A., & Yaniv, I. (1992). A case study of expert judgment: Economists' probabilities versus base-rate model forecasts. *Journal of Behavioral Decision Making, 5,* 217–231.

Brewer, N. T., & Chapman, G. (2002). The fragile basic anchoring effect. *Journal of Behavioral Decision Making, 15,* 65–77.

Brocas, I., & Carrillo, J. D. (Eds.) (2003). *The psychology of economic decisions (Vol. 1): Rationality and well-being.* Oxford: Oxford University Press.

Brody, N. (2003). Construct validation of the Sternberg Triarchic Abilities Test: Comment and reanalysis. *Intelligence, 31,* 319–329.

Brody, N. (2004). What cognitive intelligence is and what emotional intelligence is not. *Psychological Inquiry, 15,* 234–238.

Bruine de Bruin, W., Parker, A. M., & Fischhoff, B. (2007). Individual differences in adult decision-making competence. *Journal of Personality and Social Psychology, 92,* 938–956.

Buckner, R. L., & Carroll, D. C. (2007). Self-projection and the brain. *Trends in Cognitive Sciences, 11,* 49–57.

Buehler, R., Griffin, D., & Ross, M. (2002). Inside the planning fallacy: The causes and consequences of optimistic time predictions. In T. Gilovich, D. Griffin, & D. Kahneman (Eds.), *Heuristics and biases: The psychology of intuitive judgment* (250–270). New York: Cambridge University Press.

Bulgatz, J. (1992). *Ponzi schemes, invaders from Mars, and more extraordinary popular delusions and the madness of crowds.* New York: Harmony Books.

Burgess, C. A., Kirsch, I., Shane, H., Niederauer, K., Graham, S., & Bacon, A. (1998). Facilitated communication as an ideomotor response. *Psychological Science, 9,* 71–74.

Burns, B. D., & Corpus, B. (2004). Randomness and inductions from streaks: "Gambler's fallacy" versus "hot hand." *Psychonomic Bulletin & Review, 11,* 179–184.

Buss, D. M. (Ed.) (2005). *The handbook of evolutionary psychology*. Hoboken, NJ: John Wiley.

Byrne, R. M. J. (2005). *The rational imagination: How people create alternatives to reality*. Cambridge, MA: MIT Press.

Cacioppo, J. T., Petty, R. E., Feinstein, J., & Jarvis, W. (1996). Dispositional differences in cognitive motivation: The life and times of individuals varying in need for cognition. *Psychological Bulletin*, 119, 197–253.

Calvin, W. (1990). *The cerebral symphony*. New York: Bantam.

Camerer, C. (1995). Individual decision making. In J. H. Kagel & A. E. Roth (Eds.), *The handbook of experimental economics* (587–703). Princeton: Princeton University Press.

Camerer, C. F. (2000). Prospect theory in the wild: Evidence from the field. In D. Kahneman & A. Tversky (Eds.), *Choices, values, and frames* (288–300). Cambridge: Cambridge University Press.

Camerer, C., Issacharoff, S., Loewenstein, G., O'Donoghue, T., & Rabin, M. (2003). Regulation for conservatives: Behavioral economics and the case for "asymmetric paternalism." *University of Pennsylvania Law Review*, 151, 1211–1254.

Camerer, C., Loewenstein, G., & Rabin, M. (Eds.) (2004). *Advances in behavioral economics*. Princeton: Princeton University Press.

Carroll, J. B. (1993). *Human cognitive abilities: A survey of factor-analytic studies*. Cambridge: Cambridge University Press.

Carruthers, P. (2000). The evolution of consciousness. In P. Carruthers & A. Chamberlain (Eds.), *Evolution and the human mind: Modularity, language and meta-cognition* (254–275). Cambridge: Cambridge University Press.

Carruthers, P. (2002). The cognitive functions of language. *Behavioral and Brain Sciences*, 25, 657–726.

Carruthers, P. (2006). *The architecture of the mind*. New York: Oxford University Press.

Caryl, C. (2005, September 22). Why they do it. *New York Review of Books*, 52(14), 28–32.

Casscells, W., Schoenberger, A., & Graboys, T. (1978). Interpretation by physicians of clinical laboratory results. *New England Journal of Medicine*, 299, 999–1001.

Castellanos, F. X., Sonuga-Barke, E., Milham, M. P., & Tannock, R. (2006).

Characterizing cognition in ADHD: Beyond executive dysfunction. *Trends in Cognitive Sciences*, 10, 117–123.

Cattell, R. B. (1963). Theory for fluid and crystallized intelligence: A critical experiment. *Journal of Educational Psychology*, 54, 1–22.

Cattell, R. B. (1971). *Abilities: Their structure, growth, and action.* Boston: Houghton Mifflin.

Cattell, R. B. (1998). Where is intelligence? Some answers from the triadic theory. In J. J. McArdle & R. W. Woodcock (Eds.), *Human cognitive abilities in theory and practice* (29–38). Mahwah, NJ: Erlbaum.

Cavalli-Sforza, L. L., & Feldman, M. W. (1981). *Cultural transmission and evolution: A quantitative approach.* Princeton: Princeton University Press.

Cavedini, P., Riboldi, G., Keller, R., D'Annucci, A., & Bellodi, L. (2002). Frontal lobe dysfunction in pathological gambling patients. *Biological Psychiatry*, 51, 334–341.

Ceci, S. J. (1996). *On intelligence: A bioecological treatise on intellectual development* (expanded ed). Cambridge, MA: Harvard University Press.

Chapman, D. S., & Zweig, D. (2005). Developing a nomological network for interview structure. *Personnel Psychology*, 58, 673–702.

Chapman, G. B., & Elstein, A. S. (2000). Cognitive processes and biases in medical decision making. In G. B. Chapman & F. A. Sonnenberg (Eds.), *Decision making in health care: Theory, psychology, and applications* (pp. 183–210). New York: Cambridge University Press.

Chapman, G. B., & Sonnenberg, F. A. (2000). *Decision making in health care: Theory, psychology, and applications.* New York: Cambridge University Press.

Charlton, W. (1988). *Weakness of will.* Oxford: Basil Blackwell.

Chatillon, G. (1989). Acceptance of paranormal among two special groups. *Skeptical Inquirer*, 13(2), 216–217.

Cherness, C., Extein, M., Goleman, D., & Weissberg, R. (2006). Emotional intelligence: What does the research really indicate? *Educational Psychologist*, 41, 239–246.

Clancy, S. A. (2005). *Abducted: How people come to believe they were kidnapped by aliens.* Cambridge, MA: Harvard University Press.

Clark, A. (1996). Connectionism, moral cognition, and collaborative problem solving. In A. May, M. Friedman, & A. Clark (Eds.), *Mind and morals* (109–127). Cambridge, MA: MIT Press.

Clark, A., & Karmiloff-Smith, A. (1993). The cognizer's innards: A psychological and philosophical perspective on the development of thought. *Mind and Language*, 8, 487–519.

Colom, R., Rebollo, I., Palacios, A., Juan-Espinosa, M., & Kyllonen, P. C. (2004). Working memory is (almost) perfectly predicted by g. *Intelligence*, 32, 277–296.

Coltheart, M. (1999). Modularity and cognition. *Trends in Cognitive Sciences*, 3, 115–120.

Coltheart, M., & Davies, M. (Eds.) (2000). *Pathologies of belief*. Oxford: Blackwell.

Consumer Fraud Research Group (2006, May 12). *Investor fraud study final report*. Washington, DC: National Association of Securities Dealers.

Consumer Reports (June, 2007). New diet winners, 72(6), pp. 12–17. Yonkers, NY: Consumers Union.

Conway, A. R. A., Cowan, N., Bunting, M. F., Therriault, D. J., & Minkoff, S. R. B. (2002). A latent variable analysis of working memory capacity, short-term memory capacity, processing speed, and general fluid intelligence. *Intelligence*, 30, 163–183.

Conway, A. R. A., Kane, M. J., & Engle, R. W. (2003). Working memory capacity and its relation to general intelligence. *Trends in Cognitive Science*, 7, 547–552.

Corballis, M. C. (2003). Recursion as the key to the human mind. In K. Sterelny & J. Fitness (Eds.), *From mating to mentality: Evaluating evolutionary psychology* (155–171). Hove, England: Psychology Press.

Cornelius, S. W., Kenny, S., & Caspi, A. (1989). Academic and everyday intelligence in adulthood: Conceptions of self and ability tests. In J. D. Sinnott (Ed.), *Everyday problem solving* (191–210). New York: Praeger.

Cosmides, L., & Tooby, J. (1996). Are humans good intuitive statisticians after all? Rethinking some conclusions from the literature on judgment under uncertainty. *Cognition*, 58, 1–73.

Cosmides, L., & Tooby, J. (2000). Consider the source: The evolution of adaptations for decoupling and metarepresentation. In D. Sperber (Ed.), *Metarepresentations: A multidisciplinary perspective* (53–115). Oxford: Oxford University Press.

Cronbach, L. J. (1949). *Essentials of psychological testing*. New York: Harper.

Croson, R., & Sundali, J. (2005). The gambler's fallacy and the hot hand: Empirical data from casinos. *Journal of Risk and Uncertainty*, 30, 195–209.

Cummins, R. A., & Prior, M. P. (1992). Autism and assisted communication: A response to Bilken. *Harvard Educational Review, 62,* 228–241.

Currie, G., & Ravenscroft, I. (2002). *Recreative minds.* Oxford: Oxford University Press.

Damasio, A. R. (1994). *Descartes' error.* New York: Putnam.

Daniel, M. H. (2000). Interpretation of intelligence test scores. In R. J. Sternberg (Ed.), *Handbook of intelligence* (477–491). Cambridge: Cambridge University Press.

Davidson, D. (1980). *Essays on actions & events.* Oxford: Oxford University Press.

Dawes, R. M. (1976). Shallow psychology. In J. S. Carroll & J. W. Payne (Eds.), *Cognition and social behavior* (3–11). Hillsdale, NJ: Erlbaum.

Dawes, R. M. (1988). *Rational choice in an uncertain world.* San Diego: Harcourt Brace Jovanovich.

Dawes, R. M. (1989). Statistical criteria for establishing a truly false consensus effect. *Journal of Experimental Social Psychology, 25,* 1–17.

Dawes, R. M. (1994). *House of cards: Psychology and psychotherapy based on myth.* New York: Free Press.

Dawes, R. M. (1998). Behavioral decision making and judgment. In D. T. Gilbert, S. T. Fiske, & G. Lindzey (Eds.), *The handbook of social psychology (Vol. 1)* (497–548). Boston: McGraw-Hill.

Dawes, R. M. (2001). *Everyday irrationality.* Boulder, CO: Westview Press.

Dawkins, R. (1976/1989). *The selfish gene.* New York: Oxford University Press.

Dawkins, R. (1982). *The extended phenotype.* New York: Oxford University Press.

Deary, I. J. (2001). *Intelligence: A very short introduction.* Oxford: Oxford University Press.

Deary, I. J., Whiteman, M. C., Starr, J. M., Whalley, L. J., & Fox, H. C. (2004). The impact of childhood intelligence on later life: Following up the Scottish Mental Surveys of 1932 and 1947. *Journal of Personality and Social Psychology, 86,* 130–147.

Decety, J., & Grezes, J. (2006). The power of simulation: Imagining one's own and other's behavior. *Brain Research, 1079,* 4–14.

DeLong, G. R. (2004). Review of "Mental Retardation in America." *New England Journal of Medicine, 351*(5), 514–516.

DeMartino, B., Kumaran, D., Seymour, B., & Dolan, R. J. (2006). Frames, biases, and rational decision-making in the human brain. *Science, 313*, 684–687.

Dempster, F. N., & Corkill, A. J. (1999). Interference and inhibition in cognition and behavior: Unifying themes for educational psychology. *Educational Psychology Review, 11*, 1–88.

Denby, D. (2004). *American sucker*. New York: Little, Brown.

Denes-Raj, V., & Epstein, S. (1994). Conflict between intuitive and rational processing: When people behave against their better judgment. *Journal of Personality and Social Psychology, 66*, 819–829.

De Neys, W. (2006). Dual processing in reasoning—two systems but one reasoner. *Psychological Science, 17*, 428–433.

Dennett, D. C. (1978). *Brainstorms: Philosophical essays on mind and psychology*. Cambridge, MA: MIT Press.

Dennett, D. C. (1980). The milk of human intentionality. *Behavioral and Brain Sciences, 3*, 428–430.

Dennett, D. C. (1984). *Elbow room: The varieties of free will worth wanting*. Cambridge, MA: MIT Press.

Dennett, D. C. (1987). *The intentional stance*. Cambridge, MA: MIT Press.

Dennett, D. C. (1991). *Consciousness explained*. Boston: Little, Brown.

Dennett, D. C. (1995). *Darwin's dangerous idea: Evolution and the meanings of life*. New York: Simon & Schuster.

Dennett, D. C. (1996). *Kinds of minds: Toward an understanding of consciousness*. New York: Basic Books.

Dennett, D. C. (2006). From typo to thinko: When evolution graduated to semantic norms. In S. C. Levinson & P. Jaisson (Eds.), *Evolution and culture* (133–145). Cambridge, MA: MIT Press.

de Sousa, R. (1987). *The rationality of emotion*. Cambridge, MA: MIT Press.

de Sousa, R. (2007). *Why think? Evolution and the rational mind*. Oxford: Oxford University Press.

Dias, M., Roazzi, A., & Harris, P. L. (2005). Reasoning from unfamiliar premises: A study with unschooled adults. *Psychological Science, 16*, 550–554.

Dickson, D. H., & Kelly, I. W. (1985). The "Barnum effect" in personality assessment: A review of the literature. *Psychological Reports, 57*, 367–382.

Dienes, Z., & Perner, J. (1999). A theory of implicit and explicit knowledge. *Behavioral and Brain Sciences, 22*, 735–808.

Dillon, K. (1993, Spring). Facilitated communication, autism, and ouija. *Skeptical Inquirer, 17*, 281–287.

Dingfalter, S. F. (2004, November). Fatal friendships. APA *Monitor*, 35(10), 20–21.

Distin, K. (2005). *The selfish meme.* Cambridge: Cambridge University Press.

Doherty, M. E., & Mynatt, C. (1990). Inattention to P(H) and to P(D/~H): A converging operation. *Acta Psychologica*, 75, 1–11.

Dole, J. A., & Sinatra, G. M. (1998). Reconceptualizing change in the cognitive construction of knowledge. *Educational Psychologist*, 33, 109–128.

Dougherty, M. R. P., Gettys, C. F., & Thomas, R. P. (1997). The role of mental simulation in judgements of likelihood. *Organizational Behavior and Human Decision Processes*, 70(2), 135–148.

Draper, R. (2007). *Dead certain.* New York: Free Press.

Druckman, D., & Swets, J. (1988). Paranormal phenomena. In D. Druckman & J. Swets (Eds.), *Enhancing human performance: Issues, theories, and techniques* (169–231). Washington, DC: National Academy Press.

Duckworth, A. L., & Seligman, M. E. P. (2005). Self-discipline outdoes IQ in predicting academic performance of adolescents. *Psychological Science*, 16, 939–944.

Dulany, D. E., & Hilton, D. J. (1991). Conversational implicature, conscious representation, and the conjunction fallacy. *Social Cognition*, 9, 85–110.

Duncan, J., Emslie, H., Williams, P., Johnson, R., & Freer, C. (1996). Intelligence and the frontal lobe: The organization of goal-directed behavior. *Cognitive Psychology*, 30, 257–303.

Duncan, J., Seitz, R. J., Kolodny, J., Bor, D., Herzog, H., Ahmed, A., Newell, F. N., & Emslie, H. (2000). A neural basis for general intelligence. *Science*, 289, 457–460.

Dunning, D., Heath, C., & Suls, J. M. (2004). Why people fail to recognize their own incompetence. *Psychological Science in the Public Interest*, 5, 69–106.

Dunning, D., Johnson, K., Ehrlinger, J., & Kruger, J. (2003). Why people fail to recognize their own incompetence. *Current Directions in Psychological Science*, 12, 83–87.

Durham, W. (1991). *Coevolution: Genes, culture, and human diversity.* Stanford: Stanford University Press.

The Economist (2006, April 8). The avuncular state. 67–69.

Edwards, K., & Smith, E. E. (1996). A disconfirmation bias in the evaluation of arguments. *Journal of Personality and Social Psychology*, 71, 5–24.

Edwards, W. (1954). The theory of decision making. *Psychological Bulletin*, 51, 380–417.

Ehrlinger, J., Gilovich, T., & Ross, L. (2005). Peering into the bias blind spot: People's assessments of bias in themselves and others. *Personality and Social Psychology Bulletin*, 31, 680–692.

Eisenberg, D. M., Kessler, R., Foster, C., Norlock, F., Calkins, D., & Delbanco, T. (1993). Unconventional medicine in the United States. *New England Journal of Medicine*, 328(4), 246–252.

Elster, J. (1979). *Ulysses and the sirens: Studies in rationality and irrationality.* Cambridge: Cambridge University Press.

Elster, J. (1999). *Strong feelings: Emotion, addiction, and human behavior.* Cambridge, MA: MIT Press.

Engle, R. W. (2002). Working memory capacity as executive attention. *Current Directions in Psychological Science*, 11, 19–23.

Engle, R. W., Tuholski, S. W., Laughlin, J. E., & Conway, A. R. A. (1999). Working memory, short-term memory, and general fluid intelligence: A latent-variable approach. *Journal of Experimental Psychology: General*, 128, 309–331.

Englich, B., Mussweiler, T., & Strack, F. (2006). Playing dice with criminal sentences: The influence of irrelevant anchors on experts' judicial decision making. *Personality and Social Psychology Bulletin*, 32, 188–200.

Epley, N. (2008, January 31). Rebate psychology. *New York Times*, A27.

Epley, N., & Gilovich, T. (2004). Are adjustments insufficient? *Personality and Social Psychology Bulletin*, 30, 447–460.

Epley, N., & Gilovich, T. (2006). The anchoring-and-adjustment heuristic: Why the adjustments are insufficient. *Psychological Science*, 17, 311–318.

Epley, N., Mak, D., & Chen Idson, L. (2006). Bonus or rebate? The impact of income framing on spending and saving. *Journal of Behavioral Decision Making*, 19, 213–227.

Epstein, S. (1994). Integration of the cognitive and the psychodynamic unconscious. *American Psychologist*, 49, 709–724.

Evans, J. St. B. T. (1972). Interpretation and matching bias in a reasoning task. *Quarterly Journal of Experimental Psychology*, 24, 193–199.

Evans, J. St. B. T. (1984). Heuristic and analytic processes in reasoning. *British Journal of Psychology*, 75, 451–468.

Evans, J. St. B. T. (1989). *Bias in human reasoning: Causes and consequences.* Hove, England: Erlbaum.

Evans, J. St. B. T. (1996). Deciding before you think: Relevance and reasoning in the selection task. *British Journal of Psychology, 87*, 223–240.

Evans, J. St. B. T. (1998). Matching bias in conditional reasoning: Do we understand it after 25 years? *Thinking and Reasoning, 4*, 45–82.

Evans, J. St. B. T. (2002a). Logic and human reasoning: An assessment of the deduction paradigm. *Psychological Bulletin, 128*, 978–996.

Evans, J. St. B. T. (2002b). The influence of prior belief on scientific thinking. In P. Carruthers, S. Stich, & M. Siegal (Eds.), *The cognitive basis of science* (193–210). Cambridge: Cambridge University Press.

Evans, J. St. B. T. (2003). In two minds: Dual-process accounts of reasoning. *Trends in Cognitive Sciences, 7*, 454–459.

Evans, J. St. B. T. (2004). History of the dual process theory of reasoning. In K. I. Manktelow & M. C. Chung (Eds.), *Psychology of reasoning: Theoretical and historical perspectives* (241–266). Hove, England: Psychology Press.

Evans, J. St. B. T. (2006a). Dual system theories of cognition: Some issues. *Proceedings of the 28th Annual Meeting of the Cognitive Science Society, Vancouver*, 202–207.

Evans, J. St. B. T. (2006b). The heuristic-analytic theory of reasoning: Extension and evaluation. *Psychonomic Bulletin and Review, 13*, 378–395.

Evans, J. St. B. T. (2007). *Hypothetical thinking: Dual processes in reasoning and judgment.* New York: Psychology Press.

Evans, J. St. B. T. (2008a). Dual-processing accounts of reasoning, judgment and social cognition. *Annual Review of Psychology.*

Evans, J. St. B. T. (2008b). How many dual-process theories do we need? One, two, or many? In J. Evans & K. Frankish (Eds.), *In two minds: Dual processes and beyond.* Oxford: Oxford University Press.

Evans, J. St. B. T., Barston, J., & Pollard, P. (1983). On the conflict between logic and belief in syllogistic reasoning. *Memory & Cognition, 11*, 295–306.

Evans, J. St. B. T., & Curtis-Holmes, J. (2005). Rapid responding increases belief bias: Evidence for the dual-process theory of reasoning. *Thinking and Reasoning, 11*, 382–389.

Evans, J. St. B. T., & Feeney, A. (2004). The role of prior belief in reasoning. In J. P. Leighton & R. J. Sternberg (Eds.), *The nature of reasoning* (78–102). Cambridge: Cambridge University Press.

Evans, J. St. B. T., Newstead, S. E., & Byrne, R. M. J. (1993). *Human reasoning: The psychology of deduction.* Hove, England: Erlbaum.

Evans, J. St. B. T., & Over, D. E. (1996). *Rationality and reasoning*. Hove, England: Psychology Press.

Evans, J. St. B. T., & Over, D. E. (1999). Explicit representations in hypothetical thinking. *Behavioral and Brain Sciences*, 22, 763–764.

Evans, J. St. B. T., & Over, D. E. (2004). *If*. Oxford: Oxford University Press.

Evans, J. St. B. T., Over, D. E., & Handley, S. J. (2003). A theory of hypothetical thinking. In D. Hardman & L. Maachi (Eds.), *Thinking: Psychological perspectives on reasoning* (3–22). Chichester, England: Wiley.

Evans, J. St. B. T., Over, D. E., & Manktelow, K. (1993). Reasoning, decision making and rationality. *Cognition*, 49, 165–187.

Evans, J. St. B. T., Simon, J. H., Perham, N., Over, D. E., & Thompson, V. A. (2000). Frequency versus probability formats in statistical word problems. *Cognition*, 77, 197–213.

Evans, J. St. B. T., & Wason, P. C. (1976). Rationalization in a reasoning task. *British Journal of Psychology*, 67, 479–486.

Eysenck, H. J. (1994). Personality and intelligence: Psychometric and experimental approaches. In R. J. Sternberg & P. Ruzgis (Eds.), *Personality and intelligence* (3–31). Cambridge: Cambridge University Press.

Farha, B., & Steward, G. (2006). Paranormal beliefs: An analysis of college students. *Skeptical Inquirer*, 30(1), 37–40.

Farias, V. (1989). *Heidegger and Nazism*. Philadelphia: Temple University Press.

Feehrer, C. E., & Adams, M. J. (1986). *Odyssey: A curriculum for thinking*. Watertown, MA: Charlesbridge Publishing.

Feldman Barrett, L. F., Tugade, M. M., & Engle, R. W. (2004). Individual differences in working memory capacity and dual-process theories of the mind. *Psychological Bulletin*, 130, 553–573.

Fenton-O'Creevy, M., Nicholson, N., Soane, E., & Willman, P. (2003). Trading on illusions: Unrealistic perceptions of control and trading performance. *Journal of Occupational and Organizational Psychology*, 76, 53–68.

Fine, C. (2006). *A mind of its own*. New York: W. W. Norton.

Fischhoff, B. (1988). Judgment and decision making. In R. J. Sternberg & E. E. Smith (Eds.), *The psychology of human thought* (153–187). Cambridge: Cambridge University Press.

Fischhoff, B., & Beyth-Marom, R. (1983). Hypothesis evaluation from a Bayesian perspective. *Psychological Review*, 90, 239–260.

Fischhoff, B., Slovic, P., & Lichtenstein, S. (1977). Knowing with certainty: The appropriateness of extreme confidence. *Journal of Experimental Psychology: Human Perception and Performance, 3,* 552–564.

Fletcher, J. M., Shaywitz, S. E., Shankweiler, D., Katz, L., Liberman, I., Stuebing, K., Francis, D. J., Fowler, A., & Shaywitz, B. A. (1994). Cognitive profiles of reading disability: Comparisons of discrepancy and low achievement definitions. *Journal of Educational Psychology, 86,* 6–23.

Flynn, J. R. (1984). The mean IQ of Americans: Massive gains 1932 to 1978. *Psychological Bulletin, 95,* 29–51.

Flynn, J. R. (1987). Massive IQ gains in 14 nations: What IQ tests really measure. *Psychological Bulletin, 101,* 171–191.

Flynn, J. R. (1998). IQ gains over time: Toward finding the causes. In U. Neisser (Ed.), *The rising curve: Long-term changes in IQ and related measures* (25–66). Washington, DC: American Psychological Association.

Flynn, J. R. (2007). *What is intelligence?* Cambridge: Cambridge University Press.

Fodor, J. A. (1983). *The modularity of mind.* Cambridge, MA: MIT Press.

Fogelin, R. (2003). *Walking the tightrope of reason: The precarious life of a rational animal.* Oxford: Oxford University Press.

Foley, R. (1987). *The theory of epistemic rationality.* Cambridge, MA: Harvard University Press.

Fong, G. T., Krantz, D. H., & Nisbett, R. E. (1986). The effects of statistical training on thinking about everyday problems. *Cognitive Psychology, 18,* 253–292.

Foot, P. (1967). The problem of abortion and the doctrine of double effect. *Oxford Review, 5,* 5–15.

Forer, B. R. (1949). The fallacy of personal validation: A classroom demonstration of gullibility. *Journal of Abnormal and Social Psychology, 44,* 119–123.

Forgas, J. P. (1995). Mood and judgment: The affect infusion model (AIM). *Psychological Bulletin, 117,* 39–66.

Fountain, H. (2006, January 15). On not wanting to know what hurts you. *New York Times,* WK1.

Frankfurt, H. G. (2006). *On truth.* New York: Knopf.

Frazier, K. (1989). Gallup poll of beliefs: Astrology up, ESP down. *Skeptical Inquirer, 13*(3), 244–245.

Frederick, S. (2002). Automated choice heuristics. In T. Gilovich, D. Griffin, & D. Kahneman (Eds.), *Heuristics and biases: The psychology of intuitive judgment* (548–558). New York: Cambridge University Press.

Frederick, S. (2005). Cognitive reflection and decision making. *Journal of Economic Perspectives, 19*, 25–42.

Frey, M. C., & Detterman, D. K. (2004). Scholastic assessment or g? The relationship between the Scholastic Assessment Test and general cognitive ability. *Psychological Science, 15*, 373–378.

Fridson, M. S. (1993). *Investment illusions.* New York: John Wiley & Sons.

Friedman, R. (2005, April 26). Mix math and medicine and create confusion. *New York Times,* D11.

Friedrich, J. (1996). On seeing oneself as less self-serving than others: The ultimate self-serving bias? *Teaching of Psychology, 23*(2), 107–109.

Friedrich, J., Lucas, G., & Hodell, E. (2005). Proportional reasoning, framing effects, and affirmative action: Is six of one really half a dozen of another in university admissions? *Organizational Behavior and Human Decision Processes, 98*, 195–215.

Friend, M. (2005). *Special education: Contemporary perspectives for school professionals.* Boston: Pearson Education.

Frith, U. (2003). *Autism: Explaining the enigma* (2nd ed.). Oxford: Basil Blackwell.

Frum, D. (2003). *The right man.* New York: Random House.

Funder, D. C., & Block, J. (1989). The role of ego-control, ego-resiliency, and IQ in delay of gratification in adolescence. *Journal of Personality and Social Psychology, 57*, 1041–1050.

Fuster, J. M. (1990). Prefrontal cortex and the bridging of temporal gaps in the perception-action cycle. In A. Diamond (Ed.), *The development and neural bases of higher cognitive functions* (318–336). New York: New York Academy of Sciences.

Gale, M., & Ball, L. J. (2006). Dual-goal facilitation in Wason's 2-4-6 task: What mediates successful rule discovery? *Quarterly Journal of Experimental Psychology, 59*, 873–885.

Gallup, G. H., & Newport, F. (1991). Belief in paranormal phenomena among adult Americans. *Skeptical Inquirer, 15*(2), 137–146.

Galovski, T. E., Malta, L. S., & Blanchard, E. B. (2006). *Road rage: Assessment and treatment of the angry, aggressive driver.* Washington, DC: American Psychological Association.

Galton, F. (1883). *Inquiry into human faculty and its development.* London: Macmillan.

Gardner, H. (1983). *Frames of mind.* New York: Basic Books.

Gardner, H. (1999). *Intelligence reframed.* New York: Basic Books.

Gardner, H. (2006a). *Multiple intelligences: New horizons.* New York: Basic Books.

Gardner, H. (2006b). On failing to grasp the core of MI theory: A response to Visser et al. *Intelligence, 34,* 503–505.

Gardner, H., & Moran, S. (2006). The science of multiple intelligences theory: A response to Lynn Waterhouse. *Educational Psychologist, 41,* 227–232.

Gardner, M. (2001). Facilitated communication: A cruel farce. *Skeptical Inquirer, 25*(1), 17–19.

Gauthier, D. (1975). Reason and maximization. *Canadian Journal of Philosophy, 4,* 411–433.

Gazzaniga, M. S. (1998). *The mind's past.* Berkeley: University of California Press.

Geary, D. C. (2005). *The origin of the mind: Evolution of brain, cognition, and general intelligence.* Washington, DC: American Psychological Association.

Geier, A. B., Rozin, P., & Doros, G. (2006). Unit bias. A new heuristic that helps explain the effect of portion size on food intake. *Psychological Science, 17,* 521–525.

Gernsbacher, M. A., Dawson, M., & Goldsmith, H. H. (2005). Three reasons not to believe in an autism epidemic. *Psychological Science, 14,* 55–58.

Gernsbacher, M. A., & Faust, M. E. (1991). The mechanism of suppression: A component of general comprehension skill. *Journal of Experimental Psychology: Learning, Memory, and Cognition, 17,* 245–262.

Gigerenzer, G. (1996). On narrow norms and vague heuristics: A reply to Kahneman and Tversky (1996). *Psychological Review, 103,* 592–596.

Gigerenzer, G. (2002). *Calculated risks: How to know when numbers deceive you.* New York: Simon & Schuster.

Gigerenzer, G. (2004). Dread risk, September 11, and fatal traffic accidents. *Psychological Science, 15,* 286–287.

Gigerenzer, G. (2007). *Gut feelings: The intelligence of the unconscious.* New York: Viking Penguin.

Gigerenzer, G., & Goldstein, D. G. (1996). Reasoning the fast and frugal way: Models of bounded rationality. *Psychological Review, 103,* 650–669.

Gigerenzer, G., Hertwig, R., van den Broek, E., Fasolo, B., & Katsikopoulis, K. (2005). Communicating statistical information. *Risk Analysis, 25,* 623–629.

Gigerenzer, G., & Todd, P. M. (1999). *Simple heuristics that make us smart.* New York: Oxford University Press.

Gilbert, D. T. (1991). How mental systems believe. *American Psychologist, 46*, 107–119.

Gilbert, D. T. (2006). *Stumbling on happiness*. New York: Alfred A. Knopf.

Gilbert, D. T., Pelham, B. W., & Krull, D. S. (1988). On cognitive busyness: When person perceivers meet person perceived. *Journal of Personality and Social Psychology, 54*, 733–740.

Gilbert, D. T., Pinel, E. C., Wilson, T. D., Blumberg, S. J., & Wheatley, T. P. (2002). Durability bias in affective forecasting. In T. Gilovich, D. Griffin, & D. Kahneman (Eds.), *Heuristics and biases: The psychology of intuitive judgment* (292–312). Cambridge: Cambridge University Press.

Gilhooly, K. J., & Murphy, P. (2005). Differentiating insight from non-insight problems. *Thinking and Reasoning, 11*, 279–302.

Gilovich, T. (1991). *How we know what isn't so*. New York: Free Press.

Gilovich, T., Griffin, D., & Kahneman, D. (Eds.) (2002). *Heuristics and biases: The psychology of intuitive judgment*. New York: Cambridge University Press.

Gil-White, F. J. (2005). Common misunderstandings of memes (and genes): The promise and the limits of the genetic analogy to cultural transmission processes. In S. Hurley & N. Chater (Eds.), *Perspectives on imitation (Vol. 2)* (317–338). Cambridge, MA: MIT Press.

Gintis, H. (2007). A framework for the unification of the behavioral sciences. *Behavioral and Brain Sciences, 30*, 1–61.

Girotto, V. (2004). Task understanding. In J. P. Leighton & R. J. Sternberg (Eds.), *The nature of reasoning* (103–125). Cambridge: Cambridge University Press.

Girotto, V., & Gonzalez, M. (2001). Solving probabilistic and statistical problems: A matter of information structure and question form. *Cognition, 78*, 247–276.

Gladwell, M. (2000, August 21 & 28). The art of failure: Why some people choke and others panic. *The New Yorker*, 84–92.

Gladwell, M. (2005). *Blink*. New York: Little, Brown.

Glenberg, A. M. (1997). What memory is for. *Behavioral and Brain Sciences, 20*, 1–55.

Goel, V., & Dolan, R. J. (2003). Explaining modulation of reasoning by belief. *Cognition, 87*, B11–B22.

Goff, M., & Ackerman, P. L. (1992). Personality-intelligence relations: Assessment of typical intellectual engagement. *Journal of Educational Psychology, 84*, 537–552.

Goldman-Rakic, P. S. (1992). Working memory and the mind. *Scientific American*, 267, 111–117.

Goldstein, D. G., & Gigerenzer, G. (1999). The recognition heuristic: How ignorance makes us smart. In G. Gigerenzer & P. M. Todd (Eds.), *Simple heuristics that make us smart* (37–58). New York: Oxford University Press.

Goldstein, D. G., & Gigerenzer, G. (2002). Models of ecological rationality: The recognition heuristic. *Psychological Review*, 109, 75–90.

Goleman, D. (1995). *Emotional intelligence*. New York: Bantam Books.

Goleman, D. (2006). *Social intelligence*. New York: Bantam Books.

Gollwitzer, P. M. (1999). Implementation intentions: Strong effects of simple plans. *American Psychologist*, 54, 493–503.

Gollwitzer, P. M., & Schaal, B. (1998). Metacognition in action: The importance of implementation intentions. *Personality and Social Psychology Review*, 2, 124–136.

Gordon, M., Lewandowski, L., & Keiser, S. (1999). The LD label for relatively well-functioning students: A critical analysis. *Journal of Learning Disabilities*, 32, 485–490.

Gray, J. R., Chabris, C. F., & Braver, T. S. (2003). Neural mechanisms of general fluid intelligence. *Nature Neuroscience*, 6, 316–322.

Green, L., & Myerson, J. (2004). A discounting framework for choice with delayed and probabilistic rewards. *Psychological Bulletin*, 130, 769–792.

Greene, J. (2005). Cognitive neuroscience and the structure of the moral mind. In P. Carruthers, S. Laurence, & S. Stich (Eds.), *The innate mind* (338–352). Oxford: Oxford University Press.

Greene, J., Nystrom, L. E., Engell, A. D., Darley, J. M., & Cohen, J. D. (2004). The neural bases of cognitive conflict and control in moral judgment. *Neuron*, 44, 389–400.

Greene, J., Sommerville, R. B., Nystrom, L. E., Darley, J. M., & Cohen, J. D. (2001). An fMRI investigation of emotional engagement in moral judgment. *Science*, 293, 2105–2108.

Greenfield, P. M. (1998). The cultural evolution of IQ. In U. Neisser (Ed.), *The rising curve: Long-term changes in IQ and related measures* (81–123). Washington, DC: American Psychological Association.

Griffin, D., & Tversky, A. (1992). The weighing of evidence and the determinants of confidence. *Cognitive Psychology*, 24, 411–435.

Griffin, D. W., & Varey, C. A. (1996). Toward a consensus on overconfidence. *Organizational Behavior and Human Decision Processes*, 65, 227–231.

Groopman, J. (2007). *How doctors think.* Boston: Houghton Mifflin.

Hacking, I. (1995). *Rewriting the soul: Multiple personality and the sciences of memory.* Princeton: Princeton University Press.

Haidt, J. (2001). The emotional dog and its rational tail: A social intuitionist approach to moral judgment. *Psychological Review, 108,* 814–834.

Hambrick, D. Z. (2003). Why are some people more knowledgeable than others? A longitudinal study of knowledge acquisition. *Memory & Cognition, 31,* 902–917.

Hamilton, W. D. (1996). *Narrow roads of gene land.* Oxford: W. H. Freeman.

Hammill, D. D. (1990). On defining learning disabilities: An emerging consensus. *Journal of Learning Disabilities, 23,* 74–84.

Hardman, D. (1998). Does reasoning occur on the selection task? A comparison of relevance-based theories. *Thinking and Reasoning, 4,* 353–376.

Harman, G. (1995). Rationality. In E. E. Smith & D. N. Osherson (Eds.), *Thinking (Vol. 3)* (175–211). Cambridge, MA: MIT Press.

Harnishfeger, K. K., & Bjorklund, D. F. (1994). A developmental perspective on individual differences in inhibition. *Learning and Individual Differences, 6,* 331–356.

Harris, R. J., & Joyce, M. (1980). What's fair? It depends on how you phrase the question. *Journal of Personality and Social Psychology, 38,* 165–179.

Harris, S. (2004). *The end of faith: Religion, terror, and the future of reason.* New York: Norton.

Hartman, R. S., Doane, M. J., & Woo, C. (1991). Consumer rationality and the status quo. *Quarterly Journal of Economics, 106,* 141–162.

Harvey, N. (2007). Use of heuristics: Insights from forecasting research. *Thinking and Reasoning, 13,* 5–24.

Hasher, L., Lustig, C., & Zacks, R. (2007). Inhibitory mechanisms and the control of attention. In A. Conway, C. Jarrold, M. Kane, A. Miyake, & J. Towse (Eds.), *Variation in working memory* (227–249). New York: Oxford University Press.

Hasher, L., Zacks, R. T., & May, C. P. (1999). Inhibitory control, circadian arousal, and age. In D. Gopher & A. Koriat (Eds.), *Attention & Performance XVII, Cognitive Regulation of Performance: Interaction of Theory and Application* (653–675). Cambridge, MA: MIT Press.

Haslam, N., & Baron, J. (1994). Intelligence, personality, and prudence. In R. J. Sternberg & P. Ruzgis (Eds.), *Personality and intelligence* (32–58). Cambridge: Cambridge University Press.

Hastie, R., & Dawes, R. M. (2001). *Rational choice in an uncertain world.* Thousand Oaks, CA: Sage.

Hauser, M. (2006). *Moral minds.* New York: HarperCollins.

Heath, C., Larrick, R. P., & Wu, G. (1999). Goals as reference points. *Cognitive Psychology, 38,* 79–109.

Henneberger, M. (2004, July 19). A woman of the people. *Newsweek,* 31.

Herrnstein, R. J. (1990). Rational choice theory: Necessary but not sufficient. *American Psychologist, 45,* 356–367.

Herrnstein, R. J., & Murray, C. (1994). *The bell curve.* New York: Free Press.

Higgins, D. M., Peterson, J. B., Pihl, R. O., & Lee, A. G. M. (2007). Prefrontal cognitive ability, intelligence, big five personality, and the prediction of advanced academic and workplace performance. *Journal of Personality and Social Psychology, 93,* 298–319.

Hilton, D. J. (2003). Psychology and the financial markets: Applications to understanding and remedying irrational decision-making. In I. Brocas & J. D. Carrillo (Eds.), *The psychology of economic decisions (Vol. 1): Rationality and well-being* (273–297). Oxford: Oxford University Press.

Hines, T. M. (2003). *Pseudoscience and the paranormal* (2nd ed.). Buffalo, NY: Prometheus Books.

Hoch, S. J. (1985). Counterfactual reasoning and accuracy in predicting personal events. *Journal of Experimental Psychology: Learning, Memory, and Cognition, 11,* 719–731.

Hollis, M. (1996). *Reason in action: Essays in the philosophy of social science.* Cambridge: Cambridge University Press.

Holyoak, K. J., & Morrison, R. G. (Eds.) (2005). *The Cambridge handbook of thinking and reasoning.* New York: Cambridge University Press.

Horn, J. L., & Cattell, R. B. (1967). Age differences in fluid and crystallized intelligence. *Acta Psychologica, 26,* 1–23.

Horn, J. L., & Noll, J. (1997). Human cognitive capabilities: Gf-Gc theory. In D. Flanagan, J. Genshaft, & P. Harrison (Eds.), *Contemporary intellectual assessment: Theories, tests, and issues* (53–91). New York: Guilford Press.

Hsee, C. K. (1996). The evaluability hypothesis: An explanation of preference reversals between joint and separate evaluations of alternatives. *Organizational Behavior and Human Decision Processes, 46,* 247–257.

Hsee, C. K., & Hastie, R. (2006). Decision and experience: Why don't we choose what makes us happy? *Trends in Cognitive Sciences, 10,* 31–37.

Hsee, C. K., Loewenstein, G. F., Blount, S., & Bazerman, M. H. (1999). Preference reversals between joint and separate evaluations of options: A review and theoretical analysis. *Psychological Bulletin, 125,* 576–590.

Hsee, C. K., & Rottenstreich, Y. (2004). Music, pandas, and muggers: On the affective psychology of value. *Journal of Experimental Psychology: General, 133,* 23–30.

Hsee, C. K., & Zhang, J. (2004). Distinction bias: Misprediction and mischoice due to joint evaluation. *Journal of Personality and Social Psychology, 86,* 680–695.

Hudson, A., Melita, B., & Arnold, N. (1993). A case study assessing the validity of facilitated communication. *Journal of Autism and Developmental Disorders, 23,* 165–173.

Hull, D. L. (2000). Taking memetics seriously: Memetics will be what we make it. In R. Aunger (Ed.), *Darwinizing culture: The status of memetics as a science* (43–67). Oxford: Oxford University Press.

Hull, D. L. (2001). *Science and selection: Essays on biological evolution and the philosophy of science.* Cambridge: Cambridge University Press.

Hunt, C. E. (2001). Sudden infant death syndrome and other causes of infant mortality: Diagnosis, mechanisms, and risk for recurrence of siblings. *American Journal of Respiratory and Critical Care Medicine, 164,* 346–357.

Hunt, E., & Carlson, J. (2007). Considerations relating to the study of group differences in intelligence. *Perspectives on Psychological Science, 2,* 194–213.

Immelman, A. (2001, January 14). Bush gets bad rap on intelligence. Retrieved July 16, 2007 from http://www.csbsju.edu/uspp/Election/bush011401.htm.

Jackendoff, R. (1996). How language helps us think. *Pragmatics and Cognition, 4,* 1–34.

Jacobson, J. W., Foxx, R. M., & Mulick, J. A. (Eds.) (2004). *Controversial therapies for developmental disabilities: Fads, fashion, and science in professional practice.* Mahwah, NJ: Erlbaum.

Jacobson, J. W., Mulick, J. A., & Schwartz, A. A. (1995). A history of facilitated communication: Science, pseudoscience, and antiscience. *American Psychologist, 50,* 750–765.

Jacoby, S. (2008). *The age of American unreason.* New York: Pantheon.

Jacowitz, K. E., & Kahneman, D. (1995). Measures of anchoring in estimation tasks. *Personality and Social Psychology Bulletin, 21,* 1161–1167.

Jarvis, C. (2000). The rise and fall of Albania's pyramid schemes. *Finance & Development, 47*(1).

Jasper, J. D., & Chirstman, S. D. (2005). A neuropsychological dimension for anchoring effects. *Journal of Behavioral Decision Making, 18,* 343–369.

Jeffrey, R. C. (1983). *The logic of decision* (2nd ed.). Chicago: University of Chicago Press.

Jepson, C., Krantz, D., & Nisbett, R. (1983). Inductive reasoning: Competence or skill? *Behavioral and Brain Sciences, 6,* 494–501.

Johnson, E. J., & Goldstein, D. G. (2006). Do defaults save lives? In S. Lichtenstein & P. Slovic (Eds.), *The construction of preference* (682–688). Cambridge: Cambridge University Press.

Johnson, E. J., Hershey, J., Meszaros, J., & Kunreuther, H. (2000). Framing, probability distortions, and insurance decisions. In D. Kahneman & A. Tversky (Eds.), *Choices, values, and frames* (224–240). Cambridge: Cambridge University Press.

Johnson, M. K. (1991). Reality monitoring: Evidence from confabulation in organic brain disease patients. In G. Prigantano & D. Schacter (Eds.), *Awareness of deficit after brain injury* (121–140). New York: Oxford University Press.

Johnson-Laird, P. N. (1983). *Mental models.* Cambridge, MA: Harvard University Press.

Johnson-Laird, P. N. (1999). Deductive reasoning. *Annual Review of Psychology, 50,* 109–135.

Johnson-Laird, P. N. (2005). Mental models and thought. In K. J. Holyoak & R. G. Morrison (Eds.), *The Cambridge handbook of thinking and reasoning* (185–208). New York: Cambridge University Press.

Johnson-Laird, P. N. (2006). *How we reason.* Oxford: Oxford University Press.

Kagan, J., Rosman, B. L., Day, D., Albert, J., & Phillips, W. (1964). Information processing in the child: Significance of analytic and reflective attitudes. *Psychological Monographs, 78,* No. 578.

Kahneman, D. (1999). Objective happiness. In D. Kahneman, E. Diener, & N. Schwarz (Eds.), *Well-being: The foundations of hedonic psychology* (3–25). Thousand Oaks, CA: Sage.

Kahneman, D. (2000). A psychological point of view: Violations of rational rules as a diagnostic of mental processes. *Behavioral and Brain Sciences, 23,* 681–683.

Kahneman, D. (2003a). A perspective on judgment and choice: Mapping bounded rationality. *American Psychologist, 58,* 697–720.

Kahneman, D. (2003b). A psychological perspective on economics. *American Economic Review, 93,* 162–168.

Kahneman, D., Diener, E., & Schwarz, N. (Eds.) (1999). *Well-being: The foundations of hedonic psychology.* Thousand Oaks, CA: Sage.

Kahneman, D., & Frederick, S. (2002). Representativeness revisited: Attribute substitution in intuitive judgment. In T. Gilovich, D. Griffin, & D. Kahneman (Eds.), *Heuristics and biases: The psychology of intuitive judgment* (49–81). New York: Cambridge University Press.

Kahneman, D., & Frederick, S. (2005). A model of heuristic judgment. In K. J. Holyoak & R. G. Morrison (Eds.), *The Cambridge handbook of thinking and reasoning* (267–293). New York: Cambridge University Press.

Kahneman, D., Knetsch, J. L., & Thaler, R. (1986). Fairness as a constraint on profit seeking: Entitlements in the market. *American Economic Review, 76,* 728–741.

Kahneman, D., Knetsch, J. L., & Thaler, R. (1991). The endowment effect, loss aversion, and status quo bias. *Journal of Economic Perspectives, 5,* 193–206.

Kahneman, D., Krueger, A. B., Schkade, D., Schwarz, N., & Stone, A. (2006). Would you be happier if you were richer? A focusing illusion. *Science, 312,* 1908–1910.

Kahneman, D., & Tversky, A. (1972). On prediction and judgment. *Oregon Research Institute Monograph, 12*(4).

Kahneman, D., & Tversky, A. (1979). Prospect theory: An analysis of decision under risk. *Econometrica, 47,* 263–291.

Kahneman, D., & Tversky, A. (1982a). On the study of statistical intuitions. In D. Kahneman, P. Slovic, & A. Tversky (Eds.), *Judgment under uncertainty: Heuristics and biases* (493–508). Cambridge: Cambridge University Press.

Kahneman, D., & Tversky, A. (1982b). The simulation heuristic. In D. Kahneman, P. Slovic, & A. Tversky (Eds.), *Judgment under uncertainty: Heuristics and biases* (201–208). Cambridge: Cambridge University Press.

Kahneman, D., & Tversky, A. (1984). Choices, values, and frames. *American Psychologist, 39,* 341–350.

Kahneman, D., & Tversky, A. (1996). On the reality of cognitive illusions. *Psychological Review, 103,* 582–591.

Kahneman, D., & Tversky, A. (Eds.) (2000). *Choices, values, and frames.* Cambridge: Cambridge University Press.

Kanazawa, S. (2004). General intelligence as a domain-specific adaptation. *Psychological Review, 111,* 512–523.

Kane, M. J. (2003). The intelligent brain in conflict. *Trends in Cognitive Sciences, 7,* 375–377.

Kane, M. J., Bleckley, M., Conway, A., & Engle, R. W. (2001). A controlled-attention view of WM capacity. *Journal of Experimental Psychology: General*, 130, 169–183.

Kane, M. J., & Engle, R. W. (2002). The role of prefrontal cortex working-memory capacity, executive attention, and general fluid intelligence: An individual-differences perspective. *Psychonomic Bulletin and Review*, 9, 637–671.

Kane, M. J., & Engle, R. W. (2003). Working-memory capacity and the control of attention: The contributions of goal neglect, response competition, and task set to Stroop interference. *Journal of Experimental Psychology: General*, 132, 47–70.

Kane, M. J., Hambrick, D. Z., & Conway, A. R. A. (2005). Working memory capacity and fluid intelligence are strongly related constructs: Comment on Ackerman, Beier, and Boyle (2005). *Psychological Bulletin*, 131, 66–71.

Kane, M. J., Hambrick, D. Z., Tuholski, S. W., Wilhelm, O., Payne, T., & Engle, R. W. (2004). The generality of working memory capacity: A latent-variable approach to verbal and visuospatial memory span and reasoning. *Journal of Experimental Psychology: General*, 133, 189–217.

Kardash, C. M., & Scholes, R. J. (1996). Effects of pre-existing beliefs, epistemological beliefs, and need for cognition on interpretation of controversial issues. *Journal of Educational Psychology*, 88, 260–271.

Kaufman, J. S. (2001). WAIS-III IQs, Horn's theory, and generational changes from young adulthood to old age. *Intelligence*, 29, 131–167.

Keating, D. P. (1978). A search for social intelligence. *Journal of Educational Psychology*, 70, 218–223.

Keating, D. P. (1990). Charting pathways to the development of expertise. *Educational Psychologist*, 25, 243–267.

Kelman, M., & Lester, G. (1997). *Jumping the queue: An inquiry into the legal treatment of students with learning disabilities*. Cambridge, MA: Harvard University Press.

Kermer, D. A., Driver-Linn, E., Wilson, T. D., & Gilbert, D. T. (2006). Loss aversion is an affective forecasting error. *Psychological Science*, 17, 649–653.

Kern, L., & Doherty, M. E. (1982). "Pseudodiagnosticity" in an idealized medical problem-solving environment. *Journal of Medical Education*, 57, 100–104.

Kessler, R. (2004). *A matter of character: Inside the White House of George W. Bush*. New York: Sentinel.

Khan, U., & Dhar, R. (2007). Where there is a way, is there a will? The effect of future choices on self-control. *Journal of Experimental Psychology: General*, 136, 277–288.

Kihlstrom, J. F., & Cantor, N. (2000). Social intelligence. In R. J. Sternberg (Ed.), *Handbook of intelligence* (359–379). New York: Cambridge University Press.

Kimberg, D. Y., D'Esposito, M., & Farah, M. J. (1998). Cognitive functions in the prefrontal cortex—working memory and executive control. *Current Directions in Psychological Science*, 6, 185–192.

King, R. N., & Koehler, D. J. (2000). Illusory correlations in graphological inference. *Journal of Experimental Psychology: Applied*, 6, 336–348.

Kirby, K. N., & Herrnstein, R. J. (1995). Preference reversals due to myopic discounting of delayed reward. *Psychological Science*, 6, 83–89.

Kirby, K. N., Winston, G. C., & Santiesteban, M. (2005). Impatience and grades: Delay-discount rates correlate negatively with college GPA. *Learning and Individual Differences*, 15, 213–222.

Kirkpatrick, L., & Epstein, S. (1992). Cognitive-experiential self-theory and subjective probability: Evidence for two conceptual systems. *Journal of Personality and Social Psychology*, 63, 534–544.

Kitcher, P. (1993). *The advancement of science*. New York: Oxford University Press.

Klaczynski, P. A. (1997). Bias in adolescents' everyday reasoning and its relationship with intellectual ability, personal theories, and self-serving motivation. *Developmental Psychology*, 33, 273–283.

Klaczynski, P. A. (2001). Analytic and heuristic processing influences on adolescent reasoning and decision making. *Child Development*, 72, 844–861.

Klaczynski, P. A., & Gordon, D. H. (1996). Self-serving influences on adolescents' evaluations of belief-relevant evidence. *Journal of Experimental Child Psychology*, 62, 317–339.

Klaczynski, P. A., Gordon, D. H., & Fauth, J. (1997). Goal-oriented critical reasoning and individual differences in critical reasoning biases. *Journal of Educational Psychology*, 89, 470–485.

Klaczynski, P. A., & Lavallee, K. L. (2005). Domain-specific identity, epistemic regulation, and intellectual ability as predictors of belief-based reasoning: A dual-process perspective. *Journal of Experimental Child Psychology*, 92, 1–24.

Klaczynski, P. A., & Robinson, B. (2000). Personal theories, intellectual ability, and epistemological beliefs: Adult age differences in everyday reasoning tasks. *Psychology and Aging, 15*, 400–416.

Klauer, K. C., Stahl, C., & Erdfelder, E. (2007). The abstract selection task: New data and an almost comprehensive model. *Journal of Experimental Psychology: Learning, Memory, and Cognition, 33*, 688–703.

Klayman, J., & Ha, Y. (1987). Confirmation, disconfirmation, and information in hypothesis testing. *Psychological Review, 94*, 211–228.

Klein, G. (1998). *Sources of power: How people make decisions.* Cambridge, MA: MIT Press.

Klein, P. (1997). Multiplying the problems of intelligence by eight: A critique of Gardner's theory. *Canadian Journal of Education, 22*, 377–394.

Klein, P. (2003). Rethinking the multiplicity of cognitive resources and curricular representations: Alternatives to 'learning styles' and 'multiple intelligences.' *Journal of Curriculum Studies, 35*, 45–81.

Koehler, D. J. (1994). Hypothesis generation and confidence in judgment. *Journal of Experimental Psychology: Learning, Memory, and Cognition, 20*, 461–469.

Koehler, D. J., & Harvey, N. (Eds.) (2004). *Blackwell handbook of judgment and decision making.* Oxford: Blackwell.

Koehler, J. J. (1993). The influence of prior beliefs on scientific judgments of evidence quality. *Organizational Behavior and Human Decision Processes, 56*, 28–55.

Kokis, J., Macpherson, R., Toplak, M., West, R. F., & Stanovich, K. E. (2002). Heuristic and analytic processing: Age trends and associations with cognitive ability and cognitive styles. *Journal of Experimental Child Psychology, 83*, 26–52.

Koriat, A., Lichtenstein, S., & Fischhoff, B. (1980). Reasons for confidence. *Journal of Experimental Psychology: Human Learning and Memory, 6*, 107–118.

Kornblith, H. (1993). *Inductive inference and its natural ground.* Cambridge, MA: MIT Press.

Krantz, D. H. (1981). Improvements in human reasoning and an error in L. J. Cohen's. *Behavioral and Brain Sciences, 4*, 340–341.

Krantz, M. (2000, May 26). Stars above! Some investors seeking astrological guidance—really. *USA Today.*

Krueger, A. B. (2007). *What makes a terrorist: Economics and the roots of terrorism.* Princeton: Princeton University Press.

Krueger, J., & Zeiger, J. (1993). Social categorization and the truly false consensus effect. *Journal of Personality and Social Psychology, 65*, 670–680.

Kruger, J., & Dunning, D. (1999). Unskilled and unaware of it: How difficulties in recognizing one's own incompetence lead to inflated self-assessments. *Journal of Personality and Social Psychology, 77*, 1121–1134.

Kruger, J., Epley, N., Parker, J., & Ng, Z.-W. (2005). Egocentrism over e-mail: Can we communicate as well as we think? *Journal of Personality and Social Psychology, 89*, 925–936.

Kruglanski, A. W., & Webster, D. M. (1996). Motivated closing the mind: "Seizing" and "freezing." *Psychological Review, 103*, 263–283.

Kuhberger, A. (1998). The influence of framing on risky decisions: A meta-analysis. *Organizational Behavior and Human Decision Processes, 75*, 23–55.

Kuhn, D. (1991). *The skills of argument.* Cambridge: Cambridge University Press.

Kuhn, D. (1992). Thinking as argument. *Harvard Educational Review, 62*, 155–178.

Kuhn, D. (1993). Connecting scientific and informal reasoning. *Merrill-Palmer Quarterly, 38*, 74–103.

Kuhn, D. (2005). *Education for thinking.* Cambridge, MA: Harvard University Press.

Kuhn, D. (2007, Feb./March). Jumping to conclusions: Can people be counted on to make sound judgments? *Scientific American Mind*, 44–51.

Kuncel, N. R., Hezlett, S. A., & Ones, D. S. (2004). Academic performance, career potential, creativity, and job performance: Can one construct predict them all? *Journal of Personality and Social Psychology, 86*, 148–161.

Kunda, Z. (1990). The case for motivated reasoning. *Psychological Bulletin, 108*, 480–498.

Kunda, Z. (1999). *Social cognition: Making sense of people.* Cambridge, MA: MIT Press.

Lagerfeld, S. (2004). The revenge of the nerds. *Wilson Quarterly, 28*(3), 28–34.

Lakoff, G. (2004). *Don't think of an elephant: Know your values and frame the debate.* White River Junction, VT: Chelsea Green Publishing.

Lakoff, G. (2007). *Thinking points: Communicating our American values and vision.* New York: Farrar, Straus and Giroux.

Laland, K. N., & Brown, G. R. (2002). *Sense and nonsense: Evolutionary perspectives on human behaviour.* Oxford: Oxford University Press.

Langer, E. J. (1975). The illusion of control. *Journal of Personality and Social Psychology, 32*, 311–328.

Laqueur, W. (2004). The terrorism to come. *Policy Review, 126*, 49–64.

Larrick, R. P. (2004). Debiasing. In D. J. Koehler & N. Harvey (Eds.), *Blackwell handbook of judgment & decision making* (316–337). Malden, MA: Blackwell.

Larrick, R. P., Burson, K. A., & Soll, J. B. (2007). Social comparison and confidence: When thinking you're better than average predicts overconfidence (and when it does not). *Organizational Behavior and Human Decision Processes, 102*, 76–94.

LeBoeuf, R. A., & Shafir, E. (2003). Deep thoughts and shallow frames: On the susceptibility to framing effects. *Journal of Behavioral Decision Making, 16*, 77–92.

LeBoeuf, R. A., & Shafir, E. (2005). Decision making. In K. J. Holyoak & R. G. Morrison (Eds.), *The Cambridge handbook of thinking and reasoning* (243–265). New York: Cambridge University Press.

LeBoeuf, R. A., & Shafir, E. (2006). The long and short of it: Physical anchoring effects. *Behavioral Decision Making, 19*, 393–406.

Legrenzi, P., Girotto, V., & Johnson-Laird, P. N. (1993). Focussing in reasoning and decision making. *Cognition, 49*, 37–66.

Lehman, D. (1991). *Signs of the times: Deconstruction and the fall of Paul de Man.* New York: Poseidon Press.

Lehman, D. R., & Nisbett, R. E. (1990). A longitudinal study of the effects of undergraduate training on reasoning. *Developmental Psychology, 26*, 952–960.

Lemann, N. (1999). *The big test: The secret history of the American meritocracy.* New York: Farrar, Straus and Giroux.

Lepine, R., Barrouillet, P., & Camos, V. (2005). What makes working memory spans so predictive of high-level cognition? *Psychonomic Bulletin & Review, 12*, 165–170.

Leshowitz, B., DiCerbo, K. E., & Okun, M. A. (2002). Effects of instruction in methodological reasoning on information evaluation. *Teaching of Psychology, 29*, 5–10.

Leshowitz, B., Jenkens, K., Heaton, S., & Bough, T. (1993). Fostering critical thinking skills in students with learning disabilities: An instructional program. *Journal of Learning Disabilities, 26*, 483–490.

Leslie, A. M. (1987). Pretense and representation: The origins of "Theory of Mind." *Psychological Review*, 94, 412–426.

Levelt, W. (1995). Chapters of psychology. In R. L. Solso & D. W. Massaro (Eds.), *The science of the mind: 2001 and beyond* (184–202). New York: Oxford University Press.

Levesque, H. J. (1986). Making believers out of computers. *Artificial Intelligence*, 30, 81–108.

Levesque, H. J. (1989). Logic and the complexity of reasoning. In R. H. Thomason (Ed.), *Philosophical logic and artificial intelligence* (73–107). Dordrecht, The Netherlands: Kluwer Academic Publishers.

Levin, I. P., Gaeth, G. J., Schreiber, J., & Lauriola, M. (2002). A new look at framing effects: Distribution of effect sizes, individual differences, and independence of types of effects. *Organizational Behavior and Human Decision Processes*, 88, 411–429.

Levin, I. P., Wasserman, E. A., & Kao, S. F. (1993). Multiple methods of examining biased information use in contingency judgments. *Organizational Behavior and Human Decision Processes*, 55, 228–250.

Liberman, N., & Klar, Y. (1996). Hypothesis testing in Wason's selection task: Social exchange cheating detection or task understanding. *Cognition*, 58, 127–156.

Lichtenstein, S., & Fischhoff, B. (1977). Do those who know more also know more about how much they know? *Organizational Behavior and Human Performance*, 20, 159–183.

Lichtenstein, S., Fischhoff, B., & Phillips, L. (1982). Calibration and probabilities: The state of the art to 1980. In D. Kahneman, P. Slovic, & A. Tversky (Eds.), *Judgment under uncertainty: Heuristics and biases* (306–334). Cambridge: Cambridge University Press.

Lichtenstein, S., & Slovic, P. (Eds.) (2006). *The construction of preference*. Cambridge: Cambridge University Press.

Lieberman, M. D. (2000). Intuition: A social cognitive neuroscience approach. *Psychological Bulletin*, 126, 109–137.

Lieberman, M. D. (2003). Reflexive and reflective judgment processes: A social cognitive neuroscience approach. In J. P. Forgas, K. R. Williams, & W. von Hippel (Eds.), *Social judgments: Implicit and explicit processes* (44–67). New York: Cambridge University Press.

Lilienfeld, S. O. (2007). Psychological treatments that cause harm. *Perspectives on Psychological Science*, 2, 53–70.

Lilienfeld, S. O., & Arkowitz, H. (2007, April). Autism: An epidemic. *Scientific American Mind*, 82–83.

Lilienfeld, S. O., Lohr, J. M., & Moirer, D. (2001). The teaching of courses in the science and pseudoscience of psychology: Useful resources. *Teaching of Psychology*, 28(3), 182–191.

Lillard, A. (2001). Pretend play as twin Earth: A social-cognitive analysis. *Developmental Review*, 21, 495–531.

Lipsitt, L. P. (2003). Crib death: A biobehavioral phenomenon? *Current Directions in Psychological Science*, 12, 164–170.

Lipstadt, D. (1994). *Denying the Holocaust*. New York: Plume.

Locke, E. A., & Latham, G. P. (1991). Self-regulation through goal setting. *Organizational Behavior and Human Decision Processes*, 50, 212–247.

Loewenstein, G., & Prelec, D. (1991). Negative time preference. *American Economic Review*, 81, 347–352.

Loewenstein, G. F. (1996). Out of control: Visceral influences on behavior. *Organizational Behavior and Human Decision Processes*, 65, 272–292.

Loewenstein, G. F., Read, D., & Baumeister, R. (Eds.) (2003). *Time and decision: Economic and psychological perspectives on intertemporal choice*. New York: Russell Sage.

Loewenstein, G. F., Weber, E. U., Hsee, C. K., & Welch, N. (2001). Risk as feelings. *Psychological Bulletin*, 127, 267–286.

Loftus, E. F., & Guyer, M. J. (2002, May/June). Who abused Jane Doe: The hazards of the single case history. *Skeptical Inquirer*, 26(3), 24–32.

Loftus, E. F., & Ketcham, K. (1994). *The myth of repressed memory: False memories and allegations of sexual abuse*. New York: St. Martins.

Lubinski, D. (2004). Introduction to the special section on cognitive abilities: 100 years after Spearman's (1904) "General Intelligence, Objectively Determined and Measured." *Journal of Personality and Social Psychology*, 86, 96–111.

Luce, R. D., & Raiffa, H. (1957). *Games and decisions*. New York: Wiley.

Lumsden, C. J., & Wilson, E. O. (1981). *Genes, mind, and culture*. Cambridge, MA: Harvard University Press.

Lynch, A. (1996). *Thought contagion*. New York: Basic Books.

Macchi, L., & Mosconi, G. (1998). Computational features vs. frequentist phrasing in the base-rate fallacy. *Swiss Journal of Psychology*, 57, 79–85.

MacErlean, N. (2002, August 4). Do the sums—it's in your interest. *Observer (London)*, Cash 2–3.

Mackie, G. (1996). Ending footbinding and infibulation: A convention account. *American Sociological Review, 61,* 999–1017.

Macpherson, R., & Stanovich, K. E. (2007). Cognitive ability, thinking dispositions, and instructional set as predictors of critical thinking. *Learning and Individual Differences, 17,* 115–127.

Malkiel, B. G. (2004). *A random walk down Wall Street* (8th ed.). New York: Norton.

Manktelow, K. I. (1999). *Reasoning & Thinking.* Hove, England: Psychology Press.

Manktelow, K. I. (2004). Reasoning and rationality: The pure and the practical. In K. I. Manktelow & M. C. Chung (Eds.), *Psychology of reasoning: Theoretical and historical perspectives* (157–177). Hove, England: Psychology Press.

Manktelow, K. I., & Chung, M. C. (2004). *Psychology of reasoning: Theoretical and historical perspectives.* Hove, England: Psychology Press.

Marek, P., Jackson, S. L., Griggs, R. A., & Christopher, A. N. (1998). Supplementary books on critical thinking. *Teaching of Psychology, 25,* 266–269.

Margolis, H. (1987). *Patterns, thinking, and cognition.* Chicago: University of Chicago Press.

Margolis, H. (1996). *Dealing with risk.* Chicago: University of Chicago Press.

Markovits, H., & Nantel, G. (1989). The belief-bias effect in the production and evaluation of logical conclusions. *Memory & Cognition, 17,* 11–17.

Markowitz, H. M. (1952). The utility of wealth. *Journal of Political Economy, 60,* 151–158.

Marks, D. F. (2001). *The psychology of the psychic.* Buffalo, NY: Prometheus.

Marr, D. (1982). *Vision.* San Francisco: W. H. Freeman.

Matthews, G., Zeidner, M., & Roberts, R. D. (2002). *Emotional intelligence: Science & myth.* Cambridge, MA: MIT Press.

Maule, J., & Villejoubert, G. (2007). What lies beneath: Reframing framing effects. *Thinking and Reasoning, 13,* 25–44.

McCaffery, E. J., & Baron, J. (2004). Framing and taxation: Evaluation of tax policies involving household composition. *Journal of Economic Psychology, 25,* 679–705.

McCaffery, E. J., & Baron, J. (2006a). Isolation effects and the neglect of indirect effects of fiscal policies. *Journal of Behavioral Decision Making, 19,* 289–302.

McCaffery, E. J., & Baron, J. (2006b). Thinking about tax. *Psychology, Public Policy, and Law, 12,* 106–135.

McCauley, R. N. (2000). The naturalness of religion and the unnaturalness of science. In F. C. Keil & R. A. Wilson (Eds.), *Explanation and cognition* (61– 85). Cambridge, MA: MIT Press.

McClure, S. M., Laibson, D. I., Loewenstein, G., & Cohen, J. D. (2004). Separate neural systems value immediate and delayed monetary rewards. *Science*, 306, 503–507.

McDermott, T. (2005). *Perfect soldiers: The hijackers — who they were, why they did it.* New York: HarperCollins.

McElroy, T., & Seta, J. J. (2003). Framing effects: An analytic-holistic perspective. *Journal of Experimental Social Psychology*, 39, 610–617.

McEvoy, S. P., Stevenson, M. R., McCartt, A. T., Woodword, M., Haworth, C., Palamara, P., & Cercarelli, R. (2005, August 20). Role of mobile phones in motor vehicle crashes resulting in hospital attendance: A case-crossover study. *British Medical Journal*, 331(7514), 428.

McFadden, D. (1999). Rationality for economists? *Journal of Risk and Uncertainty*, 19, 73–105.

McGrew, K. S. (1997). Analysis of major intelligence batteries according to a proposed comprehensive Gf-Gc framework. In D. Flanagan, J. Genshaft, & P. Harrison (Eds.), *Contemporary intellectual assessment: Theories, tests, and issues* (151–180). New York: Guilford Press.

McGrew, K. S., & Woodcock, R. W. (2001). *Technical Manual: Woodcock-Johnson III.* Itasca, IL: Riverside Publishing.

McKenzie, C. R. M. (1994). The accuracy of intuitive judgment strategies: Covariation assessment and Bayesian inference. *Cognitive Psychology*, 26, 209–239.

McKenzie, C. R. M., Liersch, M. J., & Finkelstein, S. R. (2006). Recommendations implicit in policy defaults. *Psychological Science*, 17, 414–420.

McNally, R. J. (2003). Recovering memories of trauma: A view from the laboratory. *Current Directions in Psychological Science*, 12, 32–35.

McNeil, B., Pauker, S., Sox, H., & Tversky, A. (1982). On the elicitation of preferences for alternative therapies. *New England Journal of Medicine*, 306, 1259–1262.

Mealey, L. (1995). The sociobiology of sociopathy: An integrated evolutionary model. *Behavioral and Brain Sciences*, 18, 523–599.

Mele, A. R. (2001). *Self-deception unmasked.* Princeton: Princeton University Press.

Mele, A. R. (2003). Emotion and desire in self-deception. In A. Hatzimoysis

(Ed.), *Philosophy and the emotions* (163–179). New York: Cambridge University Press.

Mele, A. R., & Rawling, P. (Eds.) (2004). *The Oxford handbook of rationality.* Oxford: Oxford University Press.

Mellers, B., Hertwig, R., & Kahneman, D. (2001). Do frequency representations eliminate conjunction effects? An exercise in adversarial collaboration. *Psychological Science, 12,* 269–275.

Menand, L. (2004, August 30). The unpolitical animal. *The New Yorker,* 92–96.

Mesoudi, A., Whiten, A., & Laland, K. N. (2006). Towards a unified science of cultural evolution. *Behavioral and Brain Sciences, 29,* 329–383.

Messick, D. M. (1999). Alternative logics for decision making in social settings. *Journal of Economic Behavior & Organization, 39,* 11–28.

Messick, D. M., & Schell, T. (1992). Evidence for an equality heuristic in social decision making. *Acta Psychologica, 80,* 311–323.

Metcalfe, J., & Mischel, W. (1999). A hot/cool-system analysis of delay of gratification: Dynamics of will power. *Psychological Review, 106,* 3–19.

Mikhail, J. (2007). Universal moral grammar: Theory, evidence, and the future. *Trends in Cognitive Sciences, 11,* 143–152.

Millgram, E. (Ed.) (2001). *Varieties of practical reasoning.* Cambridge, MA: MIT Press.

Mischel, W., & Ebbesen, E. B. (1970). Attention in delay of gratification. *Journal of Personality and Social Psychology, 16,* 329–337.

Mischel, W., Shoda, Y., & Rodriguez, M. L. (1989, May 26). Delay of gratification in children. *Science, 244,* 933–938.

Mitchell, P., Robinson, E. J., Isaacs, J. E., & Nye, R., M. (1996). Contamination in reasoning about false belief: An instance of realist bias in adults but not children. *Cognition, 59,* 1–21.

Miyake, A., Friedman, N., Emerson, M. J., & Witzki, A. H. (2000). The utility and diversity of executive functions and their contributions to complex "frontal lobe" tasks: A latent variable analysis. *Cognitive Psychology, 41,* 49–100.

Molden, D. C., & Higgins, E. T. (2005). Motivated thinking. In K. J. Holyoak & R. G. Morrison (Eds.), *The Cambridge handbook of thinking and reasoning* (295–317). New York: Cambridge University Press.

Moore, D. A. (2007). Not so above average after all: When people believe they are worse than average and its implications for theories of bias in social comparison. *Organizational Behavior and Human Decision Processes*, 102, 42–58.

Moore, D. A., & Small, D. A. (2007). Error and bias in comparative judgment: On being both better and worse than we think we are. *Journal of Personality and Social Psychology*, 92, 972–989.

Moore, R. L. (1977). *In search of white crows.* New York: Oxford University Press.

Moscovitch, M. (1989). Confabulation and the frontal systems: Strategic versus associative retrieval in neuropsychological theories of memory. In H. L. Roediger & F. I. M. Craik (Eds.), *Varieties of memory and consciousness* (133–160). Hillsdale, NJ: Erlbaum.

Moshman, D. (1994). Reasoning, metareasoning, and the promotion of rationality. In A. Demetriou & A. Efklides (Eds.), *Intelligence, mind, and reasoning: Structure and development* (135–150). Amsterdam: Elsevier.

Moshman, D. (2004). From inference to reasoning: The construction of rationality. *Thinking and Reasoning*, 10, 221–239.

Mostert, M. P. (2001). Facilitated communication since 1995: A review of published studies. *Journal of Autism and Developmental Disorders*, 31(3), 287–313.

Muller, I. (1991). *Hitler's justice: The courts of the Third Reich.* Cambridge, MA: Harvard University Press.

Murphy, D., & Stich, S. (2000). Darwin in the madhouse: Evolutionary psychology and the classification of mental disorders. In P. Carruthers & A. Chamberlain (Eds.), *Evolution and the human mind: Modularity, language and meta-cognition* (62–92). Cambridge: Cambridge University Press.

Musella, D. P. (2005). Gallup Poll shows that Americans' belief in the paranormal persists. *Skeptical Inquirer*, 29(5), 5.

Mussweiler, T., & Englich, B. (2005). Subliminal anchoring: Judgmental consequences and underlying mechanisms. *Organizational Behavior and Human Decision Processes*, 98, 133–143.

Mussweiler, T., Englich, B., & Strack, F. (2004). Anchoring effect. In R. Pohl (Ed.), *Cognitive illusions: A handbook on fallacies and biases in thinking, judgment and memory* (183–200). Hove, England: Psychology Press.

Mussweiler, T., Strack, F., & Pfeiffer, T. (2000). Overcoming the inevitable anchoring effect: Considering the opposite compensates for selective accessibility. *Personality and Social Psychology Bulletin*, 9, 1142–1150.

Myers, D. G. (1990). *Social psychology* (3rd ed.). New York: McGraw-Hill.

Myers, D. G. (2002). *Intuition: Its powers and perils.* New Haven, CT: Yale University Press.

Naftali, T. (2007). *George H. W. Bush.* New York: Times Books.

Nathan, D., & Snedeker, M. (1995). *Satan's silence: Ritual abuse and the making of a modern American witch hunt.* New York: Basic Books.

National Highway Traffic Safety Administration (2004). *Traffic safety facts, 2004.* Washington, DC: Author.

National Safety Council (1990). *Accident facts* (1990 ed.). Chicago: Author.

National Safety Council (2001). *Report on injuries in America, 2001.* Retrieved March 29, 2002, from www.nsc.org/library/rept2000.htm.

Neisser, U. (Ed.) (1998). *The rising curve: Long-term changes in IQ and related measures.* Washington, DC: American Psychological Association.

Neisser, U., Boodoo, G., Bouchard, T., Boykin, A. W., Brody, N., Ceci, S. J., Halpern, D., Loehlin, J., Perloff, R., Sternberg, R., & Urbina, S. (1996). Intelligence: Knowns and unknowns. *American Psychologist, 51,* 77–101.

Neter, E., & Ben-Shakhar, G. (1989). Predictive validity of graphological inferences: A meta-analysis. *Personality and Individual Differences, 10,* 737–745.

Newell, A. (1982). The knowledge level. *Artificial Intelligence, 18,* 87–127.

Newell, A. (1990). *Unified theories of cognition.* Cambridge, MA: Harvard University Press.

Newstead, S. E., & Evans, J. St. B. T. (Eds.) (1995). *Perspectives on thinking and reasoning.* Hove, England: Erlbaum.

NHTSA (2000). *Vehicle design versus aggressivity,* National Highway Traffic Safety Administration, U.S. Department of Transportation (DOT HS 809 194), Retrieved February 23, 2002, from NHTSA Web site: http://www-nrd .nhtsa.dot.gov/pdf/nrd-11/DOT_HS_809194.pdf.

Nichols, S., & Stich, S. P. (2003). *Mindreading: An integrated account of pretence, self-awareness, and understanding other minds.* Oxford: Oxford University Press.

Nickerson, R. S. (1988). On improving thinking through instruction. In E. Z. Rothkopf (Ed.), *Review of Research in Education (Vol. 15)* (3–57). Washington, DC: American Educational Research Association.

Nickerson, R. S. (1998). Confirmation bias: A ubiquitous phenomenon in many guises. *Review of General Psychology, 2,* 175–220.

Nickerson, R. S. (2004). *Cognition and chance: The psychology of probabilistic reasoning.* Mahwah, NJ: Erlbaum.

Nisbett, R. E. (1993). *Rules for reasoning.* Hillsdale, NJ: Erlbaum.

Nisbett, R. E., & Ross, L. (1980). *Human inference: Strategies and shortcomings of social judgment.* Englewood Cliffs, NJ: Prentice-Hall.

Nisbett, R. E., & Wilson, T. D. (1977). Telling more than we can know: Verbal reports on mental processes. *Psychological Review, 84,* 231–259.

Norris, S. P., & Ennis, R. H. (1989). *Evaluating critical thinking.* Pacific Grove, CA: Midwest Publications.

Northcraft, G. B., & Neale, M. A. (1987). Experts, amateurs, and real estate: An anchoring-and-adjustment perspective on property pricing decisions. *Organizational Behavior and Human Decision Processes, 39,* 84–97.

Nozick, R. (1993). *The nature of rationality.* Princeton: Princeton University Press.

Oaksford, M., & Chater, N. (1994). A rational analysis of the selection task as optimal data selection. *Psychological Review, 101,* 608–631.

Oaksford, M., & Chater, N. (1995). Theories of reasoning and the computational explanation of everyday inference. *Thinking and Reasoning, 1,* 121–152.

Oaksford, M., & Chater, N. (2007). *Bayesian rationality: The probabilistic approach to human reasoning.* Oxford: Oxford University Press.

Oatley, K. (1992). *Best laid schemes: The psychology of emotions.* Cambridge: Cambridge University Press.

Oatley, K. (1999). Why fiction may be twice as true as fact: Fiction as cognitive and emotional simulation. *Review of General Psychology, 3,* 101–117.

Oatley, K. (2004). *Emotions: A brief history.* New York: Blackwell.

O'Donoghue, T., & Rabin, M. (2000). The economics of immediate gratification. *Journal of Behavioral Decision Making, 13,* 233–250.

Ohman, A., & Mineka, S. (2001). Fears, phobias, and preparedness: Toward an evolved module of fear and fear learning. *Psychological Review, 108,* 483–522.

Ones, D. S., Viswesvaran, C., & Dilchert, S. (2005). Cognitive ability in selection decisions. In O. Wilhelm & R. W. Engle (Eds.), *Handbook of understanding and measuring intelligence* (431–468). Thousand Oaks, CA: Sage.

Over, D. E. (2000). Ecological rationality and its heuristics. *Thinking and Reasoning, 6,* 182–192.

Over, D. E. (2002). The rationality of evolutionary psychology. In J. L. Bermudez & A. Millar (Eds.), *Reason and nature: Essays in the theory of rationality* (187–207). Oxford: Oxford University Press.

Over, D. E. (2004). Rationality and the normative/descriptive distinction. In

D. J. Koehler & N. Harvey (Eds.), *Blackwell handbook of judgment and decision making* (3–18). Malden, MA: Blackwell.

Ozer, D. J., & Benet-Martinez, V. (2006). Personality and the prediction of consequential outcomes. *Annual Review of Psychology, 57,* 401–421.

Pacini, R., & Epstein, S. (1999). The relation of rational and experiential information processing styles to personality, basic beliefs, and the ratio-bias phenomenon. *Journal of Personality and Social Psychology, 76,* 972–987.

Pallier, G., Wilkinson, R., Danthiir, V., Kleitman, S., Knezevic, G., Stankov, L., & Roberts, R. D. (2002). The role of individual differences in the accuracy of confidence judgments. *Journal of General Psychology, 129,* 257–299.

Parfit, D. (1984). *Reasons and persons.* Oxford: Oxford University Press.

Parker, A. M., & Fischhoff, B. (2005). Decision-making competence: External validation through an individual differences approach. *Journal of Behavioral Decision Making, 18,* 1–27.

Parsell, D. (2004, November 13). Assault on autism. *Science News, 166,* 311–312.

Paul, A. M. (2005). *The cult of personality testing.* New York: Free Press.

Paulos, J. A. (1990). *Innumeracy.* New York: Vintage.

Paulos, J. A. (2003). *A mathematician plays the stock market.* New York: Basic Books.

Perkins, D. N. (1985). Postprimary education has little impact on informal reasoning. *Journal of Educational Psychology, 77,* 562–571.

Perkins, D. N. (1995). *Outsmarting IQ: The emerging science of learnable intelligence.* New York: Free Press.

Perkins, D. N. (2002). The engine of folly. In R. J. Sternberg (Ed.), *Why smart people can be so stupid* (64–85). New Haven, CT: Yale University Press.

Perkins, D. N., Farady, M., & Bushey, B. (1991). Everyday reasoning and the roots of intelligence. In J. Voss, D. Perkins, & J. Segal (Eds.), *Informal reasoning and education* (83–105). Hillsdale, NJ: Erlbaum.

Perkins, D. N., Jay, E., & Tishman, S. (1993). Beyond abilities: A dispositional theory of thinking. *Merrill-Palmer Quarterly, 39,* 1–21.

Perkins, D. N., & Ritchhart, R. (2004). When is good thinking? In D. Y. Dai & R. J. Sternberg (Eds.), *Motivation, emotion, and cognition: Integrative perspectives on intellectual functioning and development* (351–384). Mahwah, NJ: Erlbaum.

Perner, J. (1991). *Understanding the representational mind.* Cambridge, MA: MIT Press.

Perner, J. (1998). The meta-intentional nature of executive functions and theory of mind. In P. Carruthers & J. Boucher (Eds.), *Language and thought: Inter-disciplinary themes* (270–283). Cambridge: Cambridge University Press.

Perreaux, L. (2001, May 17). Drivers all edgy: Survey. *National Post* (Toronto), A7.

Petrinovich, L., O'Neill, P., & Jorgensen, M. (1993). An empirical study of moral intuitions: Toward an evolutionary ethics. *Journal of Personality and Social Psychology, 64*, 467–478.

Petry, N. M., Bickel, W. K., & Arnett, M. (1998). Shortened time horizons and insensitivity to future consequences in heroin addicts. *Addiction, 93*, 729–738.

Pinker, S. (1997). *How the mind works.* New York: Norton.

Piper, A. (1998). Multiple personality disorder: Witchcraft survives in the twentieth century. *Skeptical Inquirer, 22*(3), 44–50.

Plomin, R., & Spinath, F. M. (2004). Intelligence: Genetics, gene, and genomics. *Journal of Personality and Social Psychology, 86*, 112–129.

Plous, S. (1993). *The psychology of judgment and decision making.* New York: McGraw-Hill.

Pohl, R. (Ed.) (2004). *Cognitive illusions: A handbook on fallacies and biases in thinking, judgment and memory.* Hove, England: Psychology Press.

Poletiek, F. H. (2001). *Hypothesis testing behaviour.* Hove, England: Psychology Press.

Politzer, G., & Macchi, L. (2000). Reasoning and pragmatics. *Mind & Society, 1*, 73–93.

Politzer, G., & Noveck, I. A. (1991). Are conjunction rule violations the result of conversational rule violations? *Journal of Psycholinguistic Research, 20*, 83–103.

Pollock, J. L. (1995). *Cognitive carpentry.* Cambridge, MA: MIT Press.

Popper, K. R. (1972). *Objective knowledge: An evolutionary approach.* Oxford: Oxford University Press.

Postman, N. (1988). *Conscientious objections.* New York: Vintage Books.

Prado, J., & Noveck, I. A. (2007). Overcoming perceptual features in logical reasoning: A parametric functional magnetic resonance imaging study. *Journal of Cognitive Neuroscience, 19*, 642–657.

Prelec, D., & Bodner, R. (2003). Self-signaling and self-control. In G. F. Loewenstein, D. Read, & R. F. Baumeister (Eds.), *Time and decision* (277–298). New York: Russell Sage.

Prentice, R. A. (2003). Chicago man, K-T man, and the future of behavioral law and economics. *Vanderbilt Law Review, 56,* 1663–1777.

Pressley, M., & Ghatala, E. S. (1990). Self-regulated learning: Monitoring learning from text. *Educational Psychologist, 25,* 19–33.

Pronin, E. (2006). Perception and misperception of bias in human judgment. *Trends in Cognitive Sciences, 11,* 37–43.

Pronin, E., Lin, D. Y., & Ross, L. (2002). The bias blind spot: Perceptions of bias in self versus others. *Journal of Personality and Social Psychology Bulletin, 28,* 369–381.

Pylyshyn, Z. (1984). *Computation and cognition.* Cambridge, MA: MIT Press.

Quinn, J. B. (2008, January 21). Help! I'm investing my 401(k). *Newsweek,* 82.

Rachlin, H. (1995). Self-control: Beyond commitment. *Behavioral and Brain Sciences, 18,* 109–159.

Rachlin, H. (2000). *The science of self-control.* Cambridge, MA: Harvard University Press.

Rachlinski, J. J. (2006). Cognitive errors, individual differences, and paternalism. *University of Chicago Law Review, 73*(1), 207–229.

Rae-Dupree, J. (2007, December 30). Innovative minds don't think alike. *New York Times,* BU3.

Raghubir, P., & Srivastava, J. (2002). Effect of face value on product valuation in foreign currencies. *Journal of Consumer Research, 29,* 335–347.

Randi, J. (1980). *Flim-Flam.* Buffalo, NY: Prometheus Books.

Read, D., Loewenstein, G., & Rabin, M. (1999). Choice bracketing. *Journal of Risk and Uncertainty, 19,* 171–197.

Reber, A. S. (1992). An evolutionary context for the cognitive unconscious. *Philosophical Psychology, 5,* 33–51.

Reber, A. S. (1993). *Implicit learning and tacit knowledge.* New York: Oxford University Press.

Reber, A. S., Walkenfeld, F. F., & Hernstadt, R. (1991). Implicit and explicit learning: Individual differences and IQ. *Journal of Experimental Psychology: Learning, Memory, and Cognition, 17,* 888–896.

Reiser, M., Ludwig, A., Saxe, M., & Wagner, B. (1979). An evaluation of the use of psychics in the investigation of major crimes. *Journal of Police Science and Administration, 7,* 18–25.

Reiss, S., & Reiss, M. M. (2004). Curiosity and mental retardation: Beyond IQ. *Mental Retardation, 42,* 77–81.

Remnick, D. (2004, September 13). The wilderness campaign. *The New Yorker*, 80(26), 57–83.

Reyna, V. F. (2004). How people make decisions that involve risk. *Current Directions in Psychological Science*, 13, 60–66.

Reyna, V. F., & Farley, F. (2006). Risk and rationality in adolescent decision making. *Psychological Science in the Public Interest*, 7, 1–44.

Reyna, V. F., & Lloyd, F. J. (2006). Physician decision making and cardiac risk: Effects of knowledge, risk perception, risk tolerance, and fuzzy processing. *Journal of Experimental Psychology: Applied*, 12, 179–195.

Reyna, V. F., Lloyd, F. J., & Brainerd, C. J. (2003). Memory, development, and rationality: An integrative theory of judgment and decision making. In S. L. Schneider & J. Shanteau (Eds.), *Emerging perspectives on judgment and decision research* (201–245). New York: Cambridge University Press.

Richerson, P. J., & Boyd, R. (2005). *Not by genes alone: How culture transformed human evolution.* Chicago: University of Chicago Press.

Ridley, M. (2000). *Mendel's demon: Gene justice and the complexity of life.* London: Weidenfeld and Nicolson.

Ritchhart, R., & Perkins, D. N. (2005). Learning to think: The challenges of teaching thinking. In K. J. Holyoak & R. G. Morrison (Eds.), *The Cambridge handbook of thinking and reasoning* (775–802). New York: Cambridge University Press.

Rodriguez, M. L., Mischel, W., & Shoda, Y. (1989). Cognitive person variables in delay of gratification of older children at risk. *Journal of Personality and Social Psychology*, 57, 358–367.

Roese, N. (1997). Counterfactual thinking. *Psychological Bulletin*, 121, 131–148.

Rokeach, M. (1960). *The open and closed mind.* New York: Basic Books.

Ronis, D. L., & Yates, J. F. (1987). Components of probability judgment accuracy: Individual consistency and effects of subject matter and assessment method. *Organizational Behavior and Human Decision Processes*, 40, 193–218.

Roseman, I. J., & Read, S. J. (2007). Psychologist at play: Robert Abelson's life and contributions to psychological science. *Perspectives on Psychological Science*, 2, 86–97.

Rottenstreich, Y., & Hsee, C. K. (2001). Money, kisses, and electric shocks: On the affective psychology of risk. *Psychological Science*, 12, 185–190.

Royal Swedish Academy of Sciences (2002a). *Advanced information on the*

Prize in Economic Sciences 2002. Retrieved August 6, 2007 from nobelprize
.org/nobel_prizes/economics/laureates/2002/ecoadv02.pdf.

Royal Swedish Academy of Sciences (2002b). *Press Release: The Bank of Sweden Prize in Economic Sciences in Memory of Alfred Nobel 2002 Information for the Public.* Retrieved August 6, 2007 from http://www.nobel.se/
economics/laureates/2002/press.html.

Royzman, E. B., Cassidy, K. W., & Baron, J. (2003). "I know, you know": Epistemic egocentrism in children and adults. *Review of General Psychology, 7,* 38–65.

Rozin, P., Kabnick, K., Pete, E., Fischler, C., & Shields, C. (2003). The ecology of eating: Smaller portions in France than in the United States help explain the French paradox. *Psychological Science, 14,* 450–454.

Rumelhart, D. E., Smolensky, P., McClelland, J. L., & Hinton, G. E. (1986). Schemata and sequential thought processes in PDP models. In J. L. McClelland & D. E. Rumelhart (Eds.), *Parallel distributed processing: Explorations in the microstructure of cognition (Vol. 2)* (7–57). Cambridge, MA: MIT Press.

Russo, J. E., & Schoemaker, P. (1989). *Decision traps: Ten barriers to brilliant decision making and how to overcome them.* New York: Simon & Schuster.

Sá, W., Kelley, C., Ho, C., & Stanovich, K. E. (2005). Thinking about personal theories: Individual differences in the coordination of theory and evidence. *Personality and Individual Differences, 38,* 1149–1161.

Sá, W., & Stanovich, K. E. (2001). The domain specificity and generality of mental contamination: Accuracy and projection in judgments of mental content. *British Journal of Psychology, 92,* 281–302.

Sá, W., West, R. F., & Stanovich, K. E. (1999). The domain specificity and generality of belief bias: Searching for a generalizable critical thinking skill. *Journal of Educational Psychology, 91,* 497–510.

Sabini, J., & Silver, M. (1998). *Emotion, character, and responsibility.* New York: Oxford University Press.

Saffran, J. R., Aslin, R. N., & Newport, E. L. (1996). Statistical learning by 8-month-old infants. *Science, 274,* 1926–1928.

Sailer, S. (2004, October 21). This just in—Kerry's IQ likely lower than Bush's! Retrieved July 16, 2007 from http://www.vdare.com/sailer/kerry_iq_lower
.htm.

Salthouse, T. A., Atkinson, T. M., & Berish, D. E. (2003). Executive functioning as a potential mediator of age-related cognitive decline in normal adults. *Journal of Experimental Psychology: General*, 132, 566–594.

Samuels, R. (2005). The complexity of cognition: Tractability arguments for massive modularity. In P. Carruthers, S. Laurence, & S. Stich (Eds.), *The innate mind* (107–121). Oxford: Oxford University Press.

Samuels, R. (2008). The magical number two, plus or minus: Some comments on dual-process theories. In J. Evans & K. Frankish (Eds.), *In two minds: Dual processes and beyond*. Oxford: Oxford University Press.

Samuels, R., & Stich, S. P. (2004). Rationality and psychology. In A. R. Mele & P. Rawling (Eds.), *The Oxford handbook of rationality* (279–300). Oxford: Oxford University Press.

Samuelson, W., & Zeckhauser, R. J. (1988). Status quo bias in decision making. *Journal of Risk and Uncertainty*, 1, 7–59.

Sanna, L. J., & Schwarz, N. (2004). Integrating temporal biases: The interplay of focal thoughts and accessibility experiences. *Psychological Science*, 15, 474–481.

Sanna, L. J., & Schwarz, N. (2006). Metacognitive experiences and human judgment: The case of hindsight bias and its debiasing. *Current Directions in Psychological Science*, 15, 172–176.

Savage, L. J. (1954). *The foundations of statistics*. New York: Wiley.

Schaefer, P. S., Williams, C. C., Goodie, A. S., & Campbell, W. K. (2004). Overconfidence and the Big Five. *Journal of Research in Personality*, 38, 473–480.

Schelling, T. C. (1984). *Choice and consequence: Perspectives of an errant economist*. Cambridge, MA: Harvard University Press.

Schkade, D. A., & Kahneman, D. (1998). Does living in California make people happy? *Psychological Science*, 9, 340–346.

Schmidt, F. L., & Hunter, J. E. (1992). Development of a causal model of processes determining job performance. *Current Directions in Psychological Science*, 1, 89–92.

Schmidt, F. L., & Hunter, J. E. (1998). The validity and utility of selection methods in personnel psychology: Practical and theoretical implications of 85 years of research findings. *Psychological Bulletin*, 124, 262–274.

Schmidt, F. L., & Hunter, J. E. (2004). General mental ability in the world of work: Occupational attainment and job performance. *Journal of Personality and Social Psychology*, 86, 162–173.

Schneider, S. L. (1995). Item difficulty, discrimination, and the confidence-frequency effect in a categorical judgment task. *Organizational Behavior and Human Decision Processes, 61,* 148–167.

Schneider, S. L., Burke, M. D., Solomonson, A. L., & Laurion, S. K. (2005). Incidental framing effects and associative processes: A study of attribute frames in broadcast news stories. *Journal of Behavioral Decision Making, 18,* 261–280.

Schneider, S. L., & Shanteau, J. (Eds.) (2003). *Emerging perspectives on judgment and decision research.* New York: Cambridge University Press.

Schommer, M. (1990). Effects of beliefs about the nature of knowledge on comprehension. *Journal of Educational Psychology, 82,* 498–504.

Schooler, C. (1998). Environmental complexity and the Flynn effect. In U. Neisser (Ed.), *The rising curve: Long-term changes in IQ and related measures* (67–79). Washington, DC: American Psychological Association.

Schwartz, B. (2004). *The paradox of choice.* New York: Ecco Press.

Schwarz, N. (1996). *Cognition and communication: Judgmental biases, research methods, and the logic of conversation.* Mahwah, NJ: Erlbaum.

Schwarz, N., & Clore, G. L. (2003). Mood as information: 20 years later. *Psychological Inquiry, 14,* 296–303.

Schweizer, K., & Koch, W. (2002). A revision of Cattell's Investment Theory: Cognitive properties influencing learning. *Learning and Individual Differences, 13,* 57–82.

Sedlmeier, P. (1999). *Improving statistical reasoning: Theoretical models and practical implications.* Mahwah, NJ: Erlbaum.

Sedlmeier, P., & Gigerenzer, G. (2001). Teaching Bayesian reasoning in less than two hours. *Journal of Experimental Psychology: General, 130,* 380–400.

Seligmann, J., & Chideya, F. (1992, September 21). Horror story or big hoax? *Newsweek,* 75.

Shafir, E. (1994). Uncertainty and the difficulty of thinking through disjunctions. *Cognition, 50,* 403–430.

Shafir, E. (Ed.) (2003). *Preference, belief, and similarity: Selected writings of Amos Tversky.* Cambridge, MA: MIT Press.

Shafir, E., Diamond, P., & Tversky, A. (1997). Money illusion. *Quarterly Journal of Economics, 112,* 341–374.

Shafir, E., & LeBoeuf, R. A. (2002). Rationality. *Annual Review of Psychology, 53,* 491–517.

Shallice, T. (1988). *From neuropsychology to mental structure.* Cambridge: Cambridge University Press.

Shanks, D. R. (1995). Is human learning rational? *Quarterly Journal of Experimental Psychology, 48A,* 257–279.

Shermer, M. (1997). *Why people believe weird things.* New York: W. H. Freeman.

Shiffrin, R. M., & Schneider, W. (1977). Controlled and automatic human information processing: II. Perceptual learning, automatic attending, and a general theory. *Psychological Review, 84,* 127–190.

Shiv, B., Loewenstein, G., Bechara, A., Damasio, H., & Damasio, A. R. (2005). Investment behavior and the negative side of emotion. *Psychological Science, 16,* 435–439.

Showalter, E. (1997). *Hystories: Hysterical epidemics and modern media.* New York: Columbia University Press.

Sieck, W. R., & Arkes, H. R. (2005). The recalcitrance of overconfidence and its contribution to decision aid neglect. *Journal of Behavioral Decision Making, 18,* 29–53.

Simon, A. F., Fagley, N. S., & Halleran, J. G. (2004). Decision framing: Moderating effects of individual differences and cognitive processing. *Journal of Behavioral Decision Making, 17,* 77–93.

Simon, H. A. (1955). A behavioral model of rational choice. *Quarterly Journal of Economics, 69,* 99–118.

Simon, H. A. (1956). Rational choice and the structure of the environment. *Psychological Review, 63,* 129–138.

Simoneau, M., & Markovits, H. (2003). Reasoning with premises that are not empirically true: Evidence for the role of inhibition and retrieval. *Developmental Psychology, 39,* 964–975.

Simonton, D. K. (2006). Presidential IQ, openness, intellectual brilliance, and leadership: Estimates and correlations for 42 U.S. chief executives. *Political Psychology, 27,* 511–526.

Sinaceur, M., Heath, C., & Cole, S. (2005). Emotional and deliberative reactions to a public crisis: Mad Cow Disease in France. *Psychological Science, 16,* 247–254.

Sivak, M. (2002). How common sense fails us on the road: Contribution of bounded rationality to the annual worldwide toll of one million traffic fatalities. *Transportation Research Part F, 5,* 259–269.

Sivak, M., & Flannagan, M. J. (2003). Flying and driving after the September 11 attacks. *American Scientist, 91,* 6–7.

Skyrms, B. (1996). *The evolution of the social contract.* Cambridge: Cambridge University Press.

Slemrod, J., & Bakija, J. (1996). *Taxing ourselves: A citizen's guide to the great debate over tax reform.* Cambridge, MA: MIT Press.

Sloman, A. (1993). The mind as a control system. In C. Hookway & D. Peterson (Eds.), *Philosophy and cognitive science* (69–110). Cambridge: Cambridge University Press.

Sloman, A., & Chrisley, R. (2003). Virtual machines and consciousness. *Journal of Consciousness Studies,* 10, 133–172.

Sloman, S. A. (1996). The empirical case for two systems of reasoning. *Psychological Bulletin,* 119, 3–22.

Sloman, S. A. (2002). Two systems of reasoning. In T. Gilovich, D. Griffin, & D. Kahneman (Eds.), *Heuristics and biases: The psychology of intuitive judgment* (379–396). New York: Cambridge University Press.

Sloman, S. A., & Over, D. E. (2003). Probability judgement from the inside out. In D. E. Over (Ed.), *Evolution and the psychology of thinking* (145–169). Hove, England: Psychology Press.

Sloman, S. A., Over, D., Slovak, L., & Stibel, J. M. (2003). Frequency illusions and other fallacies. *Organizational Behavior and Human Decision Processes,* 91, 296–309.

Slovic, P. (1995). The construction of preference. *American Psychologist,* 50, 364–371.

Slovic, P. (2007). "If I look at the mass I will never act": Psychic numbing and genocide. *Judgment and Decision Making,* 2, 79–95.

Slovic, P., Finucane, M. L., Peters, E., & MacGregor, D. G. (2002). The affect heuristic. In T. Gilovich, D. Griffin, & D. Kahneman (Eds.), *Heuristics and biases: The psychology of intuitive judgment* (397–420). New York: Cambridge University Press.

Slovic, P., Monahan, J., & MacGregor, D. G. (2000). Violence risk assessment and risk communication: The effects of using actual cases, providing instruction, and employing probability versus frequency formats. *Law and Human Behavior,* 24, 271–296.

Slovic, P., & Peters, E. (2006). Risk perception and affect. *Current Directions in Psychological Science,* 15, 322–325.

Slugoski, B. R., & Wilson, A. E. (1998). Contribution of conversation skills to the production of judgmental errors. *European Journal of Social Psychology,* 28, 575–601.

Smith, E. E., Patalino, A. L., & Jonides, J. (1998). Alternative strategies of cate-gorization. In S. A. Sloman & L. J. Rips (Eds.), *Similarity and symbols in human thinking* (81–110). Cambridge, MA: MIT Press.

Smith, E. R., & DeCoster, J. (2000). Dual-process models in social and cog-nitive psychology: Conceptual integration and links to underlying memory systems. *Personality and Social Psychology Review, 4,* 108–131.

Smith, M., & Belcher, R. (1993). Facilitated communication with adults with autism. *Journal of Autism and Developmental Disorders, 23,* 175–183.

Snow, D. N., Zurcher, L. A., & Ekland-Olson, S. (1980). Social networks and social movements: A microstructural approach to differential recruitment. *American Sociological Review, 45,* 787–801.

Sonuga-Barke, E. (2002). Psychological heterogeneity in AD/HD — a dual pathway model of behavior and cognition. *Behavioural Brain Research, 130,* 29–36.

Sonuga-Barke, E. (2003). The dual pathway model of AD/HD: An elaboration of neurodevelopmental characteristics. *Neuroscience and Biobehavioral Reviews, 27,* 593–604.

Spearman, C. (1904). General intelligence, objectively determined and mea-sured. *American Journal of Psychology, 15,* 201–293.

Sperber, D. (1994). The modularity of thought and the epidemiology of repre-sentations. In L. A. Hirschfeld & S. A. Gelman (Eds.), *Mapping the mind: Domain specificity in cognition and culture* (39–67). Cambridge: Cambridge University Press.

Sperber, D. (1996). *Explaining culture: A naturalistic approach.* Oxford: Black-well.

Sperber, D. (2000). Metarepresentations in evolutionary perspective. In D. Sperber (Ed.), *Metarepresentations: A multidisciplinary perspective* (117–137). Oxford: Oxford University Press.

Sperber, D., Cara, F., & Girotto, V. (1995). Relevance theory explains the selec-tion task. *Cognition, 57,* 31–95.

Spitz, H. H. (1997). *Nonconscious movements: From mystical messages to facili-tated communication.* Mahwah, NJ: Erlbaum.

Stanovich, K. E. (1993a). Dysrationalia: A new specific learning disability. *Jour-nal of Learning Disabilities, 26,* 501–515.

Stanovich, K. E. (1993b). It's practical to be rational. *Journal of Learning Dis-abilities, 26,* 524–532.

Stanovich, K. E. (1994a). Reconceptualizing intelligence: Dysrationalia as an intuition pump. *Educational Researcher, 23*(4), 11–22.

Stanovich, K. E. (1994b). The evolving concept of rationality. *Educational Researcher, 23*(7), 33.

Stanovich, K. E. (1999). *Who is rational? Studies of individual differences in reasoning.* Mahwah, NJ: Erlbaum.

Stanovich, K. E. (2000). *Progress in understanding reading: Scientific foundations and new frontiers.* New York: Guilford Press.

Stanovich, K. E. (2001a). Reductionism in the study of intelligence. *Trends in Cognitive Sciences, 5*(2), 91–92.

Stanovich, K. E. (2001b). The rationality of educating for wisdom. *Educational Psychologist, 36,* 247–251.

Stanovich, K. E. (2004). *The robot's rebellion: Finding meaning in the age of Darwin.* Chicago: University of Chicago Press.

Stanovich, K. E. (2005). The future of a mistake: Will discrepancy measurement continue to make the learning disabilities field a pseudoscience? *Learning Disability Quarterly, 28,* 103–106.

Stanovich, K. E. (2007). *How to think straight about psychology* (8th ed.). Boston: Allyn & Bacon.

Stanovich, K. E. (2008). Distinguishing the reflective, algorithmic, and autonomous minds: Is it time for a tri-process theory? In J. Evans & K. Frankish (Eds.), *In two minds: Dual processes and beyond.* Oxford: Oxford University Press.

Stanovich, K. E. (2009). *Rationality and the reflective mind: Toward a tri-process model of cognition.* New York: Oxford University Press.

Stanovich, K. E., Grunewald, M., & West, R. F. (2003). Cost-benefit reasoning in students with multiple secondary school suspensions. *Personality and Individual Differences, 35,* 1061–1072.

Stanovich, K. E., & Siegel, L. S. (1994). Phenotypic performance profile of children with reading disabilities: A regression-based test of the phonological-core variable-difference model. *Journal of Educational Psychology, 86,* 24–53.

Stanovich, K. E., & West, R. F. (1997). Reasoning independently of prior belief and individual differences in actively open-minded thinking. *Journal of Educational Psychology, 89,* 342–357.

Stanovich, K. E., & West, R. F. (1998a). Cognitive ability and variation in selection task performance. *Thinking and Reasoning, 4,* 193–230.

Stanovich, K. E., & West, R. F. (1998b). Individual differences in framing and conjunction effects. *Thinking and Reasoning, 4,* 289–317.

Stanovich, K. E., & West, R. F. (1998c). Individual differences in rational thought. *Journal of Experimental Psychology: General, 127,* 161–188.

Stanovich, K. E., & West, R. F. (1998d). Who uses base rates and P(D/~H)? An analysis of individual differences. *Memory & Cognition, 26,* 161–179.

Stanovich, K. E., & West, R. F. (1999). Discrepancies between normative and descriptive models of decision making and the understanding/acceptance principle. *Cognitive Psychology, 38,* 349–385.

Stanovich, K. E., & West, R. F. (2000). Individual differences in reasoning: Implications for the rationality debate? *Behavioral and Brain Sciences, 23,* 645–726.

Stanovich, K. E., & West, R. F. (2007). Natural myside bias is independent of cognitive ability. *Thinking and Reasoning, 13,* 225–247.

Stanovich, K. E., & West, R. F. (2008a). On the failure of intelligence to predict myside bias and one-sided bias. *Thinking and Reasoning, 14,* 129–167.

Stanovich, K. E., & West, R. F. (2008b). On the relative independence of thinking biases and cognitive ability. *Journal of Personality and Social Psychology, 94,* 672–695.

Stein, E. (1996). *Without good reason: The rationality debate in philosophy and cognitive science.* Oxford: Oxford University Press.

Stenger, V. J. (1990). *Physics and psychics.* Buffalo, NY: Prometheus Books.

Stenning, K., & van Lambalgen, M. (2004). The natural history of hypotheses about the selection task. In K. I. Manktelow & M. C. Chung (Eds.), *Psychology of reasoning* (127–156). Hove, England: Psychology Press.

Sterelny, K. (1990). *The representational theory of mind: An introduction.* Oxford: Basil Blackwell.

Sterelny, K. (2001). *The evolution of agency and other essays.* Cambridge: Cambridge University Press.

Sterelny, K. (2003). *Thought in a hostile world: The evolution of human cognition.* Malden, MA: Blackwell.

Sternberg, R. J. (1985). *Beyond IQ: A triarchic theory of human intelligence.* Cambridge: Cambridge University Press.

Sternberg, R. J. (1988). *The triarchic mind.* New York: Viking.

Sternberg, R. J. (1993). Would you rather take orders from Kirk or Spock? The relation between rational thinking and intelligence. *Journal of Learning Disabilities, 26,* 516–519.

Sternberg, R. J. (1994). What if the concept of dysrationalia were an example of itself? *Educational Researcher, 23* (4), 22–23.

Sternberg, R. J. (1997a). *Successful intelligence: How practical and creative intelligence determine success in life.* New York: Plume.

Sternberg, R. J. (1997b). The concept of intelligence and its role in lifelong learning and success. *American Psychologist, 52,* 1030–1037.

Sternberg, R. J. (1997c). *Thinking styles.* Cambridge: Cambridge University Press.

Sternberg, R. J. (Ed.) (2000a). *Handbook of intelligence.* New York: Cambridge University Press.

Sternberg, R. J. (2000b). The concept of intelligence. In R. J. Sternberg (Ed.), *Handbook of intelligence* (3–15). New York: Cambridge University Press.

Sternberg, R. J. (2001). Why schools should teach for wisdom: The balance theory of wisdom in educational settings. *Educational Psychologist, 36,* 227–245.

Sternberg, R. J. (2002a). Smart people are not stupid, but they sure can be foolish: The imbalance theory of foolishness. In R. J. Sternberg (Ed.), *Why smart people can be so stupid* (232–242). New Haven, CT: Yale University Press.

Sternberg, R. J. (Ed.) (2002b). *Why smart people can be so stupid.* New Haven, CT: Yale University Press.

Sternberg, R. J. (2003a). Issues in the theory and measurement of successful intelligence: A reply to Brody. *Intelligence, 31,* 331–337.

Sternberg, R. J. (2003b). *Wisdom, intelligence, and creativity synthesized.* Cambridge: Cambridge University Press.

Sternberg, R. J. (2004). Theory-based university admissions testing for a new millennium. *Educational Psychologist, 39,* 185–198.

Sternberg, R. J. (Ed.) (2005). *The psychology of hate.* Washington, DC: American Psychological Association.

Sternberg, R. J. (2006). The Rainbow Project: Enhancing the SAT through assessments of analytical, practical, and creative skills. *Intelligence, 34,* 321–350.

Sternberg, R. J., Conway, B., Ketron, J., & Bernstein, M. (1981). People's conceptions of intelligence. *Journal of Personality and Social Psychology, 41,* 37–55.

Sternberg, R. J., & Detterman, D. K. (Eds.) (1986). *What is intelligence?* Norwood, NJ: Ablex.

Sternberg, R. J., & Grigorenko, E. L. (1997). Are cognitive styles still in style? *American Psychologist, 52,* 700–712.

Sternberg, R. J., & Grigorenko, E. L. (2004). Why we need to explore development in its cultural context. *Merrill-Palmer Quarterly, 50,* 369–386.

Sternberg, R. J., & Kaufman, J. C. (1998). Human abilities. *Annual Review of Psychology, 49,* 479–502.

Sternberg, R. J., & Ruzgis, P. (Eds.) (1994). *Personality and intelligence.* Cambridge: Cambridge University Press.

Stich, S. P. (1990). *The fragmentation of reason.* Cambridge, MA: MIT Press.

Stigler, S. M. (1983). Who discovered Bayes's theorem? *American Statistician, 37,* 290–296.

Stigler, S. M. (1986). *The history of statistics: The measurement of uncertainty before 1900.* Cambridge, MA: Harvard University Press.

Strathman, A., Gleicher, F., Boninger, D. S., & Scott Edwards, C. (1994). The consideration of future consequences: Weighing immediate and distant outcomes of behavior. *Journal of Personality and Social Psychology, 66,* 742–752.

Strayer, D. L., & Drews, F. A. (2007). Cell-phone-induced driver distraction. *Current Directions in Psychological Science, 16,* 128–131.

Strayer, D. L., & Johnston, W. A. (2001). Driven to distraction: Dual-task studies of simulated driving and conversing on a cellular telephone. *Psychological Science, 12,* 462–466.

Stroud, S., & Tappolet, C. (Eds.) (2003). *Weakness of will and practical irrationality.* Oxford: Oxford University Press.

Stuebing, K., Fletcher, J. M., LeDoux, J. M., Lyon, G. R., Shaywitz, S. E., & Shaywitz, B. A. (2002). Validity of IQ-discrepancy classification of reading difficulties: A meta-analysis. *American Educational Research Journal, 39,* 469–518.

Sub, H.-M., Oberauer, K., Wittmann, W. W., Wilhelm, O., & Schulze, R. (2002). Working-memory capacity explains reasoning ability—and a little bit more. *Intelligence, 30,* 261–288.

Suddendorf, T. (1999). The rise of the metamind. In M. C. Corballis & S. Lea (Eds.), *The descent of mind: Psychological perspectives on hominid evolution* (218–260). Oxford: Oxford University Press.

Suddendorf, T., & Corballis, M. C. (2007). The evolution of foresight: What is mental time travel and is it unique to humans? *Behavioral and Brain Sciences, 30,* 299–351.

Suddendorf, T., & Whiten, A. (2001). Mental evolution and development:

Evidence for secondary representation in children, great apes, and other animals. *Psychological Bulletin, 127,* 629–650.

Sunstein, C. R. (2002). *Risk and reason: Safety, law, and the environment.* Cambridge: Cambridge University Press.

Sunstein, C. R. (2005). Moral heuristics. *Behavioral and Brain Sciences, 28,* 531–573.

Sunstein, C. R., & Thaler, R. H. (2003). Libertarian paternalism is not an oxymoron. *University of Chicago Law Review, 70,* 1159–1202.

Surowiecki, J. (2007, May 28). Feature presentation. *The New Yorker,* 28.

Suskind, R. (2004). *The price of loyalty.* New York: Simon & Schuster.

Suskind, R. (2006). *The one percent doctrine.* New York: Simon & Schuster.

Svenson, O. (1981). Are we all less risky and more skillful than our fellow drivers? *Acta Psychologica, 47,* 143–148.

Swartz, R. J., & Perkins, D. N. (1989). *Teaching thinking: Issues & approaches.* Pacific Grove, CA: Midwest Publications.

Taber, C. S., & Lodge, M. (2006). Motivated skepticism in the evaluation of political beliefs. *American Journal of Political Science, 50,* 755–769.

Taleb, N. (2001). *Fooled by randomness.* New York: Texere.

Taleb, N. (2007). *The black swan: The impact of the highly improbable.* New York: Random House.

Tannock, R. (1998). Attention deficit hyperactivity disorder: Advances in cognitive, neurobiological, and genetic research. *Journal of Child Psychology and Psychiatry, 39,* 65–99.

Taub, G. E., & McGrew, K. S. (2004). A confirmatory factor analysis of Cattell-Horn-Carroll theory and cross-age invariance of the Woodcock-Johnson Tests of Cognitive Abilities III. *School Psychology Quarterly, 19,* 72–87.

Taylor, S. E. (1981). The interface of cognitive and social psychology. In J. H. Harvey (Ed.), *Cognition, social behavior, and the environment* (189–211). Hillsdale, NJ: Erlbaum.

Tetlock, P. E. (2005). *Expert political judgment.* Princeton: Princeton University Press.

Thagard, P. (2006). *Hot thought: Mechanisms and applications of emotional cognition.* Cambridge, MA: MIT Press.

Thagard, P., & Nisbett, R. E. (1983). Rationality and charity. *Philosophy of Science, 50,* 250–267.

Thaler, R. H. (1980). Toward a positive theory of consumer choice. *Journal of Economic Behavior and Organization, 1,* 39–60.

Thaler, R. H., & Benartzi, S. (2004). Save more tomorrow: Using behavioral economics to increase employee saving. *Journal of Political Economy, 112,* S164–S187.

Thaler, R. H., Tversky, A., Kahneman, D., & Schwartz, A. (1997). The effect of myopia and loss aversion on risk taking: An experimental test. *Quarterly Journal of Economics, 112,* 647–661.

Thomas, E., & Wolffe, R. (2005, December 19). Bush in the bubble. *Newsweek,* 31–39.

Thomson, J. J. (1976). Killing, letting die, and the trolley problem. *The Monist,* 59, 204–217.

Thomson, J. J. (1985). The trolley problem. *Yale Law Journal, 94,* 1395–1415.

Thomson, J. J. (1990). *The realm of rights.* Cambridge, MA: Harvard University Press.

Thurstone, L. L. (1927). *The nature of intelligence.* New York: Harcourt, Brace.

Todd, P. M., & Gigerenzer, G. (2000). Precis of simple heuristics that make us smart. *Behavioral and Brain Sciences, 23,* 727–780.

Todd, P. M., & Gigerenzer, G. (2007). Environments that make us smart: Ecological rationality. *Current Directions in Psychological Science, 16,* 167–171.

Tomasello, M. (1999). *The cultural origins of human cognition.* Cambridge, MA: Harvard University Press.

Tooby, J., & Cosmides, L. (1992). The psychological foundations of culture. In J. Barkow, L. Cosmides, & J. Tooby (Eds.), *The adapted mind* (19–136). New York: Oxford University Press.

Toplak, M., Liu, E., Macpherson, R., Toneatto, T., & Stanovich, K. E. (2007). The reasoning skills and thinking dispositions of problem gamblers: A dual-process taxonomy. *Journal of Behavioral Decision Making, 20,* 103–124.

Toplak, M. E., & Stanovich, K. E. (2002). The domain specificity and generality of disjunctive reasoning: Searching for a generalizable critical thinking skill. *Journal of Educational Psychology, 94,* 197–209.

Toplak, M. E., & Stanovich, K. E. (2003). Associations between myside bias on an informal reasoning task and amount of post-secondary education. *Applied Cognitive Psychology, 17,* 851–860.

Torrey, E. F. (1984). *The roots of treason.* San Diego: Harcourt Brace Jovanovich.

Trends in the Well Being of America's Children & Youth, 2003 (2003). U.S. Department of Health and Human Services Office of the Assistant Secretary for Planning and Evaluation, http://aspe.hhs.gov/.

Tversky, A. (1996). Contrasting rational and psychological principles of choice. In R. Zeckhauser, R. Keeney, & J. Sebenius (Eds.), *Wise choices* (5–21). Boston: Harvard Business School Press.

Tversky, A., & Kahneman, D. (1974). Judgment under uncertainty: Heuristics and biases. *Science, 185,* 1124–1131.

Tversky, A., & Kahneman, D. (1981). The framing of decisions and the psychology of choice. *Science, 211,* 453–458.

Tversky, A., & Kahneman, D. (1982). Evidential impact of base rates. In D. Kahneman, P. Slovic, & A. Tversky (Eds.), *Judgment under uncertainty: Heuristics and biases* (153–160). Cambridge: Cambridge University Press.

Tversky, A., & Kahneman, D. (1983). Extensional versus intuitive reasoning: The conjunction fallacy in probability judgment. *Psychological Review, 90,* 293–315.

Tversky, A., & Kahneman, D. (1986). Rational choice and the framing of decisions. *Journal of Business, 59,* 251–278.

Tversky, A., & Kahneman, D. (1992). Advances in prospect theory: Cumulative representation under uncertainty. *Journal of Risk and Uncertainty, 5,* 297–323.

Tversky, A., & Shafir, E. (1992). The disjunction effect in choice under uncertainty. *Psychological Science, 3,* 305–309.

Twachtman-Cullen, D. (1997). *A passion to believe.* Boulder, CO: Westview.

Tweney, R. D., Doherty, M. E., Warner, W. J., & Pliske, D. (1980). Strategies of rule discovery in an inference task. *Quarterly Journal of Experimental Psychology, 32,* 109–124.

Ubel, P. A. (2000). *Pricing life: Why it's time for health care rationing.* Cambridge, MA: MIT Press.

Unger, P. (1996). *Living high & letting die: Our illusion of innocence.* Oxford: Oxford University Press.

Unsworth, N., & Engle, R. W. (2005). Working memory capacity and fluid abilities: Examining the correlation between Operation Span and Raven. *Intelligence, 33,* 67–81.

Unsworth, N., & Engle, R. W. (2007). The nature of individual differences in working memory capacity: Active maintenance in primary memory and controlled search from secondary memory. *Psychological Review, 114,* 104–132.

U.S. Congress House Select Committee on Aging (1984, May 31). *Quackery: A $10 billion scandal.* Washington, DC: U.S. Government Printing Office.

Valentine, D. A. (1998, May 13). *Pyramid schemes.* Presented at the International Monetary Fund Seminar on Current Legal Issues Affecting Central Banks. Washington, DC: IMF. Retrieved from http://www.ftc.gov/speeches/other/dvimf16.shtm on August 29, 2007.

Valentine, E. R. (1975). Performance on two reasoning tasks in relation to intelligence, divergence and interference proneness: Content and context effects in reasoning. *British Journal of Educational Psychology*, 45, 198–205.

Vallone, R., Griffin, D. W., Lin, S., & Ross, L. (1990). Overconfident prediction of future actions and outcomes by self and others. *Journal of Personality and Social Psychology*, 58, 582–592.

Vellutino, F., Fletcher, J. M., Snowling, M., & Scanlon, D. M. (2004). Specific reading disability (dyslexia): What have we learned in the past four decades? *Journal of Child Psychology and Psychiatry*, 45, 2–40.

Vinter, A., & Detable, C. (2003). Implicit learning in children and adolescents with mental retardation. *American Journal of Mental Retardation*, 108, 94–107.

Vinter, A., & Perruchet, P. (2000). Implicit learning in children is not related to age: Evidence from drawing behavior. *Child Development*, 71, 1223–1240.

Visser, B. A., Ashton, M. C., & Vernon, P. A. (2006). Beyond g: Putting multiple intelligences theory to the test. *Intelligence*, 34, 487–502.

von Neumann, J., & Morgenstern, O. (1944). *The theory of games and economic behavior*. Princeton: Princeton University Press.

Wagenaar, W. A. (1988). *Paradoxes of gambling behavior*. Hove, England: Erlbaum.

Waldmann, M. R., & Dietrich, J. H. (2007). Throwing a bomb on a person versus throwing a person on a bomb. *Psychological Science*, 18, 247–253.

Wang, P. (2006, October). What works in retirement planning. *Money Magazine*, 124–130.

Wason, P. C. (1960). On the failure to eliminate hypotheses in a conceptual task. *Quarterly Journal of Experimental Psychology*, 12, 129–140.

Wason, P. C. (1966). Reasoning. In B. Foss (Ed.), *New horizons in psychology* (135–151). Harmondsworth, England: Penguin.

Wason, P. C. (1968). Reasoning about a rule. *Quarterly Journal of Experimental Psychology*, 20, 273–281.

Wason, P. C. (1969). Regression in reasoning? *British Journal of Psychology*, 60, 471–480.

Wasserman, E. A., Dorner, W. W., & Kao, S. F. (1990). Contributions of specific cell information to judgments of interevent contingency. *Journal of Experimental Psychology: Learning, Memory, and Cognition, 16,* 509–521.

Waterhouse, L. (2006). Multiple intelligences, the Mozart effect, and emotional intelligence: A critical review. *Educational Psychologist, 41,* 207–226.

Watkins, S. J. (2000). Conviction by mathematical error? *British Medical Journal, 320*(7226), 2–3.

Wechsler, D. (1958). *The measurement and appraisal of adult intelligence.* Baltimore: Williams & Wilkins.

Wegner, D. M. (2002). *The illusion of conscious will.* Cambridge, MA: MIT Press.

Wegner, D. M., Fuller, V. A., & Sparrow, B. (2003). Clever hands: Uncontrolled intelligence in facilitated communication. *Journal of Personality and Social Psychology, 85,* 5–19.

Wertenbroch, K., Soman, D., & Chattopadhyay, A. (2007). On the perceived value of money: The reference dependence of currency numerosity effects. *Journal of Consumer Research, 34,* 1–10.

West, R. F., & Stanovich, K. E. (1997). The domain specificity and generality of overconfidence: Individual differences in performance estimation bias. *Psychonomic Bulletin & Review, 4,* 387–392.

West, R. F., & Stanovich, K. E. (2003). Is probability matching smart? Associations between probabilistic choices and cognitive ability. *Memory & Cognition, 31,* 243–251.

Westen, D., Blagov, P., Kilts, C., & Hamann, S. (2006). Neural bases of motivated reasoning: An fMRI study of emotional constraints on partisan political judgment in the 2004 U.S. presidential election. *Journal of Cognitive Neuroscience, 18,* 1947–1958.

Whittington, D. (1991). What have 17-year-olds known in the past? *American Educational Research Journal, 28,* 759–780.

Wilkinson, P. (1998, July 9). Juror who wanted to find truth in the stars. *Times (London).*

Will, G. F. (2005, October 5). Can this nomination be justified? *Washington Post,* A23.

Williams, W. M. (1998). Are we raising smarter children today? School and home-related influences on IQ. In U. Neisser (Ed.), *The rising curve: Long-term changes in IQ and related measures* (125–154). Washington, DC: American Psychological Association.

Willingham, D. T. (1998). A neuropsychological theory of motor-skill learning. *Psychological Review*, 105, 558–584.

Willingham, D. T. (1999). The neural basis of motor-skill learning. *Current Directions in Psychological Science*, 8, 178–182.

Willingham, D. T. (2004). Reframing the mind. *Education Next*, 4(3), 19–24.

Wilson, T. D. (2002). *Strangers to ourselves*. Cambridge, MA: Harvard University Press.

Wilson, T. D., & Gilbert, D. T. (2005). Affective forecasting: Knowing what to want. *Current Directions in Psychological Science*, 14, 131–134.

Wilson, T. D., Houston, C. E., Etling, K. M., & Brekke, N. (1996). A new look at anchoring effects: Basic anchoring and its antecedents. *Journal of Experimental Psychology: General*, 125, 387–402.

Wilson, T. D., Wheatley, T., Meyers, J. M., Gilbert, D. T., & Axsom, D. (2000). Focalism: A source of durability bias in affective forecasting. *Journal of Personality and Social Psychology*, 78, 821–836.

Wolf, F. M., Gruppen, L. D., & Billi, J. E. (1985). Differential diagnosis and the competing hypothesis heuristic—a practical approach to judgment under uncertainty and Bayesian probability. *Journal of the American Medical Association*, 253, 2858–2862.

Wolford, G., Miller, M. B., & Gazzaniga, M. S. (2000). The left hemisphere's role in hypothesis formation. *Journal of Neuroscience*, 20(RC64), 1–4.

Wonderlic Personnel Test (2002). *Wonderlic Personnel Test and Scholastic Level Exam User's Manual*. Libertyville, IL: Wonderlic, Inc.

Woodward, B. (2006). *State of Denial*. New York: Simon & Schuster.

Wright, G., & Ayton, P. (Eds.) (1994). *Subjective Probability*. Chichester: John Wiley.

Wu, G., Zhang, J., & Gonzalez, R. (2004). Decision under risk. In D. J. Koehler & N. Harvey (Eds.), *Blackwell handbook of judgment and decision making* (399–423). Malden, MA: Blackwell.

Yamagishi, K. (1997). When a 12.86% mortality is more dangerous than 24.14%: Implications for risk communication. *Applied Cognitive Psychology*, 11, 495–506.

Yates, J. F., Lee, J., & Bush, J. G. (1997). General knowledge overconfidence: Cross-national variations, response style, and "reality." *Organizational Behavior and Human Decision Processes*, 70, 87–94.

Zacks, R. T., Hasher, L., & Sanft, H. (1982). Automatic encoding of event frequency: Further findings. *Journal of Experimental Psychology: Learning, Memory, and Cognition, 8*, 106–116.

Zajonc, R. B. (2001). Mere exposure: A gateway to the subliminal. *Current Directions in Psychological Science, 10*, 224–228.

Zajonc, R. B., & Markus, H. (1982). Affective and cognitive factors in preferences. *Journal of Consumer Research, 9*, 123–131.

Zeidner, M., & Matthews, G. (2000). Intelligence and personality. In R. J. Sternberg (Ed.), *Handbook of intelligence* (581–610). New York: Cambridge University Press.

Zelazo, P. D. (2004). The development of conscious control in childhood. *Trends in Cognitive Sciences, 8*, 12–17.

Zimmerman, C. (2007). The development of scientific thinking skills in elementary and middle school. *Developmental Review, 27*, 172–223.

Zweig, J. (2002, June). What fund investors really need to know. *Money Magazine*, 110–124.

Zweig, J. (2007, February). Winning the home run hitter's game. *Money Magazine*, 102.

INDEX

Abelson, Robert, 161
accessibility, 75–78
addiction, and intelligence, 191–192
ADHD, 54
affect heuristic, 74–75, 181
affective forecasting, 184–185, 200–201
affirmative action, and framing, 97
Ainslie, George, 115, 127
Albanian financial crisis, 152–155
algorithmic mind, 29–32, 38–41, 51, 122–123, 173–177, 190–192; and intelligence, 31–32, 195–196
alternative hypothesis, ignoring, 136–140
anchoring, and adjustment, 79–81
argument evaluation, 36
Ariely, Dan, 207
attribute substitution, 23, 72–75, 122, 147–148, 181–182
Austin, Elizabeth, 192
autism, 130–131
autonomous mind, 32–33, 39–41, 171–177, 188–192; defects of, 185–188

Baron, Jonathan, 86–87, 195, 196
base rates, 144–146
Bayes, Thomas, 134

Bayes' formula, 134–136
Bayesian reasoning, 133–139, 144–146
belief bias, 120–123, 159, 182–183
belief identification, 149
beliefs: irrational, 152–160; and social psychology, 163
Benartzi, Shlomo, 204–205
bias blind spot, 109–110, 183
biased self-assessments, 109
Blair, Tony, 43
Block, Jack, 191
Boring, E. G., 50
Boyd, Robert, 59
Bruine de Bruin, Wandi, 37
Bush, George W.: cognitive characteristics of, 1–2, 42–44; fluid intelligence of, 43; intelligence of, 1–2, 6–7, 43–44; thinking dispositions of, 44

Camerer, Colin, 172
Cattell/Horn/Carroll theory of intelligence, 40–42, 50–51, 172
chance, over-reacting to, 61–62
cognitive ability, versus thinking dispositions, 31–32
cognitive miser, 23, 63–66, 176–179; and

cognitive miser (continued)
attribute substitution, 72–75; and belief
bias, 122; and defaults, 202–205; and
disjunctive reasoning, 70–72; environmental fixes for, 202–208; evolutionary origins, 64–66; and falsifiability,
143; hostile and benign environments,
82–85; loss of autonomy, 79–81, 84–
85; and mindware gaps, 147–148; and
vividness, 75–78
cognitive science, levels of analysis, 29–31
"cold" cognition, 119–120, 191
conditional probabilities, 148
conjunction error, 147–148
covariation detection, 140
critical thinking, 48, 114, 122
crystallized intelligence (Gc), 13, 40–42,
172
cultural replicator theory, 161–165

Damasio, Antonio, 185–187
D'Antonio, Michael, The State Boys Rebellion, 53
Dawes, Robyn, 148
Dawkins, Richard, 64–65, 162, 165
Deary, Ian, 192
decontextualization, and modernity,
123–124
decoupling, cognitive, 24–25, 28, 40, 50–
51, 173–177, 188–192
default heuristic, 82, 202–205
delay of gratification, 125–127
Denby, David, 9–10
Dennett, Daniel, 20; Kinds of Minds, 30
denominator neglect, 120, 182–183
descriptive invariance, 88, 93
diets, and portion size, 206–207
disjunctive reasoning, 70–72
Doherty, Michael, 139
dominance relationship, in decision
theory, 72–73

dual process theory, 21–28, 173–177; and
intelligence, 26–28; and override function, 22–23, 38–39, 41, 71, 173–174;
Type 1 processing, 21–25; Type 2 processing, 21–25
Duckworth, Angela, 37
Dunning, David, 109
dysrationalia, 10–12, 48–50, 188–193;
analogy with other cognitive disabilities,
17–19; and contaminated mindware,
157–160; definition, 18; in folk psychology, 55–57; as intuition pump, 17–19;
and mindware gaps, 150–151, 159–160;
prevalence, 66–68; pseudoscience and,
170–171; within tripartite model, 34–
35

egocentrism, 111–113, 179–180, 184
emotions, 117–119; impairment in, 186–
188
Epley, Nicholas, 95–96
Epstein, Seymour, 120
equality heuristic, 90–92
Evans, Jonathan, 159
evolution, and rationality, 64–66, 160–
161
executive function, 23; and cognitive
decoupling, 28

faith, 168–169
falsifiability, 141–144, 167–170, 201
Fenton-O'Creevy, Mark, 110
Fine, Cordelia, 101
fluid/crystallized (Gf/Gc) theory, 13, 40–
42, 50–51, 172
fluid intelligence (Gf), 40–41, 50–51; and
cognitive decoupling, 28, 50–51
Flynn, James, 52
Flynn effect, 51–52
focal bias, 173–177, 181–185, 190
Fogelin, Robert, 152

four-card selection task, 141–143, 175–176, 183

framing, 183, 190; classic research on, 92–95; and fairness decisions, 90–91; and intelligence, 98–100; and medical decisions, 91–92; and personal autonomy, 89–92; and perspective taking, 93; and public policy, 97–98; and tax policy, 86–89, 96

Frankfurt, Harry, 152

Frederick, Shane, 72–73, 190

Friedman, Richard, 206

Friedrich, James, 97

Frum, David, 2, 43

Funder, David, 191

Galton, Francis, 53

Gardner, Howard, 45–47

Gigerenzer, Gerd, 83, 205–206

Gilbert, Dan, 200–201

Gladwell, Malcolm, 115–116

Goldstein, Daniel, 203

Gollwitzer, Peter, 200

Greene, Joshua, 117–119

Harris, Sam, 165

Heath, Chip, 113

Herrnstein, Richard, *The Bell Curve*, 20

heuristic processing, 22–23, 63–64, 78–79; hostile and benign environments for, 82–85

heuristics and biases tasks, 181–185

"hot" cognition, 119–120, 191

Hsee, Christopher, 74

Hull, David, 70

hypothetical thinking, 23–25, 39–40, 51

illusion of control, 110

implementation intentions, 200

impulsively associative thinking, 181–182

informal reasoning tasks, 38

intellectual disability (mental retardation), 53–54

intelligence: as adaptive functioning, xi, 12, 51–52, 54; and algorithmic mind, 31–32; broad versus narrow definitions, 12–15, 45–47, 54, 208–209; and contaminated mindware, 157–160; critics of, 20–21, 45–50; debate about, 20–21; deification of, 54; and dual process theory, 26–28; and dysrationalia, 48–50; fluid/crystallized (Gf/Gc) theory, 13, 40–42, 50–51, 172; in folk psychology, 55–57; and framing, 98–100; heritability, 20; as imperialist concept, 47–50; malleability, 197, 208–209; and mindware gaps, 150–151; and myside processing, 113–114; overvaluing of, 195–199, 208–212; and pseudoscientific beliefs, 170–171; and reflective mind, 31–32; relation to rationality, 2–3, 12, 16, 32–33, 48–50, 98–100, 113–114, 171, 188–193; and thinking errors, 188–193; and Type 1 processes, 26–28, 71–72; vernacular definitions, 12

intelligence tests: cognitive processes missing from, x–xii, 5–6, 171, 193–194, 196–197, 209–211; ubiquity of, 3, 32

intertemporal preference reversal, 125–127

investing, 59–63, 75

irrationality, 68–69, 160–161; caused by contaminated mindware, 160–167; and delayed rewards, 125–127; as descriptive invariance, 88, 93; environmental fixes for, 202–208; and memes, 160–167; and mindware gaps, 130–133, 138–144; relation to intelligence, 188–193; social costs of, 197–199; in stock market investing, 59–63, 75; types of, 177–185

irrational thinking, taxonomy of, 177–185

Johnson, Eric, 202–203

Kahneman, Daniel, ix–xi, 62, 72–73, 79–80, 86, 92–95, 107–108, 129, 185
Kennedy, John F. Jr., 115–116
Klaczynski, Paul, 38, 104
knowledge, 40–42
knowledge calibration, 105–108
knowledge projection, 159–160
Kruger, Justin, 109, 111

Lagerfeld, Steven, 170
Lakoff, George, 97–98
Langer, Ellen, 110
Larrick, Richard, 129
lay psychology theory, 180
learning disabilities, discrepancy definitions of, 17–18
Leslie, Alan, 24–25
Levesque, Hector, 70
libertarian paternalism, 204–205
Linda problem, 147–148
Loewenstein, George, 91
loss aversion, 62

Mackie, Gerry, 169
Macpherson, Robyn, 104
MAMBIT (mental abilities measured by intelligence tests), 13–15, 45–51
maximal performance situations, 31
McCaffrey, Edward, 86–87
McCain, John, 43
McCallum, Ronald, 43
meme, 161–167; definition of, 162; faith-based, 168–169
memetics, 161–167; fundamental insight of, 162
mindware, 40–42, 67–68, 179–180; adversative, 169–170; avoiding contamination in, 167–170; contaminated, 67, 152–171; counterintuitive assumption of contamination, 166–167; definition of, 40, 129; epidemics, 152–157; and

falsifiability, 167–170; and intelligence, 192–193; motivational force of, 127–128; strategic, 148–149; survival strategies, 164–165
mindware gaps, 67, 130–149, 182–183; and intelligence, 150–151
Mischel, Walter, 191
money illusion, 77–78
moral dilemmas, 117–119
Mr. Spock problem, 185–188
multiple intelligences, 46–48
multiple personality disorder, 155–157
Murray, Charles, The Bell Curve, 20
myside bias: measures of, 38; property of cognitive miser, 104
myside processing, 101–104, 183–184; and communication, 111–112; and intelligence, 113–114; and product design, 112–113

need for cognition, 149
Neisser, Ulric, 52
Newton, Elizabeth, 112
Nozick, Robert, 8

organ donation, 202–204
overconfidence, 61, 105–110
override: cognitive neuroscience of, 117–119; of cold heuristics, 119–124; of emotions, 117–119; failure, 115–117, 180–183, 190–192; of Type 1 processing, 22–23, 38–39

paranormal phenomena, 170–171
Paulos, John, 8–9
pensions, 204–205
Perkins, David, 11–12, 40
personal finance, 59–63, 84–85
perspective taking, 93
Pinker, Steven, How the Mind Works, 21
planning fallacy, 107–108

Ponzi schemes, 152–155
possible world box, 25
Postman, Neil, 68–69
practical intelligence, 46
preattentive processes, 26, 177
prior knowledge, decoupling from, 123–124, 159
probabilistic reasoning, 42, 120, 132–136, 144–148
Pronin, Emily, 109
prospect theory, 95
pseudoscience, 170–171, 198–199
psychometric g, 172
pyramid schemes, 152–155

Rachlin, Howard, 127
Rachlinski, Jeffrey, 150–151
rationality: and contaminated mindware, 167–170; definition of, 15–17; epistemic, 16, 105–106; and evolution, 64–66, 160–161; in folk psychology, 55–57; fostering via environmental change, 202–208; instrumental, 16; and intelligence, 32–33, 48–50; malleability, 197, 202, 208–209; measures of, 36–38; mindware of, 41–42, 67–68; taxonomy of failures of, 177–185; teaching, 199–202; tests of, 4, 209–211; thinking dispositions of, 44; three requirements of, 42, 52; and tripartite model, 32–33; undervaluing of, 195–199, 208–212
rationality quotient (RQ), 4, 209–211
recognition heuristic, 83–85
recovered memories, 155–157
reflective mind, 30–32, 38–41, 51, 122–123, 149, 173–177, 188–191; and intelligence, 31–32; and intelligence tests, 195–196
reflectivity/impulsivity, 149
retirement savings, 204–205
Richerson, Peter, 59
Rokeach, Milton, 35

Rozin, Paul, 207–208
Ryan, Desmond, 157

SAT test, as an IQ test, 3
Schelling, Thomas, 86–87
Schkade, David, 185
scientific reasoning, 42
scientific thinking, 130–131, 139–144
self-control, 124–128, 182–183; and intelligence, 191–193; and precommitment, 206–207
Seligman, Martin, 37
serial associative cognition, 173–177, 181–182, 190
Showalter, Elaine, 155–156
simulation, cognitive, 23–25, 39–41, 51, 174
Sinaceur, Marwan, 85
Slovic, Paul 77
Spearman, Charles, 172
status quo bias, 82
Sternberg, Robert, *Why Smart People Can Be So Stupid*, 11, 45–47, 53, 209
Sunstein, Cass, 204
Surowiecki, James, 113
syllogistic reasoning, 120–123

Taleb, Nassim Nicholas, 59
tax policy, 86–89
temporal discounting, 125–127
Tetlock, Philip, 37
Thaler, Richard, 96, 204
thinking dispositions, 2, 31–32, 148–149, 173; and belief bias, 122–123; as predictors of rational thought and action, 36–38; within tripartite model, 34, 38–40
"think of the opposite," as reasoning strategy, 136–140, 199–200
Thomas, Evan, 43
Toplak, Maggie, 38, 104, 188
tripartite model of mind, 32–35, 38–40,

tripartite model of mind (continued)
116–117, 171–177; and dysrationalia,
34–35; expanded, 38–40
trolley problem, 117–119, 183
Tversky, Amos, ix–xi, 62, 79–80, 93–95,
129
Tweney, Ryan, 144
Type 1 processing, 63–64, 78–79, 115–116,
119, 174–180, 190–192; and intelligence,
26–28
Type 2 processing, 70–72, 115–116, 119,
174–180, 190–192
typical performance situations, 31

Ubel, Peter, 91–92
Universal Darwinism, 162, 167

ventromedial prefrontal cortex, 186–187
visceral responses, 124–127
vividness, 75–78, 85, 181

Wanger, Ralph, 79
Wason, Peter, 141, 143, 175
Wason's 2-4-6 task, 143–144
Wechsler, David, 48
weight control, 206–207
Wertenbroch, Klaus, 207
West, Richard, 55, 101, 113–114
Westen, Drew, 102
Will, George, 2, 43
willpower, 124–128
Wolffe, Richard, 43
working memory, and cognitive de-
coupling, 28

Yamagishi, Kimihiko, 76

Zweig, Jason, 60